CLIVE
PROCONSUL OF INDIA

Other books by the author

The 30th Punjabis
The Battle of Vitoria
Wellington's Peninsular Army
Charge (in conjunction with Brigadier Peter Young)
Wellington's Masterpiece, The Battle and Campaign of Salamanca (in conjunction with Brigadier Peter Young)
A History of the British Army (edited with Brigadier Peter Young)
Solah Punjab, A History of the 16th Punjab Regiment (ed.)

Frontispiece Robert, Lord Clive, by Nathaniel Dance. Since Clive was wearing the ribbon of Bath, the picture was probably painted in 1773

CLIVE
PROCONSUL OF INDIA

A Biography

by James P. Lawford

London   George Allen & Unwin Ltd
Ruskin House   Museum Street

First published 1976

This book is copyright under the Berne Convention. All rights are reserved. Apart from any fair dealing for the purpose of private study, research, criticism or review, as permitted under the Copyright Act, 1956, no part of this publication may be reproduced, stored in a retrieval system, or transmitted, in any form or by any means, electronic, electrical, chemical, mechanical, optical, photocopying, recording or otherwise, without the prior permission of the copyright owner. Enquiries should be addressed to the publishers.

© George Allen & Unwin Ltd, 1976

ISBN 0 04 923067 0

Printed in Great Britain
in 11 pt Baskerville
by Cox and Wyman Ltd
London, Fakenham and Reading

To my wife Joan
*who spent many happy years in
the Indian sub-continent*

Acknowledgements

I am most grateful to the Right Honourable, The Earl of Powis for permission to publish the extracts from the Clive papers and to reproduce the picture of Lady Clive on page 144. Colonel Alan Shepperd, librarian at the Royal Military Academy, Sandhurst, and D. W. King Esq OBE, FLA, librarian to the Ministry of Defence Library, Army Department, were both, as ever, unstinting in their assistance. Dr Charles, Assistant Keeper of the Department of Manuscripts and Records, the National Library of Wales, and Dr R. J. Bingle, Assistant Keeper of European Manuscripts at the India Office Library, and their staffs gave me most valuable help. I must also thank Mrs Archer and Miss Harrold of the Print Department, the India Office Library, Miss Evans, Librarian of the National Portrait Gallery, and R. B. Goodall Esq, Senior Photographer, The National Army Museum, for the time and patience they expended helping me with illustrations. Mr Simpson, The Librarian of The Royal Commonwealth Society and Miss Perry showed great forbearance both over my quest for books and the amount of the time they allowed me to study them.

Once again my thanks go to my daughters Diana and Sylvia for typing most of the manuscript and to Lieutenant Colonel John Ricketts MC, late of the Frontier Force Rifles, who had a family connection with Clive and with whom I had valuable discussions about his early days.

The illustrations on pages 18, 27, 34, 37, 41, 53, 58, 68, 73, 85, 93, 101, 105, 113, 116, 145, 150, 155, 157, 163, 166, 188, 203, 216, 236, 252, 255, 259, 263, 273, 290, 301, 337 and 338 are reproduced by kind permission of the India Office Library, those on pages 378, 383, 388 and 400 by kind permission of the National Portrait Gallery. The maps were drawn by F. J. Bailey, Esq.

Preface

Although the origins of the European empires may be traced back to the seventeenth century and, perhaps, to the Conquistadores of the sixteenth, the great movement that led Europe to rule much of Asia and almost all of Africa gained its momentum in the eighteenth century, and two great men, Dupleix of France and Clive of England, were largely responsible for setting it in motion. Dupleix saw the opportunities; Clive seized them.

Now the old type of Imperialism that took its pattern from the ancient Roman Empire is no more, replaced, perhaps, by newer, subtler brands, it may be worth looking once again at the life of Clive, one of the originators of European Imperialism in Asia, to see what sort of man he was, what he had to contend with, and what were his aims.

He was the supreme man of action. During most of his service in India he required and obtained the independence and dictatorial powers normally possessed only by a Roman proconsul engaged in adding a new province to the Empire; and like a Roman proconsul, he took counsel of none, bent all to his will.

So immensely positive a character was bound to create many and powerful enemies, and this has been reflected in his biographies; these range from fiery denunciations of all he did to near adulation of the man who did most to found the British Empire in India.

The contention he aroused in his lifetime will surely

live on, and no verdict on his life will be accepted as final. But whatever view may be taken of his actions and achievements, surely everyone will agree that 'here was a man', and one not unworthy of remembrance.

J.P.L.

Note on dates: The calendar was altered by twelve days in September 1752. All dates before September accord with the old calendar, all after that date with the new.

Contents

		page	
Acknowledgements		page	8
Preface			9
1	The Beginning (1725–44)		17
2	The French Capture Madras (1745–6)		35
3	Fort St David and the Siege of Pondicherry (1746–8)		61
4	The Battle for the Carnatic Begins (1749–51)		77
5	Arcot, Arni and Kauveripauk (1751–2)		100
6	The End of Chunda Sahib (1752)		122
7	Marriage and a Visit to England (1753–4)		138
8	Gheria and the Fall of Calcutta (1755–6)		153
9	The Recapture of Calcutta (December 1756–January 57)		173
10	The Battles for Calcutta and Chandernagore (January–March 1757)		192
11	The Approach to Plassey (April–June 1757)		214
12	The Battle of Plassey (June 1757)		245
13	The Aftermath (1757–8)		264
14	Governor of Bengal (1758–9)		285
15	Interlude in England (1760–4)		308
16	Reform in Bengal (1765)		327
17	The Bengal Mutiny (1766)		345

18	England Once More (1767–71)	373
19	The Last Battle (1772–4)	385

Epilogue

Clive, The Man   405

Appendixes

1	A note on spelling and pronunciation	409
2	Glossary of Anglo-Indian terms	411
3	Proposed treaty between the Company and Mir Jafar	415

Bibliography   417
Postscript   419
Index   424

Illustrations

Frontispiece   Clive by N. Dance
1	Old Styche Hall	*page* 18
2	Madras from the Sea	25
3	Mussoolas, the Madras Surf Boats	27
4	Black Town, Madras	28
5	Gentleman in Palankin	31
6	St Thomé Street, Madras	34
7	Indian Nawab and Wife	37
8	Mahratta Cavalry Commander and Wife	41
9	Fort St George, Madras, from the South	53
10	Irrigation Works near Madras	58
11	Stringer Lawrence	68
12	Pondicherry	73
13	An Indian Grandee on an Elephant	82
14	The Great Pagoda, Tanjore	85
15	The Fort of Gingee	90
16	Trichinopoly	93
17	A Muslim Matchlock Soldier	101
18	A Hircarra	105
19	Mahratta Cavalrymen	113
20	The Pagoda at Conjeeveram	116
20a	Portrait of Clive attributed to Gainsborough	141
20b	Margaret Clive	144
21	The Assembly Rooms, Madras	145
22	The East India Company Offices in Leadenhall Street	150
23	A Bombay Grab	155

14 ILLUSTRATIONS

24	Admiral Watson	156
25	The Pirate Fort of Gheria	157
26	Alivardi Khan, Nawab of Bengal	163
27	The City of Murshidabad	166
28	Captain Eyre Coote, later General, Sir	185
29	Fort William, Calcutta	188
30	Ahmad Shah Abdalli, Ruler of Afghanistan	203
31	Admiral Pocock, later Sir George	210
32	A Toddy-seller	216
33	The Landing Stage at Cutwa	236
34	The Nawab's Hunting Lodge at Plassey	252
35	Old Plan of the Battle of Plassey	255
36	The Battle of Plassey, the Frontal Attack	259
37	Meeting Between Clive and Mir Jafar After the Battle	263
38	A Patile (a Cargo Barge) on the River Ganges	271
39	Patna	274
40	Ram Narain, Governor of Patna	276
41	Murshidabad, the Great Mosque	290
42	Boats on the Hooghly	301
43	The Dutch Settlement at Chinsura	304
44	Shuja-ud-daula, Nawab of Oudh	337
45	Clive Receiving the *Diwani* of Bengal, Bihar and Orissa	338
46	The Fort at Allahabad	362
47	Portrait of Clive by Thomas Gainsborough	378
48	Lord North	383
49	Colonel John Burgoyne. Later General	388
50	The House of Lords at the Time of Clive. The Scene Depicted is the Death of Chatham	400

Maps and Plans

1	India in the Eighteenth Century	page	16
2	Southern India		38
3	Madras about 1746		52
4	Southern Carnatic		78
5	Operations round Arcot		112
6	Operations round Trichinopoly		124
7	North East India		164
8	The Hooghly River		180
9	Calcutta, the Attack on the Nawab's Camp		198
10	The Advance to Plassey		234
11	The Battle of Plassey		254
12	The Coromandel Coast and North East India		284
13	Oudh, Bihar and Bengal		346

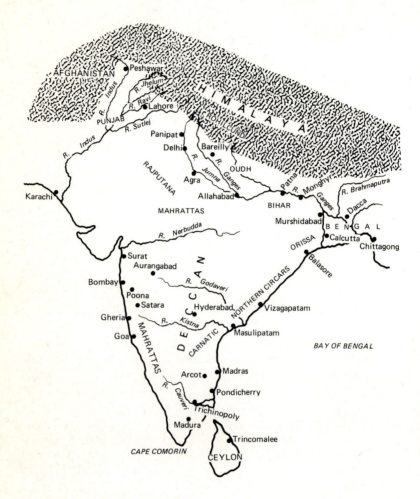

1 India in the eighteenth century.

Chapter 1

THE BEGINNING
1725-44

In 1725 George I still ruled Great Britain, Walpole was coming to the fore in government, and there had been rioting in Glasgow over a tax that the British Government had incautiously placed on beer. In London the noted thief-taker and magistrate, Johnathan Wilde, had been tried and executed as the greatest thief of all, and at Styche, not far from the town of Market Drayton in Shropshire, an infant son was born to Richard Clive, a gentleman in straitened circumstances who owned fifteen unproductive acres and practised at law with no very noticeable success. In India where the infant was to win enduring fame, the East India Company, with its trading posts at Bombay, Madras and Calcutta, was engaged in quietly expanding its activities; in that year it paid a dividend of 7 per cent to its gratified shareholders, a handsome return on their money although somewhat less than the 10 per cent of earlier years.

Rural England at this time was run by its squires, among whom Richard Clive could be numbered. They were men who frequently farmed part of their own estates, spoke the same language as their tenants, administered them as landlords, admonished them as Justices of the Peace, and generally ruled and ordered their lives. The association between the squire and his folk was not unhappy; they followed much the same pursuits, they ploughed, hunted by day and stupefied themselves with alcohol by night. The right of the squire to rule was traditional, unquestioned

1 Old Styche Hall as it was when Clive was born.

by ruler or ruled; from birth he expected and was trained to lead, and while not unmindful of his own advantage, contrived to do so with skill and discernment. Such divisions as there were in the nation arose not over class, but over religion and politics. Roman Catholics were looked on as dangerously subversive, and the new Hanoverian dynasty favoured by the Whigs had yet to strike firm roots in English soil; indeed it was suspected, often with good reason, that the Tories harboured secret hankerings for a return of the Stuarts.

The social structure of England at this time rather resembled a heavy oak chest veneered on the outside to a highly polished gloss. But the veneer was wafer-thin; underneath, the coarser-grained, enduring oak had altered little over the centuries. The great noble families were in the process of achieving a notable level of culture and sensibility. A fine lady, her sensitive feelings affronted by some uncouth exclamation or action, might fall into a swoon, especially if the right man were at hand to cut the laces of her low-cut dress; her delicate nostrils were not to be offended by the rank scent of tobacco. Her lower-born sister, however, for some comparatively trivial offence might be stripped to the waist and whipped through the streets of a town. And even the fine gentleman might have to contemplate a barbaric punishment should he venture to conspire against his lawful sovereign. The penalty for high treason was hanging, drawing and quartering. A convicted man might expect to be hanged until nearly dead, then cut down and while still conscious, watch the hangman remove his entrails and burn them before his eyes. A ferocious punishment still to be meted out twenty years later, and to remain on the statute book for Scotland until well into the twentieth century.

Underneath the surface brilliance, life was rude, tough and brutal. In London gin had begun to take the place of beer as the drink of the people, and Hogarth was recording the unfortunate results for posterity. The death rate exceeded the birth rate, and continued to do so until the Government imposed the first of the swingeing taxes on gin that have since so often vexed the devotees of that beverage. A man was expected to stand on his own feet, and there was little compassion for the weakling. The pleasures of the populace were crude and cruel. A public execution, and most executions were public, was looked upon as a pleasant diversion, drawing the crowds that in a more merciful age might be expected on the local football field; and cock-fighting was one of the more popular forms of an evening's entertainment. In an uncertain age, gambling among those who had the means held an almost irresistible attraction. The enforcement of law and order was haphazard and the streets of big cities and the country highways were infested by footpads and highwaymen; it was dangerous to travel, particularly at night. Life was cheap and for most the conditions of living hard.

This was the world that Robert Clive entered on 29 September 1725. His father, by repute a man of violent temper and limited ability, appears to have cherished no great affection for his first-born son. His wife, Rebecca, was the daughter of Nathaniel Gaskell, a citizen of some substance, who lived in Manchester. She had two sisters;

one was married to Daniel Bayley and lived at Hope Hall near Manchester, the other to the eleventh Lord Sempill. For some reason, when he was little more than two years old the unfortunate Robert was sent away from his parents to live with the Bayleys. It seems an extraordinary way to treat a son who was also the heir. Perhaps Rebecca was faced with a difficult pregnancy (she subsequently bore five more sons and seven daughters); or possibly the Bayleys wanted a child, but there is no record that anything in the way of an adoption was contemplated. Whatever the reason, the infant was thrown out by his parents. A few months after his arrival at the Bayleys he became dangerously ill. Curiously, the only letters telling of the illness were written by Mr Bayley to the Reverend King at Styche, not to the infant's father. It is possible that he also wrote to Richard Clive and the letters have not been preserved, but the omission may be significant.

The illness lasted nearly two months. On 26 June 1728 Mr Bayley in a letter again to the Reverend King writes: 'Yesterday Bob came down to the parlour for the first time. He goes on successfully with the bark and is merry and good as possible. He is poor and thin; but in a brave way and has stomach for more meat than we dare give him. . . . This afternoon Bob with some reluctance suffered his Aunt Bay to go to chapel.'

He seems to have developed an affection for his 'Aunt Bay', but he was certainly an aggressive child and probably a moody one as well. Throughout his life he suffered from fits of melancholia. If he was to be happy he needed a challenge and he needed to lead. His uncle by marriage noted that his fighting, 'to which he is out of measure addicted gives his temper a fierceness and imperiousness that he flies out upon every trifling occasion; for this reason I do what I can to suppress the hero'. The 'hero' at this time was but seven years old. It does not sound a particularly happy childhood, and when he was ten his 'Aunt Bay' died.

Probably about this time he returned to his family. Absence does not seem to have made the heart of his father grow fonder, nor would the sudden appearance of a moody elder brother be likely to appeal to the other members of his family. At an early age the young Robert had been packed off to school, and he was to pass through several establishments of learning; one senses that on each occasion his departure occasioned little sorrow to his teachers. He went first to Lostock, a small school in Market Drayton. His headmaster, one Doctor Easton, is reputed to have predicted, according to Sir John Malcolm in his memoir of Clive, that 'if his scholar lived to be a man, and opportunity enabled him to exert his talents, few names would be greater than his'. These sentiments do not appear to have been echoed by any others of those privileged to teach the young lad, and it is difficult not to suspect that the verdict was given some years after his pupil had departed, when the alleged promise had already begun to manifest itself.

At the age of eleven Clive left Lostock for the tuition of the Reverend Burslem, and about a year later he progressed to the Merchant Taylor's School in London. He lasted two years at this academy and finished his schooling with a Mr Sterling at Hemel Hempstead. He is reputed to have been 'an unlucky schoolboy', from which it may be deduced that he was often in trouble with the authorities. At home he must have made himself a thorough nuisance. He organised a gang of enterprising young hooligans who specialised in blackmailing the local shopkeepers, breaking their windows if they did not pay up. On one occasion, these spirited lads, encountering a shopkeeper who resisted their demands, dammed a gutter to flood his shop. The dam broke, 'Clive unhesitatingly threw his body into the gutter and remained there until they had repaired their work of mischief.' What his Mother said about his clothes when he returned home has not been preserved.

On another occasion he scaled the high church steeple at Market Drayton and sat nonchalantly on the top of a stone spout a few feet below the top, quite unworried by the narrowness of his perch, or the long drop below. When he had climbed down, he explained that he had gone there to obtain a particular smooth stone on the spout, which he required for some purpose that has not subsequently been revealed. He was certainly a sore trial to his father. When his son first began to come into prominence he exclaimed in some surprise, 'After all the booby has some sense'.

When his son was seventeen years old, Richard Clive secured him an appointment as a *writer* with the East India Company and packed him off to India. From the tenor of Clive's early letters, it is likely that before embarkation he received a long, stern lecture on his many shortcomings. And so when on 10 March 1743, Robert Clive boarded the East Indiaman, the *Winchester*, and the ship sailed down the Thames, it is difficult to believe that his father saw him go with any great regret. If his troublesome son came back, and this in view of the well-known hazards of the Indian climate was by no means likely, he would return almost certainly a wealthy man. In any case he was rid of him for a lengthy period. It may be conjectured that when the moment of parting arrived, both maintained their composure without undue difficulty.

And what were Clive's feelings as the *Winchester* keeled to the wind in the Channel? Possessed as he was by a restless, impatient spirit, a spirit that as a boy, and he was still little more, had made it almost impossible for others to control him; thrown out of the parental home when a baby, rejected again at the age of seventeen—what were his thoughts as the wind hummed in the rigging and the waves broke back from the side of the ship? He knew that he had been a problem to his family. He had not found it easy to make friends or inspire affection; there is no evidence that he had more than a few followers, who probably admired him for his tireless resistance to authority, but had reason to fear his uncertain temperament. He must have been conscious that he had ability above the average, but had signally failed to develop it during his schooling.

No doubt he accepted his fate as just; he was the black sheep of the family, sent overseas for his and their good. He nourished no bitterness against his parents, rather he seems to have nursed an ambition to prove them wrong, to prove in the end to be the bountiful son, not the one eternally in disgrace. And he wanted to be up and doing to dispel those periods of black depression he already knew, when nothing in life seemed of moment, nothing worthwhile.

The long-drawn-out voyage to India was something of a disaster for him. The *Winchester* was about 500 tons; no East Indiaman at that time exceeded this size, and for good reason. A British Government, anxious for the spiritual welfare of its sailors, or perhaps only resolved to give them a Christian burial, had decreed that any ship over 500 tons in size should carry a chaplain. The astute merchants of Leadenhall street had no intention of wasting their financial assets, paying for members of the church whose dividends were more likely to be realised in the next world than in this, and had laid down that none of their ships should exceed the critical size. This did not necessarily make for the comfort or the safety of their passengers.

For a period on the voyage the *Winchester* kept company with another East Indiaman, *The Princess Louisa*, but in the early hours of Tuesday 19 April, the *Louisa* struck a rock off the Cape Verde Islands. At daybreak, the dismayed observers on the *Winchester* could see only a dismasted hulk with the waves breaking over it; efforts at a rescue were foiled by a high sea, and the *Winchester* sailed on, leaving the wretched people on the *Louisa* to their fate; it was subsequently discovered that a few had managed to struggle to the shore.

At this time, ships for India used to cross the southern Atlantic nearly as far as the coast of South America to pick up the southeast trade wind to carry them round the Cape of Good Hope. Owing to an unfortunate miscalculation, on Tuesday 17 May, off the coast of Brazil 'between 3 and 4 a.m. to our great surprise found the ship to strike'. This slightly naïve remark quoted from the ship's log seems to leave a good deal unsaid. Clive himself recalls that he lost 'several of my things on the coast of Brazil, tho' I can assure you I am not the only person by many who have met with a like misfortune, it being impossible to avoid it considering the fright and confusion we were all in at the ship running on shore.'

By lightening ship the *Winchester* was eventually brought

to a safe anchorage, but the hull had been badly damaged; bad weather prevented it being moved to a place where repairs could be effected, and it was not until 22 September 1743, that it proved possible to work the *Winchester* to Pernambuco and repair the damage. While off the coast of Brazil, Clive himself had an unfortunate experience. When he was on the poop a sudden lurch threw him into the sea, 'and should certainly have drowned there being a very great sea, if the Captain had not accidentally met with a bucket and rope tied unto it which he threw out of the balcony to me, I having the good fortune to lay hold of it; I then lost the shoes off my feet and with them my silver buckles, also a hat and my wig.' So Clive wrote home to his father; characteristically he describes the incident in terms not apparently intended to excite sympathy for the dangers he had undergone, possibly he expected none, but rather to explain to his father in detail how he had come to lose some expensive items of dress.

One way or another the *Winchester* spent nine months off Brazil, and it was not until 11 February 1744 that the ship weighed anchor, saluted the fort with a nine-gun salute, and 'stood away to the northward'. Then, at last, on Friday 1 June at 7 p.m., nearly 14 months after leaving the Thames, the *Winchester* came to the Madras roads, 'dropping B Bower in 10 fathoms and a quarter. . . . At sunrise saluted the fort with nine guns and the Governor with 21'. As the cannon were booming the young Clive, not yet nineteen years of age, could look across to the misty shore of India, while the clammy heat made the sweat break out and start drenching his heavy and unsuitable clothing. It is probable that, as on most June mornings, the ship rocked gently to the long ocean swell while a sapphire sea reflected back a dazzling glare from the sunlight glancing off the waters. Just short of the shore a white line of surf would appear, then a strip of sand merging into a long low line of dark foliage. In the forefront would be seen the rusty, laterite walls of Fort St George, while to the south the sharp-sided shape of St Thomas's mount, crowned by an old Portuguese church, probably broke through the haze. It may have been a welcome sight to the youngster. It had been a disastrous voyage and his troubles were by no means over.

Not only had he lost the silver buckles of his shoes, and his wig, the unanticipated length of the journey had caused him to run out of money. As he wrote in September, 'We lay at the Brazils upwards of nine months during which time I received of Captain Stewart [the master of the ship] necessaries to the value of ten pounds and about forty shillings in

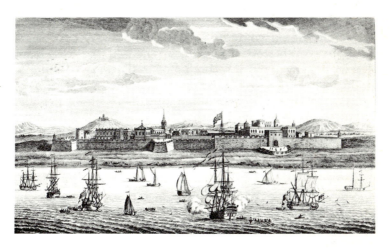

2 Madras from the sea about twenty years before Clive landed (by J. Van Ryne). Shortly after the engraving was made the walls of Fort St George were continued to the north so that the sea-gate, seen on the right of the picture, came in the centre of the fort. The hills in the background are a product of the artist's imagination. The hill with the Church is probably meant to be St Thomas Mount which should be some eight miles to the south.

money, the percentage charged making it more.' When he went ashore he found that Mr Benyon, the Governor of Madras, to whom he had an introduction and from whom he hoped for assistance, had relinquished his post and sailed for England four months before. The unfortunate youth was not merely destitute he was heavily in debt; most of his clothes had worn out during his voyage and he had been forced to buy replacements from other passengers, or as he phrased it,

'I should have been obliged to go naked'. Now he had to pay, and knowing no one ashore had to throw himself on the mercy of Captain Stewart who, thoughtfully, charged him interest at the rate of 50 per cent; he dared not borrow from local moneylenders, as the Company expressly prohibited anything of this nature, and was quite capable of returning him to England if he disobeyed its rules.

The boy, for he was no more, had not heard from anyone at home for fourteen months, and, since war had broken out with France, it was somewhat problematical when a ship with mail would come out from England. As the lonely, unhappy youth stepped ashore at the watergate with his slender baggage, and was conducted to the writers' building in the central square of the Fort, the steamy heat he was to detest burning down on him, he must have felt forlorn and forgotten. It is noticeable that the lengthy and carefully drafted letter he sent to his father that September was almost entirely concerned with explaining his borrowing and assuring him, 'I shall let no opportunity slip of improving myself in everything where I can have the least view of profit.'

Madras at this time was the principal port possessed by the East India Company along the east coast of India, the Coromandel strand as it was called. In the seventeenth century the British had followed the Portuguese and the Dutch in founding trading posts with the Great Moghul Empire. The Moghuls ruled India, generally from Delhi, and although in that century their power was still expanding, vast distances and poor communications made that power weak and diffused at the borders of their dominions. To obtain some measure of safety for their merchandise and to avoid the petty exactions of local officials, the European trading companies had generally negotiated the renting of a few square miles of territory outside existing cities, where they could trade with a degree of security and be free of official interference.

At the small village of Madraspatam in the province of the Carnatic, where the land was poor and two insignificant rivers, the Elambore and the Triplicane converged to form a lagoon by the sea, the East India Company had rented

3 Mussoolas, the surf boats of Madras. They had to be used by any one wishing to land; passengers were lucky to escape a drenching.

about five square miles from the Nawab, the title of the official ruler of the province, and the port now called Madras was created. But it had no harbour, only an open roadstead. The water was shallow and ships had to anchor nearly a mile off shore. A sudden storm could have catastrophic results, and from mid-October until the end of the year, while the northeast monsoon was blowing, it was dangerous for shipping to use the roadstead at all. Most of the cargoes had to be discharged into flat-bottomed country boats which could penetrate the surf. The combined mouth of the two rivers was useless as a harbour, as it was divided from the ocean by a sandy bar which boats could cross only immediately after the rainy season.

Nevertheless Madras was a flourishing port. Father Norbett in his memoirs, quoted in *Vestiges of old Madras*, painted a rosy picture of conditions in 1715. 'Madras or Madraspatan [*sic*] is one of the most considerable towns on the Coromandel coast. Its inhabitants and the foreigners attracted by a flourishing commerce enjoy perfect tranquillity, untroubled by wars, or the avarice of priests, or the ambitions of princes and nobles. All religions are tolerated and each has its church or temple in which any inhabitant or foreigner is free to worship in his own fashion.'

He goes on to describe the town as,

'divided into three parts. The fortress area where the garrison and the Governor reside is named Fort St George. The town proper adjoins the fort. It is very big and is inhabited by the officers, the ministers of Justice, the merchants and others of the differing nations; here one can see Armenians, Greeks, Danes, Mussulmen and Malabaris. The houses are magnificent and equal to the finest buildings in Europe. The third part which might be considered the suburbs, is open on all sides and contains a great number of Hindus and Muslims. It is claimed that the three towns amount to 100,000 souls.'

For security the Company's warehouses and the houses of most British officials of the Company had been built inside the confines of Fort St George whose ramparts stretched some 700 yards along the sea shore and perhaps 200 inland. The Fort was known as the White Town, and only Europeans were permitted to own houses within its confines. Beside its northern face was a walled town, that referred to by Father Norbett as the town proper, extending perhaps

4 Black Town, Madras—from Daniel's oriental scenery.

THE BEGINNING 29

1,000 yards further along the coast and 1,000 yards inland. This was generally referred to as the Black Town. (George V subsequently decreed that it should be known as 'George Town'.) Outside the walls of the Black Town, suburbs had grown up, of which the biggest were the Pedda Naik's Petta and the Mutial Petta. Most of the Indians lived here, but there were also a number of parks and gardens, and the garden houses, as they called them, of the wealthier European merchants. These suburbs were too extensive to be walled in, although a number of isolated redoubts and batteries were sited on the outskirts to give some form of protection.

Madras was ruled by a council consisting of a President and eight members. The President was known as the Governor, and the second member of the Council was his deputy. The President and the second member, who might normally expect to succeed the Governor, were appointed by the Court or had their appointments confirmed by it, and were generally drawn from among the senior English merchants of the port. Below the Council, and sometimes at odds with it, came the Mayor and aldermen who were elected to office by the burgesses. The Mayor and the aldermen acted as Justices of the Peace with similar powers to those in England, while the Governor and his Council acted as Quarter Sessions and a Court of Appeal. Punishment of death to an Englishman could only be awarded for acts of piracy, although the Council noted, somewhat grimly, that imprisonment under the prevailing conditions might make some prefer execution. But imprisonment, which put the Company to the expense of paying gaolers and feeding useless mouths, was looked on with disfavour, and fines which brought in money, whipping, the stocks, and the clipping off of ears were regarded as more suitable punishments.

In all this the Company's rule was absolute. The Nawab had a vague suzerainty over the area, but in practice, so long as the rent was paid, took no great interest in the affairs of the town. In general Father Norbett's praise was not unjustified. The Company's rule was just; the customs of all classes, religions and nationalities were rigorously observed, making Madras almost unique in the world at that time, and law and order maintained without partiality to any. In consequence the few derelict square miles on which Madras had originally been built now housed a thriving community; by the time Clive arrived it was estimated to amount to 200,000 souls.

The European members of the Company were divided into four classes, senior merchants, junior merchants, factors and writers. In addition, as there were no regular troops to guard the fort, the Governor in Council could enlist soldiers and grant commissions to officers, although most were commissioned by the Court of Directors in England before they came out. He could also promote them within the establishment authorised by the Company up to the rank of captain. Over its servants, civil and military, the Council exercised a paternal rule, based on the sanction that those who offended without actually committing a recognised crime could, at the discretion of the Council, be expelled and sent home to England.

The Company's idea of its responsibilities was remarkably comprehensive. It provided free boarding school for all British children between the ages of five and twelve, and similar charity schools, administered by missionaries, for all races and natives of the town. It kept a firm eye on the behaviour of its servants. Two writers who had ventured out during the night beyond the confines of the White Town, to sample presumably some illicit pleasures elsewhere, received stern justice. It is recorded in the proceedings of the Council, 'John Morgan and Conelius Moll, writers, having been several days under close confinement for keeping ill-hours in the Black Town and climbing over the battery walls next the sea at midnight, were sent for and severely reprimanded, the President acquainting them that, pursuant to the Honourable Company's orders, they should be infallibly dismissed and sent home for the next offence.' And in 1721 a Captain Fullerton was threatened with instant dismissal for 'Gaming and enticing young people to play and strip them of their money'.

However, it is apparent that the young men could still

on occasion indulge in high spirits. It is also recorded, 'We are sorry to hear that of late there has not been a sufficient decorum among our people, particularly among the young writers and factors and that there has [sic] been files of musketeers sent for to keep the peace at dinner time.' It is intriguing to speculate what could have been the activities at dinner that had to be suppressed by such extreme measures.

Since it was ruled by a President, the area surrounding Madras and under the jurisdiction of the Council was known as the Presidency. He kept considerable state, moving about in an ornate palanquin escorted by a number of soldiers, and

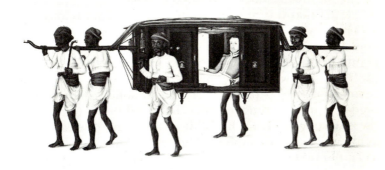

5 A gentleman taking his ease in a palankin. (Also spelt palankeen or palanquin.)

presiding over meetings with a notable degree of pomp. At this time the European population at Fort St George amounted to between 500 and 600, of whom perhaps 300 were soldiers of the garrison.

The day Clive arrived, the new Governor, Nicholas Morse, invited him to dine at his table. It must have been a difficult and perplexing occasion. Money would have been talked about in strange terms of Pagodas, Rupees and Fanams, and everyone's speech would have been interlarded with incomprehensible Hindustani. And so Clive took his place as the lowliest of the low, a newly joined writer drawing the derisory salary of £5 per annum plus a monthly allowance of 8 Pagodas, about £3 6s in the British money of the period, to pay for his food. Company servants were expected to augment their salary by private trade and any other means their ingenuity might suggest.

The daily routine would seem in some respects as suitable for a monastery as for a commercial concern. Dawn was signalled by the firing of a gun, and the first duty of the writers and factors was to attend divine service, being fined if they were absent. Breakfast in the writers' refectory might consist of bread, butter, cheese, tea, or coffee. Then commercial matters were attended to until midday, when the inferior Company servants dined together in the refectory. In the Madras Dialogues, printed in Saxony in 1750, it was suggested that this meal might include beef, pork, mutton, turkey, veal or duck, and be washed down by claret or madeira. After this meal and a nap, business was resumed at about 4 p.m. An evening service terminated the labours of the day, followed by supper which might comprise the remains of the meat served at dinner followed by a rice, sago or plum pudding, or cakes of boiled fish. After supper the entertainments of the White Town could be sampled; as already mentioned those of the Black had to be taken with some discretion. The evening's diversions consisted of little more than drinking and gambling at cards. Confined within the narrow area of British rule, it is evident that life could be very circumscribed and monotonous, and that the quality of one's companions could assume an overriding importance.

While the northeast monsoon blew, since shipping could not use the roadstead, very little business was transacted. Soon after his arrival Clive found he had virtually no work to do; he was desperately short of money and the hot damp weather was extremely unpleasant. He went down with a severe attack of fever, and when he recovered could find nothing to commend his new life; his companions were uncongenial and existence utterly miserable. He wrote home, 'I may safely say that I have not enjoyed one happy day since I left my native country.' The climate, together with unsuitable clothing and eating habits, took a heavy toll of the European population. He remarks, '. . . from the latter end of May to the beginning of November have died here not less than twelve persons, most of them young men, which reduced our number (which did not exceed fifty at the furthest) very considerably, and the major part of the rest have been visited with very severe fevers'.

The disconsolate writer was not altogether blameless for his own unhappiness. A fellow resident of Madras described him as 'inclined to be corpulent, awkward and unmannerly, his aspect gloomy, his temper morose and intractable'. His old impatience of authority had not deserted him; on one occasion it is told that when he had been compelled to apologise for his behaviour to a superior, that worthy, hoping no doubt to close the incident on a friendly note, invited him to dinner. Clive replied that, although he had been ordered to apologise, he had received no orders to accept an invitation to a meal. Such courtesy was scarcely calculated to endear him to his fellows.

Altogether the picture that emerges of Clive during these early days is that of a deeply unhappy and homesick youth, at odds with himself and his environment. He could never stand idleness and the black depression, that from time to time was to haunt him all his life, must have hung heavy on his shoulders. He had heard nothing from home, all there seemed to have forgotten that he ever existed.

One day, so Malcolm relates, a fellow writer came into his room in the writers' building to find Clive sitting by himself with a pistol on a nearby table. Clive asked his companion to take up the pistol and fire it out of the window. His companion complied, apparently, in those days the discharge of a pistol at random was nothing unusual. As the shot went off, Clive gloomily pronounced that he supposed that fate had something in store for him, as he had placed the pistol to his head and pulled the trigger twice, but on each occasion it had misfired. However, with the coming of the new year matters were to improve a little, and already the events were in train that were to write his name in great letters across the histories of England, France and India.

6 St Thomé Street; this was in the southern part of 'White Town'.

Chapter 2

THE FRENCH CAPTURE MADRAS
1745–6

As 1744 came to a close, Clive's loneliness and homesickness lingered, and it was to his uncle and Manchester that his thoughts kept returning. On 10 December he wrote to Daniel Bayley, 'If I should be so far blessed as to revisit again my own country, but more especially Manchester (the centre of all my wishes) all that I hope and desire for would be presented before me in one view.' There was still no news from England. In January he wrote again to his father, 'On the 11th December arrived here, under convoy of two men-of-war, five of the company's ships. . . . Not all the riches in India could have satisfied my desires more fully than news from my native country, but it seems fortune had elevated me to this high summit of expectation that I might in greater degree experience so heavy a disappointment. In short I was the only sorrowful person in Madras.'

The year 1745 passed quietly for Clive. He still hated his environment and agitated for a transfer to Calcutta. That he was still without news from England was perhaps not surprising. Not only was there a war with France, but later in the year wild Highland clans had surged across the border driving the red coated soldiers of George II before them. The Stuart rebellion of the '45 was a difficult time for the gentlemen of Shropshire, and much anxious thought was needed as to how they might best preserve their heads and estates. Several gentlemen from Manchester were to lose both. Fortunately Daniel Bayley was not among their number.

In peaceful Madras Clive continued at his uncongenial labours. He was at least gaining some insight into the working of a great commercial concern. Towards the end of the year he transferred to the accounts department, where he learnt a meticulousness in such matters that remained with him ever after. Nicholas Morse, the Governor, must have noticed something unusual about the youth, some talent worth cultivating; he gave him the free run of his library, an act of kindness that Clive always remembered with gratitude. So while his fellows drank and gambled he studied, an activity not likely to lessen the suspicion and dislike with which they regarded him. Perhaps it was then that he began to develop that clear understanding of Indian politics, that balanced judgement of men and events, that were to make him one of the select few among statesmen who have achieved great and permanent results and results which they intended. For although Clive gained fame as a soldier and a conqueror, he was rather a statesman than a soldier. In his military affairs he exemplified the dictum, later to be elaborated by Clausewitz, that war was the continuation of policy by other means. His battles, probably more than those of any commander before or since, were the culmination of a political strategy by which from military encounters, often trifling affairs in themselves, he obtained quite disproportionate political results.

And so, isolated from his fellows for whom he cherished little respect, he remained at his solitary studies; then later in the year his loneliness to some degree was mitigated, and in Edmund Maskelyne he found at last a friend. Soon, however, he was to leave academic studies and see instead the realities of political and military power shaping events before his eyes.

Since 1740 strong new forces had been agitating the Carnatic. Although in 1745 all might appear peaceful, beneath the placid surface there boiled a veritable volcano whose eruption could only be a matter of time. The great Moghul Empire was decaying, and as it decayed the whole political structure in India had begun to collapse. In the seventeenth century, when the Empire was still expanding, the Moghuls had imposed a Muslim military hierarchy over most of the Hindu states that they conquered converting them into provinces under a governor with the title of 'nawab'. In those Hindu kingdoms, however, where the ruling family had discreetly submitted without a struggle, the existing dynasty was often retained, the rulers keeping the ancient title of 'rajah'. In theory all nawabs and rajahs held their posts from the Emperor, and on taking office required to be confirmed in their positions by an Imperial decree known as a *firman*. But as a multitude of states and

7 An Indian Nawab and his wife.

provinces came under the Imperial aegis, two great vice-royalties were created; the viceroys had the right to appoint the governors of provinces and states, subject only to the overriding power of the Emperor.

With the passage of time most appointments became, in practice, hereditary. Further, as the Imperial power waned, the Emperors became happy to approve the appointment of anyone who made the gesture of acknowledging their supremacy by a substantial gift and a generally unfulfilled

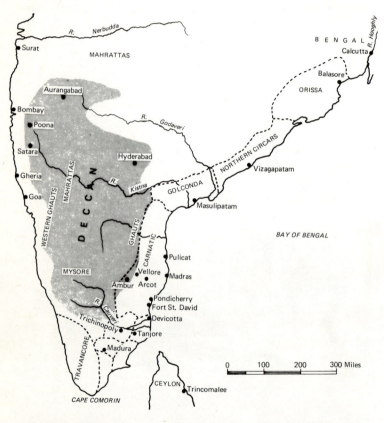

2 Southern India. The boundaries shown for states are only very approximate and have been loosely based on those given by J. W. Fortescue in his *History of the British Army*, Vol II, modified by details in contemporary accounts and maps.

promise of tribute. This practice could have vicious consequences. Any usurper who had seized his position by force and was prepared to pay sufficient money could be confident of legitimising his action; even when almost all Imperial power had gone, such was the memory of ancient majesty *firmans* still commanded respect.

All governors, even those whose territories were insignificant, maintained their own armies, both to enforce their authority and to provide their superiors with troops when required. In the eighteenth century, as the central power withered away, the rulers of states and provinces became virtually independent, settling disputes with their neighbours by force of arms rather than by reference to some nominal superior. During the first half of that century one of the greatest figures in the Empire was the Viceroy, or Subah, of the Deccan, the Nizam-ul-Mulk. By 1740 the Nizam, now an old man but still one of outstanding ability, had long been independent in all but name. He was absolute ruler over a vast tract of country comprising almost the whole of southern India.

The Deccan proper was an immense table-land that stretched southwards down the Indian Peninsula for nearly 700 miles to end about 200 miles from its tip at Cape Comorin. The edges of this enormous plateau broke down in a series of precipitous hills and tangled ridges to either coast, and these hill regions were called respectively the eastern and western Ghauts. In the west the coastal plain was narrow and generally unimportant. Three big European trading stations had been established along it, in the north, Surat, then 150 miles to the south, Bombay and 300 miles still further south, the Portuguese stronghold of Goa. In the east, however, the coastal strip was fertile and extended inland for upwards of 100 miles. Along it had grown up a number of prosperous states, many of which had formerly formed part of the once extensive kingdom of Golconda, but which now acknowledged the sovereignty of the Great Moghul, in the person of his viceroy, the Nizam. In the north of this region were the northern Circars, or provinces, with Vizagapatam as the principal port. South of the Circars, and often included with them, lay the now sadly diminished Kingdom of Golconda; it contained the mouths of the Kistna and the Godaveri, two great rivers that meandered westwards across the Deccan almost to the western Ghauts; between the two river mouths was situated the rich port of Masulipatam where the East India Company had established a trading post or factory, as it was then termed. Further south again the most important province of all, the Carnatic, stretched some 300 miles along the coast; bordered to the east by the sea and to the west by the Ghauts, its shape resembled that of an elongated and irregular rectangle.

Its capital was Arcot and it contained within its borders not only the great British trading station of Madras, but also at Pondicherry the principal station of the French. Thus both Britain and France, about to become bitter rivals for power, were largely dependent on the goodwill of the Nawab, the Muslim ruler of the province, for their continued prosperity. For the last three generations members of the same family had succeeded each other. The Nawabs had ruled well and were popular with the people, but had been somewhat lukewarm in their attachment to the Nizam and dilatory in their payments of tribute. So long as the British and French forebore from interfering in each other's affairs, the personality of the Nawab affected neither very greatly, but if a struggle for power were to develop, the attitude of the Nawab and the ability to influence his actions might be of vital importance. A hostile Nawab, by imposing a trade boycott, could ruin either of the European ports.

South of the Carnatic, near the southern tip of India were a number of minor Hindu states of which the three most important were Tanjore on the east coast, Trichinopoly inland from it, and Travancore lying along the west coast from the edge of the Ghauts to Cape Comorin. The Nizam, as viceroy to the Moghul, was sovereign over the whole of this enormous area and ruled it from his two capital cities of Aurangabad and Hyderabad. But a vast and formidable power had arisen in the northwest of his realm. The Maharatta Confederacy, set up by the great Mahratta leader Sivaji in the seventeenth century, from its twin centres at Poona and Satara had spread across to eastern India, and also down the western side of the Deccan. Mahratta armies at one time or another had marched over and plundered all the south Indian states, including the Carnatic. Had the Mahrattas been united they must have overturned the Moghul Empire and ruled all India; but the Confederacy now was one in name only, the great chieftains

8 A Mahratta cavalry commander taking his ease with his wife.

seeking to carve out kingdoms for themselves rather than enthrone one of their number.

They posed an enduring threat to the Nizam and to every state in India. Their myriad light horsemen had penetrated to Cape Comorin and swept up to the gates of Calcutta. In a famous description of them it was said,

'Nor did they, though they had become great sovereigns therefore cease to be free-booters; they still retained the predatory habits of their forefathers. Whenever their kettledrums were heard, the peasant threw his bag of rice on his shoulder, hid his small savings in his girdle and fled with his wife and children to the mountains and the jungles—to the milder neighbourhood of the hyaena and tiger.'

In 1740 they were to precipitate a chain of events in the Carnatic that led to the rise of the British and ultimately to their own downfall little more than sixty years later. That year, under the pretext that as the result of a previous invasion the Nawab owed them tribute, a large army under Raghoji Bhonsla invaded that province. The Nizam, who had been at odds with the Nawab for some time, refrained from intervening; it is even suggested that he engineered the invasion, as an ingenious way of keeping the Mahrattas occupied while at the same time contriving to chastise an insolent vassal. The Nawab gave battle near the town of Ambur. His army was utterly defeated and he and one of his two sons were killed. The victors overran the whole province seeking plunder rather than conquest.

Now the succession to the vacant Nawabship became a subject for intrigues that were to keep the Carnatic in a ferment for the next fourteen years. Initially Safdar Ali, the only surviving son of the old Nawab, was proclaimed the new Nawab; he had only a single son, a child of four years old, as his heir, but he had two sisters, one married to a prominent noble called Chunda Sahib, the other to his first cousin, Murtaza Ali Khan. If anything happened to Safdar Ali and his son, either of these would have a claim to the succession.

Chunda Sahib was, by all reports, a competent general and a gallant and chivalrous man. He was at this time Governor of Trichinopoly. In the recent past its Rajah had, over a considerable period, omitted to render the tribute to the Moghul that he owed, and the Nawab, who in this matter had the responsibilities of a tax collector, had sent Chunda Sahib with an army to instil in the Rajah a clearer idea of his duties. Chunda Sahib prosecuted this aim with no little zeal. He secured Trichinopoly by a dubious stratagem and as a reward was appointed by the Nawab to be Governor of the city.

But now that the Nawab had been overthrown, one of Raghoji Bhonsla's generals, Morari Rao, a cunning and courageous commander who was destined to flit across the history of the Carnatic for some years, supporting any faction that offered him a reasonable rate of remuneration or opportunity for plunder, thought he saw an excellent opportunity to acquire an estate; he laid siege to Trichinopoly, assuring its inhabitants that he had come to save them from their muslim oppressors. At the end of some three months he forced Chunda Sahib to capitulate, installed himself as the new Governor, and sent Chunda Sahib as a prisoner to the Mahratta stronghold of Satara, hoping in due course to collect a substantial ransom. Thus for the time being Chunda Sahib had been disposed of, but Safdar Ali's other brother-in-law, Murtaza, was still Governor of Vellore, a fort some ten miles from Arcot; he had escaped attack, presumably, because Vellore did not contain enough plunder to tempt the Mahrattas to a difficult siege.

On the death of the old Nawab, although Safdar Ali had been proclaimed his successor, the Nizam had withheld his recognition; meanwhile the Mahrattas were swarming all over the Carnatic, plundering and pillaging and demanding a huge sum of money as the price for their departure. Before embarking on the perilous task of restoring order to his chaotic province, buying off the Mahrattas, and obtaining the recognition of the Nizam, Safdar Ali thought it prudent to find a safe refuge for his family. The Mahrattas after receiving presents from the British and French, the latter thoughtfully included a handsome gift of choice French liqueurs—there were some advantages in dealing with Hindus—had left the European settlements unmolested; they were not a little influenced by the knowledge that both were fortified, and that neither would be given up without a stubborn resistance. Now Safdar Ali selected Madras as a temporary haven for his family. His choice caused something of a commotion; the council at Fort St George reported:

'On the 21st [September 1741] at midnight the Nawab sent into town his mother, his lady and his son about four years old. Their female attendance are very numerous, which has given us much trouble to find room for them. We sent our poligar [the head of the Indian community] with 200 peons and our country music to meet them at Triplicane. The Guard which the Nawab sent with them returned from thence, except 20 horse that came into the town with them. The Nawab sent notice that he intended to come into the town next afternoon. Next afternoon Mr Monson and Captain Hollond, the Poligar with 200 peons, and our country music met him at the edge of the bounds [the limits of the Company's territory]. When he came to the Triplicane bridge he stopped then and sent all his force back except about 30 horse and 100 peons; but he was met by many thousands of our inhabitants who attended him from Triplicane to the foot of the inland bridge. The Governor attended by the Council met him at the fort gate, when the guns from the ramparts saluted him with 61 guns, and the four Europe ships with 21 each. The governors of the towns to the northward of this place come in daily to pay their respects to him. 'Tis great concern to us that we are not better prepared for his reception and accommodation, but the Nawab makes it easy for us as he can, having very few attendants about him and those extremely quiet.'

Some of the ladies participated in the excitement. One of them who accompanied Governor Benyon's wife when she visited the hareem wrote an account of the episode:

'We had all the governor's attendants as well as his lady's and his music playing before us all the way and thousands of people looking at us on our way thither. When we arrived, Mrs B. was handed by a lady, who was to introduce her, through two halls which brought us into a large garden, and a pavilion at the end of it where the Nawab's lady was seated. A grand Moor lady of her acquaintance came to receive Mrs B. in the middle of the garden, and presented her to the Nawab's lady who was seated in the middle of the pavilion upon a settee covered with rich embroidery upon crimson velvet.

'I must now give you a description of her person and dress. Her person was thin, genteel and middlesized: her complexion tawny as the Moors all are: her eyes as black as possible, large and fine and painted at the edges, which is what most Moors do. Her lips painted red and between every tooth which was fine and regular she was painted black that they might look like ebony. Her attendants which were about thirty ladies were the same. Her face was done over like frosted work with leaf gold; the nails of her fingers and toes, for she was bare footed, were painted red, likewise the middle of her hands. Her hair was black as jet, very long and thick, which was comb'd back neatly and then braided; it hung a good deal below her waist; she had a fillet of diamonds round her head edged with pearls of a large size. Round her neck she had twenty rows of pearls none smaller than a pea, but a great many of them as large as the end of my little finger. Her coat, which she had on, was made of fine gold muslin close to her and a slashed sleeve; she wore a gold veil which she hung carelessly over her head and it went over her body; all the front part of it was trimmed with a row of great pearls. Her feet and ankles were if possible richer and more adorned than her arms and hands.

'She had her little son brought in to see us, the richness of whose dress, were I to describe it, you would imagine I was telling you some fairy story. But in short he was loaded with gold, pearls and diamonds. The very fan that was carried to keep the sun off him, and in make like a fire screen only four times as large, was crimson velvet all set in figures with pearls and diamonds. I own I thought myself in a dream the whole time I was there.

'I must not omit giving you a description of the Pavilion. It was very large and spacious, all the bottom covered with fine carpets and entirely hung round with muslin valens; at one end there stood the bed or rather cot, the frame and pillars of which were of solid gold, and gold gauze curtains, with a rich counterpane. At the entrance of the pavilion there was a large embroidered carpet with a pillow of the same work at each end, which was opposite to the settee the ladies sat upon, for us to walk over. There was something like an awning made of crimson silk, which went all on the outside of the pavilion and was supported with pillars of gold. She had two gold censors of incense and sandalwood that almost suffocated us with perfume.... Their numerous riches are all the enjoyment they have, for she is not suffered to go out all the year round; and when obliged to travel, is covered up in her palanquin in such a manner that no mortal can see her, and it would be death for any man to attempt to see a Moor[1] lady.'

Safdar Ali, after a brief stay, went on to Vellore to seek the help of his brother-in-law. For nearly a year he vainly negotiated with the Mahrattas who refused to moderate their demands. During this time it must have occurred to Murtaza that if an accident happened to Safdar Ali, there would be only his infant son between himself and the Nawabship. And then it may have seemed unenterprising, even improvident, to wait on nature. On 5 October 1742, Governor Benyon was woken at two in the morning by a courier with the news that Murtaza had murdered the Nawab. Benyon doubled all guards and awaited events. Murtaza now proclaimed himself Nawab and set out for Arcot. What remained of the State army and the chief nobles refused to recognise him, and Morari Rao in Trichinopoly sided with the nobles. Murtaza lost his nerve, and disguising himself as a woman fled back to the safety of his fort at Vellore. With

[1] At this time Indian Muslims were called Moors, while Hindus were often called 'Gentues' or 'Gentoos'.

great solemnity Safdar Ali's five-year-old son was proclaimed Nawab.

At this stage with most of the old dynasty disposed of and the Carnatic in chaos, the Nizam thought it time to intervene. He advanced on the province with an enormous army, said to be 120,000 strong. The Mahrattas prudently withdrew without battle.

The Nizam now displayed the statecraft for which he was famous. He declared that when Safdar Ali's son attained manhood he should be appointed Nawab, but meanwhile one of his own generals should act as Governor. The first general he selected unfortunately contracted a mysterious illness and died in great pain within twenty-four hours. The Nizam chose another, Anwar-ud-Din, to replace him. Anwar-ud-Din had shown some eagerness for the post, an eagerness which the malicious held might have had some connection with the mysterious illness from which his predecessor had died. Such matters caused the Nizam little concern, and that great man, who by now had taken up residence in Masulipatam, turned his attention to other more pressing affairs.

With Murtaza and Anwar-ud-Din looking after his interests it was clear that Safdar Ali's child was unlikely to enjoy a long life. It is asserted that Murtaza, who combined treachery and cowardice in almost equal degree, now plotted to have Anwar-ud-Din and the infant both assassinated, but that his plans miscarried and Anwar-ud-Din survived while the princeling was killed. It is not improbable that Murtaza was incompetent, but the death of the young prince was decidedly not unfortunate for Anwar-ud-Din, and to lay the blame for the murder on Murtaza might also have its uses. Whatever the truth of these unpleasing transactions, the Nizam duly authorised Anwar-ud-Din to assume the title of Nawab, appointed his eldest son, Mahfuz Khan, as deputy Nawab and his second son, Mohammed Ali, to be Governor of Trichinopoly. Mohammed Ali was to play a considerable part in the turbulent years that lay ahead. For the present, however, with Murtaza discredited the only threat to the new Nawab could come from Chunda Sahib, securely locked up by the Mahrattas in Satara; it was improbable that Anwar-ud-Din would exert himself greatly to raise a ransom.

And so, a year before Clive landed, Anwar-ud-Din had become the far from popular ruler of a distracted province. Nevertheless he managed to impose his authority, and in 1744 when Britain and France went to war over the Austrian succession, he was still its undisputed master, and suzerain over the British in Madras and the French in Pondicherry.

For a period the French company had been moribund and nearly bankrupt, but recently under active French governors it had prospered. Earlier in the century when in Europe Marlborough had been thrashing the generals of Louis XIV during the war of the Spanish succession, the British and French trading companies had contrived to remain on good terms, and avoid becoming involved in the hostilities between their two countries. As not too secure intruders in a foreign land, the policy had much to commend it.

As a result, in 1744 the fortifications both at Fort St George and Pondicherry, while strong enough to withstand a sudden onslaught, were in no condition to face a well planned attack. On the outbreak of the new war the French Governor General in the Indies, Joseph-François Dupleix, one of the truly great Frenchmen, wrote to Governor Nicholas Morse who had now been installed in Madras and suggested that neither side should engage in hostilities east of the Cape. Morse, however, knew, and suspected Dupleix knew as well, that a British naval squadron had been dispatched to Indian waters, and demurred. Dupleix now appealed to Anwar-ud-Din at Arcot. The Nawab wrote to Morse: 'As all the sea-ports are the Great Moghul's and some of them were only entrusted to the care of the Europeans in the expectation that they would behave themselves peaceably and quietly in Hindustan, you will consider it thoroughly and seriously and take care not to raise a disturbance on shore; for you shall be called to account for it hereafter in case you do.' Morse accepted the prohibition but ended his letter, 'As I have already acquainted Your Excellency that the commanders of His Majesty's ships are not under my direction, I cannot oblige myself to answer for their conduct.'

The British naval squadron under Commodore Barnett arrived shortly afterwards. Barnett agreed to respect the Nawab's orders, and called off an assault he had projected against Pondicherry which otherwise, with the poor fortifications it possessed at that time, must certainly have fallen. In October 1745, to avoid the northeast monsoon, Barnett sailed to Mergui on the Burmese coast. In January 1746, Dupleix sent a force to make a demonstration against Fort St David, a subsidiary trading post that the British had constructed at Cuddalore only sixteen miles south of Pondicherry. Some of Barnett's ships, however, appeared offshore and the French thought it wise to retire. Morse was perturbed by their action and wrote to Anwar-ud-Din, pointing out that the British had respected his prohibition and requesting confirmation that it applied equally to the French. Anwar-ud-Din replied that he was very pleased with the conduct of the British and concluded, 'You may depend upon it that the Governor of Pondicherry will not be suffered to behave in a different manner.'

During this time Barnett, while prepared to abstain from action on the Indian mainland, saw no reason why he should deprive himself of the rich pickings to be obtained in prize money if he seized French merchantmen sailing the high seas, and made some very profitable captures. Dupleix was highly incensed at these losses, particularly as he owned one of the cargoes that was captured. But he was not merely a merchant with a flair for organisation; he was a statesman who had a splendid vision beckoning him onwards. He had a far clearer understanding of recent events than the lately promoted Morse, and was not disposed to treat the instructions of the Nawab with too great a respect. He dreamed of France supreme in southern India, perhaps in the whole of India, and was far-sighted enough to foresee that the British might well be his greatest obstacle. Now he affected to consider the activities of Barnett to be an infraction of the tacit agreement with the British, and that this justified him making a riposte, the means for which were shortly to be placed within his grasp.

The French Governor of the Mauritius was a naval captain, François Mahé de la Bourdonnais. He was a man of tremendous energy and ability, but a corsair rather than a servant of the Crown. He believed in making war and in making war pay. He had no patience with long-term political objectives. The authorities of the French Company in France, knowing his temperament and dreading where it might lead him, had prevailed on the French Government to remove their naval squadron from Mauritius before the outbreak of the war. Such precautions were useless against a man like La Bourdonnais. When he learnt from Dupleix that a British naval squadron was preying on French commerce in the Bay of Bengal, he rapidly improvised a naval squadron of his own. He had one man-of-war, the *Achille*, seventy guns; round her, by arming a miscellaneous collection of merchantmen, he organised a fleet of nine vessels with armaments varying from twenty-six guns upwards, and embarked in them about 2,000 European soldiers and 1,000 African; then he set sail for Pondicherry.

While La Bourdonnais was making his preparations, Barnett, by all accounts a brave and energetic sailor, died of a fever. It was an unfortunate loss for the British. His successor, Captain Peyton, was more anxious to escape responsibility than to achieve renown; he succeeded in avoiding the latter with considerable skill. The British squadron had now been at sea for more than two years and urgently needed a refit. In early June Peyton set sail for Trincomalee on the coast of Ceylon, where there was a harbour suitable for refitting his ships. On 25 June he met La Bourdonnais' squadron sailing north towards Pondicherry. Although he had only six ships against nine, Peyton had a properly organised naval squadron and should have been able to give a good account of himself. However, in the event, after an indecisive cannonading at long range he continued for Trincomalee, leaving the way to Pondicherry open. La Bourdonnais was not slow to take his opportunity.

When he stepped ashore at Pondicherry to confer with Dupleix, the two men met with great outward cordiality but deep inward distrust; both were men of powerful personality, both unaccustomed to paying much heed to the wishes of others, and to make matters worse, it was far from clear what their relationship should be. Dupleix as Governor General of the East Indies was certain that La Bourdonnais was his subordinate. La Bourdonnais, as Governor of the Mauritius, was equally certain that no one but the King of France was entitled to his obedience. At first these divergent views remained unvoiced, and Dupleix managed to persuade La Bourdonnais to act against Madras. The French naval commander was a master of his trade. He realised it would be dangerous to move against Madras, while there was a strong British naval squadron that could strike when many of his men and much of his equipment had been placed on land. Before he attacked Madras, it was clearly desirable to cripple the British. As soon as Peyton returned from Trincomalee he sailed to engage him, but the British ships resolutely declined action and disappeared to the northward, not dropping anchor until they reached Pulicat about thirty miles north of Madras. La Bourdonnais was now in a quandary. He decided to test British reactions by bombarding British shipping in the Madras roads. Peyton not only took no notice, he sailed away to the mouth of the River Hooghli near Calcutta apparently uninterested in the fate of Madras.[1] In justice to the Royal Navy, it must be said that Peyton's flagship, the *Medway*, was leaky and the seaworthiness of the whole squadron was open to question.

La Bourdonnais now resolved to mount a serious attack on Madras. He landed a force of infantry well to the south, who could march parallel to his fleet and secure him a beachhead. Then on 3 September, Clive, if he had strolled on the ramparts of Fort St George, could have seen the French fleet come to anchor opposite St Thomas's Mount and a mass of small boats start ferrying men and equipment to the shore. The curtain had risen on the first act of the dramatic duel between the French and the British for supremacy in India. It was an act that rapidly degenerated to low comedy, verging on farce. Clive probably watched the extraordinary

---

[1] Peyton was subsequently court-martialled but acquitted.

52   CLIVE: PROCONSUL OF INDIA

antics of his seniors with an amused contempt, feeling justified in the earlier resentment he had displayed of their authority.

The fortifications of Fort St George were in a deplorable condition. A report on the ramparts of the Black Town, that had been made a few years earlier, had stated that the houses and outhouses of the suburbs which had been built

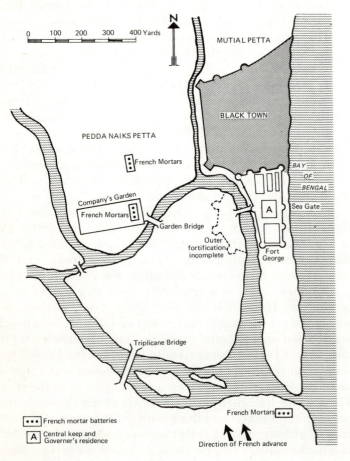

3 Madras about 1746. Based on details given in *Vestiges of Old Madras*, Vol. II, by Henry Davison Love.

against them furnished excellent cover to an attacker. On the other hand the ramparts were in such a ruinous condition that, unless they were buttressed by these houses, they would almost certainly collapse. Some 200 pieces of artillery had been mounted on the walls, but since the total number of gunners, quaintly known as the gunroom crew, amounted to little more than 100 all told, after all gunners had to be paid at regular intervals for doing nothing in particular,

9 Fort St George from the south. La Bourdonnais landed a little lower down the coast.

there was an unhappy disproportion between men and equipment. The European infantry were in little better shape. They were organised in three companies under the command of Captain Peter Eckman, subsequently described as a 'superannuated and ignorant Swede', Eckman himself claimed to have fifty-six years' service and was scarcely in the first bloom of youth. The muster roll of the Madras garrison on 1 September 1746, as quoted in *Vestiges of old Madras* makes illuminating reading:

'Muster Rolls Sept. 1, 1746........................300
Deduct:
  Portuguese sentinels, vagabond deserters from the military and ships at Goa, the worst men in the world for the service at that time............................ 23
Lewis Caldirra, a sentinel, a country Portuguese....... 1
Anthony De Cruze Rollier, a ditto................... 1
Jacob De Rovaria and Michael De Rozarrio, two drummer slave boys............................... 2
Hanibal Julian, a black, sent from England 1
Luke Schields, a Fleming, in prison for corresponding with the French and assisting prisoners to escape...... 1
Adrian Miller, deserted............................ 1
Serjeants upon the rolls not in service 3
Sentinel ditto..................................... 1
In hospital....................................... 34
Men who ought to have been there, old men and boys at the least 32
Remains (exclusive of the 23 Portuguese first mentioned) Europeans supposed to be good and effective, British subjects and foreigners Protestants and Catholics, including commissioned officers....................200'

In addition the gentlemen of the Company were formed into a militia to relieve the so-called soldiers of their routine duties.

  Fort St George, with its medieval-type towers and high vulnerable walls, was in no shape to face a systematic siege conducted on the European model. Governor Morse, well versed in commercial affairs and the day-to-day running of his community, found the situation baffling and not a little unnerving. At the inevitable council of war, a violent altercation broke out between Eckman and the Master Gunner. The Master Gunner maintained that the garrison was insufficient to man the walls of both the Fort and the Black Town. Eckman violently disagreed. Hot words were exchanged and after the majority had voted for evacuating the Black Town, Eckman threw his sword on the ground, saying, so he averred, 'Damn this sword as I have not leave to defend the place with it.' Altogether it was a scene scarcely likely to reassure a nervous governor, or spread confidence among the garrison.

On 5 September La Bourdonnais constructed a battery of ten mortars to the west of the fort. The company's peons, local Indian irregulars hired together with their commanders to man the customs posts and maintain order in the Indian Quarter, had up to this time professed great eagerness for battle; now they were ordered to storm the French battery; however, once they had left the protection of the ramparts, their ardour rapidly evaporated, and firing a few random shots they disappeared into the countryside to watch from a safe distance the events of the siege.

On 7 September the French battery opened fire. For a time the guns of the fort gave a spirited reply. It does not appear that they inflicted much damage on the French, but unhappily most of the British guns fell to pieces in the course of the action. It turned out that the gun carriages, imposing enough on the ramparts, had been made from inferior wood purchased at a cut rate, which no doubt at the time had enabled the Master Gunner to make a useful addition to his income. Now, after a few rounds, the gun carriages disintegrated putting the guns irretrievably out of action. It was probably about this time that the Master Gunner, one of the few casualties of the siege, died from heart failure. That evening all the Indian servants followed the example of the peons and decamped over the walls.

Nor was this all. The European soldiers of the garrison were also giving cause for alarm. While declaring themselves ready to defy the enemy, they gave evidence of their metal by being even readier to defy their officers. And although the Governor had considerately given them some 'fine provisions' and quantities of arrack, punch and other alcoholic beverages with which to keep up their spirits, the ungrateful wretches only seemed interested in becoming drunk, or plundering the empty houses in the abandoned Black Town.

Meanwhile the French mortars continued remorselessly

to lob their bombs over the walls of the fort. A Mr Cole has given a description of what the garrison had to endure.

'So also the house servants of all the gentlemen and ladies and most of their slaves, leaped down from the walls in the night, insomuch that the gentlemen and ladies could not get servants to dress any victuals, or bring them water to drink. Add to this the constant alarms of bombs falling causing everyone to leave victuals, drink, clothes, sleep, and everything else to run into the open air and see which way to avoid the bombs then falling. These alarms, had so harassed and fatigued the gentlemen that they were ready to die for want of sleep the third day.'

There were very few actual casualties, but clearly the garrison had become exhausted from dodging the bombs, and then there were the women and children to consider. On the evening of 8 September the Governor and his Council decided that the time had come to treat. Two emissaries were sent to inquire, rather belatedly, from La Bourdonnais why he was indulging in hostilities on Indian soil when the Nawab had expressly forbidden such activities. La Bourdonnais proved unrepentant and a period of wrangling ensued. The Frenchman was, however, worried that the British squadron might appear while the crews of his ships were ashore, and wanted to bring the whole affair to a conclusion. He showed the emissaries a battery of 24-pounder guns he had emplaced to breach the walls of the fort, and spoke darkly of the horrors that were likely to follow a storm. The emissaries were impressed. He then hinted that if the price was right, he would be prepared to sail away and leave the British in possession of Madras. Money was something that Governor Morse understood and he promptly agreed to capitulate. After some further haggling La Bourdonnais agreed to accept a ransom of 1,100,000 Pagodas (about £440,000 in the money of that time). Details of how this sum should be paid were under discussion when Dupleix intervened from Pondicherry. He now began to reveal his true intentions. The ransom would have amply compensated the French Company for the loss of their ships, but their loss had been but a pretext. Dupleix aimed at vastly more ambitious projects than milking the citizens of Madras of their wealth. He sent orders that Madras should be razed to the ground. La Bourdonnais categorically refused either to recognise his authority or to fall in with his wishes; in honour he could scarcely have complied. Dupleix, somewhat optimistically, sent three commissioners to put the recalcitrant sailor under arrest. That officer was not so easily disposed of. He ordered all the troops from Pondicherry to embark, then when he had them safely below hatches, he himself arrested the three commissioners. Acrimonious negotiations between Dupleix, La Bourdonnais and Morse dragged on. Then the weather took a hand. The monsoon broke early and on 2 October a sudden storm wrecked two of the Frenchman's ships, dismasted four more and scattered the rest. Now La Bourdonnais was anxious to be gone. He signed an agreement whereby the French undertook to evacuate Madras by the end of January and to allow the British Company meanwhile to continue trading, pocketed a sum of 100,000 Pagodas for his personal use, handed over Madras to the commissioners, and on 12 October, having reassembled what remained of his fleet, sailed for Pondicherry. Here he exchanged a few well-chosen words with Dupleix and then continued on his way to Mauritius and eventually France. His quarrel with Dupleix significantly altered the situation. Owing to his losses in shipping, he had to leave a substantial number of his soldiers behind him, a welcome reinforcement for the French, but his departure robbed Dupleix of the warships which were vital for success in this war between ports. It made it still more essential to retain Madras; and once La Bourdonnais had disappeared he repudiated the treaty.

After the capitulation, all the British in Madras had been put on parole not to carry arms against the French. When the terms of the surrender had been repudiated, it was argued that the parole was no longer valid. The prospect of being incarcerated by the French made little appeal to such as Clive. He and Edmund Maskelyne put on Indian

10 The irrigation works, Madras.

dress, escaped, and made their way to Fort St David, the only British stronghold now remaining on the coast.

With the influx of refugees that fort became abominably overcrowded; trade was at a standstill, and time hung heavy, not least for those who had escaped from Madras and who lacked almost everything in the way of clothing and money. There was little to do save gamble and drink, and Floyer, the Governor of the fort, set the pace. Clive, deprived of his library, joined in. One evening he was playing with a group of civilians and two or three officers. The officers of the Company were, with one or two exceptions, not particularly good officers and generally far from being gentlemen. On this occasion the officers taking part obviously thought the civilians fair game; they cheated blatantly, reckoning contemptuously that their opponents would never dare to protest. In Clive they had mistaken their man. At the end of the evening the others weakly paid up, but Clive refused point-blank. He claimed that the officers had won by cheating, therefore they were not entitled to their winnings and he did not intend to pay.

The word 'cheating', if not withdrawn, could only be answered in one way. Clive was obdurate, and the chief offender made the inevitable challenge. The whole affair now became so irregular, that it is impossible not to suspect that the officers were desperately trying to find a way out of their dilemma. Their bluff had been called; win or lose, a duel in such circumstances must mean ruin; yet they could not accept an accusation of cheating; to have done so would have branded them as unfit to be officers, and cowards to boot. This awkward fellow, Clive, had to be frightened into making some form of retraction. He was challenged to fight immediately; he accepted. There were to be no seconds, perhaps no one was prepared to become involved in an affair with such dangerous implications. Clive was unmoved. Taking their pistols the two adversaries went outside to settle the matter in the dark. It is not clear how the order to fire was given without seconds; perhaps they stood back to back and merely marched a set number of paces away from each other, having agreed that on a word from one of them they would turnabout and fire. Whatever the arrangement, Clive fired first and missed. His opponent withheld his fire, in itself a grave breach of duelling etiquette; perhaps he still hoped to find a way of extracting himself from an impossible situation. He walked up to him, put his loaded pistol to Clive's head, and ordered him to ask for his life. Clive did so. He then ordered Clive to retract his accusation. Clive refused. The officer retorted that unless Clive retracted he would fire. It is recorded that Clive replied, 'Fire and be damned. I said you cheated, I say so still and I will never pay you.' The officer, frustrated of his last chance of a cheap victory, withdrew, trying to cover his retreat by saying the man must be mad.

Now after the event, it is easy to suppose that the officer never intended to fire. Had he fired in such circumstances he must certainly have had to run for it or be arrested; and if Clive had died, he must have been charged with murder, and sent home to England with every prospect of being hanged. Had he only wounded Clive he must surely have been cashiered. Even if he had made his escape, at that period it was unusual for Indian Princes to employ European adventurers to train their forces, the most he could hope for was a doubtful refuge in Pondicherry. However, it is unlikely that any of those present were completely sober, least of all Clive's opponent, and his action could scarcely have been predicted with certainty. Clive stood his ground in the dark, while a man with a loaded pistol advanced on him, holding that pistol aimed at his head and, as far as Clive knew, likely to fire it at any moment. Then when Clive refused to retract he must have expected to die. On this occasion he demonstrated a quality of cold, inflexible courage that was to be one of his most enduring characteristics.

The next day Clive declined to give any evidence about the events of the night before. He said that his opponent had granted him his life and he would neither testify against him, nor associate with him. His fellows, if they still felt no great affection for the young writer, can scarcely have withheld their admiration. It was the old tale of the boy who stood up to the school bully, but framed in somewhat deadlier circumstances. And now Clive's days as a junior civil servant of the Company were nearly done.

Chapter 3

FORT ST DAVID AND THE SIEGE OF PONDICHERRY
1746–8

In Arcot Anwar-ud-Din had been watching the activities of the French with mounting distaste. To avoid the possibility that his actions might be misinterpreted, Dupleix suavely wrote to explain that he was besieging Madras merely in order to restore it to the ruler of the Carnatic. Anwar-ud-Din awaited this happy termination of the affair with some impatience and considerable scepticism. At this time he was an old man, indeed it has been asserted that he was over eighty years of age; he had spent too many years in corrupt courts, had practised himself too many devious intrigues, to treat Dupleix's assurances as much more than an agreeable form of persiflage. By early October he had assembled an army and he dispatched it under his eldest son, Mahfuz Khan, to take over Madras from the French, by negotiation if possible, by force if necessary. It was a move that was to have very significant results.

On 15 October a party of cavalrymen from the Nawab's army penetrated into the garden suburbs of Madras and started to plunder some houses. Desprémesnil, who had taken charge of the port after La Bourdonnais had departed, sent emissaries to protest; the emissaries were arrested and roughly handled. Desprémesnil, recognising the delicacy of the situation, sailed away to Pondicherry to confer with Dupleix, leaving his deputy, Barthélemy, with orders to repel any attack on Fort St George or Black Town, but not to exacerbate the situation by any overt offensive action. The Indian armies of this time were generally composed of hordes of undisciplined horsemen supported by large, antiquated, and nearly immovable cannon. Such troops were unlikely seriously to endanger an adequately fortified and garrisoned town. Nevertheless it was a bold decision that Dupleix made, when he sent instructions to Barthélemy to hold Madras at all costs, and told him that a substantial reinforcement was on the way.

Meanwhile Mahfuz Khan established camps at Triplicane and Fort Egmont, and then gradually extended his lines northwards, until he had surrounded Madras from the landward side. Some of his men occupied the suburb of the Pedda Naik Pettah, and seized the wells on which Fort St George depended for water. The French garrison soon became critically short, and Barthélemy realised that he must either recapture the wells or be compelled to surrender. On 22 October, despite his instructions, he ordered 400 men, about two-thirds of his garrison, to sally out and capture the Pedda Naik Pettah. The sally was completely successful. Some cavalry from an encampment in the suburb formed to resist the French advance; two guns the French had towed forward opened a rapid fire with grape, and the cavalry made off without attempting a charge. Barthélemy had secured his wells, but at the expense of engaging in open hostilities.

By now the reinforcement Dupleix had promised was within two days' march of Madras. Mahfuz Khan resolved to concentrate his army at St Thomé four miles to the south, intercept this force and destroy it. It seemed an excellent opportunity to teach the French a lesson where they had no walls with which to protect themselves. On 24 October the French column, about 300 Europeans and 700 Sepoys,[1] as European trained Indian Infantry came to be called, under an extremely capable Swiss engineer officer named Paradis, reached the southern bank of the wide, shallow estuary of the River Adyar near the small town of St Thomé. There they found Mahfuz Khan with an army of 10,000

---

[1] The word was derived from the Persian 'Sipahi' meaning soldier. In Africa the French corrupted the word more accurately into 'Spahi'.

FORT ST DAVID AND THE SIEGE OF PONDICHERRY   63

holding the north bank. Mahfuz Khan's army consisted almost entirely of cavalry and Paradis faced an extremely serious situation. If he retreated there could be little doubt but that swarms of wild horsemen would pour across the river, swoop down on his little column from all sides and inevitably overwhelm it; on the other hand it appeared madness to attack an army that outnumbered his by more than ten to one.

However, he knew Barthélemy had been ordered to make a sally from Fort St George towards St Thomé on 24 October to coincide with his arrival. Indian armies were clumsy and incapable of manoeuvring, a sudden surprise attack from the rear might well throw his enemy into confusion. And so, despite the disparity in numbers, Paradis boldly resolved to ford the river and attack. As the French line waded across the water, Mahfuz Khan must have found himself confronted by a perplexing situation. Should he charge into the river? Cavalry splashing about on the bed of a river would be at a severe disadvantage. On the other hand, if he ordered his ill-trained troops to withdraw so that they could charge the French as they emerged, they would certainly fall into fearful confusion, and in addition he would be obliged to abandon his guns lined along the river bank. In the face of two unpalatable alternatives Mahfuz Khan took neither, allowing the battle to develop from its own momentum.

As the French drew nearer, his artillery opened fire, but their rate of fire was deplorably slow, and the French advance continued unchecked; then, as they came to the bank, the French infantry began the well-drilled European-style volley firing which, until then, had been unknown in Indian warfare. Before the unfamiliar clangor of the volleys and the death-dealing bullets snapping and cracking through the black musketry smoke, Mahfuz Khan's cavalry panicked. The leading ranks turned and rode for St Thomé sweeping the rest along with them. Cavalry have always been more volatile than infantry; once they have been broken, control must be reimposed not only on the cavalryman himself, but also on his horse which may not share the views of his master. As the panic spread, Mahfuz Khan's whole army dissolved into a mob of fugitives trying to desperately spur their way through the narrow streets of St Thomé, while the advancing French poured volley after volley into their backs. Then the French detachment from Madras could be seen the far side of the town, and it became every man for himself. In hopeless disarray the army streamed away westwards led by Mahfuz Khan who, from the elevation of his elephant, had been well placed to observe at an early hour that all was lost. The French contingent from Madras, robbed of a major share in the victory, contented themselves with ruthlessly plundering the old Portuguese settlement of St Thomé.

As Mahfuz Khan's army rode in a jostling disorderly mob from the battlefield, the situation of the Europeans in India was dramatically changed. The marble pillars of the Moghul Empire, as it were, had been revealed as no more than lath and plaster. The combat by St Thomé, in which most of the combatants on both sides were Indian, had displayed in a glaring light the enormous gulf in military technique that separated the Indian and European armies. R. O. Cambridge, writing in 1762 had this to say:

'But they are greatly mistaken who attribute their dread of fire-arms and particularly of artillery to a dastardly disposition and an invincible timidity. The true cause lies in the inexperience of their leading men who have never understood the advantages of discipline and who have kept their infantry on too low a footing. Their cavalry are extremely unwilling to bring their horses within reach of our guns; so that they do not decline an engagement so much through fear of their lives as for their fortunes which are all laid out on the horses they ride. As an instance of the affection they contract for so serviceable a creature, Morarow (Morari Rao), the general of the Mahrattas, having his favourite horse shot, mourned for him for three days.

'Nothing is so ruinous to their military affairs as the false notion that is generally entertained among them and chiefly by their commanders in relation to the artillery ... they place their chief dependance on the largest pieces which they neither know how to manage or to move. When we march round them with our field pieces and make it necessary to move those enormous weights, their bullocks, which are at best unmanageable, if a shot come among them are quite ungovernable. But what is the greatest obstacle of all to their becoming a military people is that they are willing to save the needless expense of an army. For this reason there are few veterans, and most of their armies consist of an assemblage of various people hastily brought together from different parts; so that there can be no such thing as discipline without which numbers are but an impediment and bravery ineffectual. They can never be brought to establish either order or vigilance in their camps. At the close of the evening everyone eats an inconceivable amount of rice and many take some kind of soporific drug, so that at about midnight the whole army is in a dead sleep.'

The Europeans, therefore, had not only a great advantage in their disciplined military organisation; the emergence of the fire-arm and the artillery as the dominant weapons on the battlefield and the decline of the horseman with his sword, already evident in Europe, added immeasurably to the power of their soldiers.

The French, lacking cavalry, did not press a pursuit, and when his men had escaped from those awful muskets, Mahfuz Khan rallied them and withdrew to the neighbourhood of Fort St David, where he was to do the British no little service. Dupleix had won Madras, but he had also earned the hatred of the Nawab. Anwar-ud-Din was too supple a courtier to allow his emotions to lead him to do anything detrimental to his own interests, but he was likely to welcome any opportunity to embarrass the French or to obtain a revenge.

Clive had been in Madras while these events were in progress, it was not until after his victory at St Thomé that Dupleix finally repudiated the treaty that La Bourdonnais had negotiated with Governor Nicholas Morse; he must have seen the surprising outcome of the action, and taken note that boldness was all. It was not to be long before he himself was again engaged with the French. Fort St David was the last British stronghold on the coast, and now Dupleix was determined to destroy it.

His first attempt in December 1746 ended in a fiasco. A French force 1,700 strong, under an aged officer called de Bury, made a night march on the town of Cuddalore nestling near the ramparts of Fort St David. Somewhat exhausted by their march and unaware of the presence of an enemy, de Bury's men settled down to cooking their morning meal without the fatiguing formality of posting guards or sentries. Suddenly the cavalry of Mahfuz Khan descended upon them. As the yelling horsemen galloped down, the startled Frenchmen had no time to form their ranks. They started a headlong rush back towards the safety of distant Pondicherry. Most escaped, as their foe was less interested in sabring Frenchmen than in plundering their baggage. As soon as they saw what had happened, the British garrison at Fort St David sent out a necessarily small column to chase the fleeing enemy; Clive accompanied it as a volunteer. He noted that had the Indian cavalry persisted in their pursuit instead of going off in search of plunder, scarcely a Frenchman would have survived. However, by the time the weak British force caught up, a sufficient number had rallied to their colours to make a British attack impossible. The French repulse gave the British garrison at Fort St David a welcome breathing space, indeed it was to prove fatal to the plans of Dupleix.

For time had begun to run out for the French. The British Government had reinforced their naval squadron in the Bay of Bengal, and at last a competent officer, Commodore Griffin, had been sent to replace the inept and vacillating Peyton. Dupleix managed to buy off Mahfuz Khan, but when on 3 March 1747, Paradis marched with a considerable force finally to subjugate Fort St David, as he thrust a feeble British covering force aside and came within sight of the ramparts of the Fort he beheld the mortifying sight of British sails rising up over the horizon. Soon the British naval squadron anchored off Fort St David, and as Griffin started ferrying sailors and marines to the shore Paradis had no

FORT ST DAVID AND THE SIEGE OF PONDICHERRY 67

recourse but to beat a hasty retreat. Griffin landed 500 sailors and 150 marines as a temporary reinforcement to the garrison, and put one of his captains, Captain Gibson, in charge of the Fort. With nothing much else to do, Clive applied for a commission, being granted one dated 16 March 1747 into the '2nd Company of Foot Soldiers at Fort St David'. Edmund Maskelyne also took a commission about this time.

During the rest of the year little of note occurred; the British forces had been considerably reinforced and in the face of British naval superiority Dupleix recognised he was powerless. However, by dint of lavish presents he induced Anwar-ud-Din to withdraw from the contest, and he sent home urgent pleas for naval reinforcements.

In January 1748 Major Stringer Lawrence, after an eleven month sea voyage, stepped ashore at Fort St David to take command of the Company's soldiers. At last Clive had someone he respected to serve under. Lawrence was a singular man whose contribution to British supremacy in India has been overshadowed by that of his brilliant subordinate. Born in February 1697, he was commissioned into Major General Clayton's Regiment (Fourteenth Foot) at the age of thirty, probably after a period in the ranks; during the following eighteen years he succeeded in reaching the rank of captain, having seen service in Spain, Flanders and during the rebellion of 1745. In 1746 with no prospect of promotion, but no doubt deemed a competent company commander and an experienced regimental officer, he applied for transfer to the Company's service. After the death of Major Knipe in 1743 the post of Garrison Commander at Madras had fallen vacant, being temporarily occupied by the pugnacious but incompetent Eckman. Their dilatoriness probably cost them Madras, but on 17 December 1746, the Court of Directors brought themselves to nominate a successor and selected Captain Stringer Lawrence, 'to be major of our garrison at Fort St George upon the same terms as Major Knipe, viz two hundred and fifty pounds sterling per annum and one of the companies', little knowing that the Fort had already been captured by the French.

11 Major Stringer Lawrence. He was eventually promoted to Major General.

FORT ST DAVID AND THE SIEGE OF PONDICHERRY

And so at the age of fifty a redundant army captain arrived to take command of the Company's troops on the Coromandel coast, and revealed himself to be not only a master of organisational detail—so long as no paper work was involved—not only a commander with a fixed and rugged determination to instil a proper discipline into his troops, but also an extremely able commander in the field. It would be interesting to learn how the Court of Directors came to make such an excellent choice.

With Commodore Griffin cruising off the coast, Lawrence had some six months in which to make something out of the courageous but ill-disciplined set of ruffians that comprised the Company's army. He organised seven companies of Europeans each with a captain, a lieutenant, an ensign and eighty-one other ranks, and adopted a similar system for the Company's sepoys; until then the Indian soldiers had been nothing better than roving bands of poorly armed men under a local leader. They remained under their own officers, but British officers were now to be posted in to command them on operations. Above all he initiated a system of military law which, for the first time, made it possible to introduce proper military discipline into the Company's forces.

It was not long before his little army had an opportunity to prove its worth. In May, in answer to Dupleix's prayers, a French squadron arrived in Indian waters. Too weak to challenge Commodore Griffin, the French admiral yet managed to lure the British squadron away from its station off Fort St David; Dupleix struck at once. Suddenly French troops appeared almost under the walls of Cuddalore. It was obvious to the French that the British were alarmed, as they could be seen hauling back guns and stores from the town to Fort St David, clearly intending to move out at once. After dark however, Lawrence stealthily re-occupied the town walls. At midnight the French confidently marched up to take over what they presumed to be an empty town, only to be greeted by a totally unexpected blast of musketry and grape. The surprise was complete, and in the darkness all control broke down. The disheartened fugitives could barely be rallied short of Pondicherry. It was the first military success of any note achieved by British arms in India.

But for Dupleix worse was to follow. While his own government could only manage to send him a squadron of four ships that had to depend on the speed of their sailing for their survival, the British Government, affronted by the fall of Madras, dispatched a fleet under a noted sailor, Admiral Boscawen, with instructions to seize Pondicherry. That energetic sailor arrived at Fort St David on 29 July 1748, took over command from Commodore Griffin, and within a week had set in train the siege of the French fortress. He had indeed no time to lose if the siege was to be completed before the monsoon broke.

He had with him some thirty vessels including thirteen ships of the line; it was an unprecedented armada and Anwar-ud-Din, awed by such a display of strength, agreed to cast in his lot with the British. Boscawen had available for the siege twelve independent companies of so-called regular troops, each with a strength of 100 all ranks, about 800 marines, a contingent of sailors from the ships and the Company's European troops giving him a total European strength of 3,700; in addition there were some 2,000 Sepoys from the Company, still only semi-trained, and about 1,500 irregular horse from the Nawab. Admiral Boscawen, one of the first of interservice commanders, held command both by land and sea. His force looked formidable, but by one of those small oversights that can ruin great enterprises, he had with him no engineer officer competent to conduct a formal siege. And so a gallant admiral had to undertake a siege, the most technical of all land operations, by the light of a nature more attuned to bringing ships into action across a featureless sea.

Pondicherry now was no easy prey. Since 1744 that most able soldier and engineer, Paradis, had transformed the French fortress into an edifice more worthy of his great mentor, Vauban. And not only did Boscawen lack experienced engineers, the standard of his regular infantry companies left not a little to be desired. The raising of independent companies by drafting in men from other

FORT ST DAVID AND THE SIEGE OF PONDICHERRY   71

formed units is rarely satisfactory; commanding officers generally have a number of men with whose services they are delighted to dispense, and an accumulation of the criminal, the work-shy and the insubordinate is rarely likely to produce units of a notable quality. In this particular instance some of the 'regulars' had learned their trade under Bonnie Prince Charlie, and had accepted enlistment as an alternative to hanging.

The affair started badly. Some three miles to the south of Pondicherry the French had built a fort on the Ariancopang river. No proper reconnaissance was undertaken, but undeterred the admiral resolved to carry it immediately by boarding. The assaulting party to their surprise came upon, in the words of Clive, 'a good deep dry ditch' backed by a solid wall well furnished with flanking towers. Without ladders an assault was impossible, and the attackers suffering heavy casualties fell back before a hail of grape and bullets. The dispiriting effect of such a futile attack, the blow to the troops' confidence in their leaders, was bad enough, but now invaluable time was wasted sitting down in front of the fort, digging trenches and building batteries to reduce it by a regular siege. For a fortnight the whole army remained three miles from Pondicherry engaged in this totally unnecessary operation; the fort might well have been disregarded, as Clive later pointed out; at the most only a small covering force should have been left to keep an eye on the garrison. Nor was this all. While it was being besieged, Dupleix ordered a few cavalrymen, he had raised a troop, to make a sally. Lawrence happened on this occasion to be commanding in the forward trench; his raw troops panicked at the sight of the horsemen and ran away, leaving their angry and baffled commander to be taken prisoner. Now with their last knowledgeable soldier gone, the British might have settled down indefinitely in front of the Ariancopang fort, had not a lucky shot caused a magazine to explode, whereat the French garrison withdrew to Pondicherry.

The besiegers wandered uncertainly forward; no one quite knew what to do. Batteries were built 1,500 yards away from the ramparts of Pondicherry; this had the advantage that they were nearly out of range of the French artillery, but the British guns, once emplaced, were unlikely to be more effective. On one occasion when the guns had been run up on to their platforms in a battery, it was found that, owing to a regrettable miscalculation, a wood completely obscured the French fortifications. As blunder succeeded blunder, sickness began to exact an ever heavier toll, and the morale of the besiegers steadily declined. Clive observed, 'a strong detachment was sent to possess the French bounds which was effected with little opposition, but so prevailing was the panic among the men that in the night time the advanced sentries were continually firing without seeing anybody and very often at one another; this kept the whole detachment in alarm, and I am persuaded that the appearance of 50 of the enemy would have put us to flight.'

The French, however, were not without their misfortunes. Paradis, upon whose inspiring leadership much depended, fell mortally wounded while organising a sally. During the same sally Clive had an opportunity to display his powers; as some French, headed by a grenadier company, approached the trench he was holding, the platoons on his right and left thought fit to make a hasty departure, but Clive's platoon, some thirty men, stayed firm. They exchanged fire with the French grenadiers at a range of ten yards; the grenadiers tried to form up for a charge, but their line fell to pieces before a storm of bullets, and they ran back leaving some thirty of their comrades on the ground. Eight of Clive's men had been hit.

In the clammy pre-monsoon heat the trenches, that had been started from too far away, made slow progress, while fever decimated the ranks of the besiegers. At last a breaching battery was established about 850 yards from the walls. Not surprisingly, at this distance it could make little impression on the masonry; with no other distractions, Dupleix calmly concentrated a large number of his own guns on the British breaching battery. Instead of the besiegers silencing the guns of the fortress precisely the opposite happened, and the British battery had half its guns dismounted. At the same

FORT ST DAVID AND THE SIEGE OF PONDICHERRY

time, it became clear that the line of approach had been so badly selected, that the ground between the battery and the ramparts was too marshy to be entrenched, and would give very doubtful footing for an assault.

The monsoon season was near, his force was melting away from sickness, soon there would not be enough men on their feet to man the trenches, there could be no question of starting the approaches from a new direction, in desperation Admiral Boscawen ordered the Fleet to bombard Pondicherry from the sea. But the water was shallow, the ships

12 Pondicherry from the sea. On the left are the French Company's warehouses, in the centre the 'admiralty' and on the right the Governor's residence.

could not come closer to the shore than 1,000 yards, and at this range their guns were totally ineffective. Dupleix remarked afterwards that he suffered only one casualty, an unfortunate Malabari woman caught crossing a street. Now all chance of success had vanished. On 1 October Boscawen ordered all the stores that could not be carried away to be burnt; and on 5 October his army left their stinking and ill-fated trenches for Fort St David. Orme in his history of the war in the Deccan stated that 1,065 Europeans died in battle or from sickness. Taking into account the number of wounded this implies, and those likely to be convalescent, the little force could have had no one left standing. The figure probably represents the total number of casualties from fighting and sickness; even so, the losses were appalling enough and show that without question it was skill, not courage, that was lacking. The loss in prestige was possibly more disastrous than the loss of men. The Indian Princes were not slow to notice the glaring contrast between the defence of Pondicherry and that of Madras. It reflects no little credit on the sterling qualities of the admiral that, despite the complete failure of the enterprise, he remained almost equally popular with soldiers as with sailors, and that none called his conduct into question.

In November came the news that at Aix-la-Chapelle France and Britain had agreed on the terms of a treaty and that Madras was to be handed back by the French. It was some time before the news could be confirmed, and then arrangements had to be made for the French troops to march out as the British entered, in such a way that there was no interregnum, but at the same time no risk of the two encountering each other and restarting hostilities; it was not until 21 August 1749 that Boscawen officially took over Madras from the French Commandant, Barthélemy.

Clive had remained at Fort St David. The siege had given him much to ponder; years later in 1762, he wrote a trenchant criticism of its handling. In it he had given once again signal proof of his own personal courage, but in addition he had shown that he understood his men and knew how to gain their trust; they had stood firm when their comrades had fled; there are few clearer proofs of the quality of leadership.

In the new year Clive was to become embroiled in a curious affair. He had made a new friend, a young marine officer named Dalton, whose ship had recently been dismantled and who, being without employment, had successfully petitioned for a transfer to command one of the independent companies, obtaining at the same time promotion to the rank of captain. One day Dalton was travelling by chaise from Fort St David to Cuddalore, when he suddenly came upon the astonishing sight of two Europeans fighting in the street. He recognised one as Robert Clive and the other as the chaplain, a Mr Fordyce; they appeared to be vigorously engaged in trying to cane each other, and then as he watched Clive closed with his opponent. At this moment a Captain Lucas who had apparently been accompanying the chaplain parted the two men.

Fordyce at once lodged a formal complaint. An investigation followed. It appeared that Fordyce was accustomed to take advantage of his cloth to make disparaging remarks about his fellows. Clive, when asked for his explanation of his conduct, deposed to the effect that when he was dining with Captain Dalton on 16 February, Dalton had remarked that he had overheard Fordyce proclaim in public that Clive was a scoundrel and a coward. Nor was this the only offence. On another occasion he had heard that Fordyce had threatened to 'break every bone in his skin'. When he had met Fordyce he had demanded an explanation and, one word leading to another, had found it necessary to cane him.

Clive added that he was not the only person about whom the chaplain had thought fit to ventilate his views. 'He had aspersed the character of Mr Joseph Fowke by saying he was a dark designing villain, that he would slit his nose the first time that he met him and that he had knocked him under the table at the Governor's.' Since Fowke was a member of council these remarks were scarcely judicious. The chaplain whose mind seems to have become slightly deranged then apparently alleged that he had made the Governor himself 'shake in his shoes'.

Fordyce, when asked for his version, haughtily refused to acknowledge the authority of the Council and declined to make a statement. He was immediately dismissed for insubordination and sent home to England. It occurred to the Council that, when he arrived, Fordyce might give a different and highly coloured account of the proceeding, and it was thought prudent to write to the Court of Directors on the subject; the letter ended: 'It is not to be doubted that Mr Fordyce will set forth his own story to Your Honours, and lest the same should be to Mr Clive's prejudice we think it not improper to assure you that he is generally esteemed a very quiet person and no ways guilty of disturbance.'

The statement is of interest. Taken together with the incident to which it refers, it suggests that while Clive was undoubtedly a difficult subordinate, awkward in his dealings with others, a dangerous man to impose upon, he was far from aggressive and did not seek quarrels with those who were prepared to deal with him honourably and fairly; but that if he did feel that he had been insulted or his conduct called in question, he would be absolutely fearless in defending himself or his reputation. However, in the next few years Clive was to have more important work to do than brawling with clerics.

Chapter 4

THE BATTLE FOR THE CARNATIC BEGINS
1749-51

With the ending of hostilities between Britain and France, and the restoration of Madras, it might seem that the East India Company would be able to return to the expansion of the trade that had paid such handsome dividends during the first half of the century.

However, peace had its problems. Fort St David now contained a considerable number of European troops in the pay of the Company. A cargo of troops sent to England in place of silks and spices was hardly likely to prove a profitable enterprise, nor were the troops, now they were acclimatised, any too eager to return home to disbandment and penury, a fate the probability of which their officers, whose rank depended on the number of men they could persuade to remain and accept service with the company, did little to minimise. In addition, it was clearly dangerous to divest the coast of troops while Dupleix in Pondicherry plotted who knew what subtle moves to undermine the British.

On the other hand, to expend large sums of money so that the rapacious soldiery need do nothing more than drink and gamble away their time was hardly sound commercial practice. The merchants of the company proved equal to the occasion. They reasoned that, if they owned land for which they had no present use, they would rent it out to someone who had. The principle might well be applied to the Company's soldiers. The army could be rented out to those

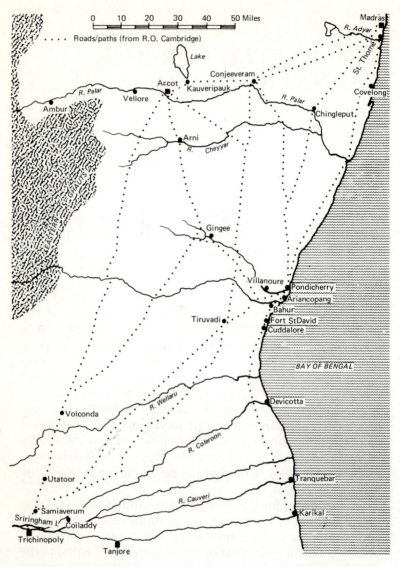

4 Southern Carnatic. Based on the map in R. O. Cambridge's *History of the War between France and England on the Coast of Coromandel*, published in 1762.

THE BATTLE FOR THE CARNATIC BEGINS 79

in need, and with skilful commercial management might not only pay for itself but even show a profit. The opportunity for proving the truth of this concept was not long in arising.

A rajah named Sahoji had ruled the small Hindu state of Tanjore for a number of years, but some seven years ago his exactions had become too oppressive for his subjects and they had succeeded in deposing him. Now he pleaded for the British to help him regain his realm; in return he promised to pay all the expenses of the expedition and to cede the town of Devicottah to the Company. Devicottah lay at the mouth of the Coleroon river, and Admiral Boscawen who had experienced the perils of the anchorages at Madras and Cuddalore hoped, somewhat optimistically, that it might have some advantages as a port. An agreement was concluded with Sahoji, and in March 1749, a force of 430 Europeans and 1,000 sepoys under Captain Cope was dispatched to restore the exiled Rajah to his dominions. Cope found that, not surprisingly, there was little support for Sahoji among the local inhabitants, and disliking the appearance of Devicottah fort he returned empty-handed. Once again the British had achieved a miserable failure. The council at Fort St David was not prepared tamely to accept such a setback; quite apart from prestige there was the question of money. A penniless rajah in exile would never be able to defray the costs of the expedition. If the Rajah could not be restored, at least Devicottah might be taken and some return received on the considerable outlay of money already incurred.

Another expedition was organised, this time under Major Lawrence. On 27 May 1749 he embarked with 800 Europeans and 1,500 sepoys and arrived off Devicottah on 29 May. By 31 May he had his small force ashore and by 8 June had constructed a battery. At this stage he ordered the battery to fire three rounds to announce its presence and then, hoisting a white flag, summoned the garrison to surrender. He concluded his appeal, according to his own account, by saying, 'As my batteries are now ready to open fire, I send this to let you know that if you open your gates and receive the troops under my command into the fort, your persons and effects will be safe and yourselves well treated, but if on the contrary you obstinately hold out the place I will beat down your wall, enter your town and then no man is to expect quarter.' The Governor of Devicottah replied, 'he was upwards of 40 years of age and had lived hitherto without reproach', that he had a garrison of 5,000 men, his fort was impregnable and he had no intention of surrendering.

After this little exchange of pleasantries, the battery opened fire and by 12 June a large breach had been blown in the ramparts. For an assault the Coleroon river had to be crossed. Lawrence's account continues:

'Mr Moore the carpenter of the train passed the river that night and made fast the rope on the other side to pass our float; as our battery was on marshy ground I was apprehensive that another day's rain would have made it impossible to attempt anything, I therefore determined to attack the place in the day. . . . As soon as we all had passed the river to the number of 700 sepoys and 400 military upon the float made by Mr Moore for that purpose, I first ordered Lieut. Clive with a volunteer platoon of 30 men at the head of 400 sepoys to drive the enemy from an entrenchment which would take our left in the flank when we stormed the breach, and 300 more sepoys to secure our right flank from a large body of Horse, which were posted there for a similar purpose. Lieutenant Clive accordingly set out for the attack, and met with a deep slough, which we knew nothing of; however, he passed it with the major part of his platoon and attacked the entrenchment; but not being seconded by the sepoys and being charged in the rear by the Horse at the same time that he was attacking the entrenchment in front, was obliged to retreat to the slough again; upon which I ordered Sergeant Brown with the forlorn hope to attack the entrenchment and Captain Dalton at the head of the grenadier company to be ready to support him; but there being no need, I immediately ordered Captain Dalton and his company followed by the main body to attack the breach, which he did, and being joined by Lieutenant Clive and the remainder of his platoon was in full possession by five o'clock; I, at the head of the main body wheeled one platoon to the right and faced the Horse in order to prevent them from flanking Dalton's company, and gave them a fire that was so successful that it killed some and put the rest in such disorder that they went off immediately. We all of us that night lay upon our arms.'

Lawrence followed up his success by occupying the Atcheveram pagoda about 5 miles distant. Pagodas at this time possessed considerable military significance. Most consisted of one or more temples enclosed in a high wall in the shape of a rectangle; the walls might often be fifteen or twenty feet tall to conceal the temples from the gaze of the vulgar. So far, except for a single charge they failed to press home, the army of the Rajah had taken only a tepid interest in the proceedings. But now Robert Orme observed, writing sometime afterwards, 'The Tanjorine army no sooner heard that the English had got possession of it (the Pagoda), than their horror at the pollution to which the temple was exposed inspired them with a resolution which neither attachment to their prince nor their notions of military honour would have produced.'

They attacked the pagoda, but despite their inspiration they quailed before the volleys of the garrison, and were repelled without difficulty. Now matters were arranged with a courtesy that did credit to both sides. The commander of the Tanjore army proffered a stately apology for being so unmannerly as to attack the pagoda, whereat Lawrence immediately offered to restore it to him—he had already come to the conclusion that it was too far from the fort to be reinforced if the attack was renewed. After such politeness further hostilities were clearly out of the question. The reigning Rajah ceded Devicottah with a region yielding an annual revenue of 9,000 Pagodas, and promised to pay Sahoji a pension, so long as the Company undertook to prevent him meddling any further in his kingdom. It was all very satisfactory, but some factious critics went so far as to suggest that the Company had sacrificed honour for a quick profit; Sahoji's views have not been recorded.

The cordiality of the Rajah was not entirely due to a sudden gush of affection for the British. In the Carnatic great and dangerous events were impending and, as owing to some disputes in the past he was on bad terms with the French, he thought it judicious to cultivate the friendship of the British. For now Dupleix had in train schemes so

13 An Indian Grandee on an elephant.

THE BATTLE FOR THE CARNATIC BEGINS 83

grandiose as to be totally outside the comprehension of the worthy merchants at Fort St David.

The great Nizam-ul-Mulk had died in 1748. His eldest son, Ghazi-ud-Din held a high post at the court of the Emperor and had no desire to abandon his lucrative position for the more hazardous life of a Viceroy. He prevailed upon the Emperor to issue a *firman* appointing his younger brother, Nazir Jang, to the vacant post. But the succession was not to go uncontested. Muzaffar Jang, a grandson of the old Nizam born to his favourite daughter, claimed that in his will the Nizam had promised him the Nawabship of the Carnatic.[1] Nazir, far too shrewd to barter away so rich a province to a possible rival, refused to acknowledge this promise and confirmed Anwar-ud-Din in his appointment.

Anwar-ud-Din, however, had been guilty of an unpardonable economy. The Mahrattas, who were no believers in charity, had been extorting from him a handsome rent for keeping Chunda Sahib in captivity. Anwar-ud-Din allowed the payments to lapse and Dupleix, seeing far-reaching opportunities opening before him, guaranteed the Mahrattas seven lakhs of rupees (about £70,000) for his release. He knew that Anwar-ud-Din and his sons would never forgive the humiliation they had suffered at St Thomé; the old dynasty was still remembered in the Carnatic with affection; if he could engineer the replacement of Anwar-ud-Din by Chunda Sahib, he could dispose of a dangerous enemy and vastly extend the influence of the French.

Muzaffar, seeking assistance from the Mahrattas at Satara, realised that in Chunda Sahib, with his connection with the French, he might find a valuable ally, and indeed with his help might be able to dispossess his uncle and take the Deccan for himself. The two princes soon came to an agreement and proceeded to raise an army of some 30,000 men; in July 1749, while the British were achieving their trumpery triumph in Tanjore, they invaded the Carnatic

[1] R. O. Cambridge: other authorities say he was willed the viceroyalty itself, although Nizam-ul-Mulk had no right to do so.

as the first step to achieving their ambitions. Dupleix at once sent a body of troops to their assistance.

At the fateful pass by Ambur, Anwar-ud-Din gave battle. Largely as the result of an assault by the French, the Nawab was killed and his army routed. His eldest son, Mahfuz Khan, was captured, but Mohammed Ali, his second son, managed to elude his enemies and take refuge in Trichinopoly, hoping to rally the southern Carnatic to his cause. Muzaffar now graciously made Chunda Sahib Nawab of the Carnatic, and the two princes continued on their way to Pondicherry, where Dupleix received them in state. It was a time for feasting, but also, Dupleix thought, a time for caution. Admiral Boscawen with a powerful fleet still lay off the Coromandel Coast, and he had no desire to try conclusions with that redoubtable sailor once again.

At Fort St David all remained placid. The Governor, Floyer, happily beguiled the hours with gambling and wine. The Devicottah expedition had finally prospered, but only after one or two vicissitudes, trade was plainly a safer way to accumulate wealth. Clive, when he returned from Devicottah, decided to throw over soldiering and once again took up his quill as a merchant; he was determined to amass that wealth which had so persistently eluded his father. His friend Maskelyne, preferring present ease to future profit, remained with the Company's army and a better rate of pay. Clive, did not sever all connection with soldiering; he accepted the civilian post of Commissary which made him responsible for feeding and equipping the Company's forces. Admiral Boscawen had been ordered to stay in Indian waters only until the French had handed back Madras. Looking at events with possibly a more prescient gaze than those whose task it was to guide the affairs of the Company, he offered to stay. The Council, blissfully unaware of the storm about to break, refused his offer; on 21 October 1749, Boscawen sailed away with his fleet.

Now Dupleix saw his chance. He equipped Muzaffar and Chunda Sahib with a sizeable contingent of French troops, and pointed out to them the urgent need to capture Trichinopoly and dispose of Mohammed Ali. The princes, however, were experiencing some financial difficulties; if they did not replenish their treasury, their unpaid soldiers would undoubtedly seek more lucrative employment elsewhere. Instead of marching on Trichinopoly, they resolved first to plunder the territories of the Rajah of Tanjore. They settled down before his capital and opened negotiations. The Rajah was overmatched in force but not in guile. Orme noted: 'The wily Tanjorine knew that by protracting negotiations he could increase the distress of his enemy and

14 The Great Pagoda at Tanjore.

in his letters expressed himself with such seeming humility that Chunda Sahib suffered himself to be amused until the middle of December.'

Dupleix, infuriated by the delay and anxious about its consequences, eventually sent a direct order to the French troops to storm the city. They achieved an initial success and the Rajah at once came to terms, agreeing to pay a substantial indemnity. However, he now procrastinated by haggling over the method of payment. 'One day he sent gold and silver plate and his officers wrangled like pedlars over the price at which it should be valued. Another day he sent old and obsolete coins, such as he knew would require strict and tedious examination.' He was still apparently trying to pay the first instalment, when Dupleix acidly informed Chunda Sahib that Nazir Jang was on the march with an enormous army and that at the least he had better secure Tanjore, as he might soon find himself in need of a refuge.

While the two princes had been duped into lengthy negotiations, Nazir Jang had consolidated his position as Viceroy, and now with an army, said to be 300,000 strong,[1] was advancing on the Carnatic to assert his authority.

Meanwhile it had at last begun to dawn on the Council at Fort St David that, if allies of Dupleix were to rule both the Carnatic and the Deccan, their own expulsion from Southern India would inevitably follow. They sent Captain Cope, that courageous officer whose most outstanding talent appeared to be the ability to endure defeat with equanimity, to aid Mohammed Ali in Trichinopoly. As Nazir approached the borders of the province he summoned Mohammed Ali, as his vassal and a feudatory of the Moghul, to bring him assistance, and on his dutiful arrival conferred on him formally the Nawabship of the Carnatic. As the united armies of Nazir and Mohammed Ali began to confront those of Muzaffar and Chunda Sahib, the issues for the British became clear beyond question. Stringer Lawrence relates:

'Muzaffar Jang and Chunda Sahib marched out of Pondicherry with their army and 2,000 Europeans commanded by Mr D'Auteuil [Lawrence could not be bothered with the troublesome French habit of using Monsieur] with a large train of artillery and a numerous body of sepoys. They took post within a few miles of Nazir Jang at whose earnest and repeated request I marched from Fort St George with 600 men, accompanied by Mr Westcott, one of the Council

[1] Although most authorities agree on this figure it seems hardly credible; allowing for camp followers, concubines and others normally found in the train of an Indian army, the total number of people on the move must have been not far short of a million. Not even the organising genius of a Marlborough or a Wellington could have fed such a multitude. It may be that 300,000 was the total figure of those present and that the number of soldiers was in the region of 100,000.

THE BATTLE FOR THE CARNATIC BEGINS 87

with a commission to treat with Nazir Jang, in which we were assisted by Captain Dalton. We joined him at Villanoure and were very graciously received, suitable to the dignity of an Eastern Prince at the head of 300,000 men, of which he declared me generalissimo. He proposed to me to attack the enemy immediately; I told him, in the eastern style, that he must be sure of victory wherever he fought, yet an attack must be attended with some difficulty and cost him the lives of many brave men, as the enemy were strongly posted and had with them a large train of artillery. But that if he pleased to march between them and Pondicherry, he might, by cutting their communication, oblige them to fight at a great disadvantage.'

Nazir disdained such basely professional manoeuvring and a battle became imminent. M. d'Auteuil now sent a messenger to Lawrence to acquaint him, 'that although we were engaged in different causes yet it was not his design or inclination that any European blood should be spilt, but that as he did not know our post, should any of his shot come that way and hurt the English he could not be blamed'.

Lawrence assured d'Auteuil that he was equally loathe to shed European blood, but added that if any French shot came his way, it could be depended upon that he would reply to it. D'Auteuil's admirable sentiments must remain a little suspect. His army was deeply discontented over matters of pay. His soldiers mutinied that night and straggled back to Pondicherry, casually leaving their gunners behind them. Lawrence continues, 'Nazir Jang soon routed Muzaffar Jang's and Chunda Sahib's armies, fell in with most of the French gunners left behind, and cut most of them to pieces. We saved as many as we could, taking them by force out of the hands of the Mahrattas and got their wounds dressed by our surgeons.'

For Morari Rao, scenting profit and probably assuming that Chunda Sahib remembered him with no great pleasure, had joined Nazir and now harried the beaten armies without mercy. Chunda Sahib escaped to Pondicherry, but Muzaffar, naïvely believing some assurances that his uncle meant him no harm, surrendered. His relative at once put him in chains, stationing an executioner in attendance to decapitate his nephew should his own safety be in any way threatened.

Dupleix's ambitious schemes appeared ruined, but in adversity the will of that indomitable man only grew greater. He redressed the grievances of his men and prepared to win by intrigue what he had lost by battle. In vain Lawrence pressed Nazir to blockade Pondicherry and force the French to submit. The Prince, well satisfied with his victory, preferred to return to Arcot to pursue his two favourite diversions, hunting and women.

As Dupleix began to forge his conspiracy, it seems likely from his future actions that Clive watched and remembered. Lawrence soon perceived what was happening.

'Ambassadors came for an accommodation (*but*) their real business was privately to concert measures with Shah Nawaz Khan, Nazir Jang's prime-minister, and the chiefs of the conspiracy which was first laid in Pondicherry by Chunda Sahib and Mr Dupleix. Though this was carried on with great secrecy, I had information that some design was afoot against Nazir Jang and that Shah Nawaz Khan was principally concerned in it. I therefore desired my interpreter to acquaint Nazir Jang with what I heard and in particular with what concerned his prime-minister. But so great were the apprehensions of the person we employed as linguist that he did not dare to say what I directed him, nor accuse a person in such high favour and power as Shah Nawaz Khan.'

It seems curious that neither Lawrence, nor presumably his European subordinates, had sufficient command of the language to take the place of the interpreter whose apprehensions were probably well founded.

Nazir wished Lawrence to accompany him to Arcot, but the soldier pleaded such a move would uncover Madras to an enemy. It seems an unlikely excuse; possibly the straightforward British officer found the stifling atmosphere of

THE BATTLE FOR THE CARNATIC BEGINS 89

intrigue in the Prince's court puzzling and uncongenial, and was anxious to be quit of it. He took the little British army back to Madras. By now it was summer and the Court of Directors in England, grown aware of the failings of their governor, summarily dismissed him. Lawrence had to act in his place until a replacement arrived. A flood of incomprehensible paper descended upon him, and he called on Clive to relieve him of its burden. He had much to discontent him. His pay was inadequate and now he heard that the Court of Directors had removed from him his power of court-martial. It was too much. He threw up his post and took ship to England. It was an unfortunate step for the British.

Dupleix began an interminable negotiation with Nazir while his conspiracy burgeoned. Then in September the Frenchman struck. Mohammed Ali's army was surprised and routed, and Bussy, one of the ablest of the French commanders, stormed the Fort of Gingee, hitherto deemed impregnable. Nazir reluctantly perceived that the time for junketing was over. Much of his enormous host had dispersed, but with a still imposing army of 60,000 men and 700 elephants he marched to recapture his fort, quite unaware that almost all his generals had been suborned by the French. In the early hours of 5 December 1750 the French stormed into his camp. Nazir thought contemptuously that they must be drunk. As dawn broke, without bothering to don his body armour, he climbed on to his elephant and rode out to superintend their destruction. He saw the part of his army commanded by the Nawab of Cuddapah drawn up as for battle, but apparently reluctant to engage. He directed his elephant to be guided to where he could see the Nawab on his elephant tranquilly surveying the scene. As he began to expostulate, the Nawab turned to a companion in his howdah and told him to shoot the Viceroy. Perhaps intimidated by his august target the man missed. The Nawab at once picked up a carbine himself and shot Nazir through the heart. The Prince toppled out of his howdah and fell to the ground. The Nawab ordered him to be decapitated, stuck his head on a spear and sent it round

15 The fort at Gingee. It is not difficult to see why it was thought impregnable.

the camp as a gory emblem of success. All fighting at once stopped, the chains were struck off Muzaffar and, to the cheers of the multitude, he was proclaimed the new Viceroy.

Muzaffar returned in triumph to Pondicherry. Now indeed it was a time for rejoicing. *Te deums*, slightly inappropriate for the victory of a Muslim, were sung; Muzaffar was enthroned in a brilliant ceremony organised by Dupleix, who appeared dressed as an Indian muslim prince and riding on an elephant. The grateful Muzaffar appointed him ruler of most of southern India, but Dupleix had sufficient judgement to decline the honour in favour of his protégé. Now he appeared to be the real ruler of the Deccan, to have dominion over a country as large as his native France and with a population as numerous. It must have been an extraordinary and intoxicating moment for the great French Governor.

In January 1751 Muzaffar marched on Aurangabad to take over his realm. Bussy accompanied him with an army of 300 Europeans and 2,000 sepoys. However, it was not to be a triumphal procession. The Nawab of Kurnool and some others of the conspirators thought they had been inadequately rewarded. The aggrieved chieftains tried to ambush Muzaffar, but the French were too much for them. Muzaffar, furious at the treacherous attack, personally pursued his fleeing adversaries. The Nawab of Kurnool, despairing of escape, turned his elephant to die fighting. Muzaffar directed his elephant to be brought up alongside that of his foe. He cut at the Nawab, but the latter, a Pathan, was too fast for him; he thrust his javelin through Muzaffar's temple. Muzaffar's men at once cut the traitor to pieces, but Muzaffar himself was dead.

In the camp that night Bussy called a conference of notables. The situation was tense. Without the contents of the treasury at Aurangabad, it would be impossible to pay the troops, and already there were ominous signs of unrest. It was vital that a new Viceroy should at once be proclaimed, so that the army might be paid. The three younger sons of the old Nizam were still alive. Nazir had incarcerated them, but had overlooked the need to dispose of them. The meeting agreed that the eldest, Salabat Jang, should be the new Viceroy, and the march was continued.

Once again the French appeared to have triumphed and, with Bussy in charge of an inexperienced young princeling, perhaps even to have improved their position. But the triumph was illusory. Dupleix had overreached himself. Only a man with the outstanding talents of a Nizam-ul-Mulk could hope to hold together the ramshackle conglomeration of states that made up the Deccan. A weakling such as Salabat Jang, helplessly relying on French bayonets, would inevitably excite the contempt and hostility of the great nobles he purported to control, a hostility that would extend to the French on whom he depended. As over the next few years the incubus of a puppet viceroy weighed down on the French, despite the remarkable diplomatic skill of Bussy, it may be conjectured that once again Clive took note.

At the time, it was not Dupleix's blunder that impressed itself on the British, but the apparently limitless extent of his power. At Fort St David, still the seat of British rule on the coast, a new governor named Saunders had taken over from the gay but indolent Floyer. He made a complete contrast with his pleasure-loving predecessor. He was dour and silent with a will of steel. Disliking the flamboyant, content to deal with his problems without spectacular gestures, his contribution to the fortunes of the British, like that of Stringer Lawrence, has been eclipsed by the brilliance of one of his newly appointed junior merchants. Clive had progressed swiftly through the Company's hierarchy and now held that rank; he could, however, foresee the perils that lay ahead, and managed to obtain for himself a brevet captaincy in the Company's army, dated 1 January 1751, while in some curious fashion being allowed to remain a civilian.

Early in 1750 he had experienced a high fever accompanied by severe pains in his stomach and had gone to Calcutta to convalesce. It may be that it was about this time that he started to take opium to deaden the pain. De Quincey in his *Confessions of an English Opium-eater* relates that a similar illness first led him to sample the drug.

He had returned in time to assist Lawrence in those administrative duties that soldier so detested and resumed his duties as Commissary, a post he held when Saunders made his first moves to counter the alarming situation that was fast developing.

After the murder of Nazir, Mohammed Ali had once again taken refuge in Trichinopoly, and Captain Cope had been sent with some troops to reinforce the garrison of that town. Mohammed Ali, in despair, offered to recognise Chunda Sahib as Nawab provided that he was permitted to retain Trichinopoly. Chunda Sahib contemptuously spurned the offer and began to assemble his army. It was clear that soon Trichinopoly once more would be besieged.

THE BATTLE FOR THE CARNATIC BEGINS

Its fortifications were strong; oblong in shape, it was surrounded by a double wall studded with towers and with a circumference of about 6,000 yards. The front wall was of masonry about 18 feet high with a ditch 15 feet deep and 30 feet wide at its foot. The inner wall, separated from the outer by 25 feet, was a properly faced rampart 30 feet wide at the bottom tapering to 10 feet at the top, and 30 feet high. Inside the city there was a ruined cross wall which separated the old town from the new, and in the centre of the old town a most extraordinary rock, crowned by a pagoda, reared up to a height computed by Lawrence to be 300 feet. The country outside was flat and open, consisting mainly of paddy fields; a man posted on the pagoda, so Lawrence wrote, could see for some forty miles around, and nearly as far as Tanjore. The Cauvery River flowed half a mile from the northern face of the fortifications and was joined by the Coleroon about three miles to the northwest of the city. For some fifteen miles to the east of the junction the rivers flowed close together to enclose a long slender island called Sriringham Island; at the eastern tip of the island a dam had been built to separate the waters of the

16 Trichinopoly.

two rivers. This dam was of great importance to the Rajah of Tanjore as he relied on it for the irrigation of his land. The Rajah therefore had excellent reasons for wishing to be on good terms with whoever might rule at Trichinopoly.

Not only were the fortifications of Trichinopoly strong. The ground outside was seamed with watercourses and, most of the year, was extremely marshy. Properly garrisoned the city would only fall through a lack of food or money. Lack of money could be as fatal as lack of food. The princely armies were made up of a heterogeneous collection of Muslim mercenaries including Pathans, Persians and even Arabs. Their loyalty depended strictly on cash; a general without money became speedily a general without troops. For considerations therefore both of food and money, it was essential that Mohammed Ali should not be cut off from at least some of the territories outside the city walls, and that these should remain loyal.

But in the face of Mohammed Ali's misfortunes, their loyalty was becoming decidedly strained. Madura, a town some eighty miles to the south, declared for Chunda Sahib; it was an evil example that the waverers might follow. Captain Cope, with his habitual optimism, volunteered to recapture it for the Prince; the offer was gratefully accepted. Cope, however, met with his usual repulse and returned to Trichinopoly in not a little haste. Unless some dramatic reversal occurred, Mohammed Ali would soon be master of no more than the city walls and his cause would be doomed.

Saunders determined to reassert the authority of the Prince in the southern Carnatic and in early April 1751 ordered Captain de Gingins, a Swiss in the employment of the Company, to take an army of 600 Europeans generally referred to as the European Battalion, and 3,000 sepoys to carry out this task. Clive was to accompany it as Commissary.

The legal situation at this time was not a little obscure. France and Britain were at peace, and any breach of that peace in India was bound to have repercussions in Europe. In fact, Dupleix subsequently accused the British of supporting a usurper; but the legitimacy or otherwise of the rival contenders for the Carnatic would have been difficult to establish; in the India of that day force not law prevailed and considerations of legality were virtually irrelevant.

Nevertheless Saunders, at this time, was reluctant to act as a principal, and de Gingins had to wait until a detachment of Mohammed Ali's army had arrived and could lend to his actions the spurious air of being in support of an ally who, by an unfortunate mischance, was at odds with the French. Mohammed Ali's troops moved with their customary lethargy, and it was not until May that de Gingins could take the field. Chunda Sahib, well aware of the British intentions, had plenty of time in which to mass his forces.

De Gingins scored an initial success and was promptly joined by Mohammed Ali's brother, Abdul Wahab Khan with 4,000 men. He continued his march southwards until he came to the important town of Volconda which lay about forty-five miles from Trichinopoly on the main road to Arcot. By now Chunda Sahib with his army was not far distant and the Governor of the fort at Volconda faced an awkward decision. His one desire, after the fashion of the Vicar of Bray, was to remain Governor of Volconda, a desire likely to be sadly compromised if he opened his gates to the side that was subsequently defeated. He tried to play for time, hoping that a battle would resolve his difficulties and make rather clearer where his allegiance ought to lie. But the two antagonists seemed in no hurry to come to grips; in desperation he declared himself neutral and closed his gates to the British.

De Gingins now was uncertain what to do. He could hardly hope to storm the fort without presenting Chunda Sahib with an excellent opportunity for attacking him in the rear; at the same time Chunda Sahib's camp, manned by some 500 Frenchmen and Indian forces considerably superior to his own, looked too formidable for him to attack. After lengthy deliberations with his officers, he finally decided to make a night attack on the town of Volconda, as an apparent first step against the fort. It was thought that this would provoke Chunda Sahib into marching to the relief of the fort, and that the British could then bring him to battle on ground of their own choosing. The town was seized without difficulty and Dalton, serving at that time under de Gingins, relates what now occurred:

'The citadel was bombarded all night, and only now and then returned to us a stone shot which did us no sort of prejudice. However, as they showed no sort of inclination to surrender, at daylight we drew off our mortars and joined the army that was lying on the plain drawn up out of cannonshot of the fort. About 8 o'clock we perceived the scouts of Chunda's army on the top of the hills that were between their camp and ours, and soon their whole army, with the French battalion of about 500 men in their front, appeared marching pretty fast to gain a deep water course that led directly to the gate of the fort. Nothing was plainer than that it was now our business to possess it ourselves before 'em, which we might easily have done, as we were much nearer it than they were. This would have put us between them and the fort. We should have been under cover and they exposed, and if they offered to advance on us over the plain, they must have lost half their people before they could get near us; but we lay still in a state of stupefaction, and saw 'em all enter the water course, and pushing hard along it to the fort.

'We then stood to our arms, and the Commanding Officer asked the officers, whether it was their opinion that we could prevent the enemy from getting in by advancing upon 'em. I believe this gave none a very extraordinary idea of [the likelihood] of success. Notwithstanding which some gave it as their opinion that a brisk push might do it, as the fire of the fort was very inconsiderable. In consequence of which the officer of the *Coffreys* [Kaffirs, i.e. African troops] showing great readiness was ordered to make what despatch he could and engage their front, and if possible stop 'em till our main body came up. I marched after him as fast as I could, in any order, with the grenadiers, three companies of sepoys from the right and a company of *Topasses* belonging to the Nawab. The *Coffreys* ran all the way as fast as they could, and attacked the French grenadiers and sepoys who led their van in so daring a manner that (assisted by the artillery from the left of the battalion and three guns of the Nawab's) they made 'em give way, and abandon their two advanced guns so precipitately that they threw the main French body into confusion; they all got into the bottom of the water course firing from thence up into the air, without doing us the least harm. Never was there a finer prospect of a complete victory; the French saw it so plainly themselves, that giving over all thought of relieving the fort, they suffered us to stop 'em and without much ado got two field pieces on to the bank to bear upon our [European] battalion which was marching down, in all appearance with a great show of resolution, to support us. But on receiving about 20 shot which killed a lieutenant and eight or nine men, the whole went to the right-about and marched towards camp in great disorder, without giving us who were advanced the least notice to retire in time.

'The officers say they could not find the Commanding Officer to receive orders what they were to do, and the men declared that the officers bid them retreat. For my part being considerably advanced from 'em, I am no sort of judge of what happened, but was never more astonished than when I saw 'em going off, even the Nawab's Horse crying out at 'em and upbraiding 'em for their shameful behaviour.

'I never saw the Nawab's Horse so animated as they were on that day. They kept close in the rear of our battalion and seemed to despise Chunda Sahib's numbers. Abdul Wahab's horse was shot under him but he immediately mounted another and headed his people. In short we had no excuse for our bad behaviour. It was a scandalous affair. On our return to camp vigorous councils did not prevail among us. The Nawab's people too, either afraid or disgusted with what had happened, were packing up their baggage and preparing to leave us.'

De Gingins withdrew his dispirited army on Trichinopoly with Chunda Sahib treading close on his heels; after one or two skirmishes he allowed himself to be shepherded under the city walls while Chunda Sahib prowled round outside. Clive, meanwhile, had taken himself off to Fort St David to collect the supplies he could see would soon be needed. In July he took a convoy from Devicottah which now served a very useful purpose and forced his way through to Trichinopoly. What he found there was deeply disquieting. The troops had lost confidence in their leaders and as Dalton remarked 'disagreements and cabals among the officers [the usual consequence of bad success] ensued, and there never was a more unhappy set of people got together nor from whom less good could be expected'.

When Clive returned to Fort St David, he told Governor Saunders in unvarnished terms that the main army of the Company was penned in Trichinopoly and in hopeless disarray; the situation looked beyond redemption. Yet Clive had a plan. It was clearly useless to send more men to Trichinopoly to join de Gingin's semi-captive army. The situation could only be retrieved by a dramatic stroke somewhere else. Most of Chunda Sahib's army was concentrated near Trichinopoly; he proposed to lead a force into the heart of Chunda Sahib's territory and capture Arcot, his capital. The plan was not merely audacious, in military terms it was suicidal. Clive with the last slender reserves of the Company, even if he succeeded in capturing Arcot, and this was by no means certain, would undoubtedly be besieged by a greatly superior army and without hope of relief be eventually compelled to surrender. It was the fate that was to overtake the French at Dien Bien Phu two centuries later.

But this was not the plan of a soldier, it was the plan of a statesman. Clive gambled that, if he achieved some initial success, he would soon find powerful allies from among the discontented, the ambitious, and from those who had good reason either to dread or hate the supremacy of Chunda Sahib and the French. It was a remarkable political assessment for a junior merchant of twenty-five years of age to make; but perhaps it was even more remarkable that Governor Saunders, on whose shoulders the ultimate

THE BATTLE FOR THE CARNATIC BEGINS

responsibility must fall, should have accepted and agreed to Clive's proposal. He must have sensed some extraordinary talent in the smouldering young man in front of him. He gave Clive leave to gather in every soldier he could find, amongst other things reducing the European garrison of Madras to a bare fifty, and on 26 August Clive with about 210 Europeans and 300 sepoys started out on his hazardous mission.[1]

---

[1] Orme, Fortescue and the official historian of the Madras Europeans put the figure at 200 Europeans and 300 sepoys. In the abstract of the Madras dispatches edited by Rodwell it is stated that Clive embarked 130 Europeans at Fort St David on the Wager, sailed to Madras and picked up eighty more before beginning his advance on Arcot. Mohammed Ali wrote to Saunders 29 July 1751 'If a disturbance could be raised in the Arcot country . . . it would confuse the enemy . . . please raise as great a disturbance as possible in Conjeeveram and countries.' This may have given Clive the idea, but the actual operation was far removed from a fund raising raid. Clive, in his evidence before the House of Commons, claimed he planned the advance on Arcot and there is no reason to disbelieve him.

Chapter 5

ARCOT, ARNI AND KAUVERIPAUK
1751-2

As Clive's 500 men with their three field guns trudged along the dusty tracks, the hot steamy heat drenching their bodies with sweat, it may be guessed that despite the climate which at other times he termed intolerable, Clive felt perhaps happier than at any time since he had landed in India. He had embarked indeed on a perilous enterprise, but one the wisdom of which he himself had judged, and over him now were no fumbling superiors. Everything depended on his skill, his courage and his resolution.

He did not hurry his soldiers. In an atmosphere resembling that of an overheated hot-house, long marches would needlessly exhaust his men. He took four days to cover the forty-six miles to Conjeeveram, a town of some importance about twenty-five miles distant from Arcot. Here he gleaned the unwelcome information that its citadel was held by some 1,100 men. A garrison that outnumbered him by more than two to one, even if only composed of peons armed with matchlocks or swords and bucklers, might still prove formidable behind the walls of a fort. Clive sent an urgent request to Madras for two eighteen-pounder siege guns and resumed his leisurely approach. On 31 August the hot moisture-laden air grew even heavier, the low clouds even darker and more threatening, then the skies broke; rain lashed down while the thunder rolled incessantly overhead and livid streaks of lightning flickered on the paddy fields. The British force tramped on, the European troops probably glad of the

ARCOT, ARNI AND KAUVERIPAUK 101

refreshing rain and the drop in temperature. The storm passed as abruptly as it came, and that night Clive halted his little army some ten miles short of Arcot. On the morrow he would meet his first great test. He had but eight officers with him, four were *writers* who had volunteered for the expedition, but knew little more of things military than how to draw their swords and shout forward, two out of the remaining four had never heard a shot fired on a battlefield; nevertheless they were ardent young men, not easily to be daunted, men he could trust; possibly they were better suited to such an enterprise than more experienced officers who might have questioned and doubted.

That night astonishing news came out of Arcot. The

17 A muslim irregular soldier armed with a matchlock musket.

garrison, noting with superstitious awe how the British had braved the thunder-storm unharmed, a clear indication that they were in league with devils, had vacated the city. Next morning at ten o'clock the little army, less than a full infantry battalion in strength, fell in and marched across the wide and barren plain surrounded by brown granite hills to where they could see the huddled houses of the city beckoning them onwards. As they entered the narrow streets, the inhabitants thronged around them, to watch, with respect mingled with friendliness, the little column threading its way steadily towards the citadel. Inside it lived some of the more prominent of the citizens and here Clive also found sums of money, amounting to about 500,000 rupees, that local merchants had banked there for safekeeping. He at once returned this money to its owners and took stringent precautions against looting.

Now he settled down to examine the situation. Boldness had reaped its reward; he had accomplished the first stage in his ambitious plan with an ease he can never have anticipated, but he knew that the real dangers lay ahead. At least it was evident that the citizens of Arcot, reputed to number 100,000, viewed the conflict between Chunda Sahib and Mohammed Ali with utter indifference, and had no intention of committing their overt support to either side. The citadel itself was in a very dilapidated condition; the city had been permitted to encroach on the glacis, the cleared area round the walls where normally no building was permitted, and in places houses overlooked the ramparts from distances as close as thirty yards.

He began to lay in provisions and repair the most ruinous parts of the walls, but it was obviously impolitic to antagonise the population by blowing down any of the houses, and the threat these constituted had to be accepted. He proclaimed Mohammed Ali the rightful ruler of the city, acted in his name, and appointed officials to collect all revenues due. Whilst employed on these tasks, he learned that the timorous former garrison had encamped by the fort at Timeri about six miles out of the city.

After three days, when the worst defects in the fortifications had been remedied, he resolved to bring them to action before they had entirely rid themselves of their superstitious fears. On 4 September, leaving one platoon to hold the citadel, he marched on Timeri. The soldiers of the former garrison formed up as though for battle, but their nerve broke, and after discharging their cannon at long range they ran off into the hills. It was idle to pursue and Clive marched his men back to the citadel.

When it was clear he had gone, however, the peons gradually filtered back from their sanctuaries in the hills and reassembled in their encampment. On 6 September Clive again sallied out to disperse them. This time they took shelter in the fort. Clive had with him only a solitary mortar; with this he lobbed a few shells into the fort, but the Governor was not to be bluffed into surrender. Without heavy guns he could do nothing more and, thwarted, he withdrew once more to the citadel. Possibly since he did not strike the fort with lightning, or show any other manifestations of an alliance with devils or evil spirits, Chunda Sahib's men began to take heart. Meanwhile Clive spent the next ten days gathering in supplies and strengthening his defences. Left unmolested, his enemy recruited their strength and, with their numbers swollen to 2,000, camped within three miles of the city; they began to boast openly of their intention to besiege the intruders.

It was the opportunity that Clive had been hoping for. On a hot, still, sweaty night he led his men out of the city to the camp. No sentries had been posted and the British entered unperceived. A crashing volley announced their arrival; it was a horrible *reveille* for their foes who fled without attempting to put up the smallest resistance. The British beat right through the camp without losing a man; at dawn not a solitary enemy soldier remained there on his feet.

News now came that Madras had dispatched the two eighteen-pounders but that, owing to the desperate shortage of men, the guns were virtually unescorted. Clive sent a force of thirty Europeans and fifty sepoys to occupy the Pagoda at Conjeeveram, the key to the route, and himself, leaving only eighty men in the citadel, went to bring in his valuable convoy. During the night that he was away, Chunda Sahib's men attempted to seize the nearly empty citadel, but the tiny garrison held firm and neither inside the fort nor outside did the inhabitants offer any assistance; at dawn the attackers prudently disappeared, before Clive could return.

So far Clive had maintained his position with comparative ease, and the series of successful skirmishes had given his men confidence in themselves and their leaders. But more important, his success was beginning to have effects far beyond the walls of the city. The Regent of Mysore, the real ruler of the state, had no desire to see a French puppet at Aurangabad and another ruling the Carnatic. Now the British had shown that their soldiers could fight and might even be able to stand up to the French, he started in earnest to negotiate an alliance with Mohammed Ali. The ubiquitous Morari Rao, encamped with his army of 4,000 veteran Mahratta horsemen just outside the borders of the Carnatic, had little to hope from Chunda Sahib save bullets; he too watched with interest to see if the British were really prepared to fight; now the actions of Clive's men had resolved his doubts, and he needed only to be assured of an adequate scale of plunder or financial reward to throw in his lot with Mohammed Ali; as time was to prove, he still nursed a secret ambition to secure Trichinopoly once again for himself. The Raja of Tanjore, as well, had little cause to remember Chunda Sahib with affection; if Mohammed Ali obtained powerful allies, he might well exact a revenge for the humiliations that Chunda Sahib and the French had made him endure.

Chunda Sahib was not ignorant of these possibilities; it was clear that a dangerous crisis confronted him. He was surrounded by enemies; let him but stumble and the whole pack would leap on his back and tear him to pieces. His friend Muzaffar was dead. Salabat Jang in distant Aurangabad had troubles enough of his own and no time or troops to spare for the Carnatic. Could he stamp on the British at Arcot the whole pack would run yelping away, mouthing protestations of eternal friendship. At Trichinopoly it was true he had penned in Mohammed Ali and the main British army, but here there was a stalemate. He lacked the strength to storm the formidable fortifications of that city, equally Mohammed Ali lacked the troops to give battle outside its walls and drive him away. If at this time Bussy with his 300 French soldiers and 2,000 sepoys had been present, the situation might well have been different and the whole war ended at a stroke. But Dupleix, entranced by the alluring prospect of French influence supreme over the whole of the Deccan, never contemplated his recall. As it was, Chunda Sahib dared not relax his blockade of Trichinopoly, but he recognised that the British, by

18 A hircarra with a message.

splitting their forces, had given him the chance to deliver a blow that might well prove mortal. He sent his son, Raja Sahib, with 4,000 men to retake Arcot.

On 8 September Richard Prince, deputy to Saunders, wrote to warn Clive that a detachment of 150 French soldiers and as many sepoys were reported to have left Pondicherry bound for Arcot. He had, however, no news of any move by either the Regent of Mysore or Morari Rao to go to the assistance of Mohammed Ali.

Clive began to feel uneasy. He was in a desperately exposed position. Too weak to fight a battle in the open, he must either retire, or expect to be besieged in Arcot at a time, as he well knew, when there were no troops in Fort St David or Madras to march to his relief. If neither the Mysoreans nor the Mahrattas allied themselves with Mohammed Ali, for the British to remain in Arcot would be to court a military disaster. Politically, a withdrawal would be nearly as disastrous; it would confirm the opinion, already held by the Indian Princes, that the British were incompetent and not particularly courageous and that to ally themselves with the British against the French was an act of political folly. Nevertheless, while the armed forces remained intact, a single battle could reverse the political situation over night.

He must have expressed his misgivings, for on 10 September Prince replied: 'We don't know what turn the expedition may have given affairs, nor what prejudice a sudden retreat may be, but you are the best judge of the situation.' Fine oracular counsel for a young untried commander not quite twenty-six years old. Clive, and Clive alone, had to make the crucial decision. He decided to gamble all on the chance that, if he put up a stout resistance, either Mysore or the Mahrattas would march to his relief. It was a tremendous risk to take; if his judgement was at fault, his own life and the lives of his men would be forfeit and the Company finally ruined.

The news from Madras continued gloomy. On 29 September Richard Prince remarked bitterly, 'I always thought the King of Mysore was not in earnest, or he would have sent his troops long ago.' But by now it was too late to withdraw.

Raja Sahib and his men were already in Arcot and on 23 September he had set up his headquarters in the Nawab's palace, a large and splendid building not far from the citadel. Clive boldly decided to storm it next day and scotch the siege before it had time to begin. But now he was no longer dealing with superstitious peons. The attackers encountered a bitter resistance. Some French guns were temporarily overrun, but eventually the British were forced back into the citadel, losing two officers and thirty Europeans out of their pitifully small numbers.

It was an inauspicious beginning. Murtaza, surveying events from his stronghold at Vellore, came to the conclusion that it was not only safe but even advisable to lend Raja Sahib his assistance. He joined the besiegers on 25 September; considering it imprudent to commit himself too firmly to one side, he suggested to Clive that if the British would make a sally from the fort, he would attack Raja Sahib's army in the rear. Clive affected to consider the proposal; Murtaza withdrew his troops from the neighbourhood of the citadel while negotiations proceeded.

Clive, however, was fully aware that if a man like Murtaza was offered an option of treacheries, it would be difficult to predict which one he would adopt, and he had no intention of reaching a firm agreement. After a time, it occurred to Murtaza that the British were only keeping him amused, and he directed his troops to play an active part in the siege. The citadel had provisions for rather more than a month.[1] Clive ordered out all civilians, and Raja Sahib, who seems to have inherited some of the chivalrous magnanimity of his father, let them pass unhindered. The Prince possessed no heavy artillery, and for a time the siege became a war of attrition between the garrison manning the walls and the marksmen in the houses that overlooked them. One midnight Ensign Glass took two men with him to blow up one of these houses, but the attempt failed and Glass, climbing back into

[1] Orme states sixty days, Cambridge three months, Abstract of Despatches one month. If Orme's figure is correct the garrison can scarcely have suffered from a shortage of rations, and Malcolm's story of the sepoys giving up their rice to the Europeans, while contenting themselves with the water in which it was boiled, joins the innumerable company of splendid myths.

the citadel on a rope, fell and severely injured himself; no further attempts were made.

Daily Clive walked round the circuit of the ramparts checking the dispositions and encouraging his men. He led a charmed life, but on three occasions the sergeant accompanying him was shot. A month went by. One by one the garrison were succumbing to gunshot wounds or sickness. Governor Saunders knew as well as Chunda Sahib how much depended on the outcome. An early trifling reinforcement under Lieutenant Innis was forced to turn back. He laboured desperately to procure sepoys and gradually assembled a small relief force under Captain Killpatrick, an officer he had previously charged with mutiny; the order sending him home had fortunately been rescinded.

However, Morari Rao, impressed by the new spirit of resolution shown by the British, had begun to stir, and the Regent of Mysore to assemble an army; perhaps more important, that dignitary had sent money to the nearly destitute Mohammed Ali, an action that had not escaped the notice of the avaricious Mahratta chieftain. But in Arcot French siege cannon had made an appearance. On 24 October a French battery opened so well aimed a fire that one of Clive's eighteen-pounder guns was dismounted and the other damaged beyond repair. Clive withdrew from the rampart the gun that could be made serviceable, to keep it intact against the possibility of a storm. Unmolested the French guns steadily blasted away at the walls. Clive resolved to make a gesture to demonstrate how little regard the garrison had for the efforts of their adversaries.

He had discovered in the fort, so Orme related, 'a vast piece of cannon sent, according to the tradition of the fort, from Delhi by Aurangzebe, and said to have been drawn by 1,000 yoke of oxen. There were several iron balls belonging to it each weighing seventy-two pounds'. Clive selected a suitable part of the ramparts and made his men build a huge mound of earth from the top of which there was a clear line of sight to the Palace. The enormous and antiquated cannon was hoisted to the top; its barrel was so corroded that at each discharge there was a chance it might blow up; a long train of gunpowder was led to its touch-hole to avoid any unpleasant consequences for the firer. It was fired ceremoniously once a day, when it was thought that Raja Sahib might be conferring with his generals in the Palace. Its effect is unknown and on the fourth day the barrel duly exploded. It had, however, given occupation and entertainment to the defenders, and helped preserve the spirit of careless defiance that was never to leave them. The loyalty of the sepoys never wavered and the Europeans, in the words of a sergeant present at the siege, 'solaced themselves with the pleasing reflection of having maintained the character of Britons in a clime so remote from our own'.

By 30 October a wide gap yawned in the southwest ramparts, but Killpatrick and Morari Rao were at last about to march, and Raja Sahib knew that his time was running out. He shrank, however, from the awful hazards of a storm; hoisting a flag of truce he proposed an honourable capitulation together with a large sum of money for Clive as a reward for his exertions. Clive treated the proposals with disdain and the guns boomed on. The Prince still cherished a faint hope that the garrison might be starved out, or lose heart and surrender. Nevertheless a new breach was battered in the northwestern face of the ramparts. Then on 9 November a detachment of Mahratta horse entered and pillaged some of the houses in the city, but finding it strongly held rode off. Now Raja Sahib dare delay no longer.

He had already delayed too long. The besieged had been given ample time to prepare. Clive had constructed entrenchments behind the breaches to seal them off, and fortified houses that overlooked them. The garrison, although undernourished and fatigued, their numbers reduced to about 80 Europeans and 120 sepoys still on their feet, yet awaited without flinching the inevitable assault. Clive had inspired the garrison with his own dynamic energy and unbending resolution, but the long ordeal had begun to sap even his strength. He was sleeping when, shortly before midnight on 13 November, a spy slunk into the citadel; he was woken to be told that Raja Sahib would be assaulting at dawn. The spy detailed the complete plan of the Prince.

The two gateways of the citadel were to be attacked by elephants with armour-plating on their foreheads; these were to break down the gates and clear the way for assaulting columns behind; in addition storming parties had been detailed to both the breaches. The signal to advance was to be the firing of three bombs. Clive calmly issued his orders and went back to his slumbers. Such was his confidence in his men that he was still sleeping when the alarm was sounded. He at once went round the ramparts; every man was at his post.

As the darkness faded, the armoured elephants moved clumsily down the streets followed by disorderly columns of infantry. Had Raja Sahib known more of ancient European history, he might not have attempted so dangerous an expedient. A volley from the walls above the gates, and the elephants turned about to make a fear-maddened charge down the streets, scattering and trampling the soldiers behind. The attack on the southwestern breach, where the ditch was flooded too deep to ford, was repulsed with equal ease. Here the vanguard of the storming party, some seventy men, crowded on a raft and tried to pole their way across. Cannon fire raked the close-packed ranks (it is said that Clive himself trained one of the guns); the attackers milled about in confusion and the raft overturned; the survivors scrambled up the far bank, and, deprived of their only means of crossing the ditch, Raja Sahib's men had to abandon their attack.

By the breach in the northwest wall the combat was fierce and prolonged; Orme relates,

'The ditch before the breach was fordable, and as many as it would admit mounted with a kind of mad intrepidity, whilst numbers came and sat down with great composure in the *fausse braye* [a lower-level wall jutting out of the ramparts] under the tower where the field piece was planted, and waited there to relieve those employed in the attack. These passed the breach and some of them even got over the first trench before the defenders gave fire; it fell heavily and every shot did execution, and a number of muskets were loaded in readiness which those behind delivered to the first rank as fast as they could discharge them. The two pieces of cannon from the top of the house fired likewise on the assailants who in a few minutes abandoned the attack, when another and another body succeeded who were driven off in like manner. In the meantime bombs with short fuses which had been lodged in an adjacent rampart were thrown into the fausse braye and by their explosion drove the crowd who had seated themselves back again over the ditch.'

The defences were manifestly too strong, and at the end of an hour the fighting died away. It was estimated that the attackers had lost 400 men, the besieged had lost but eight. At ten o'clock in the morning the guns of the French battery once more began to thunder, and from the house tops the sharper crack of muskets indicated that the marksmen had once again taken up their old positions. The garrison steeled themselves for another assault; it was noticeable that the French had yet to take part. However, at two that afternoon the fire slackened, and Raja Sahib asked for a truce while his men buried their dead, a request that Clive at once granted. About 4 p.m. the firing recommenced and at nightfall showed no signs of diminishing. About 2 a.m. next morning a single gun crashed out once, there were a few random shots, then there was silence. At daybreak the silence continued unbroken, and as the skies brightened men began to appear in the once-deserted streets, who told the incredulous garrison that Raja Sahib and his men had gone. Clive at once organised a search of the enemy's lines and found eight pieces of artillery and a large quantity of ammunition.

And so after fifty days the siege had ended. Of the garrison, forty-five Europeans, nearly a quarter of their strength, and thirty sepoys had been killed, and many more were wounded or sick. It had been a somewhat different affair from the siege of Madras. Clive's tremendous gamble had come off. The war was by no means over, but the gallant Chunda Sahib had suffered a reverse from which he never fully recovered; already an army from Mysore was on the march towards Trichinopoly and Morari Rao had gone there to join them; Killpatrick with 200 sepoys and 2,000 horsemen detached by Morari Rao was near Arcot; it had been his approach that had impelled Raja Sahib to order a retreat.

That Prince fell back on Vellore his disheartened soldiers deserting him by the hundred. Clive did not long remain inactive. Leaving Killpatrick to hold the citadel, on 18 November he marched out to take possession of the fort at Timeri, this time on the invitation of the Governor. He urged the Mahrattas to accompany him to Vellore to destroy the rump of Chunda Sahib's army, but those cost

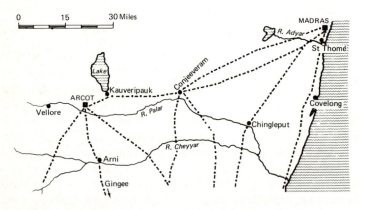

5 Operations round Arcot (extract from Map 4).

conscious warriors refused to move on the grounds that the possibility of booty was insufficient. Clive took his men to reconnoitre Raja Sahib's camp and concluded that he was not strong enough on his own to launch an attack; he had to content himself with re-establishing the authority of Mohammed Ali in the districts surrounding Arcot.

Dupleix and Chunda Sahib now tried to retrieve the situation. A mixed force of French infantry and sepoys and native cavalry with four guns was dispatched to reinforce Raja Sahib's army at Vellore. It surprised the Mahrattas, who lost only twenty of their men but much of their baggage, a grievous blow indeed. The sergeant diarist with Clive

19 Mahratta cavalrymen.

noted sardonically, 'The French used 'em so ill as to attack 'em without pre-advising 'em,'. . .

Clive was anxious to bring the French to action before they could effect a junction with Raja Sahib, but still the Mahrattas refused to move. Then on 13 December came welcome tidings, the French had with them a treasure chest. This transformed the situation; the Mahrattas at once became eager for battle; however, it was too late to prevent the junction between Raja Sahib and his reinforcements; Clive learned he had met them at Arni, a village some eighteen miles to the south. The Prince now had under his command 300 Frenchmen, 2,500 sepoys, 2,000 horse and four field guns. Clive had only 200 Europeans, 700 sepoys and 1,000 Mahratta horsemen with three field guns, but he at once marched on Arni.

On the morning of 15 December at eight o'clock, his advance guard sighted the enemy away in the distance down the Arcot–Arni road. Clive pressed on, but it soon became apparent that Raja Sahib, so far from seeking to avoid action, was advancing up the road in the direction of Arcot. At about ten o'clock, Clive halted his little force on a slight rise, and observed that the ground had certain possibilities for defence. To the right of where he stood, the road ran through a village, and on the right-hand side of the village he could see a deep, wet ditch running parallel to the road, which would furnish a useful obstacle to protect his right. On his left, about 300 yards from the village, was an extensive copse, a little forward of the low ridge on which he was standing. Below the ridge, water-soaked paddy fields, stretching away towards the French, extended from the wet ditch, across the front of the village and over to his left as far as the copse.

Clive decided to anchor his right on the village and here he placed his sepoys; in the centre he lined the Europeans and his artillery along the ridge, and in the copse on the left he sited the Mahrattas. About midday Raja Sahib's cavalry closed with the copse. The Mahrattas charged out, but French sepoys, interspersed among the enemy horsemen, opened a heavy fire and the Mahrattas recoiled. Raja Sahib's men charged in their turn but failed to break through, and on Clive's left a very brisk cavalry action began to develop.

On his right the French had been thrusting forward their guns along the road; but they had an awkward problem; it was impossible to bring the guns into action in the paddy and they were forced to fire, virtually wheel to wheel, from the roadway. In consequence their fire was ineffective, and as the road offered the only firm line of approach, the advancing French infantry soon masked their target. The French infantry, confined to the road and with a front barely four yards wide, displayed great dash, and drove in a forward post; but their front was far too narrow and they were soon checked well short of the village; now their position became very difficult; most of their number were strung back down the road in a long, thin column, making an excellent target for the British guns on the ridge. It was clear that the French had either to deploy across the paddy or retire. Over by the copse Raja Sahib's men seemed to be gaining the mastery. The French commander decided to extend into line across the paddy with his flank nearly reaching to the copse. It was an unfortunate decision. The French infantry and sepoys, floundering across the standing water in the paddy fields, soon became hopelessly bogged. Clive saw the chance for a counter stroke. He sent some European infantry and two of his guns to stiffen the Mahrattas in the copse, and himself led over two more platoons to the village. When the French extended into line they had left their guns almost unprotected. Clive ordered a charge straight down the road. To the amazement of the French, a column of infantry suddenly erupted from the village, ran impetuously down the road and had captured their guns, before the gunners had time to loose off a single effective round.

Now the French infantry, splashing about in the paddy, were in an unenviable position. British infantry shot up their left flank and rear, they had lost their guns, and they had little chance of emerging from the marsh to assault the British on the ridge in front. In considerable disorder they struggled back on to firmer ground behind them. Seeing them go, Raja Sahib's horsemen pulled back from the copse with the Mahrattas in hot pursuit. Some sort of order was restored when the French had a chance to re-form on the road, but there was no stopping the Mahrattas, in full cry after the treasure chest and the baggage. During the night the French retreated through Arni, but they had lost all their guns, their treasure chest and most of their baggage, and next day the commander of the fort at Arni declared for Mohammed Ali.

In the battle the French lost 50 men, their allies 150, hardly crippling losses, the British 8 sepoys and the Mahrattas 50 men. The morale value of the victory was, however, immense. The French sepoys flocked across to join the British in such numbers that, accepting only those who brought with them their muskets, Clive was able to form a new sepoy battalion 600 strong. It had been a brilliant little victory. With impeccable judgement Clive had selected a strong position at a glance, occupied it in a matter of minutes while his foe was in the act of advancing on him, and then exploited its advantages to administer a decisive defeat to an enemy who outnumbered him by more than two to one. It is true that, in these combats, the issue was frequently decided by the behaviour of the European troops, but even here the odds against him were three to two.

Having established Mohammed Ali's rule in the central Carnatic, at least for the time being, Clive started back for Madras. He paused at Conjeeveram. The French had occupied the Pagoda and were intercepting movement between Arcot and Madras. Clive summoned the French Commander to surrender. Now occurred a singular episode. Two of the officers who had been with Clive in Arcot, Lieutenant Revel and Ensign Glass, when returning to Madras with some wounded soldiers from Arcot, had been surprised and taken prisoner. The French, who appear to have known no English, ordered them to write to Clive and say that if he molested the Pagoda, they would be suspended from the

20 The pagoda at Conjeeveram.

ramparts; they complied, but added that Clive was not to desist from any action on their account. He did not. He probably discounted the threat, it would be suicidal for a beleaguered garrison to commit an atrocity unless they were certain of holding out, when such a threat would have been unnecessary. He brought up some heavy guns from Madras and methodically battered a large hole in the side of the Pagoda. The French, seeing their defences crumbling, vanished one night leaving their prisoners behind them. Clive continued on his way to Madras. Here he left his troops and went on to Fort St David to report.

At Trichinopoly both sides pursued a policy of studied inaction. In January 1752, troops from Mysore had begun to put in an appearance. Morari Rao who had stationed himself near the city pleaded with de Gingins to take the offensive, but despite the taunts of the Mahrattas that officer steadfastly refused to risk the hazards of a battle. Dupleix in Pondicherry, for his part, pressed on the French Commander, Law, the urgent need to storm the city, but that officer was as stubbornly wedded to inaction as de Gingins. The perfect tranquillity was only marred by Cope assaulting a minor fort; he was duly repulsed and this time lost his life. The reverse furnished de Gingins with another useful argument for doing nothing, but did not encourage Law sufficiently for him to order an assault.

Meanwhile Raja Sahib had reformed his army, and Dupleix, seeing no profit in adding to the passive masses of soldiers quietly reposing round Trichinopoly, reinforced him and instructed him to ravage the central Carnatic. Perhaps if British trade was hit hard enough they might abandon their intransigent attitude, it should at least distract their forces from Trichinopoly. Raja Sahib was happy to comply with these instructions, the opportunities for plunder should be considerable. He set up camp only seventeen miles from Madras and burnt and pillaged up to the outskirts of the city.

Clive once more took the field in late February 1752. He had with him 380 Europeans, 1,300 sepoys and 6 guns but no cavalry. Raja Sahib commanded 400 French soldiers,

2,000 sepoys, 2,500 horse and 9 guns, but despite his superiority in numbers, one experience of Clive was enough. As the British approached he dispersed his army into small columns, telling them to reassemble at Conjeeveram. Clive followed up the road, suspecting the Prince might make an attempt on Arcot. When he arrived at Conjeeveram, save for a garrison in the Pagoda that immediately surrendered, the place was empty. But now he received news from the garrison commander at Arcot, saying that he had heard that Raja Sahib was approaching. Next day Clive hastened towards that city.

Raja Sahib arrived early at Arcot hoping to seize the citadel through treachery, but his plan came to nothing. He divined that Clive would be chasing him by the Conjeeveram road, and conceived the ambitious plan of ambushing the British. He took up a position astride the main road near the village of Kauveripauk, about seven miles from Arcot. As the sun was setting, the British column, forced marching without cavalry, neared the village. Suddenly a hail of grape swept away the head of the advanced guard. For a moment there was confusion. Nine French guns had opened up from a copse of mangrove trees about 200 yards to the right of the road. About 150 yards on the left there was a wide nullah, or dry water course, into which the British dived. Now Clive had a few moments in which to think. Away to his left, he could dimly discern through the dusk long lines of horsemen cautiously advancing on the nullah; here he realised was the immediate threat. He ordered back a platoon of European infantry with one gun to guard his baggage and escort it out of danger, and ordered another platoon with 200 sepoys and supported by two more of his guns to engage the cavalry.

In the swiftly falling darkness of a tropical night the cavalry perhaps feared to press home a charge; whatever the reason the British line formed and with the onset of darkness the cavalry were helpless. But now French infantry started attacking down the nullah. As the moon began to rise a savage fire fight broke out. The French advance was halted, but in that confined space both sides hesitated to close with the bayonet, and the harsh musketry duel continued. Away down the road Clive's three remaining guns had come into action against the copse.

As the battle roared on, the situation facing the British became grave. Clive afterwards wrote,

'our field pieces drawn up on the road fired on the French cannon, but their fire was greatly superior to ours. Hitherto we had effected nothing but what was to our disadvantage, and our loss was greatly beyond that of the enemy. This made [me] determine either to attack the orchard [i.e. copse] or so far give up the point as to endeavour to find some other road which might enable the army to throw themselves between the French and Arcot.'

The copse occupied by the French had a ditch and a low bank in front. It would be a desperate measure to attack into the muzzles of their guns. Before making up his mind, Clive decided to send a small reconnaissance patrol, consisting of a Portuguese half-caste sergeant and a handful of sepoys, to see if they could find a way round the right. The patrol reported back that a practicable route existed, but that they had also discovered that the French had no sentries out on their flank and the copse might be taken from behind. This was excellent news. Clive at once detailed 200 Europeans and four companies of sepoys, the whole under Lieutenant Keene, to creep out of the nullah out of sight of the French; then, using the sergeant as a guide they were to make a wide sweep round the copse and rush it from the rear. He himself set out with this party to see it safely on its way.

But behind him, the fire of his guns had begun to falter, and the British musketry in the nullah had become ominously muted. He hurried back to find that, noticing his absence and the disappearance of many of their comrades, his men, despite all the efforts of their officers, had fallen back and were about to give way altogether; some had already disappeared into the darkness. Exerting himself to the uttermost he managed to persuade the remainder to resume their former positions. It was now well past ten o'clock and he waited anxiously for the attack on the right to materialise.

Keene and his men had been stealing stealthily forward, any noise they made being blanketed by the sound of the firing. When they had completed their circuit and Keene could see the trees of the copse against the skyline some three hundred yards away, he sent Ensign Symonds forward on his own to scout the way ahead. Groping his way through the blackness, Symonds stumbled on a trench packed with French sepoys. He was challenged; he answered angrily in French, and disappeared towards the copse before any awkward questions could be asked. In the copse he came on about 100 French soldiers engrossed in the gun duel in progress and the battle flaring up in the nullah. He slipped quietly back, taking care to skirt the trenches with the sepoys, and successfully found his way to Keene and his tensely waiting men.

In the nullah Clive waited with growing apprehension. It was past eleven o'clock, nothing had happened and he could not hope to hold on to his position much longer. Then suddenly behind the trees on the right a tremendous volley crashed out. Keene had closed undetected to within fifty yards of the French and had begun his attack. The surprise was complete. The French infantry and sepoys, appalled by the unexpected onslaught out of the shadows behind them, fled without firing a shot. Most of the French took refuge in a rest-house in the trees, but the sepoys ran out towards the road infecting all they met with their panic. With their guns silenced and the fugitives streaming through them, the remainder of the French and Raja Sahib's cavalry made off into the night, while the French trapped in the building surrendered. Raja Sahib had lost all his guns; 300 sepoys and 50 French lay dead on the battlefield, 60 French had surrendered. The British losses, 40 Europeans and 30 sepoys killed and many more wounded, were by no means slight, but the victory was decisive and the central Carnatic secure. Raja Sahib with a remnant of his army sought sanctuary in Pondicherry. The essence of Dupleix's plan was that Raja Sahib should harass the British, but avoid a decisive action.

Maddened by the ruin of his plan, it was some days before Dupleix could bring himself even to see the unfortunate Prince.

The victory had shown Clive at his greatest. Suddenly surprised by a deadly fire, he had retained control over his men, swiftly disposed them to meet the immediate threat, stabilised the situation, then launched a devastating counter-stroke. After this action the confidence of Clive's men in their leader must have become unbounded, the sepoys probably worshipped him as a god.

Soon afterwards he was summoned back to Fort St David. On his way he came across the place where Nazir Jang had been killed. Here Dupleix[1] had erected a monument to his victory. Clive paused long enough to knock it down. He reached the Fort on about 11 March to find Governor Saunders busily planning a massive offensive.

---

[1] The form of this monument is controversial. Macaulay made it a pillar, Orme a rising town called Dupleix Fatehbad. Clive himself spoke of a 'fine rest-house' presumably for travellers wishing to see the battlefield where the French had triumphed.

Chapter 6

THE END OF CHUNDA SAHIB
1752

The battle of Kauveripauk tilted the scales against Chunda Sahib. Once again Clive, in an action of apparently secondary importance, had decisively influenced the course of the war. Now, except for a few unimportant towns and forts, little remained to the Prince of the realm he had so nearly conquered, and at Trichinopoly Morari Rao and his Mahrattas, the armies of Mysore and Tanjore and contingents from minor chieftains were all ranged beside Mohammed Ali and waiting with some impatience for a lead from the British.

Governor Saunders told Clive to rest and refit his men as quickly as possible, then go to Trichinopoly and deliver the *coup-de-grâce*. But on 15 March 1752, before he had time to start, a welcome figure stepped ashore at Fort St David. The Court of Directors in London had wasted little time in meeting Stringer Lawrence's demands, had increased his pay, made him Commander-in-Chief of their armies and smartly shipped him back to India. His arrival solved a delicate problem of command. Clive, as the junior captain, must have come under the orders of de Gingins as soon as he arrived at Trichinopoly, and de Gingins was an officer, as Fortescue remarked not altogether unjustly, of 'well-proven incapacity'. But now that Lawrence had arrived the difficulty would not arise, and he was the one man who ever understood how to control and manage the impatient spirit of Clive. Lawrence himself wrote of his brilliant subordinate:

'A man of an undaunted resolution, of a cool temper and a presence of mind that never left him in the greatest danger ... this young man's early genius surprised and engaged my attention as well before as at the siege of Devicotta.' Clive liked and respected the straightforward, supremely competent old soldier, the 'old gentleman' as they called him, and accepted his authority as he accepted that of no other.

As Clive and Lawrence with a column of 400 Europeans, 1,100 sepoys and 8 guns took the road to Trichinopoly, Chunda Sahib and the French commander, Law, must have realised that their situation was rapidly becoming critical. Dupleix might have been wise to seek a negotiated settlement, but such was far from his mind. Capable as he was of the most splendid conceptions, possessed of a temperament that no failure could dismay, yet he lacked perhaps the greatest quality of all, moderation. He never accepted defeat, and magnificent as such resolution may appear, an inflexible disregard for the realities of a situation may, in the end, lead to a greater disaster than the timid vacillations of men of lesser stature.

Now he wrote to Law demanding that he should fall on Lawrence before his column could join with the forces camped round Trichinopoly. Such a course of action probably offered Law his only hope of avoiding catastrophe. But the Frenchman, who on other occasions showed himself not entirely deficient in energy, declined to stir. Perhaps he feared that if he abandoned his camp and turned his back on Trichinopoly, the Mahrattas of Morari Rao, undoubtedly among the finest light horsemen in India, might sweep down on his rearguard, plunder his baggage and endanger his whole army. A little more than twenty-five years later a British army, retiring from the neighbourhood of Poona, was to be harried by Mahratta horsemen and forced to capitulate; the peril was real enough.

Whatever the reason, Law stayed in his camp, contenting himself with reinforcing the garrisons at Coiladdy and Elmiseram, to the east of the city which commanded the route from the coast to Trichinopoly, thinking perhaps that the British, worried at leaving such strongholds along their lines of communication, might be tempted to a time-consuming and pointless siege. But the 'old gentleman' was far too astute to oblige him. Lawrence had avoided using the direct route from the north along the Arcot road, where he would have been faced by two opposed river crossings and, as Law had guessed, had crossed the Coleroon River well to the east to strike up the road from the coast. This ran under the guns of Coiladdy and Law hoped, if Lawrence bypassed the fort, to catch him on the restricted front between Elmiseram and the Cauvery, compelling him to give battle with an enemy stronghold behind him. But Lawrence swung wide intending to skirt both forts the far

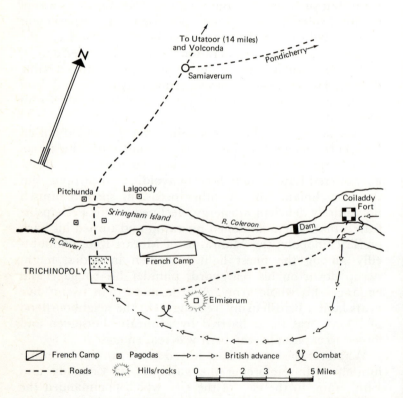

6 Operations round Trichinopoly based on details in Cambridge, Fortescue, and Orme.

side from the river, and come up on Trichinopoly from the southeast.

On 28 March, although owing to an error of his guides he came too close to Coiladdy and suffered a few casualties from gunfire, he camped for the night some ten miles east of the city, intending to enter it next day. De Gingins, profiting from the inertia of the French, dispatched Captain Dalton to meet him with 200 Europeans, including the incomparable grenadier company, 400 sepoys and 4 guns, and arranged for their move to be screened by the cavalry of the allies. Dalton marched at daybreak. Lawrence continued his wide sweep to the south and was joined by Dalton at midday, followed shortly by the allied cavalry withdrawing hastily before Chunda Sahib's horsemen.

As the British plodded on through a stiflingly hot afternoon, they saw in the distance the French forming line on the plain outside the city with Chunda Sahib's cavalry taking post on their left. Clive rode forward to reconnoitre. He came across a rest-house, with some outbuildings constructed of masonry, about 800 yards in front of the French line, which for some reason they had neglected to occupy. He reported his discovery to Lawrence who at once ordered him to take forward the grenadier company and nine guns, seize the buildings and engage the French.

The sun burned down, bathing the men in sweat, as Clive led them forward. The British guns dropped into action and the French replied with twenty-two of their own. For half an hour a gun-battle raged that Orme described afterwards as 'without doubt for the time it lasted, the hottest that had ever been seen on the plains of Hindustan'. During this time Lawrence brought up the rest of his army and deployed it to support Clive. The British were behind cover, the French in the open, and the French line began to waver without ever coming to close quarters. Chunda Sahib's cavalry remained firm and threatened a charge, but a round shot decapitated their leader, Allum Khan, and they drew back discouraged. Then the whole army withdrew. The British, continuing on their way, reached Trichinopoly by nightfall. Seven men died from heatstroke, and perhaps the clammy heat had something to do with the lack of resolution displayed by the French. The action had been almost entirely decided by the guns. It was a characteristic of the armies in India that they were equipped, proportionately, with far more artillery than was customary at that time in Europe, and that the guns were used to far greater effect.

That evening in Trichinopoly Lawrence and Clive deliberated their next move. Lawrence wanted to strike at once, but his allies had this in common with the generals of ancient Greece and Rome: they had an inveterate faith in omens, and now apparently the soothsayers and astrologers pronounced the omens unpropitious. Lawrence with some difficulty swallowed his impatience. He observed, 'Ready and resolute as the country people appear in council, they are ever slow and dilatory in execution. Superstitiously tied down to fasts and feasts, lucky and unlucky days, nothing spurs them to act till those ridiculous customs are complied with, which seldom happens before the opportunity is lost. Thus three or four days were thrown away, and the enemy apprised of our designs . . . decided to retreat to the island.'

The French and their allies, numbering about 600 French and African soldiers, 1,800 sepoys and 15,000 native cavalry took up a position by two large pagodas situated on the western half of Sriringham Island about a mile to the north of Trichinopoly. The island was protected on all sides by the waters of the Cauvery or the Coleroon; but the protection was double-edged; there were only a limited number of crossing places, and difficult as the island might be to assault it was equally difficult for the French to leave; it would be easy to blockade. Lawrence boldly resolved to split his forces and station a strong detachment north of the Coleroon to block the approaches from Pondicherry and Arcot, designing to starve out his adversary. His plan had its dangers. Law might rapidly concentrate his troops against the British detachment north of the river, and if Dupleix sent reinforcements from Pondicherry, the British might be crushed like a walnut between nut-crackers before Lawrence could cross the two rivers and bring assistance. There was only one man

Lawrence could trust for so perilous a task. As he said afterwards, 'I promised myself great success from the activity and vigilance of Captain Clive.' There was, however, the problem that Clive was the junior of his captains. The Mahrattas solved it by refusing categorically to serve under any other officer. Lawrence continues, 'I detached him with 400 of my best Europeans, 200 sepoys and 4,000 cavalry to take post on the other side. We now endeavoured to cut their supplies which they mostly received from the other side of the Coleroon, their communication being open that way quite to Pondicherry.'

By the village of Samiaveram about six miles north of the river, Clive came on two pagodas about 400 yards apart and on either side of the road to Arcot and Pondicherry. He took possession of both, fortified their gates and linked them by redoubts commanding the road both from the north and the south. An attack by a small body of French from Sriringham on 6 April was beaten off without difficulty. Lawrence visited him on 8 April and the two concerted plans to attack the Pitchunda pagoda on the north bank of the Coleroon, which commanded the main crossing place to the western part of the island.

During the next few days Clive consolidated his position, only leaving it to capture a fort at Lalgoody which commanded a minor ford and which he found to his jubilation to contain a large quantity of grain. Then disturbing news came from the island; the French apparently were marching to the east and it was uncertain what they proposed to do. Clive conjectured they might be manoeuvring to cross the Coleroon lower down, intending to wheel westwards and fall on him with the whole of their army. He wrote to Lawrence asking for reinforcements. Lawrence answered him reassuringly, saying that he would 'be on their backs' if the French moved against him, but sent no men.

Then on 14 April Clive heard that d'Auteuil, with about 100 French soldiers, 500 sepoys and 500 Horse, was escorting a large convoy of supplies, and had reached Utatoor about fourteen miles to the north down the Pondicherry road. Dupleix, appreciating the perilous situation in which Law had contrived to place himself, had dispatched all the supplies and men he could assemble to his relief. He had put d'Auteuil in charge with orders to take over command from Law so that Law, as he ingenuously phrased it, could rejoin his wife '*qui ne désire que le moment de vous tenir dans ses bras*'. Only a Frenchman could have put an order for supersession in quite such terms. D'Auteuil proposed to fetch a wide circuit to the east to avoid Clive, and it was Law's preparations to cover him on to the island that had caused the original alarm.

Clive dared lose no time consulting with Lawrence. He afterwards wrote: 'The intercepting of this convoy was of the greatest consequence; the fate of the two armies [Chunda Sahib's and Law's] in a great measure depended on its arrival or non-arrival.' But if he was to go to Utatoor, it was vital to conceal his move from the French on the island, or Law might exploit his absence to capture Samiaveram and open the road to Pondicherry. He waited until nightfall, then, leaving his camp still standing, hastened towards Utatoor. Now occurred a most astonishing comedy of errors. Clive was within four miles of Utatoor when he learnt that there was no sign of the French. Suspecting he might have been duped, he doubled back arriving at Samiaveram next morning after an exhausting march of twenty miles.

Despite Clive's precautions, however, spies told Law of his move, and the Frenchman sent a party of eighty French soldiers and 500 sepoys after dark on 15 April to occupy the empty camp, as he supposed, at Samiaveram. The party marched quite unaware that Clive had returned. At Samiaveram Clive had placed his Europeans and most of his sepoys in the larger of the two pagodas. In the smaller, about 400 yards away on the other side of the road, he had merely stationed a guard, while he himself slept at a rest-house nearby. The Mahratta cavalry were camped round both the pagodas.

The French party had with them a number of British deserters under an ex-Irish sergeant called Kelsall whom Dupleix had made an officer. They tramped through the hot, sticky night and sometime after midnight reached

Samiaveram, expecting to find a virtually unguarded camp. As they approached the outskirts they were challenged by a sepoy sentry. Kelsall answered in English that they were reinforcements sent by Major Stringer Lawrence and the sentry let them pass. They threaded their way through part of the Mahratta camp. The Mahrattas, happily snoring away, ignored them, but as they came to the smaller pagoda, they were challenged by the sentry of the guard there, and also by the sentry over Clive's sleeping place in the rest-house. They answered both with a volley. The Frenchmen then charged into the smaller pagoda, while the sepoys stayed outside firing into the night at nothing in particular. Clive, wakened by the sudden crash of musketry, leapt out of bed, buckled on his sword and rushed over to the large pagoda, where he found his men hastily snatching up their arms. In the dark it was impossible to see what was happening; shots were going off in all directions; but no one seemed to be assaulting the large pagoda, and Clive began to suspect a false alarm, started by a nervous sentry firing at shadows. However, he led about 200 of his Europeans out of the pagoda and went to investigate. He came on a line of sepoys firing down the road in the general direction of the Mahratta camp, an action unlikely to endear them to their allies. Clive, now certain it was all a false alarm, lined up his Europeans behind the sepoys in case of trouble, and went angrily forward to stop the firing before any damage was done, failing in the darkness to note that the sepoys were not his own. The sepoys, probably accustomed to wrathful Europeans shouting out incomprehensible orders in broken Hindustani, did not perceive he was British. The pantomime continued for a few moments, then one of the sepoy officers, suddenly recognising Clive was an enemy, slashed him with his sword. Clive, thinking he had to deal with a mutineer, turned on him furiously and the man fled to the small pagoda with Clive in hot pursuit.

By the entrance to the pagoda Clive was astounded to run into a group of six indubitable Frenchmen. The French were no less astounded at the sight of a British officer with a drawn sword and in his shirt-tails chasing one of their sepoys.

Clive was the first to recover. He calmly told the Frenchmen, as he afterwards related, that 'If they would look about them, they would see they were all surrounded and would certainly be cut to pieces if they did not surrender immediately.' Three surrendered at once, but the others ran back into the small pagoda. Clive returned to fetch up his European troops. The sepoys had disappeared; it had suddenly dawned on them that the line behind them was British and they had coolly formed up and marched away; Clive's men, under the impression that they were British sepoys, let them go without firing a shot.

Clive placed his three prisoners in charge of a sergeant. The sergeant, probably not too imaginative a man, fell in an escort and took the prisoners over to the small pagoda to put them in charge of the guard. He was staggered to find that the pagoda was packed with Frenchmen. The French were equally staggered to have a British NCO appear out of the darkness and deliver three of their comrades into their safekeeping; the sergeant reacted quickest and made good his escape before the French could lay hands on him.

Now Clive knew he had to deal with a serious attack. Uncertain of the strength or intentions of his enemy, he thought it necessary to regain the small pagoda at once, and ordered a party to attack it. The sole entrance was by a small gateway admitting only two men at a time, and the French defended it valiantly. After losing fifteen men, Clive called off the assault, and, stationing a platoon to watch the exit, deployed the rest of his men round the walls of the pagoda to shoot any Frenchmen who might try to escape.

By now it was dawn, and as the darkness faded it became at last possible to see what was happening. The French commander, realising he was trapped and courageously deciding to break out, charged out of the pagoda at the head of his men. Clive's platoon slammed home a volley, felling the French officer and those close beside him; the remainder ran back to the shelter of the pagoda. Clive ordered guns to be brought up. His wound was paining him and he felt weak from loss of blood, but seeking to avoid a senseless slaughter he hobbled forward, leaning on a sergeant,

THE END OF CHUNDA SAHIB 131

to point out to the French the futility of further resistance. Kelsall, standing near the gateway and knowing he would receive short shrift if he surrendered, picked up a musket and fired a shot at Clive; the sergeant supporting him fell dead.[1] The French still in the pagoda, fearing that after such an outrage they could expect no mercy if they continued to resist, forced the English deserters to lay down their arms, and then all capitulated.

The Mahrattas, at last fully aroused, leapt on their horses and rode off after the retreating French sepoys. They caught up with them well short of the Coleroon. The sepoys, seeing a mass of horsemen about to descend on them, panicked and dispersed. The Mahrattas galloped after the fugitives and hewed them in pieces. When they returned, the Mahratta leader remarked that all the sepoys had been killed. Orme drily observed, 'It is certain that none of them ever appeared to contradict this assertion.' Clive went back to his rest-house to find his Muslim servant dead and two musket balls lodged at the foot of his bed. Next day he received congratulations from Lawrence, who directed that Kelsall and three others of the deserters should be hanged forthwith, and tenderly hoped that Clive's wound would not spoil his good looks. It does not appear to have been very serious, as Clive remained at his post.

With the French on the island demoralised by this disaster, Lawrence thought it safe to send a detachment under Dalton to deal with d'Auteuil, still rumoured to be in the neighbourhood of Utatoor. Towards evening the gallant ex-marine, to the surprise of both, suddenly encountered d'Auteuil near the outskirts of the town. Dalton, although outnumbered, made such a display of force that he bluffed the Frenchman into abandoning his convoy and making a hurried retreat to Volconda.

Now the last hope for Chunda Sahib had vanished. Clive closed up to the Coleroon and laid siege to the Pitchundah

---

[1] Clive stated that he was supported by two sergeants and the same shot killed both; when asked how this was physically possible, he replied that he was leaning forward at the time. Even so his account is scarcely credible, and it seems likely that he was merely embellishing a good story.

Pagoda. The whole enemy camp on the island was open to his guns firing from the north bank of the river, and he bombarded it, spreading panic among a host of followers, concubines and other non-combatants. On 10 May the Pitchundah Pagoda surrendered and the situation of those on the island, already short of provisions, became desperate. Monakji with the army from Tanjore blockaded the island from the east, the Mahrattas from the west, Lawrence from the south and now Clive was firmly established across the routes from the north. Dalton, after dealing with d'Auteuil, joined forces with Clive and in order to avoid any trouble over seniority, generously insisted on serving as a volunteer without rank.

Chunda Sahib's soldiers had been drifting away. On 14 May, recognising that the end was near, he called in his chiefs, thanked them for their past services and offered them all he possessed in payment. He regretted that this would still leave him in their debt and promised to repay them if fortune turned again in his favour. The chiefs asked Mohammed Ali for permission to have a free-conduct through the lines. Despite the angry protests of his allies, Stringer Lawrence insisted that the request be granted.

Law, however, with the remnant of Chunda Sahib's army that still stayed loyal, refused to capitulate and took refuge in the two pagodas on the island. On 18 May Lawrence crossed on to the island and made preparations to besiege them. A distraught Dupleix urged d'Auteuil at Volconda to make one last effort at a relief. D'Auteuil advanced. Clive turned on him like a tiger, drove him back to Volconda and forced him to surrender, returning to Sriringham Island on 29 May. That night Chunda Sahib made a bid to escape. He thought his best chance was to slip away eastwards, and head for the French port of Karikal. In exchange for a large sum of money a Mahratta officer offered to guide him through the lines of the Tanjore army. As soon as Chunda Sahib was in his power, however, he betrayed him to a Tanjore army patrol and pocketed the money. Chunda Sahib was at once put in chains. A violent argument broke out among the allies as to who was to guard him. Lawrence offered to take him in charge but his offer was rejected and the Raja of Tanjore, as Lawrence observed 'put an end to the dispute by cutting off his head, which was done the 3rd of June'.

Lawrence remarked of Chunda Sahib that 'in private life he is said to have been a man of great benevolence, humanity and generosity'. His crime had been that he had depended on the support of the French. On the same day that Chunda Sahib was murdered Law accepted the inevitable and surrendered. In the Sriringham Pagoda, a force of about 1,000 Rajputs in the service of Chunda Sahib, horrified by the possibility that the inner temple of the pagoda might be defiled by unbelievers, proclaimed their intention to defend it to the death. The British, admiring their courage and their devotion to their beliefs, replied that they would not enter the temple and allowed the Rajputs a free passage.

Dupleix's great schemes appeared utterly to have collapsed; but in the Carnatic situations changed overnight. Success had a baneful effect on the allies. The Regent of Mysore demanded the cession of Trichinopoly, which had been agreed as the price of his support. Mohammed Ali blandly replied that no one could have taken such a proposition seriously, but that he might be prepared to consider it, after the rest of the Carnatic had been subdued, an answer little to the taste of the Regent. Morari Rao, designing to obtain the city for himself, assiduously urged on each the justice of his cause, hoping to provoke them into destroying each other. Dupleix started to intrigue with all three. For two more years the war was to continue, for two more years battles were to be fought on the sodden, bloody plains round Trichinopoly. For it was an extraordinary war. Neither Madras nor Pondicherry could be attacked, as France and Britain were at peace; the vital European component of each army was so small that the sudden arrival of a ship from Europe with troops, or its loss in the Indian Ocean, could dramatically alter the situation and reverse a decision arrived at on the battlefield. Both Mysore and Morari Rao were to ally themselves with the French, but all Dupleix's combinations were to be frustrated by the stern determination of Lawrence and his indomitable British soldiers.

Yet although the fighting was to go on, the British triumph at Trichinopoly in 1752 made a lasting impression on the Directors of the French Company in Paris. Despite the glowing prophecies of their Governor-General, the war seemed unending, and a high military reputation made a very poor substitute for dividends. At last, convinced that Dupleix would never abandon his grandiose projects for the more profitable pursuits of trade, they resolved to supersede him, and dispatched to India a new Governor-General, Godeheu, with instructions to send home their errant servant, in chains if necessary.

Dupleix, however, accepted his fate without a struggle, and Godeheu at once opened negotiations to bring the ceaseless and financially crippling strife to an end.

The British were happy to comply and a treaty was drawn up. The first article read,

'The two companies, English and French, shall renounce forever all Moorish government and dignity and shall never interfere in any difference that may arise between the Princes of the country.'

and Article 9

'Neither Nation shall be allowed to procure, during the truce, any new grant or cession, or to build forts for the defences of new establishments. It shall only be lawful to repair and rebuild fortifications now subsisting in the establishments they possess at this time, in order to prevent their entire ruin.

'Signed at Fort St George 31 December 1754 and at Pondicherry 4 January 1755'.

The war had apparently been fought to a draw, indeed it might be maintained that the French gained the more valuable territory, but, most significant of all, it was Mohammed Ali who remained Nawab of the Carnatic. The whole issue was briefly to be revived during the Seven Years' War, but the knell had sounded over Dupleix's glorious dreams, and, paradoxically, his mantle was to descend on Robert Clive, the man who did most to frustrate his boundless ambitions. Dupleix returned to France to meet with disdain and die in penury and want. It was a warning that Clive, who in so much else followed in his footsteps, might have done well to heed.

After Law had surrendered, Clive left the army and returned to Madras. His health had been troubling him and his affairs probably needed his attention. By now he had amassed a fortune of some dimensions. His period as Commissary when he had been responsible for supplying the army with food at a rate of six fanams per man per day, had proved not unprofitable—after some rather acrimonious debate the figure was subsequently lowered to four fanams—and he had established a lucrative partnership with Robert Orme trading between Madras and Calcutta. Possibly at this time he met Edmund Maskelyne's attractive sister, Peggy, newly out from England. His friends still serving with the army commented on a sudden lack of letters from their erstwhile comrade, but it is difficult to say whether this was due to the charms of Peggy, or a breakdown in health, perhaps as a reaction to months of intense strain.

Few of the letters Clive wrote at this period have been preserved. It may be significant that George Pigot at Vizagapatam, with whom he was to have many dealings in the future, wrote to him on 11 July: 'Pray Clive let the September ship carry you home and entertain our friends in Shropshire with an account of our fights and frays . . . you are doubtless now so rich that I can accept a few bags. . . . I have not a line from Madras these last two months, you gentlemen there have so much entertainment that you never think of us poor people in the north.'

The last is a cry not to go unheard in the days to come. The letter suggests that as early as May Clive was meditating his return to England. However he had one more service to perform.

The French still possessed two forts in the Central Carnatic, one at Covelong on the coast, about twenty-five miles south of Madras, the other at Chingleput some twenty-five miles inland from it and a similar distance from the important centre of Conjeeveram. From the two forts they had been actively fomenting resistance to the rule of Mohammed Ali. The Prince asked Saunders for help. Lawrence with the main army had just beaten the French at the Battle of Bahur near the boundary of the French concession at Pondicherry. He was still in that neighbourhood anxiously watching developments at Trichinopoly, where the three rivals were jockeying for position, while Dalton who had the unhappy task of commanding the British garrison trusted only the muskets of his men.

Saunders, wishing to assist the Nawab, contrived to scrape together 200 newly arrived English recruits, termed by Fortescue 'the sweeping of the streets of London', and 500 newly raised and very raw sepoys. Clive volunteered to take command. The Council at Madras debated the legality of attacking the two French possessions and cheerfully concluded that, since the French had acquired them illegally in the first place, it was virtually their duty to restore them to their rightful owner, the true Nawab, Mohammed Ali.

When on 16 September Clive approached Covelong fort and demanded its surrender, the Governor pointed to the lilies of France flying over the battlements and ordered him not to fire on the flag of a friendly nation. Clive unemotionally began to construct a 24-pounder battery within 300 yards of the walls. At first he had no little trouble with his own troops, who displayed an unbecoming tendency to run away at the sight of the French. Orme reported that on one occasion 'one of the advanced centries [sic] was found some hours after, concealed in the bottom of a well'.

But the tremendous personality of their commander and his utter disregard of danger soon communicated itself to his men. Within a few days Covelong surrendered; before he gave in, the Governor of the fort had sent earnest appeals to the garrison at Chingleput for assistance. They arrived after the surrender, but mistook the green and white colours of the Nawab, now fluttering over the fort, for those of France. Clive guessed their error and, as he afterwards wrote, 'ordered the greater part of the troops to conceal themselves behind the rocks, bushes and houses that lay in their way. Mr St Germain, the Commandant of the Chingleput fort with twenty-five Europeans and two field pieces were either killed or taken prisoner'. This time Clive's soldiers had fought with the resolution of veterans. Chingleput, deprived of most of its garrison, capitulated as soon as a breach had been blown in the walls of the fort without attempting to withstand a storm.

Clive returned to Madras, having shown that, with troops that many commanders would have hesitated to lead into battle, he could still be victorious. He had fought his last action in the Carnatic.

Chapter 7

MARRIAGE AND A VISIT TO ENGLAND

1753-4

Clive was now twenty-seven years old and famous. His countrymen both in India and England well understood the magnitude of his achievements, his father wrote to tell him that the Directors in London toasted him as 'General Clive'; but later historians have tended to decry him, to suggest indeed that he captured Arcot by a lucky fluke and so came to prominence at a time when a British success was virtually assured; others have pointed out that when he left India the task was only half completed. Now that his period of active service in the Carnatic had come to an end, it may be appropriate to try to assess what he had accomplished.

In the long run British supremacy in India owed much to sea-power, but in 1751 and 1752, as England and France were at peace, the warships of neither could take part in the conflict. During these two crucial years the early foundations of British power in India were laid by the land forces of the East India Company, and in particular the land forces commanded by Clive; of course, much had still to be done to make these foundations secure. It can be argued that in June 1752 the war had two more years to run and that it was Stringer Lawrence, not Clive, who brought it to a successful conclusion. But in the space of nine months Clive utterly frustrated the plans of the French; he inflicted some four defeats on their soldiers and by a rare union of military and political skill brought about a combination of Indian Princes and chiefs that finally doomed the cause of Chunda

Sahib, the only rival to Mohammed Ali who possessed any claim, either legally or through the affection of his subjects, to rule in the Carnatic. Clive not only beat the French, he outmanoeuvred Dupleix in the council chamber where previously the Frenchman had known no peer. After he left the Carnatic, it took the more pedestrian talents of Saunders and Lawrence two more years to complete the task he had so splendidly begun; but by the end of 1752 that task appeared nearly done, and it seems reasonable to contend that, had Clive not left India when he did and his health had allowed him to play an active part, the diplomatic reverses, that led both Mysore and Morari Rao eventually to ally themselves with the French, would almost certainly have been averted. A brief summary of what he accomplished in nine months may serve to substantiate this claim.

In June 1751 he had been present with de Gingins at Volconda, but he had no part in that inglorious affair, he was the commissary, a non-combatant with no standing in the councils of those responsible for the battle and its wretched aftermath. He did not take the field as a soldier until the main British army was locked up in Trichinopoly and the French were everywhere triumphant.

But from the moment in September when he marched on Arcot everything changed. The very success of his brilliant campaign has served to obscure the courage and foresight of those who planned it. To Saunders must go the credit for authorising the plan, but from then onwards everything depended on Clive. He had staked his life and the lives of his men on the correctness of his judgement, not only of the military but also of the political possibilities. Fortune favoured him initially, and then, when Raja Sahib arrived with his army, he undoubtedly blundered.

The characteristics of a great general are mostly inborn. He must possess a stubborn resolution that does not degenerate into blind obstinacy, a cool detached brain that can weigh up the essentials of a situation without emotion or pre-conceived ideas; he must have an unshakeable composure, but beneath it a volcano must burn that can set his men alight; above all he must have judgement and this he can rarely learn without sampling the realities of command in battle.

When on 24 September Clive led his men out of the citadel to drive Raja Sahib away, he made an error that might have cost him Arcot. Yet despite the reverse and the heavy casualties they suffered, Clive's men never lost confidence in their leader, nor he in himself. Having learnt his lesson, that courage and determination are no substitute for calculation and skill, he never needed to learn it again. Half a century later at the Sultan Pettah Tope, outside Seringapatam, the young Arthur Wellesley, the future Duke of Wellington, was harshly taught a similar lesson; he too never needed to be taught it again.

But after that one mistake, Clive can scarcely be faulted. Despite the awful strain of a prolonged siege in which his garrison lost more than half their strength—fearful casualties by any standard of fighting—once the siege had been raised he at once took to the field, and his men shrugged off the memory of their ordeal as if it had never been; and then at the battle of Arni they finally shattered the myth of French invincibility. His victory spurred the lethargic allies of Mohammed Ali into action and caused a host to assemble at Trichinopoly which, after his victory at Kauveripauk, became too formidable for Law and Chunda Sahib to oppose in the field. As a result, after the arrival of Lawrence and Clive at Trichinopoly Law and Chunda Sahib allowed themselves to be herded on to Sriringham Island and destroyed almost without putting up a fight.

During the whole of this period Clive dominated the war. But he did so after his own fashion. Instead of concentrating the Company's troops into a single army and seeking a mighty confrontation with the main army of the French, as any exponent of classical military strategy must have done, he fought a series of peripheral actions through which he created political conditions that made an eventual French catastrophe almost inescapable. This may have been partly due to the chance that, if he had joined the main army, he would have come under the paralysing command of the de

Gingins, but it must also be attributed to the skill with which he directed his military actions to the achievement of his political aims.

When considering his prowess as a commander, it can be objected that his battles were skirmishes won against an Indian enemy who, however courageous, so lacked the technical ability of the European soldier as to be as helpless as the ancient Britons before the legions of Rome. But unlike most of his successors, his victories were also won against the soldiers of France, against soldiers justly dreaded throughout the continent of Europe.

That the scale of his battles was small cannot be denied.

20a Portrait of Clive attributed to Gainsborough.

He never knew the problems of commanding great numbers of men, he was untroubled by subordinates who misinterpreted orders, and all the other frictions that plague large armies. His victories were personal affairs after the style of a Caesar, rather than the great combinations of a Marlborough or a Napoleon, and it must be conceded that he never fought against a truly worthy opponent. His right to join the ranks of the Immortals among military commanders, therefore, cannot be unquestioned; here the verdict can only be 'not proven'. But that in nine months he transformed the British situation in the Carnatic can hardly be disputed.

And what of Clive himself, an undoubted hero at the age of twenty-seven? Something of a change for the black sheep who had sailed to India on the *Winchester* on 10 March 1743. The society in which he had been plunged while little more than a boy, the society that must have moulded him, resembled that of no other in the world. Something has been written of the effect of the British on India, rather less of the effect of India on the British and in particular on the British who dwelt in that country. They lived in a curious almost claustrophobic community. Cut off by language from most of those around them, meeting few women and no elderly or adolescents of their own race, knowing each other as a schoolboy knows his class-mates, they developed their own conventions and values, communicated among themselves easily and with few words, and forgot the petty insincerities, the little artificialities so necessary to the easy functioning of a larger more variegated society. It was as though they were part of a large, adult and mainly male family which rarely encountered strangers and only accepted those who conformed to its standards. It was an aristocratic family in the sense that all its members were men of authority, but one, generally speaking, without artists, without leisure to cultivate to any degree the graces of living or indulgence in philosophic speculation. But then it was a society of transients in which few expected to stay long.

Its impression on the young lad must have been accentuated by his ventures into the still more enclosed society of the British soldier in India. In wartime, soldiers, whose lives

MARRIAGE AND A VISIT TO ENGLAND 143

depend on the decisions taken by their superiors, value competence above all else. A man such as Clive, of outstanding ability and courage, would receive the adulation of his men, his opinions would be unquestioned, his pronouncements final. And in a small community where he would meet none with talents equal to his own, a certain imperiousness and arrogance would inevitably be born. With good reason he would pay little attention to opinions that differed from his own, and can hardly be censured if he treated criticism as little more than a personal affront.

In addition, his experiences of Indian princes and their courts cannot have been without their effect. From them he would learn a love of the splendid gesture, a princely and prodigal style of living, a tradition of openhanded generosity to friends and adherents, and an unrelenting animosity to enemies.

Having arrived in India at the age of eighteen after an unsatisfactory schooling, with no background of past education and culture on which to base his values, his character must have been shaped in large measure by his surroundings. And now wretched in health, but with an unlimited faith in his own attainments, Clive longed to return to England, to bask in the admiration of his countrymen, and perhaps to seek wider fields to conquer in a climate more congenial.

In October 1752 he submitted a formal request to be allowed to return. At first there was delay over granting him a passage. Morari Rao was siding with the French and Lawrence, complaining that Saunders interfered ceaselessly with his plans, had once again resigned. The old gentleman was, however, persuaded to soldier on, and Clive's health, so he assured the Council at Madras, would never mend while he had to endure the heat and fevers of India.

There can be little doubt that by this time he had started to take opium to ease his suffering. Perhaps when he left for England he may have decided to break himself of the habit. A letter dated 6 March 1754 signed by Walsh, Maskelyne and Vansittart, who were looking after his affairs in India, reads: 'Having no hopes of disposing of your two chests of opium here we have consigned them on the Selangore sloop to the eastward on your account and directions to sell them for whatever they will fetch.'

By February 1753 he had recovered sufficiently from his ailments to lead Margaret Maskelyne to the altar of the English church in Fort St George. His bride's father worked as a civil servant in Whitehall, but her family had connections with the East, as an uncle had died in Sumatra and two aunts found matrimony in India. She had three brothers. Two were elected fellows of Trinity College, Cambridge, and one of them, Nevil, was to reach the eminence of Astronomer Royal. The third, Edmund, who was Clive's

20b Margaret Clive. Attributed to Nathaniel Dance. Probably painted in 1773.

friend, seems to have been ignored by nature when it came to talent and to have led a life that was more entertaining than memorable.

Edmund had written to Margaret, assuring her with brotherly candour that she was more likely to make a good match in India than by remaining at home. When Clive, the young hero of the moment covered in glory and by no means deficient in wealth, proposed to her, she must have reflected that although her brother might be lacking in academic distinction, when it came to practical matters he possessed a certain perception.

She was small with a small-featured face, and there is little evidence to show how attractive she might have been; in Madras at that time any young English girl by reason of her age and sex would have been thought attractive. Clive himself, with his heavy forehead and tendency to corpulence, his abrupt manner and impatience of the conventional courtesies, was unlikely to be superficially attractive to women, although the sense of power radiating from his personality might well have intrigued the more mature. He,

21 The Assembly rooms, Madras, built on the race course.

himself, does not appear to have been much interested in the feminine sex. The French, who had no great cause to love him, suggested that at a later date, when he was in Calcutta unaccompanied by his wife, he was not entirely impervious to the beauty of the local courtesans, but there is little evidence that his wife or any other woman had much influence on his life.

Margaret herself seemed to take after her brother Edmund more than the brilliant mathematician, Nevil. She carried on a long correspondence with Carnac, one of Clive's friends who had a somewhat chequered career, winning two notable battles and being promoted major general only finally to be dismissed the service. In it she reveals herself as a pleasant, kindly, gregarious woman, fond of music and not entirely deficient of a sense of humour. She frankly found high policy boring and beyond her comprehension, but loyally accepted the demanding and sometimes uncongenial activities inseparable from political life. She probably loved but stood in awe of her masterful husband, ministered to his more material needs, but had little influence over his thoughts and actions. She remains today a little obscured by the mighty shadow of the man she married.

On 23 March Clive and his bride sailed for England; Robert Orme accompanied them on the voyage. Clive left instructions for some 50,000 Arcot rupees, about £5,000, to be turned into diamonds, or paid into the Company's account in Calcutta so he could draw the equivalent when he was in England, and this seems only part of his fortune.

On 14 October the Clives landed in England, the ugly duckling had turned into a swan with plumage of the rarest. All England rang with his exploits, and his father and mother gratefully sunned themselves in his glory. The greatest men in the Kingdom wished to meet him and hear of his deeds. Heady stuff for a young man of only twenty-seven. It was ten years since he had seen his family, and it may be guessed that the first meeting followed the normal pattern of such affairs. There would be the first shock of recognition, then the usual remarks how this one had grown and that one had filled out, finally everyone would loudly proclaim how little anyone had changed.

But of course everyone and everything had changed. Life in India, at that time a voyage often of twelve months or more away, might well have been that on a different planet. The exile, with his memories of England as it was ten years before, would find his dress looked on as quaint and outmoded; when he hastily ordered replacements, his taste would be uncertain and his clothes subtly wrong. When he spoke he would use phrases and forms of speech long since discarded, and much of what he talked about would be almost unintelligible to his hearers. His stories would centre round odd places called pagodas and choultries, and towns with unpronounceable names; to make the confusion worse, outlandish Hindustani phrases would come tumbling out, and he would use extraordinary words such as punkah, bazar and bearer, and Nawab, Rajah and rupee, that no reasonable person could be expected to understand. At first his conversation might have a certain exotic fascination, but soon it would bore and finally seem tiresome and affected.

Such hazards particularly faced those returned from the East, at that time known to so few; clubs had yet to be established where the exile could relax among friends who understood his language and the places and people he spoke about. Conversely the exile would have difficulty in understanding those who had never left England. The small change of conversation, the references to people and events familiar to the speaker but unknown to him, the fashionable phrases that had been coined in his absence, new attitudes and ideas, all these he would find novel, puzzling and disconcerting. If he went to the theatre he would fail to grasp the significance of allusions that were convulsing his companions. And some of the new customs to his fresh eye might well appear foolish and ridiculous, although he would be well advised to refrain from voicing his opinions.

An educated and sophisticated man who had reached maturity before leaving England might recognise the pitfalls, and know that the country he was in differed profoundly from the idealised vision that had gradually formed in his mind during the long years away. He would patiently allow time to educate him into ways and places that appeared so treacherously familiar; he would realise that he was a stranger in a strange land and must gradually accustom himself to the mysterious ways of the natives.

For Clive, whose education had been scanty, who had left his country at the age of seventeen and had now returned wealthy and famous, life would have been peculiarly difficult, had he perceived the difficulties. Most probably at first he did not, and however farouche he might appear to London society, his personality had an impact nothing could diminish. And so he came home, a celebrity, to the unfamiliar familiar, and threw his money about with the traditional prodigality of the Indies, a prodigality that had already become part of his nature. He paid off the mortgage on the Styche estate, settled money on his parents and set up house in London. His early days were triumphant, his father holding him up to the admiration of all with the unbalanced enthusiasm he had previously displayed in his strictures. Clive bought himself a carriage and pair, and his lavish, rather ostentatious style of living excited the usual petty sarcasms and sneers from the malicious and those with a reputation to sustain as wits. His clothes, even for that age, were too loud, and no doubt fine ladies said after the Clives had left their houses, 'Isn't he odd? And my dear, did you notice her dress? And isn't his father too awful?'—or the eighteenth-century equivalent.

The Directors of the Company, however, welcomed him without reservation. He was voted a diamond-hilted sword which he refused to accept until a similar honour was done to his old comrade in arms, Stringer Lawrence, and his advice was sought on matters of high policy.

Once he had settled down and family affairs had been arranged, he began to cast about him for new paths to distinction. Politics were clearly the road to power. He joined the ultra-whig faction headed by Lord Sandwich whose culinary contribution to picnics has achieved more lasting fame than any service he contrived to render to his country.

MARRIAGE AND A VISIT TO ENGLAND

It might have been expected that one well versed in the devious ways of the Orient would be equally well qualified to understand the not particularly straightforward political arts practised in the England of that day. But perhaps the exile, dreaming of a native country becoming with the passage of time ever more perfect and remote from the chicanery with which he was surrounded, failed to realise that deviousness in politics knows no national boundaries. He stood for the Borough of St Michaels in Cornwall. There appear, by modern standards, to have been remarkably few electors, but these few must have had decidedly expensive tastes for the cost of the election far exceeded expectation. In the upshot, he won the seat receiving the notable total of thirty votes as against twenty-five cast for his opponent. But the Duke of Newcastle, who headed the newly elected Government, did not much fancy the result and a petition was lodged against it. In those days such petitions were less concerned with legal points than with the respective Parliamentary strength of the rival parties. Both sides mustered their forces for a contest in the Commons.

The first fine glitter of his return by now was fast fading, and Clive with much of the fortune he had previously thought so impressive already expended, began to suspect that India and its ways might have more attractions than he had at first been prepared to admit. His health was restored, and the Company was making some interesting proposals. The bitter war in the Carnatic showed no signs of abating, and the Directors despaired of peace while the Viceroy of the Deccan, Salabat Jang, remained the office boy of Bussy and the French. Now, however, the powerful Mahratta Confederacy, their traditional rivalry with the Viceroy exacerbated by a growing hatred of the French influence at his court, wished to destroy both, yet hesitated to face Bussy's soldiers without having some European infantry with which to match them. They asked the British for assistance.

The Directors cogitated long. They concluded it would be folly to miss such an opportunity; even if Salabat Jang were not dethroned he might well be induced to dispense with the

French. Clive concurred. For reasons of geography, an expedition against Aurangabad, particularly in conjunction with the Mahrattas, was best mounted from Bombay. But then who should command it? It was unlikely that Lawrence could be spared from the Carnatic. Would not Clive like to return to his former fields of glory? There was, of course, a problem of rank. The British Government, awake at last to the value of their acquisitions in India, had posted a regular infantry battalion, the 39th, to Madras and its colonel might well feel entitled to be given the command.

22 The East India Company's offices in Leadenhall Street.

But if Clive was prepared to accept the appointment, the Directors could arrange for him a commission in His Majesty's army, but only while serving in the East Indies; thus began the curious and long-standing delusion that those who won battles in the East would be baffled by the intricacies of warfare in Europe; even Wellington back in England after his splendid victories at Assaye and Argaum was deemed incapable of commanding an infantry division in Europe without the aid of a competent second-in-command.

After Clive had dealt with Bussy, it was proposed that he

MARRIAGE AND A VISIT TO ENGLAND 151

should return to the Carnatic and become a member of the council at Madras. The present Governor, Saunders, had intimated he wished to retire; George Pigot would be appointed to succeed him as Governor and Clive become Second-in-Council, Deputy Governor and Commander of Fort St David at Cuddalore. His initial contract would be for five years. The offer opened attractive, if eastern, vistas of power and affluence. Clive was not inclined to dismiss it out-of-hand. Rumours of it percolated to Lord Sandwich who wrote with perhaps justifiable indignation in March 1755, 'I heard for the first time last night that you was [sic] to have a Lieutenant-Colonel's commission which greatly surprised me as your seat in Parliament would therebye be vacated. . . . If you would write me a letter in answer to this one to tell me you are determined not to vacate your seat, I might possibly retrieve some of the ground this report may have made me lose.' Possibly feeling this was a little bald, Sandwich added after he signed the letter 'I am in good spirits and not at all diffident of success'.

Clive deferred his decision until after the petition was heard. The Commons made it easy for him, they rejected his election. Next day he accepted the Company's offer. He was gazetted a Lieutenant-Colonel in His Majesty's Forces in the East Indies with effect from 31 March 1755. Robert Fox, writing on 29 March from Holland House to ask where the commission should be sent, cordially added, 'I sincerely wish you all the success which your great character makes all your friends sure you deserve.'

In April 1755 Lieutenant-Colonel and Mrs Clive embarked on the *Stretham*. In the convoy were three companies of Royal Artillery, and as the Colonel and his lady set foot on the deck a nine-gun salute boomed out across the waters. It was all a little different from the time twelve years ago when he had embarked a solitary, friendless youth bound for a distant land where he was as likely to find his grave as his fortune. By now the Clives had two baby sons and these they left behind them, the parting must have caused anguish to Margaret. Robert, however, had learnt that, if he wished to reach the highest ranks in his native country, without enormous wealth the way was likely to be hard indeed. And so, he went back to India to seek fresh riches. The air of England might suit his health, but the atmosphere of India went better with his purse. His second tour in India was to bring him wealth and enduring fame.

Chapter 8

GHERIA AND
THE FALL OF CALCUTTA
1755–6

This time the voyage was fast and uneventful and in November 1755, the *Stretham* dropped anchor in the beautiful harbour of Bombay. Both the Clives were returning to a land where they were known and had friends. As early as 1754 there had been rumours in Madras they were contemplating coming back. Ann Bourchier, wife of the Secretary to the Council in Madras, wrote on 1 November 1754 to Margaret Clive:[1]

'I hope Mr. Clive has found the good effects of a cold climate and quite recovered in which I am myself interested as I find on that depends your making a similar visit next year. I assure you my dear Peggy I propose a good deal of satisfaction on your return to India, and as you may call at Madras I hope you will find it convenient to accept of the two little rooms which shall always be at your service. Your friend Sally remains a spinster but much against the inclinations of all the single gentlemen I imagine. . . .'

Clive had been sent to Bombay to command the expedition against Salabat Jang should Lawrence still be required in the Carnatic; there is little evidence, however, that

---
[1] This letter shows Clive considered a return to India before standing for Parliament and refutes Macaulay's suggestion that it was lack of money that compelled his return.

Lawrence ever seriously considered leaving the province and Clive arrived in Bombay as commander-in-chief designate.[1] But even before he embarked Saunders and Godeheu had signed a truce that, at least for the time being, ended the war in the Carnatic. One of its articles expressly prohibited either Company intervening in disputes between Indian princes. The truce did not bind the Council at Bombay which was in no way subordinate to the Governor of Madras; but if it were ratified by the Court of Directors in London, the expedition against Salabat Jang might have to be recalled before matters had reached a conclusion, an act which the Mahrattas would certainly look upon as a betrayal and which would damage the reputation of the British throughout India. The Mahrattas were far too powerful for the Council to risk incurring their enmity. As Clive himself wrote, 'Acting by halves, or making cats paws of the Mahrattas, may ruin the Company's affairs in these parts.' Besides, despite the remarkable diplomatic ability of Bussy, his presence and influence at Aurangabad excited the hostility of the great nobles of the Deccan as well as that of the Mahrattas. It was by no means impossible that Salabat Jang might find himself obliged to expel the French to avoid a large scale insurrection.

These arguments carried the more weight in that, since the territory of the Mahrattas lay between them and the dominions of the Viceroy, the Council at Bombay cared little about what transpired at Aurangabad and had a pressing problem much nearer home. An admiral who commanded the Mahratta fleet during their struggles against the Moghul Emperors, perceiving the advantages of private enterprise over the public service, had turned pirate with the enthusiastic support of his men. For the past fifty years he and his successors had extended their sway along the west coast of India; with their shallow draught vessels known as

---

[1] Both Malcolm and Forrest suggest that the Duke of Cumberland insisted that if Lawrence could not command, Scott, an Engineer officer in Calcutta at that time, should lead the expedition. Scott died shortly after arriving in Madras in May 1754 and his death must have been known to the Directors before Clive accepted their proposals.

GHERIA AND THE FALL OF CALCUTTA 155

23 A Bombay grab, the vessel most used by the pirates of Gheria.

'Grabs', they operated in packs which were known to attack even convoys escorted by warships.

Piracy, as such, was not frowned on by the chiefs of the Mahratta Confederacy, themselves never known to refrain from an opportunity to plunder, but when the ruling pirate chief, Tulaji Angria, in a rash moment refused to pay them tribute, their views changed abruptly and they proclaimed it was time to extirpate the pirates, a view that owed something to the stories they had heard of the immense wealth that the pirates had secreted in their stronghold, Gheria, about 170 miles south of Bombay.

At this time Vice-Admiral Watson with a strong squadron lay at anchor in Bombay harbour. Although rumours of the impending war with France were circulated by every new arrival from Europe, the French naval forces in the Indian Ocean were weak, the war in the Carnatic was ended, and Clive, the most successful British commander in India, was at their disposal. A better opportunity for dealing with

24 Admiral Watson.

Tulaji Angria could hardly be expected, and the tales of the pirate treasure were not lacking in attraction. The Council cancelled the expedition to the Deccan and proposed instead an attack on Gheria. Watson and Clive accepted the new proposal with some enthusiasm; neither disdained an opportunity for prize money. It was agreed that the naval squadron should bombard the pirate fortress from the sea while Clive, in conjunction with the Mahrattas, assaulted it from the land.

And so began a relationship between Watson and Clive that was often uneasy, sometimes acrimonious, but which was singularly fruitful for their country. Watson had been sent to the East Indies to watch over British interests. He was a vice-admiral,[1] the naval equivalent of a lieutenant-general, and far outranked anyone else in that part of the world. As a servant of the Crown he probably regarded the so-called Governors, appointed under no greater authority than that of a bunch of businessmen in London, with a tolerant disdain. Personally he was utterly fearless, able and autocratic—timid men rarely reached his rank. He could be choleric and arbitrary; but there was nothing small-minded about him, and he was completely devoted to the good of his service and country. No doubt he looked upon the soldiers as strange land animals, who generally got into difficulties from which they expected the Navy to extricate them. Clive he almost certainly regarded with suspicion as an amateur soldier and rather bumptious young man.

25 The pirate fort at Gheria.

He had under him a powerful fleet for those waters. He had four ships of the line, *Kent*, *Tyger*, *Cumberland* and *Salisbury*, a twenty-gun ship, *Bridgewater*, and the sloop *Kingfisher*; in addition the Company placed under his orders the *Protector* of forty guns, three frigates, *Revenge*, *Bombay*

---

[1] He did not know of his promotion at this time; the Crown confirmed the appointment of governors, a mere formality.

Grab and *Guardian*, and four bomb ketches with which to shell the fortress and any shipping that might be lying within the pirate harbour.

    Clive's men were embarked and on a fine cold weather morning on 11 February 1756 the fleet dropped anchor opposite Gheria. Tulaji Angria panicked at the sight of so formidable an armada, and hastily took refuge with the Mahrattas, hoping to negotiate a settlement that would preserve for himself at least some of his possessions. His lieutenants, displaying a less prudent if more gallant spirit, opened fire on the British. The broadsides of the battleships thundered a reply while the bomb ketches lobbed their bombs into the pirate fleet with devastating effect. The casualties were few but the noise was appalling, and the pirates soon offered to treat. A lengthy wrangle ensued while Clive landed his men. The Mahrattas had failed to put in an appearance, and Tulaji Angria's presence in their camp led Clive to suspect that they were waiting until the fire from the British ships had subdued the fort, when, with the connivance of Tulaji, they would enter the stronghold and escape with the booty. To prevent such an unfortunate event, Clive cordoned off the fort from the landward side.

    After some twenty-four hours of inconclusive argument Watson lost patience and reopened fire, upon which the fortress promptly surrendered, and Clive took possession. Treasure amounting to some million rupees was recovered. The Mahrattas, tardily approaching, despite their agitated protests were prevented from passing the cordon and, since they had contributed nothing to the siege, were excluded from sharing in the proceeds. They do not seem to have borne much malice, they probably admired Clive for having divined their intentions and outmanoeuvred them.

    The fortifications at Gheria were destroyed and such vessels of the pirate fleet as had survived the action were burnt. The operation had been eminently successful, but the division of the spoils occasioned a dispute between the Army and the Navy. The Naval officers contended that as Clive was a Lieutenant-Colonel his share should be the same as that of the post captains on H.M. ships, while the Army officers maintained that as Commander-in-Chief of the land forces it should equal that of Rear-Admiral Pocock, the Second-in-Command of the Fleet. No doubt, the Naval officers pointed out that the Navy had done all the fighting, and the Army, in its customary fashion, had only woken up when it came to the division of the loot. It was a difficult situation for Clive. He was a young and newly promoted Commander-in-Chief and his prestige with his officers would depend on how he handled the affair. Unless he insisted on his rights at the outset the Navy would treat his authority with contempt. He pressed the point of view of his officers. Watson ruled against him, but offered to pay him sufficient out of his own share to make Clive's equal to that of Pocock. This Clive declined, saying he had only advanced his claim as a matter of principle and was not prepared to enrich himself at the expense of the Admiral. It was the first of a series of incidents in which Clive had to battle with Watson to secure a proper recognition of his authority. It is perhaps one of the greatest tributes to the characters of both these masterful men that such disputes, arising fundamentally from the ill-defined relationship between the Company and the Crown, were never allowed to mar the harmony of their actions when their cause or country was at stake.

Now that the expedition against the Deccan had been abandoned and the pirates crushed, Watson decided to sail for Madras. Clive took passage with him. He arrived in June to find that, as anticipated, Saunders had gone home, and his friend George Pigot was now the Governor. Clive accordingly became the Deputy Governor, Second-in-Council and Commander of Fort St David.

Events in the Carnatic had taken an interesting turn. Salabat Jang, yielding to the pressure of his nobles, was proposing to expel Bussy and the French. He had written asking for British assistance. The conscience of the Council at Madras being somewhat more elastic than that of Bombay, steps had already been taken to organise an expedition. But now came disturbing news from Calcutta. The old Viceroy of Bengal, Alivardi Khan, had died and been succeeded by a young, capricious and aggressive Prince, so the Council at Calcutta affirmed, and he was threatening to expel the British from Bengal. He had already confiscated the trading station at Cossimbazar near his capital, Murshidabad, and help was urgently required.

The request was exceedingly unwelcome. Rumours of the imminent outbreak of a European war grew daily in strength, and it was reported that in France a large fleet destined for Pondicherry was being fitted out. It was not the moment to strip the Carnatic of troops, and that shrewd officer, Watson, was not prepared to adopt any policy which required him to split his fleet and risk a general action with some of his ships away in Bengal. The Council, too, were reluctant to miss the excellent opportunity they had been offered to destroy French influence in the Deccan, and Calcutta must surely be able to withstand a siege by an Indian Prince unsupported by a European siege train. It was resolved to send Major Killpatrick with 200 soldiers from the Madras European battalion in a merchantman, the *Delaware*, to the aid of Calcutta. Killpatrick had already booked his passage home to England, but he agreed to stay on, a decision that prevented him ever seeing his native land again.

Then on 16 August came appalling news. Calcutta had fallen. To understand what happened and the course events were to take in the future, it is necessary to consider something of the past history of Bengal. The provinces of Bengal, Bihar and Orissa formed the second great viceroyalty of the Moghul Empire, the viceroy of which was customarily entitled the Nawab of Bengal.

Bengal itself had been a great and prosperous province until devastated by a vicious civil war during the forties. The two great arteries through which flowed most of its commerce were two of the largest rivers in India, the Ganges and the Brahmaputra. Near its mouth the Ganges flowed into an extensive delta and here the River Hooghly was one of its main channels to the sea. The Hooghly, despite shifting shoals that made it a nightmare to navigators, could accommodate large ships for the first sixty miles from the sea, and gave a reliable water route inland to the main

GHERIA AND THE FALL OF CALCUTTA

channel of the Ganges. Not far from the junction of the Hooghly (or Baghirathi) and the Ganges, and on the banks of the former, lay Murshidabad, the capital city of Bengal.

In the late seventeenth century the East India Company had been ceded some four miles of land on the east bank of the Hooghly, about 100 miles south of Murshidabad and forty miles from the mouth of the river. Here a British settlement was established that subsequently came to be called Calcutta. The French founded a trading station of their own at Chandernagore about 18 miles upstream, and the Dutch one at Chinsura, another three miles up the river. The French and Dutch settlements were only out-stations of their eastern trading empires, but Calcutta, after some vicissitudes, developed into a large and flourishing port with its own Council equal in standing to those at Madras and Bombay. From Calcutta trading stations were established at Cossimbazar a mere six miles from Murshidabad, at Patna on the Ganges, which was the capital of Bihar, and at Dacca an important city in eastern Bengal. Internal disorders subsequently led the company to evacuate its factory at Patna.

In 1716, in return for a large sum of money, the Company obtained a *firman* from the Moghul Emperor Farrukhsiyar which, among other privileges, exempted the Company from paying customs duties on any of its goods. The relevant part of the *firman*, as recorded in Orme, reads:

'The English Company have been exempted from Customs throughout the Empire excepting the port of Surat, and in the port of Hooghly they pay annually 3,000 rupees in lieu of customs. . . . The command which subjects the world to obedience is issued forth. Whatever goods and merchandise their agents may bring or carry by land or water in the ports, quarters and borders of the provinces, know them to be customs free and let them have full liberty to buy or sell. Take annually the stated peshkush [tribute] of three thousand rupees and besides that make no demands on any pretence.'

To be accorded this exemption merchandise had to carry a pass known as a *dustuck* signed by the President of the Council. Such goods, moving duty-free through his province, clearly deprived the Nawab of Bengal of valuable revenue, but, more important, if the *firman* could be construed as applying to goods moved by any merchant of the Company on his private as well as the Company's account, and covered the inland trade as well as the European, its effects would be disastrous to the merchants of all other nationalities. If a British merchant could purchase goods in Patna, say, to bring them to Calcutta for sale, and these were exempt from all the many transit tolls to which others would be liable, he would gain a ruinous advantage over his competitors.

The Nawab of Bengal, Murshid Ali Khan, at the time the *firman* was issued firmly interpreted it as extending the duty-free privilege only to bonafide goods of the Company, which were being exported to or imported from Europe. When he died, however, and was succeeded by Sujah-ud-daula, the merchants of the Company started to use *dustucks* for their own private internal trade, and the more venal of the Presidents were known to hawk *dustucks* to Indian merchants trading in Calcutta; it was a construction of the *firman* bound to lead to trouble. Sarafaraz Khan succeeded him.

He did not reign long. A central Asian named Alivardi Khan, stated variously as of Afghan or Turcoman descent, who had achieved power in the services of the old Nawab, rebelled, killed Sarafaraz in battle in 1739 and usurped the viceroyalty. His action started a long and bloody civil war in which the Mahrattas under Raghoji Bhonsla intervened on the side of the old ruling house. For the next ten years Mahratta horsemen rode over the province looting and burning. In 1742, worried by the chaotic conditions in the province, the Indian merchants in Calcutta, at their own expense, dug a large ditch, afterwards known as the Mahratta Ditch, round the boundary of the city; either money or enthusiasm ran out and the ditch was never completed, about a quarter of the original trace remaining to be dug. The Mahrattas, however, never penetrated far into the delta of the Ganges, and Calcutta survived the turbulent

26 Alivardi Khan, Nawab of Bengal.

years unscathed. Eventually Alivardi Khan, eschewing any form of European help, by a mixture of cunning, treachery and bribery gradually won the ascendancy. In 1751 he obtained an Imperial *firman* confirming him in his position as viceroy in exchange for a large gift of money and a promise of an annual tribute which he subsequently omitted to pay. In 1753 he came to terms with the Mahrattas, and for a brief period there was peace in Bengal. He died on 10 April 1756 without an heir.

His brother, Haji Ahmad, sired three sons before he perished in battle. Alivardi Khan made the eldest Governor of Dacca, the second Governor of Patna, and the youngest

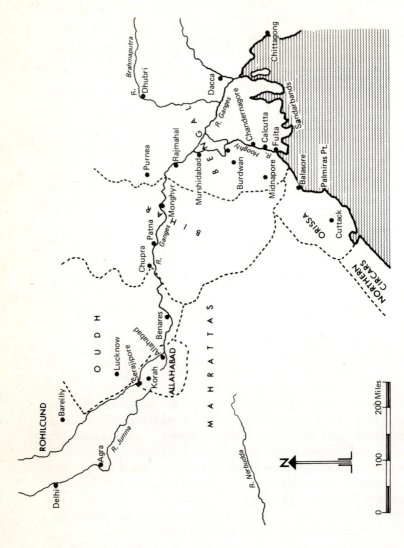

7 North East India. The boundaries between states are only very approximate.

Governor of Purneah; he also married his half sister to his Commander-in-Chief, Mir Jafar Ali Khan. Despite his tumultuous life, Alivardi Khan outlived his three nephews, and at his death the succession lay between their offspring, so far as hereditary claims were concerned. Alivardi Khan himself had adopted the eldest son of his second nephew, the Governor of Patna, as his heir; this was a young man about twenty-six years of age called Siraj-ud-daula. His eldest nephew, the Governor of Dacca, died without issue but his widow, the Begum Ghasiti, had adopted the infant son of a younger brother of Sirah-ud-daula, called Mourad-ud-daula, and she, with the aid of her late husband's chief minister, Raj Ballabh, put forward the claims of her adopted child. Alivardi Khan's youngest nephew also had a son, Shaukat Jang, who had succeeded his father as Governor of Purneah; he also advanced a claim to the viceroyalty.

As soon as Alivardi Khan died, Siraj-ud-daula proclaimed himself Viceroy. To the surprise of the Europeans, Mir Jafar and the prominent men in the province supported him, he assembled a large army and by the middle of May both the Begum and Shaukat Jang acknowledged his supremacy without a struggle. But even before his reign began events were in train that were to embroil him with the British. Alivardi Khan, during his last days, had called in Raj Ballabh from Dacca to Murshidabad to act as his chief minister. When Raj Ballabh saw that the Viceroy had little longer to live, distrusting Siraj-ud-daula, he sent his son Krishan Dass, together with his wives, and it was reputed an enormous quantity of treasure accumulated by various unorthodox means while he was a minister, to seek asylum in Calcutta.

Siraj-ud-daula discovered this perfidious act while his great-uncle lay near death. The angry young Prince sent a letter to Calcutta ordering the British to surrender Krishan Dass, the treasure and the wives. His courier, when he arrived at Calcutta, first called on Omichand, a prominent and wealthy Hindu merchant. At this time the British were accustomed to dealing with the viceregal court through leading Indian merchants who had the right to attend on the

27 The Great Mosque in the city of Murshidabad.

Nawab at his *durbar*, a session of his court when he gave audience to his subjects. Omichand had been such an intermediary, but owing to the abuse he had made of his position had fallen into disfavour with the Council at Calcutta.

When the courier subsequently presented himself to Roger Drake, the President of the Council, Drake, according to his own account, suspected an intrigue instigated by Omichand and, assuming the letter to be a forgery, did not open it; instead he brusquely ordered the courier to leave Calcutta. It is difficult to understand why Drake did not, at the least, read the letter and lay it before the Council. Siraj-ud-daula, while heir apparent, had viewed with some concern the virtual independence of the European settlements, a concern enhanced by the events that had taken place in the Deccan. He intended to be absolute master in his own dominions and with the intolerance of youth had railed against the weakness of his great-uncle in failing to assert his authority properly over the Europeans.

The refusal of the British to surrender Krishan Dass and his treasure, and the insolent way in which the refusal had been made, seemed to him to be an intolerable flouting of his authority. He had at his disposal a splendid army, his

GHERIA AND THE FALL OF CALCUTTA

antagonists had submitted so far without even a fight, and now was the time to settle with the interlopers from Europe, bearing in mind that they brought some useful money into his Kingdom. The French at Chandernagore and the Dutch at Chinsura had both acknowledged his accession with suitable gifts. The British, however, had ignored his orders and were cheating his revenue by what he considered the flagrant abuse of the system of *dustucks*. Moreover, his spies told him that the British were actively engaged in strengthening the fortifications of Calcutta, no doubt the better to defy his authority. It was time the British learned who ruled in Bengal. Through an intermediary named Khwaja Wajid, a wealthy Armenian merchant, he again demanded the surrender of Krishan Dass, the restriction of the system of *dustucks* to bonafide exports and imports, and the dismantling of all fortifications.

His demands placed the Council in a quandary. They thought the Prince capricious, vain and dissolute and doubted his ability long to remain in power. If they surrendered Krishan Dass they might be antagonising a future ruler of Bengal; to dismantle their fortifications, in view of the almost certain war with France, would be to invite the fate of Madras during the previous one, and leave themselves defenceless when the civil war they anticipated came to break out; as for the *dustucks*, the right to them had been negotiated with the Emperor and this could not be abandoned, but some compromise might be possible over their use.

It was no easy situation nor would it seem to have been handled with very much skill. Watts, the experienced British Chief at Cossimbazar anticipated that some compromises and perhaps some gifts in suitable quarters might be needed, but never contemplated matters coming to open hostilities. On the other hand, the speed with which events moved argues that the Nawab had already made up his mind and was prepared to accept nothing short of total submission. Drake rejected all the demands in terms that are now uncertain; what is certain is that the refusal threw the Nawab into a tremendous rage, and on 28 May he concluded a letter to Khwaja Wajid, whose purport he wished communicated to the British 'I swear by the Great God and the prophets that unless the English consent to fill up their ditch and raze their fortifications; I will expel them totally out of my country.' It was the cry of an angry, headstrong young man, not the considered view of a statesman. The date of the letter is significant; seven weeks after his accession he made demands on the British which any of his counsellors would have told him must be unacceptable; he then made no attempt to negotiate, but proceeded at once to take military action.

The events now in train had results so momentous both for the history of India and Britain that it may be worth briefly considering the legal aspects. Alivardi Khan, a Central Asian, usurped the Nawabship, but eventually obtained legal recognition from the Emperor on conditions that he subsequently failed to fulfil. On Alivardi Khan's death, Siraj-ud-daula seized power. But he held it only by force of arms. The British rights in Bengal were enshrined in a treaty duly negotiated with the Imperial Court. Legally, the treaty could only be altered or enforced by the Emperor himself, or his properly accredited agent. Siraj-ud-daula had no standing in the matter. He had received no Imperial recognition, and the Wazir, a high official of the Imperial Court, was even then assembling an army to restore the authority of the Moghul in Bengal; a threatened Afghan invasion, however, prevented him marching. At this time legal considerations had little significance, but if Siraj-ud-daula's right to rule depended on arms he could not complain if it was resisted by arms.

The Council probably expected a lengthy and perhaps expensive negotiation, but by the end of May they suddenly realised a menacing situation had begun to develop. On 25 May 1756, Messrs Watts, Collett and Batson at Cossimbazar wrote to the Council: 'The Nawab receiving a letter from the Governor, [presumably Drake's letter refusing his demands] was extremely angry and immediately sent orders to Rai Durlabh [his Dewan or Treasurer] to stop our business at Cossimbazar'. On 31 May they reported,

'Ghulam Shah, a considerable Jemadar [senior military officer] with his forces are come upon the factory and put stop to all provisions coming in.' On 2 June, 'All intercourse with the country people has been put a stop to. We have great reason to expect we shall soon be attacked.' The situation deteriorated rapidly. On 3 June Vernet, the chief of the Dutch establishment at Cossimbazar, writing perhaps with a certain relish, told how the Chief of the British community, 'had allowed himself to be prevailed upon by the lamentations of his wife so far as to write a cowardly letter to Durlabh Rai, and at the invitation of the said Durlabh Rai, he went in his nightdress, like one distracted, having only two foot soldiers before him. Durlabh Rai received them very courteously and conducted them to the Prince who immediately ordered them to be pinioned.'

The unfortunate Watts was then called on to sign an agreement, on behalf of the Company, to surrender Krishan Dass together with Raj Ballabh's treasure and wives, to dismantle all fortifications at Calcutta and to pay inland tolls on all goods in transit. Vernet in his narrative makes the interesting remark, 'these matters would not have gone so far if they had stuck to their first defiant attitude, for the Prince was so dejected and frightened that he had not the courage to order a shot to be fired.' In another letter he speaks scathingly of the 'cowardly behaviour of the English'. Watts still hoped a way might be found of settling the dispute; with his tiny garrison of 100 men resistance looked futile, and if active hostilities could be avoided, he thought that, at even that late hour, a peaceful settlement might still be contrived.

Possibly the Dutchman was right. Certainly the easy capture of Cossimbazar served only to encourage the Nawab; it was clear that he had only to threaten and even the arrogant British would bend to his will. On 5 June he set out for Calcutta and on 14 June his leading troops reached the outskirts of the city; by 17 June they had penetrated the streets and had begun to make contact with the fortifications. Calcutta was garrisoned by the same undisciplined mob of fugitives from justice and seedy adventurers as had formed the Company's troops in Madras before the days of Stringer Lawrence. Shortly after the siege began, Governor Drake thought it judicious to embark on a ship without wasting the time of his colleagues by informing them of his intentions. Captain Minchin, the Garrison commander, also saw certain advantages in commanding from a distance, and he too took ship.[1] A number of the garrison, for various unlikely reasons, followed suit. On 20 June 1756, Fort William surrendered. Some of the garrison who stayed at their posts had fought with courage, and there had been individual acts of heroism, but in general it had been a sorry affair; it excited the contempt not only of the Nawab but also of the Dutch and French.

The remnants of the garrison spent the night in a small airless room where many died of suffocation; the atrocity became famous under the title of the 'Black hole of Calcutta', but it appears to have occurred through negligence and incompetence rather than from any deliberate intent. When compared with the more sophisticated atrocities of the twentieth century, it pales into insignificance. However, it entered into the folklore of the British in India, and some 150 years later Curzon, the then Viceroy, re-erected a derelict monument to mark the occurrence. Perhaps it was an early exercise in propaganda to convince the British soldier of the perils of defeat, or perhaps, the eighteenth century in some matters had higher standards of conduct than the twentieth.

Those of the garrison that had escaped and the women and children, who had been mostly embarked before the siege began, dropped downstream in the ships and encamped on an unhealthy stretch of land near the mouth of the Hooghly by the village of Fulta. Originally, the disembarkation had been intended to last only the time needed to reprovision the over-crowded ships for the voyage to southern India; but once established ashore there was a reluctance to move. Then Killpatrick arrived with his 200 soldiers. He had too few to attempt to retake Calcutta, but he gave the settlement an element of security. Drake realised that if he went elsewhere his authority would vanish, and neither he, nor a

[1] Minchin was subsequently dismissed from the Company's service.

GHERIA AND THE FALL OF CALCUTTA 171

number of others, wished to be questioned too closely about the part they played in the fall of Calcutta. They stayed on.

Siraj-ud-daula, seemingly unmindful of the likely consequences of his actions, left them unmolested. Placing one of his favourites, Manikchand, as Governor of Calcutta he started back to Murshidabad, on the way thoughtfully exacting heavy fines from the Dutch and the French for failing to help him against the British. The British trading post at Dacca discreetly surrendered, and except for the fever-ridden and desolate huts at Fulta the British presence in Bengal was virtually at an end.

In Madras the extent of the calamity that had befallen the Company in Bengal and the dangerous implications it had for British prestige throughout India were recognised immediately. The reconquest of Calcutta took precedence over all else. Besides, surprisingly enough, no positive news had been received about a war in Europe, and now that the northeastern monsoon would soon be blowing, it would be impossible for a French reinforcement of any size to reach Pondicherry for several months. Admiral Watson, although still nervous of French naval intentions and reluctant to allow his fleet to be divided, agreed to sail with all his ships to recapture Calcutta. The question as to who should command on land raised some delicate problems. Colonel Adlercron, a crusty sixty-year-old, commanding the 39th Foot was prepared to go with his men provided he went as Commander-in-Chief. But Adlercron declined to acknowledge the authority of the Governor, and his attitude had already provoked several disputes with the Council. In a few month's time Pondicherry might be reinforced and it would become vital to the security of Madras to recall the troops sent to Bengal. Adlercron now refused to guarantee that he would return if required to do so by the Governor. The Council decided the command must be given to someone who accepted their authority and gave it to Clive, with the proviso that while operating in that province he remained under their orders; a proviso that was to give offence to the Council in Bengal. Adlercron promptly refused to allow any of his men to join the expedition. That he was petty and small minded it is hard to deny, but it is possible to sympathise with the hurt feelings of the professional soldier who thought himself slighted by a parcel of merchants and required to put his men under someone he probably regarded as a jumped-up and untrustworthy adventurer. Admiral Watson had little patience with such an attitude and promptly demanded soldiers to travel on his ships as marines. Adlercron dared not defy the Admiral and three companies of the 39th were embarked. These marines, of course, were under the admiral, not the land forces commander, a cause of friction in the future.

And so on 16 October 1756, Admiral Watson sailed with his fleet for the Hooghly, conveying with him an expeditionary force consisting of 5 companies of the Madras Europeans which together with the artillery and train totalled 570 Europeans, 3 companies of the 39th, about 270 men, approximately 1,000 trained Madras sepoys, and 300 Lascars who were camp followers rather than soldiers.

Clive, before embarking, wrote to Drake with typical generosity, 'I have desired my attorneys to pay you the interest arising from all my houses in England and the Bishop of Clintforth annuity which is all in my power at the moment having lost nearly £3,000 on the Doddington.' Imperious and occasionally overbearing Clive might be, but no friend in need ever called on him in vain. To his father he wrote: 'The expedition, if attended with success, may enable me to do great things, it is by far the grandest of my undertakings.'

Chapter 9

THE RECAPTURE OF CALCUTTA
December 1756–January 57

For Siraj-ud-daula 1756 was proving a miraculous year. He had but to lift his hand and his enemies collapsed at his feet. His character at this distance can scarcely be delineated with certainty; that British writers, both at this time and later, looked on him with little favour might perhaps be expected, and the qualities of arrogance, avarice, capriciousness, cruelty and cowardice they attributed to him so freely may owe something to a partisan point of view. But it is undeniable that, in a short space of time, he contrived to make himself odious both to his ordinary subjects and to many of the foremost men in his realm. Brought up in the stifling atmosphere of an Indian court where most would find it dangerous to oppose his will, surrounded by toadies and flatterers, segregated from contact with the realities of living, unless he possessed a character far above the ordinary, he was bound to be, at the least, vain, foolish and self-willed, and no judge of men or affairs. Yet he must have possessed some quality of charm, a certain ability and native shrewdness, or it is difficult to account for the ease with which he succeeded his long-lived great-uncle.

His miraculous year was not yet over. The British had been humiliated; they were sheltering at Fulta, presumably meditating flight to Madras. It seemed unnecessary to molest them further, and now that they knew who ruled in Bengal, they might be permitted to resume that trade that enriched not only themselves but the province and its ruler.

He wrote rather naïvely to Governor Pigot at Madras on 30 June 1756: 'It is not my intention to remove the mercantile business of the company belonging to you out of the Subah (viceroyalty) of Bengal.' After a few vitriolic comments about Governor Drake whose character he did not admire he added, 'I gave leave to Mr Watts who is a helpless, poor and innocent man to go to you'.

As he returned to Murshidabad with the handsome fines which he had exacted from the Dutch, Danish and French settlements swelling his exchequer, he boasted that he had driven out the British and made the other Europeans pay his expenses. He did not rate the Europeans above a pair of 'slippers', and drew parallels between himself and Tamburlaine the Great.

He was soon to be required to exert his genius again. Shaukat Jang, the Governor of Purneah, whose friends already seriously doubted his sanity, had taken advantage of his cousin's absence in Calcutta to aquire a *firman* from the Emperor appointing him viceroy in exchange for a substantial gift and rather less substantial promises. Siraj-ud-daula, unabashed by the Imperial script, regarded the *firman* as nothing more than a declaration of war. Early in October he marched on Purneah and on 16 October came upon his cousin with his army drawn up for battle near the town of Rajmahal. The Nawab confided the battle to his military commanders, while he discreetly took up his station some three miles to the rear.

The Indian battles of the day had the characteristics of a gigantic game of chess. There was a recognised opening gambit, a long, noisy and generally harmless artillery duel. Then a certain amount of fighting took place and a few pawns were removed from the board, but the aim of both sides was to checkmate the king, or in practical terms, slay the enemy commander. Once this had been accomplished, the game was finished and the soldiers of the defeated army generally offered their services to the victor. He was, after all, the one most likely to have the financial resources to pay them.

Now Siraj-ud-daula adopted a ruse to which most of his

THE RECAPTURE OF CALCUTTA 175

peers would have scorned to stoop. He dressed up some of his relatives in his clothing and dotted his army with spurious nawabs. These might be expected to confuse the enemy and if, as he suspected, some of his own army held him in little affection, might also serve to trick them into revealing their treacherous intentions prematurely. The ruse worked well. Shaukat Jang, seeing as he thought his cousin, led a wild charge to engage him in personal combat, fell into a trap and was killed. Siraj-ud-daula emerged from his secluded headquarters and was promptly hailed as the victor. He returned in triumph to Murshidabad. Nothing, perhaps, reveals more clearly the depths of venality which the Imperial Court had plumbed than the speed with which Siraj-ud-daula, in exchange for the equivalent of about £2 million, was issued with an Imperial *firman* confirming him Viceroy of Bengal. Possibly some at the Court thought that a rapid turnover of viceroys was good for business and brought in valuable revenue to the normally empty Imperial coffers.

Siraj-ud-daula was now the undisputed master of Bengal. It had been a wonderful year, and he might be pardoned for thinking himself a man of destiny under a divine protection that rendered him immune from the ills of common mortality. As a divinely inspired ruler he considered he deserved from his subjects not service but worship, and he began to treat his nobles as though they were slaves who existed but to minister to his godlike desires. Mir Jafar and others among his leading generals and ministers suffered and waited.

Meanwhile during the rains of August the wretched, faction-ridden British community at Fulta stubbornly refused to leave. After some misgivings about its legality outside the bounds of Calcutta, the old Council was revived with Drake as President and Governor. Drake still cherished a desperate hope that, if help was speedily forthcoming from Madras, Calcutta would be retaken and the news of its recovery, sent by express to Suez and thence overland to the Mediterranean, might overtake that of its fall. So happy a result would avert the danger of the Company's shares crashing on the London stock exchange, and might induce the directors not to inquire too vindictively into the events that had occasioned the misfortune.

But from the Coromandel coast nothing stirred. The Council resolved to send Manningham, one of its number, to Madras to press for immediate action. The proposal caused an immediate outcry among those who had taken a nobler part in the siege; these pointed out with some force that, since Manningham had viewed the scene from the safety of a ship, he was in no position to know what had happened. Nevertheless Drake had his way and Manningham departed.

At Fulta matters began to improve. Manikchand, the Governor of Calcutta, far from making any effort to expel the British authorised the opening of a market at Fulta, he owned some property in the area and was not averse to adding to his income. Killpatrick arrived, and people felt more secure. As September faded into October, the rains ceased, the land began to dry out and the weather became cooler. Then on 23 October the sloop *Kingfisher* brought tidings that Admiral Watson and Clive, with powerful forces, were on their way. Spirits rose and the Union Jack was hoisted; but it was not until 15 December that Clive and Watson stepped ashore at Fulta. The sailor, fearing the incidence of sickness likely in closely packed ships during the unhealthy months of August and September, had wisely postponed sailing until October. By sailing late the fleet encountered the northeast monsoon, and high seas and contrary winds had turned a journey frequently done in fifteen days into one of two months.

Shortly before their arrival, instructions had been received from London, ordering the councils at Bombay, Madras and Calcutta to form secret select committees, so as to expedite business and prevent important policy decisions being broadcast to potential enemies. At Fulta a Committee was accordingly formed consisting of Drake, Watts, Becher, and Holwell who took the place made vacant when Manningham departed to Madras. Watson and Clive were invited to join; Clive accepted, but Watson, although he sometimes sat in at meetings, never served as a member;

perhaps, as the senior officer of His Majesty's forces in the East Indies, he considered that to do so might imply that he acknowledged the Committee had some jurisdiction over his actions, or perhaps he merely found committee meetings tedious and not to his autocratic taste.

The situation that confronted the British commanders at Fulta was far from easy. Sickness had so reduced Killpatrick's detachment that he had only thirty men fit for service; even when the volunteers from Calcutta and its outstations were added, his force amounted to not more than a hundred men. The *Marlborough*, a poor sailer and in a leaky condition, had dropped astern of the fleet and after 16 November had been seen no more. *Cumberland* had failed to weather Palmiras point near the Balasore roads, gone aground, and after being refloated had vanished into the bay of Bengal; the failure of these two ships to make the Hooghly deprived Clive of about 250 Europeans, 400 Sepoys and almost all his artillery and stores. But this was only part of his problem. Watson regarded him as little more than a fractious subordinate who was there to do his bidding, and the members of the select committee were certain that on their shoulders lay the ultimate responsibility for policy. Clive would have to battle with more than Siraj-ud-daula if he was to realise his ambitions.

The day he arrived he wrote to Manikchand thanking him for the aid that he had given the British at Fulta. He continued, 'I doubt not but as you have hitherto professed to a desire to serve the Company, you will at this time when their affairs must require it retain the same disposition in their favour.' It was highly desirable that Manikchand should not be alarmed before the British were ready to move. To Siraj-ud-daula, however, he wrote in sterner terms, 'You must make proper satisfaction for the losses sustained by the Company, their servants and riots (peasants), return their factories and invest them in their ancient priveledges [*sic*] and immunities. By doing this piece of justice you will make me a sincere friend and get eternal honour for yourself and save the lives of many thousands.' Such admirable but financially unrewarding sentiments were unlikely to weigh much with the Nawab, but Clive presumably thought they gave a touch of polish to an otherwise somewhat bald ultimatum.

Manikchand, however, to whom Clive sent a copy of his letter, exclaimed in horror at the mode of expression and was kind enough to redraft it for the British commander. Clive obligingly rewrote his missive without altering its substance. These courtesies can have deceived no one, but at least matters were being conducted with a due regard for form. Siraj-ud-daula had the bad taste to ignore the correspondence, but did little to secure his conquest; perhaps in his dreamworld he thought that Manikchand with his rabble, 2,000 strong, would be sufficient to repel the British.

From the Dutch settlement of Chinsura Dr Forth, who had attended Alivardi Khan on his death bed, kept the Council posted about the movements and intentions of his successor. He reported on 17 December that on hearing of the arrival of the British, Manikchand had sent to the Nawab asking for instructions. Forth wrote, 'The Faujdar of Hooghly [the commander of the troops at Hooghly] was despatching letters to the same purport. They have both received their orders the 16th, Manikchand to go to Budge-Budge, the faujdar to Tannah and to defend these places. The former is gone and with him most of the forces in Calcutta having left about 500 in the last; the faujdar sets out tomorrow.' Tannah fort was on the Hooghly about ten miles below Calcutta while Budge-Budge was another five miles downstream.

Forth went on to say, that ships were being filled with sand which it was intended to sink in the narrow channel opposite Tannah fort. However to offset this depressing information he added, '... if we are firmly established in Calcutta ... and would get the Nawab in chains, the whole country would be glad of it, for that at present they have nothing they can call their own, his mind is taken up with nothing but the getting of money, it did not signify by what means. His other favourite passions, drinking and women.'

Speed was clearly essential. If the Hooghly were blocked and Siraj-ud-daula with his army at Calcutta, the task of the

British would be wellnigh impossible. There could be no question of waiting for *Cumberland* or *Marlborough*. Clive himself was unwell. He wrote to Major Killpatrick:

'A violent cold and slight fever has reduced me to committing to writing what I should have been glad to execute in person.... I take it for granted we shall march from Budge-Budge to Calcutta by land. It would save the trouble of embarking if we could do the same from Fulta.... There are many other things which do not occur to me which may fall within your knowledge, in short I leave everything to your prudence and discretion for the present.... It would be a singular service if you could prevail on the Bazar people to follow us up the river to Budge-Budge.'

Preparations were hastened. Watson held a Council of War on his flagship, *Kent*, to plan the capture of the first obstacle to the advance, the fort at Budge-Budge. It was decided that the King's troops and the Company's Europeans should embark on the ships while the sepoys marched overland. The Europeans would disembark at Mayapur, about twenty miles up the river from Fulta and about five miles below Budge-Budge, and join the sepoys. Clive with all the Company's troops would then make a night march bypassing the fort to the east, occupy a position about two miles to its north, and isolate it from Calcutta. In the morning the fleet would bombard the fort, while Clive with his men would intercept any reinforcements and prevent the garrison from escaping. Clive disliked the idea of a night march over unknown country and suggested that his men should be taken to their position in boats; he was, however, over-ruled; he still had to establish the right to have his opinions respected.

On 27 December the expedition set out; it consisted of *Tyger*, *Kent* and *Salisbury*, ships of the line, *Bridgewater* and *Kingfisher*, two companies of the 39th numbering about 120 men, 400 Europeans of the Company's army and 500 sepoys accompanied by two field pieces and a cart for ammunition. As there were no bullocks to draw the guns and

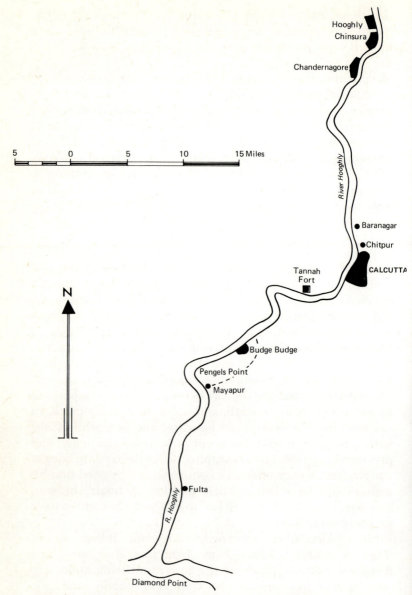

8 The Hooghly River. Taken from the contemporary Map by Rennell as published by C. E. Hill in his book *Bengal in 1756–7*.

THE RECAPTURE OF CALCUTTA 181

cart these were transported in boats. On the morning of 28 December the Fleet anchored opposite Mayapur and by 2 p.m. the Company's Europeans were ashore; 3 p.m. the fleet weighed anchor and sailed for Pengel's Point a little over two miles from Budge-Budge.

While the fleet slowly made its way upstream, Clive organised and rested his men for the night march. The two field pieces and the ammunition wagon were something of an embarrassment; since there was no transport for them Clive had to detail men to haul them; he was not prepared to risk an engagement without artillery. Some locals were recruited as guides and about 6.30 p.m., as the shades of the rapid tropical sunset were falling, the little column marched off.

All through an interminable night the men plodded on along narrow paths intersected by water courses and bordered by swamps; those dragging the guns and ammunition cart faced almost insuperable difficulties and caused much delay; the guides, however, obstinately protested that every wearisome detour was necessary if the advance was to go undetected. Dawn broke and still they tramped onwards. At about 7.30 the distant crash of gunfire announced that the ships were engaging the fort, and at 8 a.m. the weary men gratefully halted just short of the Budge-Budge–Calcutta road and some 1,000 yards from the bank of the river. About two miles downstream it was possible to see the upperworks of the ships. *Kent* was firing broadsides towards the riverbank while *Tyger* and *Salisbury* were manoeuvring to bring their guns to bear. To the left of the riverbank, dry paddy fields, the rice had long since been harvested and the fields formed a firm and level plain, stretched for nearly 2,000 yards to where a few mud huts marked the edge of Budge-Budge village; beyond the huts a cluster of trees masked the outlines of the fort. To the north and east the paddy was bounded by low bush jungle.[1]

[1] Accounts are contradictory. The only two eyewitness accounts are those given by Eyre Coote and Clive's military journal, the latter agrees with an account signed J. C. possibly John Carnac.

When his tired men had assembled, Clive took stock of the situation. He disposed his company of Calcutta volunteers across the road where it entered the jungle to watch for any movement from Calcutta, and at 9 a.m. dispatched Captain Pye with the grenadier company and the sepoys to occupy the huts at the edge of the village. Pye advanced down the riverbank and Watson, seeing his column, signalled Captain Eyre Coote with his company of the 39th to disembark. Coote occupied an empty earthwork near the fort; Pye finding the huts deserted and seeing a flag fluttering near the fort, pressed on and joined Coote. Coote at once put him and his men under his command. At this time he says in his journal,

'I could see plainly that there was a narrow road into the interior fort and that the gate was made of wooden bars, so that I thought we might enter without difficulty—especially as the men-of-war had silenced their batteries. I therefore ordered a march to be beat, and was advancing to storm the fort when word was brought to me that Captain Weller, who was my senior, was landed with the troops from the Salisbury and desired me I would halt until he came up which I did.'

Heavy firing could be heard from the northeast of the village, and, while Coote was explaining the situation, a messenger hurried up to say that Clive had been attacked by a large body of horse and foot and desired the sepoys to march to his assistance. Coote wanted to continue his attack on the fort, but Weller, to his annoyance, insisted that all the troops should go to Clive's assistance.

While the volunteers were blocking the road to the north and Pye moving south to the village, Clive had taken the balance of his European battalion, about 270 men under Killpatrick, to a position about 2,000 yards northeast of the village close to a deserted hamlet. Orme states that he went to a hollow, Coote and the log of the *Tyger* (the action was seen from the foretop) both refer to a plain. Most probably his position was in some dry paddy fields; since they were

THE RECAPTURE OF CALCUTTA 183

destined to be flooded in the rainy season the fields would tend to be lower than the jungle to the east and north.

Clive must have felt secure; the volunteers were to his north, Pye with his grenadiers in the village to the south, to the west lay the river, and in his long night perambulation to the east no enemy had been encountered. He ordered his men to pile arms and rest in any shade they could find, without taking the precaution of putting out piquets into the bush jungle to the east. By the hamlet he placed his two guns so that they could sweep the exits from Budge-Budge and the Calcutta road. However, his Indian guides must have been treacherous. Manikchand with a mixed force of horse and foot about 2,000 strong had been encamped two miles to the east of Budge-Budge, and the guides must have gone to great pains to avoid the British discovering his camp during the night. Next morning they probably reported to the Indian commander and guided his men to Clive's position, for Manikchand with his army managed to approach it unobserved.

His matchlock men gathered quietly in the jungle bordering the paddy and in the empty hamlet. A crashing volley announced their presence, while the hamlet spewed a crowd of men who rushed the guns before Clive's gunners could man them. The British infantry ran to snatch up their muskets and there were a few ugly moments of confusion. Clive, as ever ice-cold in moments of peril, checked an incipient panic and sent off a messenger towards the village to ask for the sepoys. His men, all veterans from Stringer Lawrence's campaigns, quickly recovered their order and formed into line. In places the matchlock men closed in to twenty yards, but the British line held firm and the immediate danger was over. Hearing the firing, the volunteer company from the Calcutta road came up; although the matchlock men maintained a heavy fire they fortunately did not know how to use the guns they had overrun. Now Clive directed the volunteers on the guns, while he led an advance by three platoons on the hamlet. The British swept forward with immense dash; the volunteers recaptured the guns while Clive took the hamlet with the bayonet.

Meanwhile masses of cavalry started to form on the plain, and an enemy commander on an elephant, whom Clive identified as Manikchand, could be seen urging the cavalry to charge, but without much noticeable effect. The British gunners brought the recaptured guns into action, and the cavalry, suffering casualties, began to give ground. Then Manikchand himself received a ball through his turban and the 39th and sepoys came into sight. The Indian commander turned his elephant and his men fled in disorder towards the jungle. The British chased after them, came up with the fugitives by a creek, and inflicted about forty casualties as they scrambled across. Here the British halted their advance, reformed their ranks, and marched back to the position that Coote had originally taken up by the fort.

It had been a brisk affair while it lasted. Clive estimated that Manikchand lost about 200 men while the European battalion lost eighteen, mostly in the first few minutes. The bold charge of the matchlock men had undeniably caught the British off guard, but Manikchand on the other hand had been shocked by the speed with which the British had recovered from their original surprise. He told Siraj-ud-daula he had been confronted with a new type of Englishman, and indeed the well trained and disciplined troops from Madras bore little resemblance to the ragged mob that had manned the ramparts of Calcutta.

By now it was well on into the afternoon. From the fort there came a desultory musketry fire, but its guns were silent and in places the ramparts had collapsed. The ships were only firing single guns when a target appeared. Watson ordered ashore 150 seamen to lead an assault and two 9-pounder guns to give the finishing touches to a breach. Clive had himself ferried out to *Kent* to confer with the Admiral. He and his men were utterly worn out and he wanted to defer the storm to next morning. He returned to the bivouac by the fort to find that Weller, feeling ill, had returned to *Salisbury*, and that Coote was in command of all the 39th ashore. It was an unhappy circumstance.

Coote was an Irishman, the youngest of six brothers, and with his way to make in the world. At this time he was

28 Captain Eyre Coote, later General, Sir.

thirty-one, the same age as Clive. As a regular officer he probably believed he was as qualified to command as his titular superior. He was able, determined, pugnacious and argumentative, the type of man who would, on principle, contradict an opinion advanced by anybody else. His military career had begun badly. He was serving with the 27th Foot during the Jacobite rebellion, and was thought to have shown rather too fine a turn of speed when leaving the stricken field of Falkirk. He was court-martialled and in the end justly exonerated, but no doubt he felt there was still something of a bar sinister across his military record and was anxious to erase it. He had only been a short period in India and was likely to regard the Company's army with suspicion if not downright contempt. Tact was unknown to him. When, in 1761, he captured Pondicherry, he hoisted the Union Jack and proclaimed he had captured it for the King and not the Company. He received short shrift from Governor Pigot at Madras, who merely observed that the army would receive no pay until Pondicherry was handed over. It was an argument that Coote, for once, found convincing. He was clearly a man who, by temperament, was almost certain to clash with Clive, and the situation was aggravated by the ill-defined positions they held. Adlercron had only agreed to his men accompanying the expedition if they went as marines, and had explicitly refused to put them under the command of the Company.

Now Coote, who had spent the previous night comfortably on board ship, approached Clive and suggested that an immediate storm should be ordered. The details of the argument that ensued are unknown, but it was likely to have been acrimonious, as at the end Coote expressed concern about the seamen and the men of the 39th who would have to spend the night in the open, a curious argument for a soldier and not one likely to commend itself to Clive who faced a similar hardship. He curtly replied that if Coote wished to have his men re-embarked he should take the matter up with the Admiral. At this stage it may be imagined that Coote gave the type of salute he reserved for Company officers and took a boat out to *Kent*.

Now occurred a comedy that made both the soldiers look a little foolish. The Navy, facing a hard night ashore, had taken the precaution of bringing their rum ration with them, and at about 8 p.m. a sailor named Strahan, enlivened by his tot and possibly one or two culled from the more abstemious of his mess-mates, took advantage of the darkness to wander up to the fort and inspect it. Everything seemed quiet, so drawing his cutlass he climbed up some debris and stepped out on to the top of the rampart. Here he found two or three peons quietly sitting, perhaps around a hookah, and gossiping. Shouting to his comrades to join him, Strahan plunged in with his cutlass. About a hundred seamen, not all of whom were sober, with the agility of their service clambered up the breach, and in the dark a wild scrimmage took place. Four seamen were wounded, it is not clear by whom; the most serious casualty was Captain Dugald Campbell who was shot dead by a roving seaman while posting a sepoy guard over the magazine of the fort; apparently the seaman mistook the sepoys for enemy. Coote sourly recorded in his journal,'. . . and thus the place was taken without the least honour to anyone'.

The Naval reaction to this affair can be imagined without difficulty. While the Army dilly-dallied and complained of feeling tired, a party of semi-intoxicated seamen had captured their fort for them. Coote, back on his ship, would have had to submit to the witticisms of his nautical comrades, and no doubt when next he met Clive commented, in what he considered suitable terms, on Clive's refusal to permit a storm.

Admiral Watson, who had strong views on discipline, had Strahan brought before him, presumably on a charge of violating Naval discipline by capturing an enemy fort without first obtaining permission. The spectators must have had difficulty in maintaining their gravity, but clearly Watson made some telling points about the virtue of a strict regard for orders, as Strahan was heard to mutter as he left: 'If I am flogged for this here action, I will never take another fort by myself for as long as I live, by God.'

The cannon were put out of action, the fort demolished and on 1 January 1757, the fleet continued up the river. Tannah fort was found abandoned, and early next morning Clive and the Company's troops disembarked to march on Calcutta, while the fleet sailed on to bombard Fort William from the river. The action at Budge-Budge seems to have been enough for Manikchand. Fort William fell after a feeble resistance before the marching troops could come up, and Watson sent Coote ashore to take possession. He gave him written instructions: 'You are herebye required and directed to garrison the fort of Calcutta with His Majesty's troops. In the evening I shall be on shore and you are not to quit your post or deliver up your command until further orders from me.'

Eyre Coote interpreted his orders with his usual good sense and tact. When the leading troops of the Company

29 Fort William, Calcutta before it was resited by Clive.

approached, he barred the fort to them, arresting their commander for good measure. The news, not surprisingly, threw Clive into a towering rage. He went to the fort, pushed his way past a sentry who had the acumen to realise when things were beyond his control, and stormed up to Coote to inquire what he thought he was doing. Coote blandly presented his written orders. Clive hotly replied, 'The Admiral has no authority to place an officer inferior to me in charge of the fort.' He went on to tell Coote bluntly that if he did not obey his orders he would put him under arrest. Clive was a Lieutenant-Colonel of His Majesty's forces, if only in the East Indies, and Coote had no ambition to face another General Court-Martial. He accepted Clive's ruling, but requested permission to write to the Admiral to tell him what had occurred, a request that Clive could hardly deny.

The precise wording of Coote's letter can only be deduced from the results it produced. He must have accused Clive of forcing a sentry placed under the authority of the Admiral, and of treating the Admiral's authority with contempt. The letter had the result that no doubt the author intended. Watson fell into as great a rage as Clive and sent the captain of his ship, Speke, ashore to find out what precisely had happened. Speke seems to have shared his commander's feelings. He asked Clive on what authority he assumed command of the Fort. Clive replied sharply, '... by being Lieutenant-Colonel and Commander-in-Chief of the land forces'. A heated exchange followed and Speke, baffled, returned to *Kent*. The angry Admiral now wrote a letter that included the phrase, 'if you still persist in continuing in the fort you will force me to take such methods as will be as disagreeable to me as they possibly can be for you'.

Speke armed with this missive returned, and, to make sure the Admiral's meaning was correctly interpreted, added that if Clive did not withdraw, the Admiral would fire on the fort. Clive was not the man to yield to threats and the statement was plainly absurd. Speke returned once more unsuccessful. Now Speke tried his hand at letter writing. He began in what he may have thought a conciliatory vein but went on, 'As by forcing the guards placed in the fort by his orders you have offered him [Watson] a personal affront and through him to His Majesty's authority, the duty he owes to himself as an officer trusted with the care of His Majesty's honour in supporting of his forces will not admit of his promising anything till you have first, by withdrawing the troops under your command, acknowledged the insult you have unadvisedly offered.' He concluded with an invitation to Clive to step aboard the *Kent* to discuss the matter further.

Clive declined the invitation. He had no intention of bearding an infuriated admiral on his own quarter deck; possibly he remembered La Bourdonnais clapping Dupleix's Commissioners in irons and feared he might have to continue the discussion under a similar disadvantage. Besides, as the man in possession, his position was nearly impregnable. At this point, Watson began to ponder the situation; he was indubitably in the wrong; the Commander-in-Chief of the Land Forces was supreme on land; Clive held a regular commission and Coote had no right to defy him. He had allowed a sudden spurt of anger to place himself in an impossible situation. He discarded his hot-headed ambassador, Speke, and sent for Latham, the captain of the

Tyger and a personal friend of Clive, and irritably told him to settle the matter.

By the time Latham arrived Clive had recovered from his first gust of fury. The two friends talked the matter over calmly. Clive had vindicated his authority, and now the problem was to find a formula that would allow Watson to withdraw without humiliation. They came up with an ingenious solution. A vice-admiral unquestionably outranked a lieutenant-colonel. When the Admiral was on land Clive was prepared to recognise him as his superior officer. If Watson were to come ashore himself, Clive would be happy to hand over the keys of the fort to him personally, but to no other.

Latham returned to Watson who promptly assented to the proposition; by now he must have been uneasily aware that to some the whole affair might appear ridiculous, and all he wanted was to bring it to an end in a reasonably seemly manner. He landed next day, took the keys from Clive, and handed them over to Governor Drake as the representative of the Company. It may appear a petty and ludicrous quarrel, but it was of considerably importance. Clive had shown he had to be treated with the proper consideration his position warranted, even the ebullient Coote, awkward as he could be, never challenged his authority again. When his wrath had abated, it is almost certain that Watson understood the stand that Clive had made and realised he was not a man to be bullied, even by a senior admiral in the Navy.

Calcutta had been won, but the city had been damaged and the Company's goods had been plundered; the problem now was to force Siraj-ud-daula to make restitution. At Clive's insistence, on 3 January 1757 Drake on behalf of the Company and Watson on behalf of King George II formally declared war on the Nawab. This conferred on the British the rights of a belligerent, they could blockade Bengal and legally interfere with the commerce of the French and Dutch settlements if they continued to trade with an enemy of His Britannic Majesty's Government. Then on 5 January, to bring the war home, some 700 men under Killpatrick were sent up the river in *Bridgewater*, *Kingfisher*, and a bomb ketch appropriately named *Thunder*, to raid the considerable town of Hooghly some 25 miles above Calcutta.

There were grave navigational problems in sailing so far up the river. The captain of the *Kingfisher*, in the forthright naval fashion, kidnapped a Dutch pilot off a brigantine to guide him, leaving his Admiral to deal with the subsequent extremely acrimonious correspondence with the Dutch authorities, who feared they would be incriminated with the Nawab. Even so *Bridgewater* ran aground, and it was not until 10 January that the little expedition made Hooghly.

Now Killpatrick, with considerable good sense, gave Coote a free hand to take the town. Coote executed a skilful attack and captured it without difficulty, destroying a quantity of grain that might be useful to the Nawab should he advance on Calcutta. That Prince could not resist such provocation. Gathering an enormous army he began a leisurely advance towards Hooghly. The real battle for Calcutta was about to be fought.

Chapter 10

THE BATTLES FOR CALCUTTA AND CHANDERNAGORE
January–March 1757

Almost immediately after the recapture of Calcutta, definite news was received that France and England were once more at war. On 7 January 1757, the Select Committee passed a resolution proposing a policy of neutrality with the French at Chandernagore. The proposal was referred to the Admiral, who promptly declared he would only support it if the French consented to ally themselves with the British against the Nawab, a proviso he can hardly have expected them to accept. But the Admiral assumed that the French, with the small forces at their disposal at Chandernagore, would be afraid to denude their settlement of troops while the British fleet lay moored off Calcutta.

The French, not surprisingly, rejected any idea of an alliance with the British. Since the two countries were already at war in Europe, it seemed a curious suggestion and one that might lead to some peculiar and anomalous situations. On the other hand they offered no help to the Nawab. Partly this may be attributed to Watson's ships, but their policy owed more to the overweening arrogance displayed by Siraj-ud-daula and his officials after the capture of Calcutta. The French concluded that, if the Nawab drove the British out of Bengal, with nothing to curb his power his avarice would be the ruin of all the European settlements; they still recollected without pleasure his exactions after the fall of Calcutta. If the British humbled him and he came to them as a suppliant, it might be a different matter.

But it was not only the French in Chandernagore that had to be considered. Bussy, despite the numerous intrigues against him, was still the trusted counsellor of the Viceroy of the Deccan, Salabat Jang. That Prince, always in financial difficulties, had in 1753 granted Bussy the governorship of the Northern Circars, so that he could pay his troops from the revenues of the province. The Northern Circars extended for some 400 miles along the Coromandel coast and in the northeast bordered on Orissa, one of the three provinces that made up the viceroyalty of Bengal. Bussy was now master of this long coastline and could enter Bengal at will. At present all his resources were absorbed propping up the shaky regime of Salabat Jang, nor was his rule in the Circars entirely unchallenged. Despite his high-sounding titles and the eminence of his position, Bussy knew that he left the Deccan at his peril; neither French influence nor Salabat Jang would long survive his absence. But if he became disillusioned with a princely master who was little more than a leech sucking away the strength of the French, if he was prepared to forgo his present hollow grandeur, he might move to Bengal and, securely based on Chandernagore, try to build a less ephemeral empire. Or if he could reconcile the warring factions in the Deccan he might feel free to extend French influence in Bengal. The Nawab with Bussy as his ally would be formidable indeed. It was dangerous to ignore the French, but Watson who, once he had made a decision, was as immovable as a pyramid in Egypt, had blocked all hope of tying the hands of the French by diplomatic means.

At this moment the situation appeared to Clive to be one of unrelieved gloom. He still lacked field guns or gunners, with his puny army he confronted a viceroyalty with twice the population of England, and he had no Indian ally to provide him with cavalry. Britain and France were at war and he distrusted the Admiral's opinion that the French would refrain from helping the Nawab. The fleet was the only asset of the British and Watson's ships of the line, owing to the depth of water they drew, could not navigate the Hooghly upstream of Chandernagore. To crown it all, in Calcutta his authority was questioned and his designs frustrated. In something like despair he wrote to Governor Pigot at Madras. 'The mortifications I have received from Mr [*sic*] Watson and the gentlemen of the squadron, in point of prerogative, are such that nothing but the good of the service could induce me to submit to them. . . . Added to all, the gentlemen here seem much dissatisfied with the authority I am vested with . . . I am sorry to say the loss of private property and the means of recovering it seem to be the only object which takes up the attention of the Bengal gentlemen. . . .' Without field guns he could not contemplate any offensive action. He continued, 'The want of them [the artillery] puts it quite outside my power to undertake any considerable enterprise against the Nawab, we can only chuse [*sic*] some advantageous spot of ground near the riverside, entrench and there wait for him.' He began to fortify a camp by the Chitpur Tank, a large embanked artificial lake near the village of Baranagar about two miles northeast of Calcutta. He instructed his agents to realise all his remaining property in India [he had lost £2,500 over the fall of Calcutta] and remit the proceeds to England by means of bills of exchange. The next few weeks were going to be extremely dangerous; there seemed little merit in risking his money as well as his life.

As the Nawab with his army approached the town of Hooghly, Killpatrick embarked his men and sailed down the river to rejoin Clive. Now the Nawab had a crucial decision to take. If he had the wit to stay where he was the game was his. At Hooghly his position was unassailable. Watson's battleships could not penetrate so far up the river and Clive's little army, without the support of the fleet, dare not venture far from Calcutta. If he contented himself with throttling the trade of the Company, the British had no remedy and must come to terms. But the savaging of the town of Hooghly had been designed to provoke him to retaliation, and he allowed his emotions to lead him into the trap; he began a leisurely advance towards Calcutta, volubly declaring all the while his readiness to treat. Since he was admirably placed to do so at Hooghly his protestations are open to doubt; it seems more likely that they were little more than a verbal smokescreen to cover his advance and conceal his real intentions.

As he came on, the war by letter waxed hotter. On 21 January Clive wrote to Khwaja Wajid detailing four points which the Nawab must meet if he desired a settlement. He would have first to reimburse all losses caused by his attack on Calcutta; second, restore all past privileges to the Company; third, permit Calcutta to be fortified; and, fourth, give the Company permission to coin rupees valid throughout Bengal.

The last demand reveals one of the great problems of the Company. It suffered from what in modern parlance would be called an adverse balance of payments. Britain's main export at this time, broadcloth, in a tropical climate had a decidedly limited appeal. In consequence the Company had to pay for much of its purchases in silver or gold. War with Spain that justified the looting of treasure ships from South America might occasionally be helpful, but South American specie, unhappily, was sometimes hard to come by. The provision of adequate supplies of precious metal was a problem that haunted the Company for many years to come, and indeed bedevilled trade between Europe and Asia for nearly a century. However, if precious metals could be minted into coins, their value would be considerably enhanced and the quantity of bullion required from England in some measure reduced.

Clive's demands look excessive when compared with the weakness of his strategic situation; but the Company was a trading concern, its losses had been great and if they were not recouped the Company might well be bankrupted. It was pointless to demand anything less. Meanwhile Watson, as the representative of His Britannic Majesty, fired literary broadsides in support of Clive; but the Nawab, still protesting his willingness to treat, steadily drew nearer. It was becoming evident that gunpowder, not paper, would resolve the issue.

In Calcutta itself, the dispute between Clive and the Select Committee over his independent authority as Commander-in-Chief, answerable only to Madras, flared to a head. On 18 January 1757, the Committee sent him a letter in which they required him 'to recede from the independent powers given you by the Committee of Fort St George and subject yourself to the orders of this Presidency ... [and] comply with and follow whatever plans of military operations the Select Committee may judge proper to point out'.

The letter concluded, 'but if you are determined to abide by the independent powers given you by the Select Committee of Fort St George ... we must not only represent to our honourable Masters such a refusal on your part as an infringement of the authority they have invested in us, but must exculpate ourselves from any bad consequences attending it, by protesting against you and the said Select Committee.' Signed Roger Drake, junior, William Watts, Richard Becher, J. Z. Holwell.

Despite his tribulations, or because of them, Clive had been learning to exercise a modicum of tact and patience. In his reply he conceded a few minor administrative points, but politely yet firmly rejected the central proposition: 'I do not intend to make use of my power for acting separately from you without you reduce me to the necessity of so doing, but so far as concerns the means of executing those powers, you will excuse me, Gentlemen, if I refuse to give them up. I cannot do it without forfeiting the trust reposed in me by the Select Committee of Fort St George.'

With Watson Clive had a more fruitful correspondence. From sickness and other causes the strength of his European troops had declined to about 300. He asked to be loaned the companies of the 39th at present on the ships. Watson at once complied. Further he swore he would not take the fleet from Calcutta until matters had been settled.

By 25 January the Nawab's advance guard had reached a point some eighteen miles away. But five days earlier the Marlborough had at last appeared with the artillery and between 300 and 400 sepoys; it was also learnt that Admiral

Pocock with Cumberland, having failed to weather Palmiras Point had put in to Vizagapatam, where his providential arrival had stopped Bussy sacking the British factory there. Instructions were sent to him to sail to Calcutta as soon as he could. Five hundred European troops were on their way from Bombay.

By 1 February, Clive was satisfied that his camp by Chitpur Tank was securely protected by earthworks and that the defences of Fort William were fit to withstand a siege. He was confident he could hold Calcutta. But there were rumours that Bussy was making warlike preparations and it was not certain whether he intended to return to the Carnatic or adventure into Bengal. A settlement with the Nawab was urgently needed.

On the same day the Nawab wrote offering to restore their old privileges to the Company and compensate British merchants for their losses; he asked for two envoys to be sent to him so that terms might be agreed. But despite his apparent reasonableness, still he came on. On 2 February, burning villages, marking the light hearted approach of his advance guard, could be seen from the Chitpur camp. On 3 February disorderly columns of troops started to stream across the plain towards Calcutta, and on 4 February the plain to the east was choked with columns of cavalry, infantry, elephants and guns, and a vast camp began to sprout just to the east of the Mahratta ditch. The numbers of Siraj-ud-daula's army have been variously estimated at figures ranging from 25,000 to 75,000. He probably had about 20,000 fighting men with thirty guns.

The same day Siraj-ud-daula wrote reassuringly to Clive reiterating his offer; he asked for two envoys to meet him at Nawabgange about six miles from Calcutta. Clive sent Walsh and Scrafton. The two Britons experienced some difficulty in finding the Nawab's headquarters. To their astonishment they found him already inside the boundaries of Calcutta, comfortably installed in a pavilion pitched in the garden of Omichand's house, the city side of the Mahratta ditch. When they did find him, their difficulties were not at an end. The Prince affected to believe that they had come to assassinate him and refused to see them. They were eventually granted an audience late in the day, and at once made it clear that there could be no negotiations while the Nawab's army was encamped outside Calcutta.

The Nawab was evasive, made an oblique reference to a monetary present for Clive and suggested that negotiations should be resumed next day. Convinced he was only playing

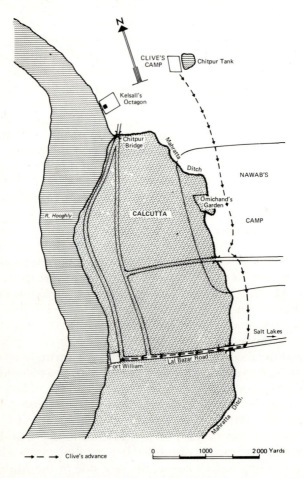

9 The Attack on the Nawab's Camp. Based on information in Robert Orme's *History of Military Transactions of the British in Industan* (4th edition).

BATTLES FOR CALCUTTA AND CHANDERNAGORE 199

for time so that his troops could occupy the city undisturbed, the two envoys slipped away under cover of darkness and reported their findings to Clive. To Clive it was evident that the moment for decision had arrived. Nearly all the native workmen and servants had vanished, the bazaars were empty and food becoming scarce. Next morning the Nawab's army would surely take possession of the city, and at Arcot he had seen that, when fighting in streets, well-trained troops, unable to manoeuvre freely and shot at from unexpected directions, forfeited most of the benefits of their training. He decided he must strike at once. It was too late to mount a night attack when darkness would severely handicap the enemy's cavalry, but in the early morning a mist rolled in from the river which generally cleared at about eight o'clock in the morning; he determined to launch an attack under its cover. He went on board *Kent* to confer with the Admiral. Any scheme for attacking the enemy appealed to that stalwart sailor and he generously agreed to loan Clive 600 seamen.

Clive returned to his camp to perfect his plans for his incredibly bold venture, the odds against him were at least ten to one. He estimated that two-thirds of the Nawab's army was outside the Mahratta ditch and one-third inside. He proposed under cover of the fog to break into the camp outside the ditch, then beat through it to where a road on a raised causeway crossed the ditch into the city about a mile beyond Omichand's garden. He hoped to reach the causeway at about eight o'clock when the fog ought to be lifting. With the enemy outside the ditch in confusion, he intended to re-enter the city by the raised road and thrust back towards Omichand's garden and the Nawab's headquarters. He had at his disposal, including the 39th and his gunners, about 600 European soldiers, 800 sepoys, six field guns and a howitzer; to this total 600 seamen could now be added.

At one o'clock in the morning the seamen under Captain Warrick came ashore at Kelsall's Octagon, and at two marched into Clive's camp, where they found the soldiers formed up in the darkness and waiting. Half the seamen, to their fury, were detailed to drag the guns and carry ammunition; Clive had no draught animals for his artillery. At about three o'clock the little column set off. The sepoys furnished the advance guard and the rear guard; immediately behind the advance guard came Coote commanding a picked grenadier company improvised from the 39th; behind him followed the rest of the Europeans organised as a single battalion, and behind them the seamen and the guns.

As the sky lightened, thick fingers of fog began to blot out the fading stars, and at six o'clock the advance guard broke into the Nawab's camp by some unguarded horse-lines. But the alarm gongs sounded and a confused action broke out. Coote, always happy to decry the Company's troops, observed,

'Our sepoys in front began to fire but in some confusion. I was not without apprehension of being broke by them. I therefore endeavoured to make them advance as fast as I could and sent a piece of cannon to come in my front. While this was doing, a shower of arrows came amongst us with some fire rockets, one of which unfortunately fell on one of the Company's grenadiers, who were in my rear, and blew up almost the whole platoon; immediately after this, a body of their choice horse came riding down on us sword in hand; as there was a great fog we did not perceive them until they came within ten yards of us.'

Undismayed, the infantry loosed a volley and the cavalry went about and disappeared into the surrounding gloom. Taking courage from the attack of their horse, Siraj-ud-daula's men using banks, hedges and walls as cover, or merely depending on the fog to protect them, formed a shifting ring of flame round the British. The British column never faltered; but in the clammy all-pervading fog, land marks disappeared, the guides became uncertain and lost their way, and the ranks fell into ever greater disorder. Eight o'clock came and the fog showed no signs of dispersing; it was not until nine that it began to lift. Coote recorded . . . 'Found ourselves nearly opposite the Nawab's quarters which was behind an entrenchment made by the English many years ago for the defence of the town against the Mahrattas [The Mahratta ditch]. Here we could see their greatest force lay and they began to cannonade us briskly. They sent some bodies of horse to surround us, but they never attempted to come near for us to fire our musketry at them.'

But with his men well short of their objective and in great confusion it was evident to Clive that his plan had miscarried. When the column did come to the raised causeway, the entrance to the city was found to be barricaded and strongly held. While the British tried to form up for an assault, the Nawab's guns in Omichand's gardens raked their disordered ranks with deadly effect. There was no hope of launching a properly ordered attack, and Clive decided to follow the ditch round for another mile to where the wide, straight Lal Bazar road crossed it.

The ground over which the little column was now moving consisted of small dry paddy fields intersected by numerous low banks, or bunds, marking the boundaries between fields. Hauling the guns over these was a difficult and time consuming task, and meanwhile the British were fully exposed to view, making an excellent target for the Nawab's guns; at the same time the enemy horse and foot, encouraged by an apparent British withdrawal, vigorously harassed the rear guard. The British guns were dropping into action, firing a few rounds then moving to come into action again further on. The carriage of one broke and the barrel of another split.[1] Coote noted, 'Ensign York with a platoon of the King's was ordered from the front to the rear in order to recover the cannon; when he arrived he found the rear in some confusion and another piece of cannon in great danger of being taken, as there was a body of horse and foot pressing upon it; it being at some distance from the battalion; he then marched beyond the gun and drew up his platoon in rear of it and by keeping up a constant fire secured the gun till it was drawn to the front.'

[1] This according to Captain Warrick's account of the action. Characteristically Coote suggested that one gun was abandoned because the Navy grew tired of hauling it. He may, of course, be right; the seamen bitterly resented being used, as they termed it, as coolie labour for the guns.

The Lal Bazar road at last came into view, but where it crossed the ditch a body of cavalry barred the way. A few rounds of grape disposed of them, and his army successfully filed over to the city side of the ditch. Here Clive formed line of battle with the ditch in front. There was a fierce exchange of artillery fire, but the Nawab's men hesitated to close, and after half an hour broke off the engagement.

Clive marched his weary and battlestained troops back to the security of Fort William, arriving at noon; here they rested during the afternoon then returned to their camp, marching in at about seven o'clock that evening, somewhat disheartened by the confusion of the morning and the heavy casualties they had suffered, which amounted to some 200 killed and wounded. Clive, himself, as was his custom, appeared wherever the battle was hottest, and both his ADC and his secretary had been killed by his side. Siraj-ud-daula, however, had lost nearly 1,000 men and the incredibly bold sally by the British had badly shaken his nerve. He realised he had no hope of taking Calcutta, and the next day he withdrew to place a safe distance between himself and that dangerous man, Clive.

Watson at once wrote to Clive suggesting an immediate pursuit and sending Speke to press his opinion. He added gratuitously, 'I think, too, it might not be amiss if you was to consult some of your officers.' Clive had no intention of forfeiting all he had gained by such a rash enterprise, but was beginning to understand how senior officers should be handled. He courteously replied, '. . . as you wish I would consult my officers on this occasion. . . . I have called a Council-of-War and a copy of which I enclose you. Be assured Sir I am very desirous my conduct should be such as may meet with the approbation of the world.' Clive could manipulate a Council-of-War at least as deftly as any company chairman a meeting of his shareholders.

Siraj-ud-daula had received a rude shock. He had not the strength of character to withstand a reverse and, owing to his lack of consideration and habit of abusing and insulting his ministers, had antagonised all his most experienced advisers. While he was pondering his next move disquieting

30 Ahmad Shah Abdalli, Ruler of Afghanistan; later he adopted the family name of Durani.

news came from Delhi. The Afghans, under Ahmad Shah Abdalli, had defeated the Emperor and captured his capital. Ahmad Shah had proclaimed himself Emperor, and it was reported that the vanguard of his army was on the move eastward toward Oudh and Bengal. Here was an enemy that menaced his rule and very existence. The British, after all, were but traders who posed no permanent threat to his province and indeed enriched it. He could settle with them without compromising his sovereignty, and if the Afghans bore down on Bengal, the magnificent British infantry, of whose quality he had just received such unwelcome evidence, might be a very useful addition to his army. Clive's claims had not been unreasonable and, when times were easier, onerous conditions no doubt could be repudiated.

Clive was as ready as the Nawab to treat. For him, too,

the future was dangerous and obscure. Madras had sent him at great risk to themselves and he had undertaken to return as soon as Calcutta was secure. The French might soon launch a damaging attack in the Carnatic, and it was imperative that the Bengal entanglement should be ended before the onset of the southwest monsoon made sailing to Madras unduly hazardous. Besides, how long could the French at Chandernagore be trusted to remain neutral? And if the treaty was not to be the prelude to further hostilities, it must be sufficiently moderate not to be a cause of future grievance. As he wrote to the Directors in London on 22 February: 'Jealousies instilled into him [the Nawab] by the French agents made it necessary for us to conclude the treaty with him out of hand, as well as to convince him of our moderate views.'

On 9 February, four days after the action outside Calcutta, a treaty was signed. It confirmed the *firman* granted by the Emperor Farruksiyar, and reiterated the Company's right to free trade in the following terms: 'All goods passing or repassing through the country by land or water in Bengal, Bihar or Orissa with English *dustucks* shall be exempt from any tax, fee or imposition from the *choquedars, zemindars* [local officials and gentry] or any other.' It was also agreed that compensation should be paid for the previous British losses (said to amount to £2 million), but the losses suffered by private individuals were not fully catered for. No restrictions were to be imposed on the fortifications at Calcutta and the construction of a mint was permitted. In addition, 'Admiral Watson and Colonel Robert Clive on the part and behalf of the British Nation and Company do agree to live in good understanding with the Nawab, to put an end to troubles and be in friendship with him, whilst these articles are observed and signed by the Nawab.' On their side the Council at Calcutta, 'Do agree and promise in the most solemn manner that ... we will never offer protection to any person having any accounts with the Government, nor ever act contrary to the tenor of the articles granted by the Nawab'.

Provided they were respected, the articles contained all

the British desired. As might be expected, some of the more short-sighted and avaricious of the merchants in Calcutta clamoured that the treaty was far too moderate, and wished to know why heavier terms had not been imposed.

However, the treaty had been signed and peace restored. Watts was dispatched to Cossimbazar to reopen the Company's factory there and reconstruct the old trading post at Patna. Somewhat unwisely, Omichand had again been admitted to favour and was appointed to assist Watts in representing the Company at the Nawab's Court at Murshidabad. Only the problem of the French remained.

Bussy's movements in the Deccan were, as yet, shrouded in mystery, but while Chandernagore remained in French hands it was a focus for all who wished ill to the British, and there could be no certainty that Bussy would not compose his difficulties and add Bengal to his laurels. Both Watson and Clive were certain that Chandernagore had to be destroyed. For a period after 25 February the tides in the Hooghly would make it impossible for Watson's ships to reach the French settlement; the stranding of *Bridgewater* had illustrated vividly enough the hazards of navigation on that river. The British must strike at once.

But while preparations were in hand Siraj-ud-daula intervened. He expressly prohibited an attack on Chandernagore, and inquired, rather querulously, why Watson kept his ships at Calcutta after the peace had been concluded. Watson and Clive accepted the prohibition, they did not wish to upset the newly signed agreement nor lay the British open to a charge of bad faith. Now Clive considered that if Chandernagore could not be destroyed it must be neutralised. There had been a long tradition that, whatever happened in Europe, navigation on the Hooghly should not be impeded nor any hostilities be permitted among the European settlements that bordered the river. Such, of course, had also been the tradition in the Carnatic until Dupleix violated it, and relying on tradition was not enough. However, the French were perfectly ready, if not eager, to treat.

The articles of a treaty of neutrality were drawn up and were agreed between the representatives of both Companies, all that remained was for the agreement to be signed. Now Watson, who up to this time had been placidly indifferent, suddenly declared that, before he signed, he must be certain that Governor Renault at Chandernagore had the authority to execute a treaty binding on the French throughout the East Indies. Renault had to confess that he had not, and that only the French Governor-General at Pondicherry was competent to do so. Watson at once insisted that, before he signed, the treaty must be ratified by the French Governor-General. To refer the matter to Pondicherry would take up to three months, and there was no certainty that the Governor-General would agree to it. Watson's attitude effectively wrecked the negotiation. Clive wrote to Pigot in Madras of the admiral's objection, 'which I imagine will put a stop to the whole negotiation and make us think of other measures for settling the differences in this province. My concern is that by the uncertainty . . . I can take no measures for the immediate return of part of the troops to the Coast.'

The admiral's refusal had a certain logic. In his view, a treaty that was not binding on the French Company as a whole could be too easily overturned, but his sudden intrusion into the negotiation placed Clive and the Select Committee in an awkward dilemma. It was suggested to Watson that, if he did not agree to a treaty of neutrality with the French at Chandernagore, then, logically, he must attack their settlement. Quite unmoved, he rejected the proposition. Now it was almost certain that Clive would be unable to leave Bengal before the monsoon broke. The Admiral's intransigence may have significantly affected the history of India. Clive was wrathful about his attitude and ventilated his feeling to the Select Committee, 'I think he has taken the consequences of all miscarriages on himself. . . . If I am not misinformed he runs counter to His Majesty's instructions which require that he should give attention to all representations made to him by the Company's agents in India for their service.'

Once again fate, in the shape of the Afghans, took a hand. News came to Murshidabad that their long-threatened thrust against Bengal had begun. In great alarm Siraj-ud-

BATTLES FOR CALCUTTA AND CHANDERNAGORE 207

daula wrote to the British imploring assistance. On 8 March 1757 Clive started marching towards Murshidabad, but with his gaze veering towards Chandernagore. His spirits rose. He wrote cheerfully to Robert Orme, 'I am going to Patna, or Delhi, or somewhere'. But how could he march up the Ganges to Patna and leave a potentially hostile Chandernagore squarely across his lines of communication? While Watts pressed this point on the Nawab at Murshidabad, Clive approached Chandernagore, saying airily that he would not begin hostilities without doing them the courtesy of telling them first, a remarkable piece of effrontery as at that time he had fewer European troops than the French. He also assured the Nawab that he would not attack Chandernagore without his permission.

However, he remained near Chandernagore awaiting his reinforcements from Bombay, now reduced to 450 fit men; these had disembarked at Calcutta and were being ferried up the river in contingents about 100 strong; the last contingent did not arrive until 14 March. Meanwhile he passed the time exchanging acid notes with Renault about the large number of British deserters he had managed to entice away. The European battalions of both Companies were a heterogeneous mixture of nationalities, and many of the soldiers felt only a tepid attachment to the country whose service they had entered.

At Murshidabad 10 March was a day of decision. The savage Afghans were rumoured to be near the borders of Oudh and the Nawab, a prey to the most extreme apprehension, was prepared to agree to almost anything to obtain help from the British. Watts wrote to the Select Committee: 'The Nawab said that he could not write but desired me to inform you that if you were determined to attack the French he would not meddle or give them the least assistance . . . he only requests to be informed of your sentiments three or four days before you begin action.' The Nawab, himself, wrote to Watson: 'If your enemy with an upright heart claims your protection you will give him his life, but then you must be well satisfied of the innocence of his intentions; if not, whatever you think right, that do.'

Watson received the letter on 12 March and interpreted it as giving him a free hand with the French. The same day he had received from England an official copy of the Declaration of War on France, together with instructions to harass the French in every way possible. He at once ordered the Fleet to sail for Chandernagore, as soon as the tides permitted.

On the evening of 13 March, when he knew that Watson was on the way, Clive read the declaration of war to his men and summoned Renault to surrender. The Frenchman, of course, refused and at three o'clock on the morning of 14 March his grenadiers were at the gates of Chandernagore. The French had no perimeter wall round the settlement, but had erected some batteries on its outskirts and with 2,000 Bengali troops from the garrison at Hooghly made available by Nand Kumar, the Governor, prepared to do battle. Clive, however, had suborned Nand Kumar with a substantial present (12,000 rupees) and after a few random shots his men withdrew. The French put up a stout resistance, but their batteries, owing to this defection, were isolated and in danger of being cut off; during the night they withdrew all their troops into their citadel, Fort D'Orléans.

The French garrison was a polyglot mixture made up of about 250 soldiers, some sailors and all the French officials capable of bearing arms, totalling about 500 Europeans plus 300 Sepoys.[1] The fort had been constructed on the banks of the Hooghly in the shape of a square with a bastion at each corner and sides 200 yards long. The walls were thin masonry and inadequately protected by banks of earth, especially on the riverward side. Each bastion mounted sixteen guns, five on each of the two outer faces and three on each of the two inner ones. They had blocked the river approaches by sinking four ships in the channel, chaining a boom across it from bank to bank, and siting a battery to command it.

---

[1] According to M. Renault. Watson gave the strength as '500 Europeans and 700 blacks' and Clive, while agreeing with the European strength, estimated the black troops at 600 in one letter and 700 in another. The French figure is the most likely to be correct.

While Watson's ships slowly navigated the river Clive closed in on the fort. The French fought stubbornly and against their accurate fire progress was slow and difficult. He managed to construct two batteries within 200 yards of the two landward bastions, but the fire of the French nearly demolished one and silenced the other. Clive waited for the fleet without risking unnecessary casualties by pressing a siege for which he was not properly equipped.

On 18 March the ships hove into view and anchored off the Prussian Gardens, about two miles below the fort. On 19 March Watson demanded the surrender of the fort. Satisfied with the course of events on the landward side and confident the big British ships could not penetrate any further up the river, Renault refused; but in the fort counsels were divided, and as a compromise he offered to ransom it. Watson dismissed the offer and set about clearing the obstructions. A party of seamen had already cut the chains holding the boom and towed it away. On the night of 19 March another party in boats rowed to where three French ships were anchored above the fort; it was suspected the French would use these as fire ships; the seamen cut their mooring and let them drift firmly aground on a shoal. On the same night the position of the blockships was charted and it was found possible for ships to pass between them. The French subsequently suggested that strong tides had shifted them. On the night of 20 March, under a heavy fire from the river battery, a passage through them was buoyed.

Watson relied on neap tides for his attack, as otherwise his lower deck guns could not elevate sufficiently to bear on the walls of the fort. High tide was unsuitable on 22 March, and the attack was timed to go in the following morning. All through the night Clive maintained a steady bombardment with a solitary 13-in. mortar he possessed, and armed his two batteries with 24-pounder guns he had captured from the French during the first day's fighting. He crammed the roofs of houses near the ramparts with infantrymen. At six o'clock in the morning he opened fire on the fort, while off Prussian Gardens Watson's ships set their sails before a strong south wind, weighed their anchors and glided slowly forward over the grey tinged and muddy waters of the river. *Tyger* led, flying the flag of Admiral Pocock, who, having arrived in *Cumberland* at Calcutta, had been rowed night and day up the river so that he could take part in the action. *Kent* followed and then *Salisbury*.

Skilfully piloted, the ships threaded their way through the blockships, under a heavy fire from the French battery

31 Admiral Pocock, later Sir George.

on the riverbank. Without replying they sailed majestically onwards their gun ports open and the guns run out. As *Tyger* drew level with the battery the Frenchmen spiked their guns and ran back into the fort. *Tyger* came to anchor opposite the further of the two bastions fronting the river; but the tide must have turned, as, when *Kent* hove-to opposite the wall between the two bastions and dropped her anchor, it dragged and she dropped downstream as far as the south-

BATTLES FOR CALCUTTA AND CHANDERNAGORE 211

ward or nearer of the two bastions, crowding out *Salisbury* which in consequence could not bring her guns properly to bear; it was an unfortunate mishap which deprived Watson of nearly a third of his firepower. At a quarter to seven the Admiral hoisted a red flag to the head of his main mast and the broadsides of the two ships crashed out.

In the bright early morning sunlight a deadly duel began. The range to the fort was little more than fifty yards and neither side could miss. Some of the roundshot from the French guns smashed clean through both sides of the British ships. A torrent of shot virtually cleared the quarter-deck of *Kent*. Captain Speke was severely and his son mortally wounded by the same ball. Eyre Coote, who had re-embarked with his men on *Kent*, lost fourteen out of his detachment of thirty lining the deck. Watson continued to pace his quarter-deck unmoved. One of his surviving officers exclaimed that a Frenchman was carefully training his gun on the Admiral. Watson replied, 'Why then, they shall have a fair shot,' and halted until the ball flew by, then resumed his pacing. A cable broke and for a few minutes the ship veered towards the fort before being brought under control. Three 32-pounder guns were dismounted, the main mast received five hits, the mizzen as many. A fire broke out and a few men panicked, but it was swiftly dowsed. The rigging hung from the masts in shreds. Ahead the *Tyger* suffered nearly as severely, and a roundshot striking the deck showered Admiral Pocock with wooden splinters and covered him with blood, although he was not seriously hurt. Then, after two terrible hours, the fire of the French guns slackened and about nine o'clock stopped. As the gunsmoke cleared a white flag could be seen on the ramparts. The two French bastions were little better than heaps of rubble and part of the wall between had fallen in. The bodies of French gunners could be seen scattered about their broken cannon. *Kent*[1] was a wreck and some seventy of her crew had been killed or wounded, including practically all the officers; *Tyger* had lost over sixty men.

In the fort some 200 men lay dead or wounded. A few of

[1] *Kent* was subsequently brought down to Calcutta, condemned and scrapped.

the younger men vowed they would die in the breaches, but to Governor Renault such heroics seemed senseless. The fort must be stormed before nightfall, already Clive's men were forming up; his counsels prevailed. Coote going ashore to ascertain the French proposals noted, 'when I got into the fort everything seemed in very great confusion; in about a quarter of an hour I returned to the Admiral with the Governor's son and a letter concerning the delivery of the place.'

On the landward side Clive's batteries, practically unopposed, had blasted a great hole in the southeastern bastion, and he was preparing to storm when he heard that the French had surrendered. His casualties had been trifling. Watson granted the French generous terms. All officers could go free on parole, although the soldiers and sailors would have to become prisoners of war while hostilities continued between England and France. The sepoys could disperse to their homes. The officials of the Company were at liberty to depart with their personal belongings. Perhaps his long ordeal on the quarter-deck and the appalling damage suffered by his ships had shaken even his iron nerve. In a moment of unusual pettiness he objected to Clive signing the articles of the capitulation in addition to Pocock and himself, on the grounds that the army had contributed nothing to the capture of the fort, a statement palpably false. Clive, however, insisted and, for once, Watson relented.

The results of the action were far-reaching. The capture of the contents of the French warehouses went some way to meeting the losses in Calcutta, but more important the French had no base of any size left in Bengal. Law remained at Cossimbazar; but the factory there was unprotected, although some of the sepoys and a number of the soldiers from Chandernagore, who, so Clive asserted, broke out after the white flag had been hoisted, joined him there.

In Murshidabad Siraj-ud-daula watched the course of events in an agony of indecision. The threat from the Afghans had receded. Too late, he yielded to the entreaties of Law and sent an army of 16,000 men under Rai Durlabh to relieve the beleaguered fort, but Durlabh was in no hurry

BATTLES FOR CALCUTTA AND CHANDERNAGORE 213

and was still some distance away when the French gave in. The situation of the Prince was unenviable, his problems far too difficult for a man of his limited capacity. The Afghans might come in the autumn, the Mahrattas were always a threat, and now the manifest reluctance with which he had permitted the British to operate against Chandernagore excited their distrust without saving the French. If he had stifled his fears of the Afghans and exerted himself to aid the French, Chandernagore would never have been attacked. On the other hand, had he assisted the British he would have won their trust and gratitude and his position would have been secure. Neither Clive nor Watson wished to break the treaty if they could rely on his good faith.

But perhaps the most far reaching result of all was that now there could be no question of either Clive or any of his men returning to the Carnatic before the Autumn. Watson, with his damaged ships, could not consider sailing before the monsoon had blown itself out. Clive, with an army at his disposal and nothing in particular to do, was unlikely to fill in his time by wining and dining in the comfortable mansions of Calcutta.

Chapter 11

THE APPROACH TO PLASSEY
April–June 1757

Clive's army was composed of contingents from Bombay, Madras and Calcutta. He had served recently in all three Presidencies and seen that, although ready enough to give each other assistance in an emergency, the three councils were parochial in outlook and little interested in problems that did not affect them directly. The Council at Bombay had displayed little enthusiasm for the expedition against Bussy in the Deccan and had leapt at a chance to cancel it. In Madras affairs in the Carnatic, not unnaturally, bulked large, and the crisis looming in Bengal had gone unperceived until far too late. Now the Company was becoming a power in India, it was abundantly clear that there must be some form of central authority, if its resources were to be deployed to best advantage.

The Court of Directors in London was too distant to deal with rapidly changing situations; a Governor-General on the French model was required, who would be supreme over all the British settlements in the East Indies. The unrivalled opportunities such a post offered excited Clive's imagination. Its holder would exercise more untrammelled power than the King of England himself. The problems were first to impress on those in authority in England the pressing need to create such a post and secondly to indicate unmistakably the man most qualified to hold it.

Perhaps this alluring vision floated before Clive's eyes as he sailed for Bengal. The difficulties he had encountered there had demonstrated beyond reasonable doubt the correctness of his view; after his success in bringing the Nawab to terms he thought the moment propitious to canvass it discreetly in England. He wrote to his father on 23 February, 'I am desirous of being appointed Governor General of India, if such an appointment should be necessary . . . however, I would have you manage the affair with great prudence and discretion'. He also ventilated his idea to William Mabbot, one of the Company's senior directors. His father was scarcely the best of men to put forward so radical a concept, or any concept at all, and although the vision doubtless tantalised him during much of his time in India, he was never destined to see it crystallise into reality. Warren Hastings became the first to attain such eminence, and then the Government hedged his powers with such limitations that most of his finest designs were frustrated, and for what he did accomplish a grateful country in due course made him stand trial.

But, although such desires might lurk at the back of Clive's mind, more practical problems called for his attention. After the fall of Chandernagore he quartered his army in the town for a few days, but his men developed so marked a taste for arrak, the cheap local spirit, that, although the heat of April was becoming unpleasant, he removed them from temptation by camping them a mile to the northward of the town. He wanted to keep his army as far up the Hooghly as he could to impress its presence on Siraj-ud-daula.

He had dealt French power in Bengal a heavy blow; he wrote to Pigot, '. . . the taking of Chandernagore is of more consequence to the Company, in my opinion, than the taking of Pondicherry itself', but the French still had their factory at Cossimbazar where their chief, Jean Law, elder brother of the Jaques Law who had been forced to surrender at Sriringham, had easy access to the Nawab. There could be no security while the French remained in Bengal, seeking every opportunity to undermine the British. And now, to his indignation, he heard that as a result of Admiral Watson's misguided leniency, Renault had reconstituted the French council within the boundaries of the Dutch settlement at

32 A toddy-seller; the sort of shop that Clive's soldiers found only too attractive in Chandernagore.

Chinsura and was issuing instructions to the remaining French possessions in Bengal. Clive had not been consulted about the terms of the capitulation and this was conduct he could not tolerate. He declared that the parole to be observed by the French officers applied equally to the officials of their Company, and that since these officials had violated their parole, they were no longer entitled to its protection. He ordered a force of sepoys to Chinsura, and the Dutch, helpless in the face of British might, allowed the Frenchmen to be arrested and taken to Calcutta. The legal justification for Clive's action may be somewhat flimsy, but the distinction between officials and soldiers, at this time, was decidedly fine; England was at war with France and whatever the terms of the capitulation, if the French indulged in actions hostile to the British they might expect retaliation. It could of course be argued that, since Chinsura was administered by the Dutch under the suzerainty of the Nawab, Clive's action was illegal unless he first obtained sanction from the Nawab. Such legal niceties, however, had become scarcely relevant after the breakdown of the Moghul Empire.

The problem of Renault had been solved, but there still remained Law at Cossimbazar. On 29 March Clive wrote to the Nawab, 'It is absolutely necessary that your Excellency should deliver up to us the persons and effects of the French at Cossimbazar.' The wretched Prince wriggled and protested. He had an uncertain and violent temperament that caused him to be feared by all who had to deal with him, his uncontrollable rages had alienated almost all the great men of his realm, and he was capable of appalling cruelty,[1] but he was the child of his emotions and incapable of self-discipline or stability of purpose. Now he was torn between anger that the British should presume to dictate to him and fear of what they might do if he did not comply with their requests. At one moment he let the French fortify their factory and talked of impaling the unfortunate Watts, then he sent his own men to demolish the fortifications the French had erected. He ordered them to withdraw to Patna, then countermanded the order and told them to return, only to revert to his original decision. While maintaining a cordial correspondence with Clive, he negotiated with Bussy, and urged his governors to give that general every assistance could he be persuaded to march into Bengal.

Clive faced much the same situation as had Dupleix in his relations with Anwar-ud-Din, when he had defied that Prince's orders and first attacked Madras, then routed his army at St Thomé. Was it reasonable to suppose that Siraj-ud-daula would not avenge his humiliation at the first opportunity? The experienced Watts at Cossimbazar had no doubts on the matter and reiterated his view that the vacillating and inconstant Prince could on no account be trusted. And indeed he was writing to Bussy: 'I am advised you have arrived at Echapore, this news gives me pleasure, the sooner you come here the greater satisfaction I shall have in meeting you. What can I write of the perfidy of the English; they have without ground picked a quarrel with M. Renault and taken by force his factory. I will take care to oppose and overthrow their proceeding.' These sentiments

---

[1] A Frenchman reported that on one occasion Siraj-ud-daula had a pregnant woman cut open so that he could see what an embryo looked like.

contrasted starkly with his letter to Clive on 26 March which began, 'The particulars of your victory at Frankedongy (Chandernagore) which I have been impatient to hear, gave me inexpressible pleasure . . .'.

For the time being Clive could discount any threat from Bussy; the Frenchman was fully occupied in maintaining a tenuous grip on the territory he endeavoured to rule. Clive mentioned to Pigot, 'We have information that Monsieur Bussy has lost 200 Europeans besides many blacks in taking some Rajah's fort in that neighbourhood. If this news be true, he will find it difficult enough to maintain himself in Golcondah without detaching either to the northward or the southward.'

But circumstances might change. A French presence near Murshidabad was a standing danger. The readiness of the Nawab to expel the French from his dominions would show clearly enough what faith could be placed on his professions of friendship. Both Clive and Watson bombarded him with letters. At this time they could do no more. Without an Indian ally, a British advance from Chandernagore could not be contemplated.

Siraj-ud-daula never fully understood Clive's desire to have the French evicted, and almost certainly wished to retain them as a counterpoise to the perilously increased power of the British. He dared not refuse Clive outright, but tried to procrastinate by raising objections. He protested that if the French left the Viceroyalty, the Emperor would lose the revenues he obtained from the taxes on their commerce, a rather implausible objection, the Emperor had received little revenue from Bengal over the past few years.

The Select Committee, however, guaranteed that they would make good any loss of revenue incurrred by the departure of the French. Then the Nawab found another difficulty in that the French Company was heavily in debt to a number of his subjects. Clive offered to repay the loss from French goods they would be forced to leave behind them. At last Siraj-ud-daula gave way. Watts wrote to Clive on 16 April, 'The French left their factory and marched through the city today. They had about 100 Europeans. I have sent spies into their camp to entice away as many soldiers as I can.' But the Nawab could never resist doing things by halves, and accordingly neither succeeding in doing what he wanted nor receiving any benefit from his compliance with the wishes of others. He sent Law to Patna, the capital of his province of Bihar, not, as might be expected, to join Bussy in Golcondah, an action that at once aroused the suspicions of the British. In justice to the Nawab, he did so at the pleading of Law, who represented that if he went towards Golcondah the British might intercept him on the line of march.

While relations with Siraj-ud-daula continued to be unsatisfactory, there had been an interesting development in Murshidabad itself. The Seths, an immensely rich family of bankers with connections over most of eastern and central India, had decided that the Nawab had to be overthrown. Their business interest had suffered severely from the unsettled conditions of the past year, and they were certain that if Siraj-ud-daula was once firmly in power, the avaricious Prince would confiscate most of their wealth. At this time Murshidabad seethed with intrigue and it is impossible now to unravel the tangled skein of hate, ambition and personal enmity that the Seths sought to weave into a coherent conspiracy. According to Jean Law they acted with a skill and deviousness that would not have disgraced Machiavelli. They conceived that to prevent Bengal lapsing into anarchy and civil war after the Prince had been deposed, the British must be among the prime movers of their conspiracy; they, therefore, exerted themselves to the utmost to embroil the British and the Nawab, not scrupling to incite the Prince against the British at every opportunity in the hope of provoking a rupture. Omichand, in view of his relationship with the British, became one of the objects of their attention although never admitted into their inner councils.

Watts at Cossimbazar innocently wrote to Clive on 11 April 1757,

'Almost every individual of the Nawab's ministers are [*sic*] our enemies from our not having gratified them; this they resent and as they have but little regard for the Nawab, they care not what rash measures they precipitate him into; they are always raising his apprehensions of us, and affirm that when we have got what we want, we shall in the rains attack him; they are also continuously crying up the French power; sometimes Bussy with a large army is entering the province, at others the French are arrived at Pondicherry with 17 ships of war . . .'.

Watts thought this unfortunate prejudice against the British could be remedied by a not excessive sum of money discreetly laid out. Apparently oblivious of his past misdemeanours, Watts found Omichand a man 'of a superior understanding . . . I therefore consult him on all occasions'. From Omichand he had gained an inkling that some plot was being hatched; in rather veiled terms he continued,

'Omichand and I have had many conversations on a subject I did not know how to address you about. I opened myself to Scrafton and from him learn that Omichand's and my endeavours for yours and the Major's service will not be disagreeable.

'It is hinted to me, as if it would be proposed to the committee, for our army to march this way, but hope no such proposal will be listened to, as it will be violating our treaty with the Nawab who is complying with his part of it, though not as expeditiously as we could wish; it will be throwing the country again into confusion and probably prevent the Company's getting an investment for another year, the consequence of which may be fatal to them; nothing but an open and apparent breach by the Nawab in his contract ought to induce us to rekindle a war in this province.'

Scrafton, chief designate of a factory at Luckipore, was passing through Cossimbazar en route for Dacca, but he had found the political complexities at Murshidabad so fascinating that he had tarried there, appointing himself Clive's unofficial representative in the capital. He thought Watts was something of an old woman, a view he may have shared with Clive. From Watts' letter it may be inferred that, after a discussion with Scrafton, he realised Clive knew something of the plots in Murshidabad and did not entirely disapprove.

The situation was not entirely new. Early in the year some disaffected nobles had made overtures to the British, but at the time these had been firmly rejected. Now Watts understood that, if the conspiracy against the Nawab was widely enough based, Clive might consider associating the Company with it, a course of action that Watts himself viewed with some reserve.

At this stage Clive was probably only taking care to keep in touch with affairs in Murshidabad without committing himself or the Company in any way; but he was too far-sighted to believe that, if an attempt was made against the Nawab, the British could avoid being involved, one way or another. The goodwill of the Nawab was essential to the well-being of the Company. If Siraj-ud-daula met his commitments to the Company and rid himself of the French, it might be possible to rely on his good-faith and in the autumn ship the Madras troops back to the Carnatic, where already their absence was the subject of harsh comment and accusations of ill-faith. If, on the other hand, Siraj-ud-daula was overthrown, it was of the utmost importance that his successor should be well-disposed to the British. Clive watched and waited.

On 12 April Scrafton wrote, 'There is great probability that the French have taken service with the Nawab' and went on to suggest that in the confused atmosphere in which he lived, it might be as well if letters were written in cypher. Yet despite Scrafton's letter the Nawab informed Clive, 'I have ordered Monsieur Law and his people out of my subaship [viceroyalty] and have wrote expressly to my *naibs* and *phousdars* never to let these people whom I have turned out to reside in any part of my province.' Admirable sentiments but ones hard to reconcile with the decision to send Law to Patna, and his instructions to the Governor of that city to give him every consideration.

On the same day Watts wrote, 'The Nawab, before our success at Chandernagore, threatened in the presence of Ranjit Rai [a representative of the Seths], and others to impale me or cut off my head, and yesterday he repeated these threats in the presence of Jagat Seth [the most influential of the Seths] Manikchand, Khwaja Wajid, Mir Kassim, Ranjit Rai and Omichand.' Watts made light of the threats, but no doubt they gave him some uncomfortable moments; the Nawab was unlikely to be restrained on humanitarian grounds.

Scrafton, himself, had no doubts that the Nawab could and should be unseated. He expressed his opinions to Walsh who had become Clive's secretary, 'Give me that power, and I dare swear that in ten days I could settle that you shall be joined by a large force as soon as you have marched two days to the north; send me your terms and my life on it I do my part well.' And on 21 April he wrote, 'The army [the Nawab's] is daily increasing. In the fit he was in two days ago he ordered Mir Jafar to march and promised him six lakhs the instant he advanced beyond their present encampment, and to make it ten if he was victorious [over the British]. The next day he starts at the danger and countermands the march.' Almost daily the evidence accumulated that in his relationship with the British Siraj-ud-daula was torn between terror and hatred.

He had now elevated a new favourite, Mohan Lal. Mohan Lal had been ill for some months, poisoned, it was said, by some ill-disposed person, and many considered that the illness had affected his mind. Clive wrote to him to ensure that he knew where his sympathies ought to lie; 'as the Nawab gives great attention to what you say, I desire you will give him such advice as is consistent with his honour and the good of his country. In so doing you will gain the character of a faithful servant and make the British your friends.'

Watts, however, never wavered in his opinion that it was an illusion to repose any trust in the Nawab, and pressed his opinion on Clive, 'The Nawab is at heart our bitter enemy and you may be assured will join with what French he can collect together and attack us whenever he is disengaged from the apprehension of the Pytans [Afghans] and the My Rajah [the leader of a rebellion in Bihar]'. At the same time the conspiracy spread. The Seths to safeguard their possessions employed a General of 2,000 horse named Khudadad Yar Lutuf Khan, a prominent and wealthy nobleman at the court of the Nawab; they now proposed him as a successor to Siraj-ud-daula. The increased powers given to Mohan Lal and the arrogant way he used them had deepened the general discontent. On 24 April Scrafton wrote, for once disregarding protocol and addressing Clive direct, 'Omichand's mind is big with some great project. He told me yesterday he was bound to secrecy, but to keep ourselves in readiness and when matters were ripe he would let you know. I can give a pretty good guess. It is in conjunction with Jagat Seth to set up Khudadad Yar Lutuf Khan.' Scrafton, eager for the Company to join the conspiracy, ventured to censure his superior, Watts, for his timidity. But then issues always seem clearer to subordinates without the ultimate responsibility for making the decision.

On 19 April Admiral Watson had himself written to the Nawab scolding him in high terms for not answering his letters. 'I was more particularly entitled to a speedy reply from my high rank and station; and I cannot help looking upon your neglect in this matter but as a slight offered to the King my master.' The Admiral disdained the language of diplomacy and continued, 'As soon as Cossimbazar is properly garrisoned, to which place our troops will speedily begin their march, I desire that you will grant a *dustuck* for the passage of 2,000 of our soldiers by land to Patna.'

Siraj-du-daula, not surprisingly, had no intention of allowing British troops up the Ganges to Patna, Clive might suddenly decide he had to hold Murshidabad to secure his line of communications. He lacked the breadth of vision to realise that his refusal to expel the French was poisoning his relations with the British, and that he had to decide, once and for all, which of the two warring nations he would support. He sent his answer to Clive. 'As by your marching this way, the treaty must be infringed and the kingdom suffer, on this account I write you, so that if you do send an army this way, it is you who break the treaty and I am blameless. I have directed my generals when they receive accounts of your having begun your march to set out to meet you.'

That settled the matter, but at his capital discontent had now reached fever heat and the city was alive with rumours. It was said that the My Rajah had defeated the Nawab's army and that the Afghans were at Agra and on the point of invading. It seemed almost certain that the Nawab would march into Bihar to protect that province and put down the rebellion. The conspirators laid elaborate plans. If the Nawab left Murshidabad, Khudadad Khan would seize it and Clive bring his army up the Hooghly and join him. Clive waited impatiently for the revolt to break out, his army poised and ready. Watson wanted him back in Calcutta for consultations. He replied, 'You may be assured, Sir, some great revolution will happen before long, and I hope much to the advantage of the Company.' He added that he dared not leave Chandernagore.

But inexplicably nothing happened. The Nawab did not leave Murshidabad, the Afghans did not march and the conspirators lacked the courage to put their plan into operation. Weak and vacillating he might be, but Siraj-ud-daula in his violent rages could be an exceedingly dangerous man. It became clear that the conspirators would not act without the open support of the British, and that Khudadad Yar Lutuf Khan lacked the stature needed in a candidate for the Viceroyalty. Once again a fog of uncertainty descended. Clive made clear to Watts, 'I will not willingly undertake anything which may occasion a rupture without I am obliged to it.'

However, he wrote to Pigot on 30 April, 'The opinion here is universal that there can be neither peace nor trade without a change of government.' Now came an important new development. Mir Jafar Ali Khan, Commander-in-Chief of the Nawab's army, had been insulted beyond bearing by the deference he had been compelled to render Mohan Lal and now he announced himself ready to lead the revolt, provided that he could be assured of British support.

Blazing April gave way to the furnace heat of May, while the Select Committee deliberated on whether formally to link the Company with the conspirators. On 1 May the decision was recorded in the minutes of its meeting.

'The Nawab is so universally hated by all sorts and degrees of man . . . and a revolution so generally wished for, that it is probable the step will be attempted, and successfully too, whether we give assistance or not. In this case we think it would be a great error in politics to remain idle and unconcerned spectators of an event, wherein by engaging as allies to the person designed to be set up we may benefit our employers and the community very considerably, do a general good and effectually traverse the designs of the French.'

It only remained to draw up an agreement acceptable to both parties. Until the conspirators were ready to move, inevitably, nothing could be done that would arouse the suspicion of the Nawab, and the cloying insincerities of the subsequent correspondence between Clive and Siraj-ud-daula cannot fail to evoke a feeling of distaste; but they were quite unavoidable and can have deceived neither. Siraj-ud-daula, too, was playing a double game and doing his utmost to persuade Bussy to lead a French army into Bengal.

The leaders of the new conspiracy, in addition to the Seths, Mir Jafar and Khudadad Yar Lutuf Khan who was apparently unworried by his diminished status, included Rai Durlabh, the second Minister in the realm, and Mir Kassim, one of the leading generals. While these were being approached, to allay suspicion Clive settled his Bengal troops into billets in Chandernagore, and sent the remainder of his army back to Calcutta; they could come up the river in a couple of days when the time came; and Clive always intended to act in support of a revolution, not to be the prime mover. Arrangements were also made to evacuate all the factories in Bengal at short notice before hostilities commenced. He directed Watts on 2 May, 'enter on business with Mir Jafar as soon as you please'.

While Watts 'entered on business', a strange envoy arrived in Calcutta. The servant of a traveller newly arrived in the city, secretly approached Governor Drake and revealed himself, so he claimed, to have been sent by Balaji Rao, the Peshwa or hereditary chief minister of the Mahratta Confederacy, to offer the British the assistance of 70,000 Mahratta horsemen, who, he said, were ready to invade Bengal. Clive in a letter to Watts doubted the authenticity of the offer 'the absurdity of the Mahrattas entering the country when the rains are near makes me suspect Narain Singh [the Nawab's spymaster] has some notion of what is going forward and sent the man to sound us'. Again on 12 May he reiterated the opinion that the supposed envoy was a spy sent by the Nawab to probe the intentions of the British.

By 14 May nothing had been concluded in Murshidabad and Clive became impatient and a little anxious. He pressed the need for haste on Watts. 'In fifteen days the rivers may rise and the scheme be impracticable. . . . For God's sake let us have no unnecessary delay, let me know at once if Mir Jafar is resolved. Remember he can bring 22,000 Mahrattas in the field.' Watts had submitted an agreement to Mir Jafar, but matters hung fire; then events took a dangerous turn. Omichand was behaving in a curious fashion. He had obtained two lakhs of rupees from the Nawab by an intrigue that resulted in the disgracing of Ranjit Rai, the agent of the Seths. It was an act that must incur the enmity of the Seths and disclosed unsuspected stresses among the conspirators. Then, when Watts showed him the draft agreement with Mir Jafar, he disagreed with it violently and went on to make some absurd demands for himself. Watts related,

'he . . . insisted on my demanding for him 5 per cent on all the Nawab's treasure which would amount to two crore of rupees, besides a quarter of all his wealth. These and many other articles, in which his own ambition, cunning and avaricious views were the chief motives, he positively insisted on and would not be prevailed upon to recede from one article. Perceiving his obstinacy would only ruin our affairs and that we would alarm the jealousy and lose the good opinion of all people, and that the accomplishment of his treaty, if agreed to, would take some years, Mir Jafar likewise having expressed an utter distrust and disgust at his being in any ways concerned in the treaty, and delays are dangerous, I therefore had a meeting with Mir Jafar's confidant [Mirza Omar Beg] who sets out today with the accompanying articles, which he says he is sure Mir Jafar will comply with.'

On 17 May the Secret Select Committee considered the alarming news contained in Watts' letter. Clive had inserted a clause in the draft agreement giving Omichand, as a reward for his services, the right to 5 per cent of the Nawab's treasury, a figure Watts thought unduly high. Now, in view of his outrageous claim and the manner in which he made it, the Select Committee considered he had lost all rights to be rewarded. In the minutes of the meeting held on 17 May it is recorded

'The article in favour of Omichand the Committee think should be totally left out, as his behaviour merits disgrace and punishment at our hands than such a stipulation on his behalf.

'It was then considered how we might deceive Omichand and prevent a discovery of the whole project, which we run the risk of should we refuse to insist on the unreasonable gratification he expects and demands, and on the other hand it would be highly improper to stipulate much less demand with any obstinacy, such extravagant terms from Mir Jafar for a person who can be no service in the intended revolution. So on the other it would be dangerous to provoke a man of Omichand's character by seeming to take no care at all of his interests and slighting his weight and influence, which prompt him to make a sacrifice of us and ruin our affairs entirely.

'For these reasons we think it will be necessary to form a double treaty both to be signed by Mir Jafar and by us; in one the article in favour of Omichand is to be inserted, in the other left out.'

The two treaties were accordingly drawn up and signed. Watson, while aware in general terms of what was happening, had taken no hand in the matter; now, while perfectly ready to sign the true treaty, he declined to sign the fictitious one. It is uncertain precisely how it was done, it has been suggested that Watson's signature was forged with or without his permission, but Omichand was satisfied that Watson had assented to the fictitious treaty which gave him all he wanted. It is perhaps just credible that in a matter of such crucial importance Watson, happily isolated on his flagship, never bothered to find out how the problem was solved; but it seems more reasonable to suppose that he had some idea of what was done, or took care not to find out.

The affair of the two treaties has been looked on as an indelible stain on the character of Clive, and he was called on to explain it years later before the House of Commons. His defence will be considered later, but the circumstances in which the decision was made may appropriately be considered now.

Watts stated that Mir Jafar would not agree to Omichand's terms, therefore, if the Select Committee accepted them the conspiracy would lose its head and inevitably fall apart. The monsoon would break sometime next month, and from then until the middle of October military operations would be impossible. If, therefore, the revolution did not begin in the next few weeks it would be delayed until October, a delay that must prove fatal, and result in the details of the plot and the British complicity in it coming to the notice of Siraj-ud-daula—Law drily remarked that he was about the only person who seemed unaware it existed.

It had been known since last autumn that a powerful French reinforcement had been ordered to India (the Comte de Lally with a complete French regiment and nine ships of the line left Brest in March 1757, but the expedition was much delayed by adverse winds and the lethargy of the French admiral). It was by no means impossible that it would arrive that autumn to find the Carnatic virtually unprotected, Bussy in full control of the Northern Circars, and the Nawab the implacable enemy of the British. If this happened the British situation in India would be all but hopeless. In addition, the conspirators at Murshidabad and Watts and his staff would probably be executed, and not gently.

On the other hand, if Omichand's demands were rejected, he would almost certainly recoup his losses by betraying the conspiracy to the Nawab and the same disastrous situation come about. If Omichand's proposals could neither be accepted nor rejected, the question arises whether or not some middle course might have been adopted. Here the time factor was decisive; quite apart from the question whether Omichand would have moderated his demands to a figure acceptable to Mir Jafar, taking into account what he might hope to gain by betraying the conspiracy to the Nawab, there was no time for such an unlikely and hazardous negotiation before the rains broke.

However, it might be argued that these considerations are less important than upholding a moral principle, that the double treaty was a dishonourable expedient and nothing could justify it. The force of this argument can scarcely be denied; yet even in ordinary life in such a case some form of deception is regarded as acceptable. Omichand was indulging in the most common form of blackmail—'pay up or I tell'. In the present day it is not generally considered wrong, in such circumstances, to try and trap the blackmailer, by making him an offer of payment and inveigling him into a room, suitably garnished with concealed policemen, to prove his guilt in the eyes of the law. Nevertheless, Watson's refusal to sign the spurious treaty appears to reflect on the conduct of Clive and the Select Committee. Watson had remained apart from the negotiation. His ships could not penetrate above Chandernagore and he had little interest in affairs out of reach of the Navy. He and his squadron had already been recalled to England, and after a year spent mainly on board ship, he had little idea of the complexities of Indian politics. He knew that double treaties were dishonourable and had no intention of associating the British Government or the Royal Navy in what appeared to be a dishonourable transaction. Having taken no part in the original intrigue, he could close his eyes to the probable consequences of his refusal. However, when all rationalisation is done, the episode is repugnant, but the pressures on Clive and the Select Committee can at least be understood.

Matters dragged on. The Nawab must have known something was afoot, already it was the talk of the bazaars. Watts was finding it almost impossible to communicate with Mir Jafar, and Clive thought of an expedient. The Select Commitee still doubted the credentials of the Mahratta envoy, but were anxious not to offend his masters should he be genuine. They had, therefore, given him a non-committal answer, suggesting the matter could be raised again after the rains if the conduct of the Nawab remained unsatisfactory. Clive saw in this an opportunity to reassure the Nawab about the intentions of the British and at the same time make contact with Mir Jafar. Scrafton had been withdrawn from Cossimbazar some days earlier. Watts, not unnaturally, resented his presence and the role he was playing. Clive now sent him to the Nawab ostensibly to reveal the Mahrattas' proposals, but with the real task of seeking an interview with Mir Jafar to discover his plans. Scrafton duly obtained an audience with the Nawab, who, to his surprise, took the news about the Mahrattas seriously and considered what dispositions he might adopt. Scrafton, however, failed in the most important part of his mission, and on 25 May wrote to tell Clive that all his endeavours to secure a private interview with Mir Jafar had been foiled.

By now the pre-monsoon heat would be approaching its greatest intensity, the days burning hot and the nights bringing little relief. The unsuitable clothing of the Europeans would generate prickly heat in swathes, and the resultant itching drive men near to madness. A blanket of silence seemed to have descended on Murshidabad. The strain on the nerves of even such a man as Clive was fast becoming unendurable. The monsoon must break in a few days and nothing had been decided. It was impossible to delay longer and he began preparations for an advance. He asked Watson for 200 sailors to garrison Chandernagore and 100 to march with him and help man his guns. Watson was reluctant; he disliked the whole enterprise; but he was not the man to decline a request for help. He finally agreed, but warned Clive that if he again used seamen as coolie labour to haul his guns, as he had done in Calcutta, he might expect a mutiny.

May ended without the eagerly awaited news that Mir Jafar had signed the treaty. The sun glared down out of a brassy sky and the tension was becoming wellnigh intolerable. On 1 June Clive wrote to Watts, 'I hope there had been nothing done that makes you fear Mir Jafar will prove treacherous.'

At last a letter came from Cossimbazar, but the news it contained was far from welcome. Watts wrote on 3 June that Rai Durlabh had objected to the articles, and he suggested that his objections must be met as 'Mir Jafar appears only a tool in the hands of Rai Durlabh, therefore if we can agree with the latter all may yet be well.' Not much comfort here, but worse was to follow. 'I do not find Mir Jafar has as many Jemadars as he boasted of,' and 'We can expect no more assistance than that they will stand neuter ... if you think you are strong enough, I am of the opinion we had better depend on ourselves and enter no contract with such a set of shuffling, lying, spiritless creatures.'

Clive's feelings can easily be imagined. Watts knew very well that he never contemplated advancing on his own; and what could he mean about not entering into a contract, when a contract signed by the Company was already in Mir Jafar's possession, damning evidence if he decided to show it to the Nawab. Boiling with impatience and anxiety, Clive wrote back on 5 June, 'You assured Mr Scrafton that Omichand once gone you had no further obstacle to a conclusion. Then why this delay? Surely you are deceived by those you employ, or you have been deceiving me ...'

Clive can be visualised in his house in French Gardens at Chandernagore, tormented by the heat and suffering from an agony of frustration and uncertainty. Had Watts been chasing a will-o-the-wisp all the time and merely succeeded in fatally compromising the Company? He wrote again the same day, his anguish breaking into anger. 'I find you have been duped throughout the whole. You have now no more to do than to get the articles back again which you have been so imprudent as to trust to their hands, for I will not embark on any undertaking with such a set of cowardly rascals.'

But now when affairs seemed at their most hopeless, a faint ray of light pierced the black confusion. Mir Jafar signed the articles[1] and on 6 June Watts wrote,

'Ranjit Rai informs me that Jagat Seth has secured Khudadad Yar Lutuf Khan who will act in conjunction with Mir Jafar. Rai Durlabh has confessed that Omichand has been tampering with him and told him that if we were once permitted to march this way, we should not quit Murshidabad these three years; in short no device has that cunning serpent left unessayed to mar our affairs, because he had not the managing of them himself. Permit me to request expedition or Ghazi-ud-din [the chief minister of the Moghul Emperor, at that time in Oudh] and the Emperor's son who are expected here in two months will endanger our scheme . . . I think we may depend on the sincerity of Mir Jafar.'

On 7 June Watts reported he had dispatched the articles to Calcutta and asked permission to withdraw from Cossimbazar; but he said nothing about Mir Jafar's plans. On 9 June he wrote again, 'Affairs here are very near come to a conclusion. Mir Jafar is turned out of the Nawab's service. Threatening messages continually pass between them. Whether we interfere or not it appears affairs will be decided in a few days by the destruction of one of the parties.'

[1] The Articles are given in Appendix 3.

THE APPROACH TO PLASSEY 233

It was enough. On 10 June 1757 Clive decided to march. He asked Watson for *Bridgewater* to overawe the garrison at the town of Hooghly and ordered up the troops from Calcutta. On 11 June he gave Watts permission to evacuate Cossimbazar. The news of his departure would ring like an alarm gong announcing that the British intended to strike; now there could be no turning back.

On 12 June Killpatrick disembarked with his men at Chandernagore. He had left only about fifty fit men and a number of invalids to defend Calcutta. The outbreak of open fighting between the troops of the Nawab and those of Mir Jafar had yet to be confirmed, but with the monsoon bound to break in the next few days Clive had no alternative but to advance at once on Murshidabad. He sent a letter to the Nawab listing a number of grievances about his failure to implement his treaty with the British, and added that he was, himself, going to Cossimbazar to seek redress. It was only a formality designed to justify his action to the outside world; it might also prove useful if for any reason he subsequently found it necessary to disclaim a hostile intention and open a negotiation. That day, 13 June, he marched north.

He left behind him about 100 seamen to garrison Chandernagore and took 59 more to help man his artillery. His army consisted of two improvised battalions of European infantry each 400 strong, some 190 gunners and train including the 50 seamen to work eight 6-pounder field guns and a howitzer, and 2,200 sepoys, some of them newly recruited in Bengal.

It was desperately late in the year to begin operations; the risks that Clive faced were such as to appal the most courageous. While he had been operating near Calcutta he could always shelter under the guns of the Fleet, or seek refuge in Fort William. Now he might have to confront overwhelming odds with nothing to fall back on. His strength lay in his artillery and infantry. Indian gunners, it had been said, fired at the incredibly slow rate of one round every fifteen minutes, whereas Europeans could fire without difficulty, two aimed rounds in a minute. It is difficult to envisage how Indian gunners contrived to be quite so slow, perhaps they took a few thoughtful pulls at their hookahs in between rounds; but supposing their rate of fire to be one round every 6 minutes, European gunners would be able to fire twelve rounds to their one, and six European guns could produce the same volume of fire as

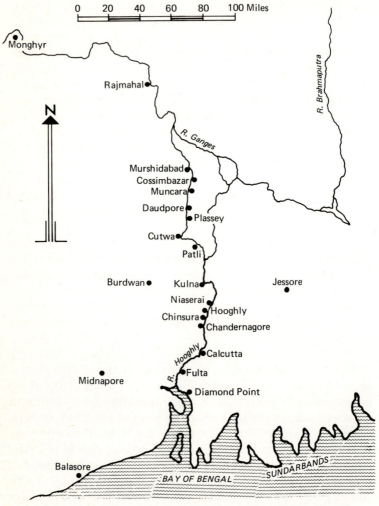

10 The Advance to Plassey. Based on details given by Robert Orme.

seventy-two Indian; even with this ratio the advantage would lie with the Europeans, as their fire would be more concentrated and easier to control and their guns more mobile.

The superiority of his European trained infantry was almost as great. Using the more dependable flintlock musket and firing in well-disciplined volleys, they had an immeasurable advantage over the undisciplined Indian levies, armed with the slow firing and unreliable matchlock. The main strength of Indian armies lay in their cavalry; but even here mercenary troopers, whose wealth consisted of their horses, had time and again refused to risk their mounts against the well-aimed grape of the European artillery. An Indian army of almost any strength was as likely to break a European battle line as a horde of Trinobantes the line of a Roman legion. But the European army had an Achilles heel, its baggage train. If the Indian cavalry hovered outside the range of grape, a mere 300 yards, by threatening the baggage train they could paralyse all movement and turn any retreat into a catastrophic rout.

Hitherto, except when operating under the guns of a fleet, the French and British had always relied on an Indian ally to provide them with cavalry, both to guard against this danger and to bring them information. When in similar circumstances Dupleix had made his bold stroke against Nazir Jang in the Carnatic, Chunda Sahib with his cavalry had accompanied the French army.

Clive had relied on Mir Jafar to supply him with cavalry, but now he was plunging into the unknown without a solitary trooper to bring him information. He knew nothing of the Indian general's plans nor of what was happening in Murshidabad. It was not impossible that Mir Jafar had made his peace with Siraj-ud-daula and that the British were marching to their destruction.

In the almost intolerable heat the little army pursued its way. His Europeans, artillery and baggage he transported in boats, but the sepoys perforce had to march. The Governor of Hooghly, after some equivocation, allowed him to pass and on the evening 13 June he camped at Niaserai

33 The landing stage at Cutwa.

some thirteen miles up the river from Chandernagore. On 14 June he reached Kulna, a bare twelve miles further on; in that fierce heat it was essential to husband the strength of his men. Despite the shortness of the march a Jemadar and the equivalent of a complete platoon of Madras sepoys deserted. At three o'clock that afternoon Watts, Collett and Sykes appeared after a dangerous and exciting ride from Cossimbazar. Watts was accompanied by Mirza Omar Beg as the personal representative of Mir Jafar.

They were in high spirits; they said that Mir Jafar's party was increasing daily in strength and had been joined by Khudadad Yar Lutuf Khan and all the artillerymen. His anxieties relieved, Clive informed the Select Committee that night, 'There is the greatest probability of a happy issue to the expedition'. On 15 June, incredibly, the heat grew even worse, unshed rain filling the atmosphere with moisture. The Europeans had disembarked and in a march of only five miles that evening, sixteen men fell out. That night Clive promoted Archibald Grant of the 39th Foot to the rank of major. Next day the Europeans were re-embarked, and in the next two days some twenty-two miles were covered, the army arriving at Patli on the evening of 17 June. Clive had thought it judicious to promote Eyre Coote to major on 16 June.

Still totally without any positive information, Clive resolved to proceed with caution. He kept the main body of his army in camp at Patli with the baggage, while he pushed forward Coote with a detachment of 200 Europeans and 500 sepoys to secure his next objective, the fort at Cutwa, fourteen miles up the river. Coote set out in boats at midday on 18 June. He disembarked his men three miles short of the fort at ten o'clock that evening, and advanced warily towards it. The fort commander was one of the conspirators, nevertheless his garrison opened fire when the British troops drew near. Early on the morning of 19 June Coote executed a skilfully planned attack, feinting with his sepoys and driving home with his Europeans. After firing a few random shots at long range the garrison fled. Coote took possession of the fort, but it was disturbing that he had encountered resistance. The fort commander clearly desired to safeguard his position should the conspiracy fail.

On 18 June, after Coote had departed for Cutwa, Clive at last received a letter from Mir Jafar written on 16 June. Mir Jafar thanked him for a letter and continued, 'I understand you marched the 25th [of the month of Ramadan] agreeable to your contract. I broke the chain of service. On the news of your coming the Nawab was much intimidated and requested at such a juncture I should stand his friend. On my part, agreeable to the circumstances of the times, I thought it advisable to acquiesce with his request, but what we have agreed must be done. I have fixed the first day of the moon for my march. God willing I shall arrive.' The rest of the letter was devoted to some meaningless good wishes for Clive's health and an anxiety that the correspondence should be kept secret.

It was a puzzling letter. It seemed clear that Mir Jafar had not yet broken with the Nawab. Presumably the reference to agreeing to be his friend was a subterfuge he thought necessary for some reason and 'what we have agreed must be done'. But other than these somewhat contradictory statements the letter gave virtually no useful information. Mir Jafar was marching the first day of the moon, this must be the new moon that would signal the festival of Id; it would fall on 19 or 20 June depending when the new moon was seen. He said nothing about his own intentions and his letter revealed nothing about the strength of the Nawab's army, its location, or his intentions. Above all it was completely silent about where Mir Jafar proposed to meet Clive and provide him with the cavalry he so desperately needed. Clive replied diplomatically, if insincerely, the same day, 'I have received your letter which gives me the utmost satisfaction after the great pain I suffered from your silence'. He ended with a plea, for more information, 'Write me what you intend to do and what it is proper for me to do. On mutual intelligence depends the success of our affairs so write me daily and fully.'

Next morning, 19 June, he heard that Coote had captured Cutwa fort and early that afternoon he marched the rest of his army forward to be reunited with Coote that evening. No letter from Mir Jafar awaited him at Cutwa and almost despairingly he wrote, 'I think it absolutely necessary that you should join my army as soon as possible, come over to me at Plassey or any other place you judge proper with what force you have. Even 1,000 horse will be sufficient and I will engage to march immediately with you to Murshidabad.'

The same night he addressed a letter to the Select Committee at Fort William, explaining the fearful uncertainties that confronted him. The heat and the strain of the past few weeks had worn him down, and in unprecedented fashion he ended his letter, 'I desire you will give me your sentiments freely how you think I should act, if Mir Jafar can give us no assistance.'

On 20 June he rested his army at Cutwa and waited anxiously for news; that day the monsoon broke. As the merciful rain sluiced down, the temperature, as always, must have dropped sharply and spirits have risen. For the next few days existence would be tolerable, then the heat and the moisture would combine and the fiery furnace of the past few weeks be exchanged for the sweltering humidity of a Turkish bath. For the moment the rain brought inexpressible relief, but it also served notice that the campaigning season was nearly at an end. Soon torrential rain would fill the paddy fields and turn the roads into rivers of mud.

Yet still there was nothing to show that Mir Jafar had broken with the Nawab. As he sat waiting in Cutwa fort with no cavalry or reliable information of any sort, Clive was like a man groping his way across a darkened room knowing that sooner or later he must trip and fall. Who did Mir Jafar intend to betray? Clive had with him almost every soldier from the army in Bengal and substantial contingents from Madras and Bombay. How much longer dare he risk the larger part of the Company's military resources in India in this absurd and perilous game of blind-man's buff, with an enemy immensely stronger than himself and with friends, if friends they were, afraid to show their hands. It was time an element of sanity was introduced into this lunatic intrigue dreamed up by Watts. There was plenty of grain in the fort and it was rumoured that the granaries in the villages nearby were full. He could remain at Cutwa during the monsoon like a brooding eagle crouched at the gates of Murshidabad. His very presence might unnerve the young Prince and let the British retire from this tangled affair with a modicum of honour.

If Siraj-ud-daula remained unmoved, then in the autumn the Mahrattas could be invited in and a proper plan of campaign concerted with reliable allies. The more Clive considered the matter, the more certain he became that to advance further, unless certain that Mir Jafar intended to join him, would be an act of arrant folly.

But if he abandoned the conspiracy and stayed at Cutwa, the grounds for his decision would almost certainly be questioned, particularly by those in Calcutta who bore him ill-will. It would be wise to have his decision backed by the formal declaration of a Council of War. He ordered one to assemble at his quarters the next morning, 21 June 1757. That night no courier rode in, and next morning no messenger stumbled into the fort to disturb his breakfast. Nothing had changed. His mind made up, Clive went to preside over the assembled Council. It consisted of the three majors, all the captains, the captain lieutenants, and Lieutenant Hayter RN commanding the detachment of sailors, eighteen individuals in all.

The proceedings opened with an element of comedy introduced by the Navy. Lieutenant Hayter claimed precedence over all the Company's captains, and when Clive refused his claim he declined to take any further part in the Council. It is doubtful if his withdrawal deprived the members of any illumination on their problems, but it has a certain magnificence. The Navy considered its precedence of greater importance than debating an issue of life and death. Such men would be hard to beat.

Having disposed of the Royal Navy, Clive outlined the situation. The Nawab had an army of 50,000 men, Mir Jafar could be depended upon for nothing more than remaining neutral, Law with a body of Frenchmen (probably not much more than 150 Europeans and the same number of sepoys) was within three days' march. The issue was whether to make an immediate attack on the Nawab or to remain in Cutwa during the rains, after which the Mahrattas might be induced to enter the country as allies. He did not invite discussion, but posed the question in the following terms: 'Whether in our present situation without assistance and on our own bottom it would be prudent to attack the Nawab or whether we should wait until joined by some country power?'

Clive then took the lead and himself voted against an attack. Killpatrick came next and dutifully followed his example. Coote, of course, was not to be suppressed and as usual disagreed with his commander. With a deference that rings slightly false, he said that, since he differed from his commander, he ought to give his reasons. He went on,

'We have hitherto met with nothing but success which consequently has given great spirit to our men, and I am of the opinion that any delay might cast damp. Secondly, the arrival of Mr Law will not only strengthen the Nabob's [Nawab's] army, but likewise weaken our force considerably, as the number of Frenchmen we have entered into our service after the capture of Chandernagore will undoubtedly desert to him upon every opportunity. Thirdly, our distance from Calcutta is so great that communication from thence will be cut short and therefore give no room to hope for supplies. Therefore in my opinion we should come to an immediate action, or if that is considered impracticable, we should return to Calcutta, the consequence of which must be our disgrace and the inevitable destruction of the Company's affairs.'

He then voted for an immediate attack.

In a nutshell, Coote argued that it was impossible to remain at Cutwa during the rains, a retreat would be disastrous, therefore there was no real alternative to going forward. Although the motion not to move was carried by ten votes to seven, it was significant that four out of the six Bengal army officers present voted with Coote for an immediate attack.

Clive had obtained the decision that he wanted, but almost at once he began to doubt its wisdom; despite the way the question had been framed, a substantial minority had voted in favour of an immediate action, and that minority included a majority of the officers most experienced in local conditions. Clive did not often relish opposition, but on this occasion it must have been both surprising and invigorating. The resolution had been worded in such a way that it did not preclude the possibility of continuing the advance, and now when he came to forward the proceedings to Calcutta he watered it down still more, writing in his covering letter, 'I wait only for some encouragement from Mir Jafar to proceed.'

But no encouragement came. As the day wore on Clive's doubts multiplied. He drafted another letter to the Select Committee purporting to ask for advice, although it must have been obvious that, whatever its tenor, it would surely be too late to be of any service. Perhaps he wished to clear his mind by setting out his conclusions in writing, or perhaps he wished to have the views of the Select Committee recorded on paper at that time, so that some of the lambs in wolves' clothing in Calcutta could not bay him in the future. He began:

'Since my last, another letter has been delivered to Mir Jafar and no answer returned in writing. I am really at a loss how to act. . . . The Nawab's forces at present are not said to exceed 8,000 men . . . if we attack them it must be entrenched and ourselves without any assistance. In this place a repulse must be fatal, on the contrary success may give the greatest advantage . . . perhaps he may be glad to offer us an honourable peace . . . there still remains another expedient of sending an embassy to Ghazi-ud-din Khan or the Mahrattas to invite them. I beg you will let me have your sentiments how I should act.'

As he considered his 'another expedient' it must have seemed increasingly dubious. It meant waiting until the monsoon rains were finished, and who could guess what would then be the situation in Bengal, or anywhere else for that matter. But an attack on the detachment of 8,000 men reported to be entrenched in the camp some three miles beyond Plassey could have promising results. A repulse did not bear thinking about. Plassey was on the Cossimbazar island formed by two arms of the Ganges delta; if he was compelled to withdraw, hounded by the enemy cavalry at every step he would have to recross the river; in such circumstances few of his army would ever see Calcutta again. If, however, he routed the defenders and captured the camp, it might spur Mir Jafar to declare himself; if he did not, Siraj-ud-daula was far too foolish to realise the strength of his position; he would almost certainly panic, and conclude a peace on terms sufficiently advantageous for the British to claim a success and gloss over their failure to obtain the true objectives of the expedition. Without cavalry the advance to Plassey would be dangerous, the whole enterprise bristled with dangers, but it was not in Clive's nature to concede defeat by default. Some time in the late afternoon or evening that day[1] he resolved to override the decision of

---

[1] The circumstances in which Clive made this decision have been disputed. Scrafton claimed that after receiving a letter from Mir Jafar at 3 p.m. next day, 22 June, Clive decided to disregard the decision of the Council of War and that the army marched at five o'clock that evening for Plassey. Forrest, in his biography of Clive, accepted Scrafton's version and accordingly stated that Clive decided to ignore the decision of the Council of War only after he had received Mir Jafar's letter. Yet the timings make this impossible. If Clive did not decide to march to Plassey until after he received the letter at 3 p.m., his army could never have marched out at 5 p.m. a mere two hours later. To examine this in more detail; Clive received the letter at 3 p.m., say by 3.10 p.m. he took the decision to move. He would then have to prepare his orders, consider his order of march, scales of ammunition to be carried, action to be taken if the river crossing was opposed, or enemy met en route, allocation of boats to baggage, etc., etc. He could not have issued his orders until 3.30–3.45 p.m. and they would have taken perhaps half an hour to issue. In addition all sorts of other problems would have arisen, a battalion would have had a working party out bringing back grain and not due back until 5.30 p.m., the only officer with the key to the reserve ammunition would have disappeared into Cutwa village to find a blacksmith to repair some damaged muskets and so on. Even if by some miracle of organisation such difficulties were overcome, a panic move at short notice would be the worst possible prelude to a hazardous night march over unreconnoitred country.

Apart from the question of military probability, there is plenty of evidence to show that Clive must have made up his mind before 3 p.m. on 22 June. On 22 June he wrote two letters to Mir Jafar. But why should he write two replies to Mir Jafar

the Council of War and to attack the camp at Plassey. He summoned his officers and outlined his plan. It must have been on the following lines.

Next morning, 22 June, at dawn a strong detachment under Coote would cross the river, take up a position on the far bank to protect the crossing and reconnoitre the routes forward. Owing to the danger of attack by cavalry the march to Plassey would be carried out almost entirely at night; the main body should leave Cutwa at five o'clock in the evening, join Coote and the whole continue to Plassey. A British subaltern with a platoon of Europeans, 100 sepoys and all the unfit men and surplus baggage would be left in the fort.

---

at a time when every moment of his time would be occupied? It seems logical to suppose that he wrote his first letter in the morning before he heard from Mir Jafar, yet in this letter he announced he would be crossing the river 'this evening' (the two letters are quoted on pp. 249, 251.

Finally Eyre Coote in his journal recorded that the army crossed the river at six o'clock in the morning of 22 June, halted the far side of the river and went on to Plassey that evening, while Clive's military journal stated that the army marched for Plassey at 5 p.m. that night. The two statements are not irreconcilable. Coote was probably sent across the river early in the morning to secure a bridgehead and cover the crossing of the main body in the evening. It would be a sound way to carry out a difficult and dangerous tactical manoeuvre. Orme in his history stated that Clive changed his mind an hour after the Council of War. This is probably too soon. The whole issue was bedevilled by a somewhat irrelevant argument as to whether or not it was on Coote's advice that Clive advanced; a decision and the responsibility for a decision rests squarely on the shoulders of the commander, not on his advisers.

Chapter 12

THE BATTLE OF PLASSEY
June 1757

In Murshidabad at the beginning of June Siraj-ud-daula, for the first time since the British recaptured Calcutta, felt relaxed and at ease. The Mahrattas could attempt nothing before the autumn and he had heard that the Afghans were withdrawing from Delhi; Ghazi-ud-din, the Wazir of the Emperor, had responded favourably to his overtures; and the British had broken up their camp near Chandernagore and the majority gone back to Calcutta. The fast of Ramzan had started when no true believer may eat, or more taxing drink, between sunrise and sunset; it was therefore no time for activity, although towards the end of the month-long fast, particularly when, as on this occasion, it occurred just before the monsoon, men sometimes went a little mad.

But now Siraj-ud-daula enjoyed a few days of tranquillity, the last tranquil days of his life. It was true he was at odds with Mir Jafar; on 4 June he had deprived him of his post as Commander-in-Chief and sent men to arrest him, who had been repelled by Mir Jafar's retainers. However, he intended to disband most of his army, leaving only a detachment at the great entrenched camp near Plassey which had been constructed by Rai Durlabh. It would save him some money, and indeed it seemed a pointless extravagance to pay his soldiers their arrears of pay; they could always be paid if they had to be recalled, and it would make them more anxious to rejoin if the need arose.

There had been a rumour that the British meditated some mischief, and he had at once dispatched messengers to tell Law to return, but the bazar was always buzzing with rumours and nothing seemed to happen. Law, himself, after so many orders and counter-orders, supposed this to be yet another false alarm and continued on his way to Patna, arriving on 3 June to a warm welcome from the Governor, Ram Narain. He did, however, order his deputy, St Frais,[1] who had come to him after the fall of Chandernagore, to go to Murshidabad with an escort of forty Europeans, both to show his readiness to assist the Nawab and to re-establish contact with his Court. When St Frais reached Murshidabad, he found the Nawab in no hurry to see him, and it was not until 8 June that he was granted his first audience.

Then, so Law recorded in his journal, St Frais observed, 'Siraj-ud-daula had not the least suspicion of the English, and did not even wish to have any, for this troubled a tranquillity for which he had so long sighed and which he had enjoyed for a few days only'. On 19 June Law received a letter dated 10 June purporting to come from the Nawab and bidding him remain in Patna. Afterwards he suspected it to be a forgery. At the time, the slowness of its delivery made him wonder if the messenger had been bribed. If the letter was a forgery, there would seem to have been a certain lack of co-ordination among the conspirators, if they also arranged to delay it. Whatever the reason, Law started back from Patna too late to have any influence on events.

The disappearance of the British from Cossimbazar on the night of 12 June sounded a knell in the ears of the Nawab. Clive, the man he most feared, was on the march. Forgetting for the moment his cruelty and duplicity, it is possible to feel a pang of pity for the doomed young Prince, sitting in his palace surrounded on every side by treachery. On 13 June he wrote with some dignity to Admiral Watson;

'According to my promises and the agreement made between us I have duly rendered everything to Mr Watts except a

---

[1] Spelled in Jean Law's journal 'Sinfray'. The pronunciation, of course, is the same.

very small remainder ... notwithstanding all this, Mr Watts and the rest of the Council at Cossimbazar fled away in the night. This is an evident mark of deceit and of an intention to break the treaty. I am convinced it could not have happened without your knowledge and without your advice. I praise God that the breach of the treaty has not been on my part. God and his prophets have been witness to the contract made between us, and whoever first deviates from it will bring upon themselves the punishment due to their actions.'

He hastily ordered his army to reassemble and then humbly took himself to Mir Jafar's palace to seek a reconciliation.

Mir Jafar, generally recognised in the past as an honourable and upright man,[1] was perplexed by almost insoluble problems of personal conduct. He owed his position to Alivardi Khan and had married his half-sister. On the old Nawab's deathbed he had pledged himself on the Koran to be faithful to Siraj-ud-daula. He had honoured the pledge and made certain that the young Prince succeeded to the viceregal throne, or *musnud* as it was called.

But since then Siraj-ud-daula, unable to control his temper, had spat on him and reviled him; he had been made to swallow insults that he felt no man could endure with honour; he had been compelled to do obeisance to Mohan Lal; finally he had been deprived of his post as Commander-in-Chief, and only the exertions of his own retainers had saved him from imprisonment. Now, when the Prince came imploring his forgiveness and help, and reminded him of the holy oath he had sworn to his great uncle, Mir Jafar must have been deeply perplexed. And the appalling heat at that time of year, combined with the excruciating thirst engendered by a strict observance of Ramzan, must have made rational thought almost impossible. He described the action he took in a curiously worded letter dated 19 June, to his agent Mirza Omar Beg, at that time with Clive.

[1] Jean Law's journal. Yet Law had no reason to be grateful to Mir Jafar.

'I was to be with him on three conditions. I consented to it. One that I would not enter his service, secondly I would not visit him and thirdly I would not take post in his army. As he wanted me he consented. But I took in writing from all the commanders of the army and artillery, that when they had conquered the English they should be bound to see me and my family safe wherever I chose to go. By the blessing of God I will pray on the Id day at the Cuttlee mosque, and shall then join the army.'

Mir Jafar's meaning seems as confused as was probably his mind. His words imply that he no longer contemplated allying himself with Clive, but that he would neither support nor oppose the Nawab. In return, the Nawab's generals had guaranteed him and his family a safe-conduct to the refuge of his choice, after they had defeated the English. Meanwhile he and his men were to remain with the army. This last proviso may seem a little strange, but, after the fashion of the great nobles in medieval Europe, the great men of the realm maintained their own private armies. Possibly Siraj-ud-daula did not like to leave Mir Jafar and his men at Murshidabad while he was away fighting the English, and Mir Jafar, as a mark of good faith, assented to accompanying him.

The Indian General must have been racked by hopelessly conflicting loyalties. When Siraj-ud-daula threatened his life and his honour, he could scarcely be blamed for conspiring for his overthrow. When, however, the Prince pleaded for his aid and reminded him of his oath, his conscience must have been vexed. It is true that he should have considered all this before, and recognised that once he had signed the treaty there was no turning back, but it would almost certainly be wrong to attribute his apparently pusillanimous conduct to fear. A British victory was ardently to be desired as it solved all his perplexities, but he was doubtful how far, in honour, he could promote such an end.

In his letter to Mirza Omar Beg he also mentioned that the Nawab's soldiers, mutinous over the Nawab's refusal to pay them, refused to leave the capital. The Prince must have realised that economy, however praiseworthy in general, was mistaken at such a time, and doled out sufficient to persuade them to march. On the morning of 20 June his army left the neighbourhood of Murshidabad and encamped the same evening at Muncara. Here Mir Jafar joined it and wrote an undated letter to Clive, for in it he remarked that the Nawab had marched to Muncara that day.

Possibly hearing that Clive had halted at Cutwa, on 21 or 22 June the Nawab decided not to remain at Muncara, but to advance to his entrenched camp near Plassey. The gloomy, distraught young Prince seemed intent on rushing to meet his doom. Law observed that he should have remained at Murshidabad, imprisoned Mir Jafar and Rai Durlabh and awaited his return from Patna. Such a policy, if it were possible, must have frustrated the British design, but perhaps the wretched Nawab had so alienated his subjects and army that, after his failure to arrest Mir Jafar, he doubted his ability to master those he suspected of plotting against him, and sought to commit his army to battle before its members could turn on himself or each other. But he is unlikely to have thought out a plan; he probably drifted along on the impulse of the moment. By the evening of 22 June he bivouacked about Daudpore, some six miles from his camp near Plassey; with his large army said to number 15,000 horse, 35,000 infantry and about 50 guns his bivouac area must have been extensive and have stretched a considerable distance to the south.

On the morning of 22 June, Clive, still uncertain if Siraj-ud-daula had even left Murshidabad, wrote to Mir Jafar. 'I am determined to risk everything on your account. . . . I shall be on the other side of the river this evening. If you will join me at Plassey I will march half way to meet you . . . but if you cannot go even to this length to assist us, I will call God to witness the fault is not mine, and I must desire your consent to concluding a peace with the Nawab.'

Perhaps feeling with good reason unable to trust his ally too far, he did not mention his intention of marching on Plassey himself. Then at three o'clock that afternoon, as he

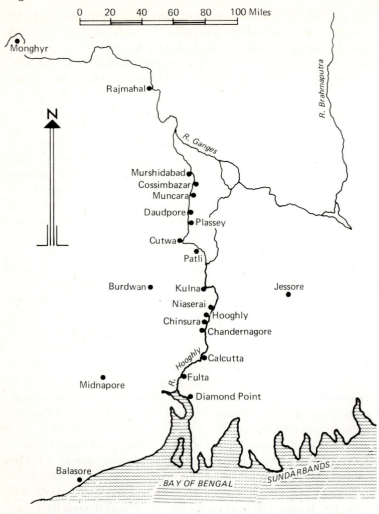

was preparing to leave Cutwa, an undated letter from Mir Jafar was delivered; it read:

'I have received your letter advising the taking of Cutwa and was highly pleased. . . . The Nawab marched today from Tarrackpore and has pitched his tent at Muncara near the bridge. The Nawab's intention is to have his entrenchment at Muncara, therefore the sooner you fall on him the better before his design can take place. When you come near I shall then be able to join you . . . when I am arrived near the army I will send you privately all the intelligence.'

If the letter is sincere Mir Jafar must have once again changed his mind. To Clive the letter was more than welcome. It gave him his first positive information about the Nawab, and if the Prince's army was entrenching a position at Muncara fifteen miles north of Plassey, he could strike at the entrenched camp next morning without fear of interference. There was no longer any purpose in concealing the object of his move. Before setting out he scribbled a reply, 'Upon receiving your letter I am come to a resolution to proceed immediately to Plassey. I am impatient for an answer to my letter by the trusty man.' (Presumably the letter he had sent that morning by a reliable emissary.)

His anxieties in some measure abated, he set out for Plassey. Rain fell steadily and it was a fatiguing and unpleasant march. As the column plodded on through the black night with the rain sheeting down out of the darkness, it became very strung out, and although the head reached Plassey grove just before midnight, the last files did not stumble in until three o'clock in the morning of 23 June 1757.

The position that Clive had selected lay about a mile south of the Nawab's entrenched camp; its main feature was a large orchard of mango trees near the river, which was bordered by an earth bank and ditch making it virtually a readymade entrenchment. It was 800 yards long, 300 yards wide and roughly rectangular in shape; its long sides ran nearly parallel to the river, its northwestern corner being only 50 yards and the southwestern 200 yards from the riverbank. Just to the north and actually on the bank had been constructed a hunting lodge for the Nawab surrounded by a wall. To the west lay the river, but otherwise the hunting lodge and the orchard lay in a flat, open plain some three or four miles in extent. Clive, himself, occupied the hunting lodge and placed 500 men in its grounds; the

34 The Nawab's hunting lodge at Plassey, after a water-colour of 1801.

remainder of his damp, bedraggled army bivouacked with his baggage in the orchard; his boats, which he had prudently brought with him, were beached on the riverbank nearby.

As with the dawn the eastern skies began to lighten to reveal a dark and overcast sky, the rain eased off. From the roof of the Hunting Lodge the Nawab's entrenched camp could be seen unexpectedly close. Its edge nearest the British consisted of a low breastwork and ditch jutting out eastwards for about 200 yards from the bank of the river, before turning sharply to run northeast. No messenger had met Clive at Plassey and nothing had been seen of Mir Jafar's army. Just before dawn, Clive sat down in the hunting lodge and by the light of a candle scrawled what he may well have thought to be his final plea to his enigmatic fellow conspirator. 'Whatever could be done by me I have done. I can do no more. If you will come to Daudpore I will march from Plassey to meet you, but if you won't comply with this, pardon me, I shall make it up with the Nawab.' He handed the letter to Mirza Omar Beg, who dispatched it at seven o'clock that morning.

But a little after six o'clock, before the letter had even gone

THE BATTLE OF PLASSEY 253

the watchers on the roof of the hunting lodge discerned movement in the plain; about three miles to the northeast a moving dark cloud had come into view that steadily expanded and drew nearer.[1] Earlier that night it had been reported that Rai Durlabh with a body of troops was encamped at Daudpore, but as the cloud began to break up into distinct bodies of troops, a multitude of horsemen, infantry, bullock trains drawing guns, and gorgeously caparisoned elephants flowed across the plain. Before the awestruck watchers on the roof the whole of the Nawab's army, 50,000 strong came into view. It must have been a terrible moment for Clive. Mir Jafar had betrayed him and lured him into a trap. Before that host of cavalry a retreat in daylight would be disastrous, he had to put up a bold front and then under cover of darkness, slip back down the river to Cutwa and thence to Calcutta. However, there was no time to consider what would happen when he and his army slunk back to Calcutta, the immediate peril was too great for time to be wasted in futile regrets and recriminations.

He formed his European infantry into four grand divisions each of about 180 men, appointing Killpatrick, Grant, Coote and Gaupp as the divisional commanders, and divided his sepoys up into two wings each a thousand strong. On the left, with their flank resting on the hunting lodge he placed one wing of the sepoys, in the centre a few yards forward of the orchard his Europeans, and on the right flank, projecting out into the plain, the other wing of the sepoys; in the intervals between divisions and units his field guns poked their muzzles. To make the greatest possible showing he held no reserve whatsoever, and the slender scarlet line,

[1] Orme writes, 'The continued sound of drums, clarions and cymbals which always accompany the night watches of an Indian army convinced them they were within a mile of the Nawab's army.' This makes nonsense of Clive's letter. If the whole of the Nawab's army had been identified in front of him there would be no point in giving Mir Jafar a rendezvous at Daudpore, six miles to the north, and Clive would have made his plans to deal with the situation before dawn. When Clive wrote his letter he must have assumed that the entrenchment was not too strongly held, and that the main enemy army was still at Muncara. The news that Rai Durlabh was at Daudpore might have encouraged him to think that the conspirators had at last acted and that Mir Jafar was at hand.

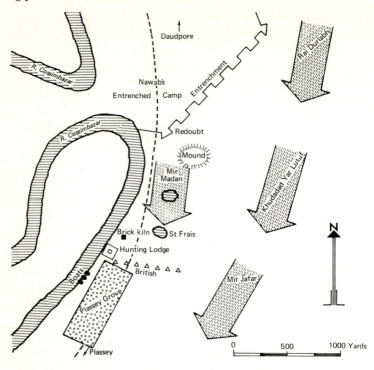

11 The Battle of Plassey. The shape of the river has been taken from Rennell's map, and the remaining details drawn from the distances given in contemporary accounts, selecting the most probable where they clash. The British here called the Bhagirathi the Cossimbazar River.

three ranks deep, from its left by the hunting lodge to its right in the plain stretched about 1,000 yards.

At about eight o'clock a solitary 24-pounder boomed out from the entrenched camp; its ball, ricocheting over the ground, tore off the arm of a grenadier in the 39th. The battle had begun. Soon in front of the British line long bullock trains appeared, the bullocks harnessed in pairs and hauling the heavy guns affected by all Indian armies; cannon began to crown every slight rise in the ground, but separately and at some distance from each other. Behind the cannon massive bodies of infantry and cavalry took their station; in the plain

THE BATTLE OF PLASSEY 255

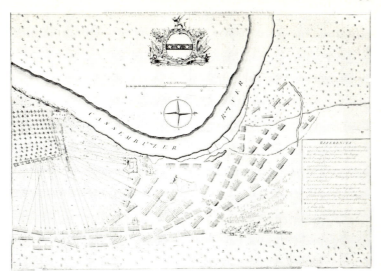

35 An old plan of the Battle of Plassey, probably made a few years after the event. It shows the dispositions after Clive had withdrawn his men into the orchard.

to the east more heavy columns of foot and horse started to menace the open British right flank and behind them away to the northeast long trains of oxen could be perceived dragging forward innumerable cannon accompanied by yet more infantry and cavalry. Clive pointed only three of his guns at the enemy in front,[1] deploying the remainder to compel the cavalry threatening his right to keep their distance.

A brisk artillery duel broke out. Then, on the embankment of a large artificial pond only 300 yards from the British line, a well-drilled battery of four guns came smartly into action. St Frais with his forty Frenchmen, turned gunners for the occasion, had joined the battle; now about twelve guns were pounding the British line from in front.

When his men fell-in for battle, Clive had noted that they jested and seemed utterly unimpressed by the immense numbers confronting them. The whole army radiated confidence and an eagerness for battle. Clive wondered if,

[1] Letter to the Select Committee of 24 June.

after all, a retreat would be necessary, he had never retreated before, had written to Mir Jafar in lofty terms about joining him with 5,000 men who had never turned their backs, should he do so now? With the men he commanded anything was possible; he resolved to hold the position by day then attack the Nawab's army under cover of darkness.

But meanwhile the fire from St Frais's guns, half protected by the embankment and in a commanding position, was beginning to smash gaps in his ranks. There was no merit in leaving his men to be knocked over like nine-pins. An assault on the French guns meant offering a still more vulnerable right flank to the cavalry in the plain, and would also deprive his men of the benefit of the defensive position he had chosen so shrewdly. Except for the three guns in front he ordered the rest of his men to withdraw within the orchard while preserving their battle order. Now with its left flank protected by the river, the men under cover, and its right guarded by the long eastern edge of the orchard, the small British army could face any attack with composure; in particular the orchard, with the bank and ditch on its borders and the trees behind, formed a singularly unpromising target for a charge by cavalry.

In the orchard some embrasures were hacked out for the guns, then the infantry lay down in comparative safety. In front the enemy hung well back behind their guns and out of range of the British 6-pounder field guns; Clive's two field guns and a howitzer with some audacity moved out to some brick kilns about 150 yards in front of the hunting lodge, and brought them under a hot fire. However, as the enemy cavalry slowly encircled his right, the guns became too exposed and Cliver ordered them back behind cover.

While the cannon boomed on, the enemy cavalry, keeping discreetly out of range of the British artillery, gradually extended round the right-hand face of the orchard, while at the same time long trains of oxen with their cannon crawled across the plain, swung round in succession, and dropped their guns into action, gradually forming a great arc round the right flank of the British. As through the morning the guns thundered on, it is not difficult to envisage the scene.

THE BATTLE OF PLASSEY 257

The grey lowering skies, the little humps in the plain with the tiny figures clustered round, and behind rank on rank the horses of the cavalry tossing their heads and stamping impatiently, with here and there a general watching the battle from his elephant.

From a little hump there would be a sudden spurt of flame followed by a puff of white smoke and the dull thump of the discharge, to be succeeded by the whining note of the roundshot rising to a crescendo before burying itself with a thump into the bank, or else slamming into the trees overhead bringing boughs and trunks crashing to the ground. Then there would be another spurt of flame over to the right, then one over to the left, and the roundshot whirring and cracking overhead.

To the inexperienced the scene would be intimidating enough, but to Clive's veteran soldiers, assured of their relative safety, it probably sounded a battle music that made the blood tingle in their veins. As the cannonade continued Clive called for his field officers and captains to assemble, then for some reason abruptly cancelled his order. He felt comfortable enough. His men were concentrated behind cover in a strong position; they could never be broken by any troops that the Nawab could bring against him, and at night he would go over to the attack. All might yet turn out well. About midday an alarming report came in that the enemy had penetrated right round the orchard to the boats behind. A party of sepoys was sent to investigate and found the report false. At about the same time the heavens opened and for more than half an hour the rain lashed down. It seemed a wonderful opportunity for the enemy cavalry to attack, while the firing pans of the British infantry were wet and their muskets incapable of firing. The mass of cavalry between the entrenched camp and the orchard swayed forward, but the British gunners kept their powder dry and before their steady fire the attack petered out. During the brief advance, Mir Madan, the general commanding the sector and the ablest of those still loyal to the Nawab, was mortally wounded and Mohan Lal's son-in-law, Bahadur Ali Khan, killed.

The Nawab's artillerymen had been unskilful in warding off the rain, and their guns fell silent. The mass of enemy in front, discouraged by the death of their general and the lack of artillery support, started to drift back towards the entrenched camp. It appeared to Clive that the enemy had abandoned any serious intention of mounting an attack; he returned to the shelter of the hunting lodge and forbade any forward movement without his permission. St Frais, his gunners also suffering from the dampness of their powder, seeing the infantry and cavalry behind him disappearing in the direction of the entrenched camp perceived he was in danger of becoming isolated and followed their example.

A sudden stillness descended on the battlefield. Killpatrick, noting the enemy had evacuated the commanding bank by the artificial pond, despite his orders took his division forward with two guns and occupied it, driving away a few stragglers. Clive was about to change his drenched garments when he learned what was happening. In a justifiable rage he rushed out to expostulate, and for a moment seemed to contemplate putting his old comrade under arrest. But he quickly recovered his poise; to retire might be fatal; he sent Killpatrick back to take command in the orchard while he remained at what might be a crucial position.

He ordered up Eyre Coote with his division and two more guns. But as Coote came up St Frais at a redoubt near the entrance to the entrenched camp brought his guns again into action. The battle flared up. Horse and infantry poured out of the camp and formed in front of the British by the pond. Clive now was in something of a dilemma. With his right flank in the open an easy target for the cavalry, he dared not advance far from the protection of the orchard. He ordered his troops still manning the right-hand face of the orchard to advance into the plain. Without hesitation his men left their cover, but the enemy cavalry were not provoked into a charge and were too far away for the British infantry to assault, a somewhat hazardous undertaking at any time. Since his men had merely become a target for the enemy guns, he ordered them back into the orchard.

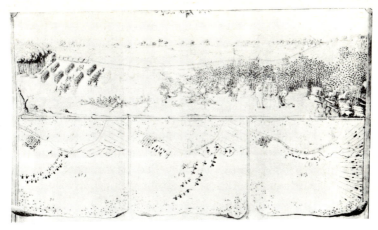

36 The Battle of Plassey. The scene depicted appears to represent the counter-attack by the Nawab's army after Killpatrick had made his advance. The British troops are, however, shown unduly close to the orchard. The contrast between the disordered host of Siraj-ud-daula and the ordered ranks of Clive's army is striking.

Two or three times he rode over to Killpatrick to tell him to bring forward the remainder of the army, but each time he countermanded the move—with that mass of cavalry in the plain it appeared inexcusably rash. But meanwhile the battle by the pond was going well. St Frais's guns still seemed to have been affected by the rain and were causing few casualties. The four British guns, however, had been extremely effective. When the enemy artillery which had retired within the camp tried to come out again, the British guns played on their bullocks with such success that most were left stranded. With great courage, enemy horse and infantry pressed forward within 150 yards of the British line, but, unsupported by their own artillery, they could not withstand the showers of grape from the British guns and the well-aimed volleys from the infantry. The enemy commanders on their elephants were both conspicuous and vulnerable, and four or five were picked off, the great beasts that carried them spreading disorder among the ranks behind.

Some enemy had taken cover behind a second artificial pond about 600 yards from their camp. Clive saw that the enemy in front of him were wavering, and perhaps by now he had begun to suspect that the cavalry in the plain had no intention of joining the battle; or perhaps with that intuitive feeling that distinguishes a great commander he sensed that the moment of decision had arrived. It was now about four o'clock in the afternoon. Despite his earlier resolve to wait for nightfall he decided to advance at once. He ordered forward his European and sepoy grenadier companies to assault the second pond; with levelled bayonets they swept forward; their enemy did not wait for them. Clive had with him only about 350 Europeans and two or three companies of sepoys, but the enemy was reeling backwards and now was the time to strike. He directed Coote and his men to attack the French guns, and himself led the remainder of his men towards a low mound that overlooked the angle of the breastwork where it turned northeast. Already the enemy were streaming from the battlefield in droves, and the two charges met with little resistance; the Frenchmen, smelling defeat, abandoned their guns and left the battlefield without firing another round. As the British stormed into the camp all resistance collapsed. It was then about five o'clock and the battle was over.

Clive called up Killpatrick, thrust right through the camp and pressed on towards Daudpore. Since he had no cavalry and men formed in ranks inevitably moved considerably slower than men running for their lives, the pursuit inflicted few casualties, but most of the army that had remained loyal to the Nawab was utterly dispersed. All his baggage and some forty of his cannon were captured. At Daudpore, six miles to the north, Clive halted the pursuit; it was probably between seven and seven-thirty in the evening; here Killpatrick joined him with the rest of the army; of Siraj-ud-daula there had been no sign.

That morning Siraj-ud-daula had ensconced himself in a tent in the entrenched camp. It is not clear what he was intending to do that day, whether he knew Clive was at Plassey Grove, or whether he thought that he was still at

Cutwa. When the battle began, the knowledge he was fighting Clive seems to have paralysed him.[1] He stayed inert in his tent, incapable of action. He may have had a moment of jubilation when he heard that the British were retreating into the orchard, but it must have been very short lived. Then sometime about noon Mir Madan, the only general he could really trust, was brought into his tent to die. Early in the afternoon, in desperation, he sent for Mir Jafar and implored his aid. Mir Jafar can have had nothing but contempt for the Prince skulking in his tent instead of riding out on to the battlefield mounted on his elephant. He subsequently recounted that the Nawab threw his turban at his feet and implored his assistance. He coldly advised his Prince to withdraw within the entrenched camp, and rode away. The advice was sound enough, but he could see that the nerve of Siraj-ud-daula was already shattered, and he sent a message to Clive, telling him that if he attacked that night the battle was his. His messenger never arrived until the fighting was finished.

During the afternoon the noise of firing outside the camp reached a new intensity and came steadily nearer to Siraj-ud-daula's tent. As it became clear that the entrenched camp itself was threatened, terror overcame him, and at about four o'clock he called for a riding camel and bolted for Murshidabad to be the first to announce his own defeat. Once it was known that he had gone, according to the accepted convention of the day, the battle was over and the British had won.

Thus Clive gained the most famous of his victories and the cost on both sides was remarkably light. The Europeans had some twenty-eight men killed and wounded of whom eleven were gunners, while the sepoys suffered fifty-two casualties. The losses in Siraj-ud-daula's army were estimated at about 500. Like all Clive's battles, Plassey had been a curious affair, differing profoundly from the studied, formal and

---

[1] Scrafton has a vivid description of the Nawab alone in his tent the night before the battle. Since Clive did not leave the neighbourhood of Cutwa until five o'clock that evening, it is doubtful if either commander expected to fight a battle next day.

murderous encounters customary in Europe. The numbers of the Nawab's army that remained loyal to him on the day possibly amounted to about 12,000 including all the artillerymen, but of these no doubt a number were disgruntled over his failure to pay them except under duress. As the casualties, relative to the forces engaged on both sides, were so light there has been a tendency to regard the battle as little more than a skirmish, which Clive virtually won by the defection of the conspirators before it began. It was a mistake that his contemporaries never made; after Plassey, the knowledge that Clive had taken the field with an army was sufficient for his foes to concede him victory without going through the formality of actually fighting a battle.

At Cutwa he had been confronted with an unnerving number of imponderables; he knew nothing about the strength or intentions of his enemy; he might well have been betrayed and marching towards disaster. He had grave doubts, but preserved the balance of his judgement and did not take counsel of his fears. If, in 1745, he had been with Bonnie Prince Charlie in Derby, it is not too much to suppose that the Jacobites would have marched on London—and captured it.

But not only did he advance from Cutwa, he did it with such superb tactical skill that, when he was surprised by an army ostensibly 50,000-strong, he was able to stand and fight in a defensive position from which he could defy almost any odds. Had he been caught at a disadvantage, it is not unlikely that at least some of the conspirators might have forgotten their pledges and redeemed their treachery by being foremost in the field. Clive's victory was the triumph of a great soldier and statesman, but he owed not a little to his soldiers, who, ignorant of complicated conspiracies, watched unperturbed an army nearly twenty times their strength deploy before them, and then executed everything that was demanded of them with never a backward glance.

That evening Mir Jafar asked Mirza Omar Beg to come out to him with Watts, for it was urgent to concert plans for the future, and next morning he went to Daudpore. Not surprisingly, as he rode into the British camp on his elephant

37 The meeting between Clive and Mir Jafar at Daudpore. Clive's horse appears to dislike elephants.

he felt a little nervous about his reception. He had done nothing during the battle but send futile messages to Clive, which never arrived until the battle was concluded. Clive, however, at once reassured him and greeted him as Nawab.

But Mir Jafar's devious political contortions were to have immense significance and fatally to undermine his power when he succeeded Siraj-ud-daula. To all India, it appeared that a tiny British army, on its own, had unseated one of the great viceroys of the old Moghul Empire; there were now few who doubted that the British were the true arbiters of power in Bengal. However understandable his scruples, Mir Jafar's hesitations scarcely marked him out as possessing those qualities of foresight, resolution and decision he would need to rule his great realm. Clive had conquered his kingdom for him, and the relations between King and king-maker seldom run smoothly. Clive's problems and those of the Company were far from being over.

Chapter 13

THE AFTERMATH
1757-8

When Clive welcomed Mir Jafar at Daudpore, he must have looked back on the past six months almost with incredulity. At Fulta in December he had joined a disconsolate British community tolerated by the Nawab only on account of its insignificance. Now that community was the real, if undeclared, master of a realm with a population of perhaps 20 million.

It was an extraordinary reversal of fortune, and one in which chance, on occasion, seemed almost to play the dominant part; paradoxically, even Clive's disagreements with Admiral Watson worked in the long run to his benefit. While the French held Chandernagore a British advance on Murshidabad was inconceivable. Clive, conscious that a firm alliance between the Nawab and the French must prove fatal for the British, twice tried to neutralise the Hooghly river; each time Admiral Watson thwarted him, not through his own understanding of the complex Indian political scene, but rather because he never grasped how precarious was the British hold in Bengal.

Then, after Watson had blocked any possibility of coming to terms with the French, fate, as it were, produced its next *deus-ex-machina* in the shape of the Afghans; the fortuitous threat of Afghan aggression enabled Clive to turn Watson's prohibition that he had so resented into an essential stepping stone to the overthrow of Siraj-ud-daula. Even after he had destroyed the French at Chandernagore and opened the road to Murshidabad, he never meditated conquest.

Initially, he was only concerned with expelling the French from Bengal, on the assumption that Calcutta could never be safe while they retained a foothold in the province. But Siraj-ud-daula persistently flirted with a French alliance and the British could not rely on his friendship. Clive came to the conclusion that he had to be replaced, and when some of the foremost men in his kingdom conspired to unseat him, Clive leapt at the opportunity they offered.

But he intended no more than to support a suitable aspirant to the viceroyalty, in the expectation that he would remain the friend of the British, after the fashion of Mohammed Ali in the Carnatic. He never expected to overthrow Siraj-ud-daula single-handed. He, and Watson to a still greater degree, doubted that such an enterprise could succeed with the limited military resources available to them. It was Watts' letter telling him that an open break had occurred between Siraj-ud-daula and Mir Jafar that virtually compelled him to move. Then the indecision and dilatoriness of the Indian conspirators led him to a position from which he had no real alternative but to go forward. For perhaps twenty-four hours at Cutwa, the immense dangers that surrounded him caused him to hesitate, then he plunged on to a victory more overwhelming than any he could have dreamed of.

Yet although it might appear that at times Clive was virtually dragged forward at the chariot wheels of fate, by recognising the trend of events, by accommodating himself to it and finally exploiting to the full all the opportunities it opened to him, he revealed perhaps the most valuable attribute of a great statesman, the ability to see in which direction the currents of history were flowing. But even after Plassey, he did not entirely comprehend the significance of what had occurred. On 30 June he wrote to the Select Committee that he had told Mir Jafar's Court, 'For our parts we should not interfere in the affairs of government, but leave that wholly to the Nawab; that so long as his affairs require it we should keep the field, after which we should return to Calcutta and attend to trade which was our proper sphere and our whole aim in these parts.'

But Mir Jafar's nobles knew better. When on 29 June he marched at the head of 200 Europeans and 300 Sepoys into Murshidabad, a city he later described as being as large and rich as London, the great men of the realm with their vast wealth and hordes of retainers thronged round him, and it was his favours they were seeking. It must have been one of the most intoxicating moments of his life. Mir Jafar himself appeared dazed by the swift change in his fortunes; when Clive entered the audience chamber of the palace, he rose to greet him and wished Clive to lead him to the *musnud* and proclaim him Nawab. Then, all his nobles hailed him and did him homage.

And now to the victor his spoils, and almost at once disappointment. Siraj-ud-daula's treasury had barely a quarter of what had been confidently anticipated. The Select Committee had not undervalued either its own or the Company's services. In the treaty Mir Jafar had offered: to the Company and merchants in Calcutta to recompense them for their losses, 177 lakhs, distributed at 100 to the Company, 50 to the British merchants, 20 to the Hindu and 7 to the Armenian; to the armed forces, 40 lakhs to be split equally between the army and the navy. In a separate agreement the members of the Select Committee were to receive 12 lakhs, and the remaining members of Council 6. Clive himself was given a present of 16 lakhs, Watts 12 and Scrafton, 2. Thus Mir Jafar owed a grand total of 266 lakhs of rupees or approximately £2,660,000. Unfortunately there were only 140 lakhs in the treasury. Out of this Mir Jafar would also have to pay his troops and meet the current expenses of government.

He suggested to Clive that the Seths should be asked to arbitrate, a proposal that Clive readily accepted, for he had reason to believe as he told the Select Committee, 'great sums have been secreted and made away by his [Siraj-ud-daula's] ministers. It would have been an invidious and difficult task for me to have sifted into these affairs'. Jagat Seth ruled that the Nawab should meet half the British demands immediately, two-thirds in money and one in plate and jewels, and the remainder by yearly instalments over the next three years. Clive and Mir Jafar accepted his ruling. The sums of money were undoubtedly large, but on the other hand the Nawab had the revenues of a state over twice the size of England on which to draw.

While the conference had been in progress, Omichand had waited a little apart; now he approached to claim his share. He was brutally told that his treaty was a trick and he got nothing. Orme relates, 'These words overpowered him like a blast of sulphur; he sunk back fainting and would have fallen to the ground had not one of his attendants caught him in his arms . . . they conveyed him to his house where he remained many hours in stupid melancholy, and began to show some signs of insanity . . . his mind every day more and more approaching idiotism . . . in this state of imbecility he died about a year and a half after the shock of the disappointment.'

It is an affecting story. There is another one, that immediately after Plassey he and Rai Durlabh repaired hot foot to the treasury and helped themselves liberally to its contents, contributing not a little to the dearth of currency subsequently discovered. It is also of interest that Clive in August was writing to the Select Committee about employing Omichand as one of their agents over a salt-petre transaction; he thought the employment unwise, not on account of Omichand's 'imbecility', but because of his intriguing nature, which suggests that Omichand made a quick recovery. It is doubtful if Omichand's sad fate requires the shedding of a tear.[1]

Clive had no trouble collecting his own present. Testifying before Parliament a number of years later, he said that after meeting all his expenses he cleared about £160,000. The morality of his action in accepting this gift has been questioned and needs to be considered. Clive himself was never in doubt. The Company paid its servants a derisory salary, on the assumption they would augment it as they could. There was nothing at that time to prohibit the acceptance of presents, and he did not attempt to conceal what he

---

[1] Mervyn Davies in his book *Clive of Plassey* states Omichand lived to a ripe old age.

had done. Clive's standards of conduct were absolute, and he never did anything that offended against his own code; he was, however, no moral philosopher, and did not aspire to a higher code of ethics than was practised by those with whom he associated. Marlborough and Wellington received huge sums of money and high honours from their own and foreign governments, and the practice of voting successful military commanders sums of money was only discontinued after the Second World War. Servants of the Crown who accepted rewards without the consent of their government or allowed their actions to be influenced by the prospect of such rewards would, of course, be regarded as corrupt. But Clive throughout acted in the best interests of the Company, and the Company at the time did not disapprove his actions, it saved the Directors the expense of themselves awarding him a substantial sum of money. The practice of accepting such presents could clearly have vicious consequences, and in due course came to be forbidden. But if, as Macaulay maintained, retrospective legislation is always bad, the same must be true of retrospective moral judgements; a man is surely entitled to be judged by the standards of his day.

His officers suffered from no qualms of conscience and almost immediately set him a problem. He convened a Council of War to settle how the money given to the army should be divided. The army officers unanimously voted that the naval contingent that had accompanied the army to Plassey should count against the relatively smaller amount of money allotted to the navy. This mean attitude infuriated Clive, and he dissolved the Council of War. His officers then, seriously misjudging their commander, sent him a remonstrance. Clive put the bearer of the remonstrance under arrest, and bluntly told the others that he had negotiated the reward for them, and that unless they changed their attitude they would receive nothing.

The officers apologised and the incident was closed. Where Clive thought himself to be in the right he was utterly inflexible, no matter what the opposition. It is easy to be censorious of the soldiers, but they soldiered for cash, not a country to which many of them did not belong; their lives were hard and generally short, and they resented anything they thought infringed their right to money which they considered their due; a spirit not wholly unknown in a later age.

Meanwhile Siraj-ud-daula paid the price of failure. When he heard that Mir Jafar was approaching, he fled the city in disguise and hurried up the Ganges, hoping to meet Law; but on the way a man who had good reason to remember him, the Prince had sentenced him to have his nose cut off, recognised him and denounced him to the local governor who, anxious to show his zeal for the new Nawab, at once took him prisoner. He was brought back to Murshidabad on 2 July. Mir Jafar had agreed with Clive to spare his life, but his son Miran, a vicious and bloodthirsty youth, had other views. He hired an assassin who cut down Siraj-ud-daula with a sabre. As the unfortunate man lay dying he is reputed to have said, 'Enough. That is enough. I am done for and Kuli Khan's death is avenged.' Hussain Kuli Khan had been one of the chief ministers at Dacca, and Siraj-ud-daula had procured his murder in 1756 to clear his own way to the *musnud*.

Siraj-ud-daula was no more, but there still remained Law and his party of French. Law had reached Rajmahal when he heard that Siraj-ud-daula had been taken and promptly turned round to head for Patna. Now Clive perceived a chance to rid himself of an officer who was both a troublesome subordinate and a competent commander. He dispatched Coote up the Ganges with orders to capture Law and disperse his band of followers.

During perhaps the most trying season of the year, Coote set off on a pursuit that might well rank as a minor epic. In the steaming monsoon heat his Europeans were almost incapable of marching, and he could only move up the river in boats. Boatmen were hard to find and then in a storm a number of boats were wrecked. His Europeans mutinied and he doggedly carried on the chase with his sepoys. Law, however, it was reported had 200 French soldiers and 300 sepoys with him, and Coote dared not leave his Europeans far behind. He restored some form of discipline among them

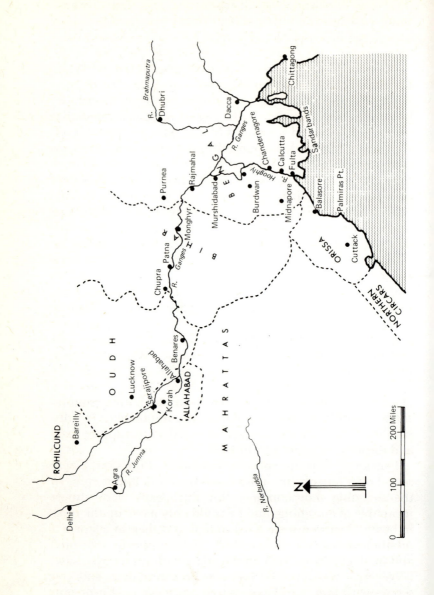

by flogging thirty of the worst offenders. Then his sepoys quietly grounded their arms and announced that they would go no further; the attitude of Ram Narain's troops in Bihar was extremely uncertain; and to add to his joys, letters from Clive in Murshidabad queried his slowness and observed that he, Clive, had received complaints about the conduct of his troops that made him 'blush'—a somewhat unlikely statement.

38 A *patile*. A cargo boat used on the Ganges in Upper Bengal. Doubtless Eyre Coote used this type of unhandy craft during his chase of Jean Law.

By sheer force of character he drove his men onwards through a hostile countryside, eventually reaching Patna to find Law gone. Ram Narain blandly explained that, since he had received no orders to detain the French, he had not hindered their departure. The Governor had too many troops for Coote to make a suitable rejoinder, and he pressed on after Law. The Frenchman crossed the border into Oudh where it was plainly unwise for Coote to follow. Clive recalled him to Patna on 13 August, thus bringing to an end a pursuit that had covered nearly 400 miles.

While Clive stayed in Murshidabad helping Mir Jafar to

establish his authority, he received from the Select Committee the answer to his letter asking for their advice, which he had written on the eve of Plassey. The letter they sent has been lost, but in the minutes recording their discussions as to how they should answer Clive, it was recorded, 'No thoughts can be entertained of making a fresh treaty with the Nawab . . . though the Committee are for trying a decisive engagement, they would not recommend that step without a pretty good prospect of success . . .' and much more in a similar vein. Presumably the letter to Clive reflected the general sense of the minutes. When he asked their advice Clive had with him Watts, Scrafton and Mirza Omar Beg, the only three with any up-to-date knowledge of affairs in Murshidabad; the Select Committee, isolated in Calcutta, could not hope to give him any useful guidance; they would have been wise to confine themselves to trusting to his judgement and assuring him of their support in whatever decision he took. Anything else was bound to be so hedged round with provisos as inevitably to assume a delphic ambiguity. The issue had been triumphantly decided and Clive might well have ignored the letter; instead he replied: 'Gentlemen I have received your letter of the 23rd inst., the contents of which are so indefinite and contradictory that I can put no other construction on it than an attempt to clear yourselves had the expedition miscarried . . .'.

A letter written in such terms could serve no useful purpose save to antagonise its recipients. Clive merely indulged a momentary, and unjustified feeling of irritation. It was one of his less happy characteristics that he never understood the dangers of giving free rein to an emotion when writing a letter. This time, beyond probably causing a few angry or rueful remarks by the members of the Select Committee, it had no baneful results, but a later intemperate letter was to cost him dear.

At the beginning of August all appeared quiet at Murshidabad and he felt able to return to Calcutta, where his wife Margaret had just arrived from Madras. On 16 August of that month Watson died after a brief illness. All in Calcutta mourned his death. Clive observed of him,

'... his generosity, disinterestedness and zeal for the service must forever endear his memory to the Company'. At this time news came from the Northern Circars that in revenge for the capture of Chandernagore, Bussy had sacked the British factory at Vizagapatam. The Northern Circars were the responsibility of the Madras Presidency and the Council there lacked the troops to attempt a reprisal.

Clive himself had acquired the fortune he wanted and now fixed his gaze on returning to England. He wrote to his father on 19 August. 'Mrs Clive takes her passage upon the *Tyger*, Captain Latham, and will sail from hence in six weeks taking Bombay on her way. I propose leaving this place in January. ... If I can get into Parliament I shall be very glad, but no more struggles against the ministry. I chuse to be with them.' He wrote to Mr Belchier; 'I wait for nothing but the settlement of these provinces to begin my voyage for old England which I hope will be some time in January. As this good news may set my father upon exerting himself too much and paying too many visits to the Duke of N. and Mr Fox and other great men, I desire you will endeavour to moderate his expectations ... you know the merit of all actions is greatly lessened by being too much boasted of.' For once Clive's foresight failed him; it was to be another three years, all but a month, before Margaret and he saw England again.

When the rains ended he intended to march on Bihar and confirm Ram Narain's allegiance to Mir Jafar, but meanwhile he turned his energies to selecting a site for a new Fort William with adequate fields of fire, and put in hand its construction in accordance with the latest techniques, so that the miserable experience of 1756 might never be repeated. But when after the monsoon he retraced his steps to Murshidabad, he found that his army which he had left at Cossimbazar, as it was more healthy than Calcutta, had disintegrated. His soldiers had spent their prize money 'not wisely but too well' and most were in hospital. His experienced and trustworthy second-in-command, Killpatrick, had died of a fever.

Coote's small detachment at Patna had been recalled

39 Patna.

early in September, and Coote himself, in poor health after his exertions, was gone to Calcutta. His regiment departed from India that autumn and Coote went home towards the end of the year. Clive was not unhappy to see his able but cantankerous subordinate depart, and Coote was glad to end a relationship that he doubted would further his career.

The poor health of the European soldiers was the more unfortunate in that Mir Jafar faced a very serious challenge to his rule. Ram Narain had revolted, and in Bengal itself, two powerful noblemen, the rajahs of Purneah and Midnapore, defined his authority and threatened open hostilities. The Nawab suspected his fellow conspirator, Rai Durlabh, of having instigated the risings in Bengal, and the latter, in peril of his life, fled from Murshidabad. The situation had largely arisen because Mir Jafar, as was customary, replaced many of the existing rulers of provinces and districts by his relatives and friends, making the remainder fear that they would soon be supplanted.

As far as Bengal was concerned, the presence of Clive at Murshidabad and the sight of a few sepoy companies proved sufficient without any need for bloodshed. Clive guaranteed to the rebellious rajahs that if they submitted they would be allowed to retain their positions, and this was sufficient to bring them to heel. The quarrel between the Nawab and the Treasurer ran more deep, but Clive with patience and an unrelenting resolution induced a reconciliation. Now only Bihar remained. Ram Narain was backed by a large province and might enlist the aid of the powerful and ambitious Nawab of Oudh, Shuja-ud-daula. A strong force had to be assembled, not only to overawe Ram Narain, but also to deter Shuja-ud-daula from any ill-advised adventures.

With the cooler weather of November the health of Clive's men began to mend, and in the Carnatic the scanty forces of Madras appeared to be holding their own. By the end of December, it should be possible to take the field, meanwhile Clive thought it opportune to place the repayment of Mir Jafar's debt to the Company on a satisfactory footing. He had no illusions about the difficulty to be expected in extracting money from the Nawab, once he was firmly established on his throne. He suggested that it would save a good deal of unnecessary administrative work, if the Nawab assigned the revenues of specific regions to the Company until the debt was liquidated. Mir Jafar did not share Clive's enthusiasm for administrative efficiency, but he realised clearly enough that it was beyond his powers to subdue Bihar on his own, and with some reluctance he assigned the revenues of Burdwan, Nuddea and Hooghly to the Company until the debt was repaid.

By the end of January the armies had assembled and on 2 January 1758 three armies, those of the British, Mir Jafar

40 Ram Narain, Governor of Patna

and Rai Durlabh took the field, each viewing the other two with a certain degree of suspicion. Clive anxious to avoid bringing on an armed conflict, persuaded Mir Jafar to promise he would retain Ram Narain as Governor of Bihar if he swore his allegiance. He then wrote to Ram Narain informing him of the Nawab's offer, and inviting him to come into the camp and make his peace with Mir Jafar. Clive assured him of his safety, and it is noticeable that all the Indian Princes unhesitatingly accepted Clive's word.

When Ram Narain had entered the camp and was within his grasp, Mir Jafar thought better of his offer and decided to make his brother-in-law, Mir Kassim, Governor. Clive drily informed the Select Committee, 'I represented to him the impossibility of retracting the promise he had made through me to Ram Narain . . . my discourse had weight with him and Ram Narain is confirmed.' As a sop to Mir Jafar, Ram Narain was appointed only Deputy Governor of Bihar with Miran as his nominal superior. Clive improved the occasion by securing for the Company a monopoly of the salt-petre trade of which Patna was the centre; the bargain was fair and the price fixed high, but it made certain that the bulk of a lucrative trade was reserved to the Company, something not much to the liking of the other European traders, especially as salt-petre was an essential ingredient of gunpowder.

With affairs in the viceroyalty settled, Clive returned to Murshidabad by the middle of May 1758. He had good reason to feel satisfied. Without firing a shot he had settled the vexed question of Mir Jafar's payments to the Company, and asserted his authority throughout his realm; at the same time he had established a number of powerful officials who depended on the British for their protection and would form a valuable check should Mir Jafar think of indulging in foolish adventures. Mir Jafar, perhaps, had less reason to feel pleased; yet although the British guiding reins might occasionally chafe, there were certain undeniable compensations for an elderly Nawab whose interests were beginning to centre on the comforts of the body rather than the excitements of the battlefield. So long as he respected his obligations he had an ally whom the boldest in his realm feared to challenge; and besides, outside his borders lay the kingdom of Oudh and the menacing Mahratta hordes of Balaji Rao; both would think long before going to war with an ally of Clive. The relationship between Mir Jafar and Clive was unusual and shot through with antagonisms; yet despite occasional asperities, both cherished a curious respect and affection for each other. They each knew the character of the other so well that, even when most suspicious of each other's designs, an underlying, if unacknowledged, bond of sympathy remained.

While Clive had been engaged in enforcing Mir Jafar's authority in his realm, those indefatigable 'fixers' the Seths were busily employed in Delhi securing its legal recognition at the Court of the Emperor. A *firman* was duly issued and in addition the Emperor was graciously pleased to appoint Clive an *Omra* or Imperial Councillor, and a nobleman with the rank of a commander of 6,000 infantry and 5,000 horse, a position of some splendour that carried with it an income of three lakhs a year, payable, of course, not by the Imperial Court, but by the Viceroy in whose domain the nobleman resided; for the time being Clive forbore from demanding his salary from Mir Jafar.

He was not to remain long in Murshidabad. While he had been away pacifying Bihar, the French fleet had emerged out of the Indian Ocean and disgorged its contents into Pondicherry. It consisted of nine ships of the line under Admiral d'Aché and it had landed the new French Governor-General, the Comte Lally de Tollendal, a Franco–Irish soldier who had acquired a reputation on European battlefields and was confident he could show the inefficient French rabble in Pondicherry how war should be waged; he had with him his regiment, 1,000-strong. Pocock had sailed for Madras in February and been reinforced by a squadron from England under Commodore Barnett, but he still had only seven ships of the line against the French nine. However on 29 April, the day after Lally and his men had completed their disembarkation, he engaged d'Aché in battle. One French ship ran aground and the others, it was believed, suffered heavy losses in men, but the action had been indecisive, and the British ships had suffered such damage to their rigging that they needed time for repairs before they would again be fit for action.

Garbled rumours of the affair reached Calcutta, spreading alarm among the citizens who peered down the Hooghly, almost daily, expecting to see the topsails of the French ships looming up over the riverbank. On 22 May, Manningham, a member of the Select Committee, wrote to Clive, 'I need not intimate to you the critical state of the Company's affairs . . . I own I heartily wish for your assistance; you will have weight, none else seem to have any . . .'.

Clive went immediately down the river to Calcutta. He left three sepoy battalions at Cossimbazar and brought two with him, each 1,000-strong. As he stepped from his boat on to the landing stage, he entered a city seized by fear. The buoys had been removed from the ship channel in the river and all navigation was stopped. He had no patience with such panic measures which would only spread doubt and alarm through Bengal. He ordered the buoys to be replaced, re-opened the river to traffic and directed that immediate attention should be paid to the construction of a dock for repairing ships. The nervous Council at Calcutta continued the feverish drilling of all able-bodied men, and called in all personal fire-arms and shotguns to arm their garrison.

On 20 June, at this moment of crisis, a letter came from the Directors in London recalling Drake to England to explain the loss of Calcutta nearly two years before; they nominated a new Council, omitting Clive's name as they thought him in Madras, and changing the old system of governors, replacing it by one where the four senior members of Council took it in turn to be president for periods of four months. Ridiculous at any time, now when strong consistent leadership was vital the new system invited disaster. The Council, led by Drake, urged Clive to accept the Presidency and to disregard the Directors' instructions.

At first Clive demurred. He wrote to Drake on 28 June 1758, 'I think it is plainly discovered that the Presidency of

Bengal was by no means intended for me by the Court of Directors,' adding, 'I cannot sufficiently express my sense of the disinterestedness which you and the other gentlemen have shown in this generous offer.' He was worried that if a new governor was appointed by the Directors and he had to surrender the appointment, the people of Bengal would misunderstand and think him disgraced, a circumstance that could have grave implications.

However, it was clear he had to accept, there could be no other solution. On 5 July he wrote to Amyatt, the chief at Patna, 'After much persuasion I have accepted the Presidency ... whenever the French squadron is superior we may expect a visit, but not before.' Clive with his clear strategic sense perceived that in the first instance the issue would be decided at sea, and although the situation in the Carnatic might appear critical he had good reason to place his faith in the Royal Navy. On 6 July his friend Captain Latham in the *Tyger* wrote to him:

'The fate of the Company seems to depend on the arrival of supplies. If their's arrive before our's I fear Madras must fall ... they expect every hour one ship of 78 guns with several of their armed and loaded Indiamen. If they arrive our affairs will wear a very cloudy appearance; they have eight sail of the line and two fire ships ... our force is seven and the Protector.

'They outnumber us greatly in guns and men, but our people, I hope are so much better that we shall have little to fear from a second action. ... The Gentlemen here tell me that we shall see you here in September.'

Madras had asked Clive to return. He is reported to have expressed no desire to face the regular battalions of France in the field. For him to leave Calcutta, where his presence was vital, to serve as second-in-command to Stringer Lawrence would have been an act of arrant folly. On 14 August, having taken up his post as Governor of the Calcutta Presidency and thereby severed his connection with Madras, he expressed his views on the situation to Governor Pigot, displaying remarkable prescience.

'I do not find M. Lally is able to take the field with three thousand men. When the expected forces arrive [a British Regiment the 79th or Draper's Foot was expected shortly from England], and are joined to those at Madras and Trichinopoly we shall be 2,500-strong, and I do not think victory depends so much on equality of numbers as conduct and resolution. From the several accounts I have received of Mons; Lally I do not entertain that high regard for him which he seems to have gained on the coast . . . [his troops] were not draughted out of the regiments of France, but are composed of foreigners and deserters . . . by this time the superiority of our force at sea I take for granted is beyond dispute, and of consequence our forces must be more than those of the French . . . a victory on our side must confine the French within the walls of Pondicherry and when that happens nothing can save them from destruction but a superior force at sea . . . their great want of money is well known . . . if they cannot raise sufficient money to pay their forces, they must disband their blacks and the whites will disband themselves. I find M. Lally has gone south . . . I sincerely believe the French will meet with some disgrace before Trichinopoly.'

These were indeed prophetic words. On 2 August Pocock again brought d'Aché to action. After a bitter combat, the French ships were so mauled that they had to seek the protection of the guns of Pondicherry. As a result of their fearful experience, d'Aché and his captains were unanimous in their view that they could not again fight the British. Despite the angry protestations of Lally, on 2 September d'Aché and the French fleet departed for Mauritius, leaving Pocock master of the seas off the Coromandel coast.

While this was happening, Lally, desperate for money, revived the old treaty between the Rajah of Tanjore and Chunda Sahib. He demanded fifty-six lakhs, which he asserted the Rajah owed the French under that treaty, and marched on Tanjore to compel the Rajah to comply with his demand. The Rajah of Tanjore knew of old how to cope with this type of situation, and happily opened a lengthy negotiation. Major Caillaud, commanding the British garrison at Trichinopoly, dispatched 1,000 well-trained sepoys to assist in the defence of the city. On 2 August Lally, utterly exasperated by the expert procrastination of his wily adversary, directed his batteries on the city. He met a fierce resistance. On the afternoon of 9 August the garrison of Tanjore made a sally aided by a great number of polyghars, minor local chieftains from the territories nearby, who brought a multitude of irregular cavalry into the field, and the sepoys sent by Caillaud. The French appear to have been indulging in a siesta and a picked group of Tanjore horsemen penetrated to Lally's headquarters. John Call, chief engineer at Madras, related to Clive 'One trooper made a cut at Lally; he parried it with his arm; [then] Lally ran under the belly of the horse, got a kick in the guts, and the fellow who attempted to demolish him was cut down . . . the batteries were soon demolished and the guns spiked . . . but 2,000 Europeans were not to be broke by a rude multitude . . . However, M. Lally was so satisfied with the drubbing he got that he marched off that night or early next morning.'

It was not so much the 'drubbing' he received that caused Lally to depart, as the news that d'Aché had been defeated, and that Pocock with his ships was cruising off the port of Karikal on which he depended for his supplies. Lally had no reserves of food or ammunition, problems of supply he deemed beneath the dignity of a general; now he had no alternative but to retreat. This unlooked-for reverse disheartened his troops and gravely damaged the reputation of his army. Nevertheless, despite the defection of his fleet and this setback, Lally remained confident he could conquer the Carnatic and throw the British out of India. D'Aché had left behind him some marines, and prize-money he had obtained by capturing British shipping, and he had recalled Bussy with some of his troops from the Northern Circars. Now he embarked with some success on the conquest of the Carnatic.

The aged Stringer Lawrence watched the activities of the French with a cool, experienced eye. While Lally marched on Arcot, he massed every available soldier for the defence of Madras; then, thanks to the British naval superiority, on 14 September a wing of the 79th Foot, disembarked at Madras. In the Carnatic all was at stake, but Lally had weakened the French hold on the Northern Circars and taken away Bussy, the only Frenchman who understood the tortuous politics of the Deccan. He had given an opening to an opponent whose judgement was as sure as his own was faulty.

12 The Coromandel Coast and North East India.

Chapter 14

GOVERNOR OF BENGAL
1758–9

August 1758 was to be a momentous month for Clive. As it opened, while Lally invested Tanjore menaced Trichinopoly and lost his best chance of taking Madras, and the British fleet, its ships refitted, prepared to engage the French, in the intrigue-ridden city of Murshidabad a covert battle for power broke the surface. Scrafton, holding the new appointment of British Representative at the Court of the Nawab, warned of trouble in a letter dated 23 July, which he prefaced with a personal complaint. 'Pardon me, Sir, when I say the contempt and slights put on me by yourself and more particularly Mr Watts when at Muradbagh have deprived me of all influence in the city,' the hot and humid monsoon weather had clearly taken its toll of Scrafton's temper, and with Watts, his chief at Cossimbazar, his relationship had never been happy. But more ominously, he went on to remark that Rai Durlabh was in great personal danger.

During the advance on Patna, Rai Durlabh had put 10,000 men in the field, and if pushed to it might involve Bengal in a new and serious civil war. Moreover he was a friend of the British; if Mir Jafar were allowed to attack him with impunity, others at present depending on the friendship of Clive for their safety would take alarm and might look elsewhere for protection. The Seths were implicated in the plot. They disliked Rai Durlabh's methods as treasurer and found Mir Jafar's patronage less rewarding than they had hoped. They contemplated oversetting the Nawab. To disgrace Rai Durlabh and provoke a rupture between Mir Jafar and the British at the same time would indeed be a triumph.

But while Murshidabad simmered and bade fair to boil over at any moment, extraordinary news had come from the Northern Circars. Taking advantage of the departure of Bussy with 600 French soldiers, a local chieftain, Ananda raj, had swooped down on Vizagapatam, captured it and hoisted the Union Jack. Bristow, a British agent at Ingeram, wrote to Clive on 29 July:

'Rajah pretty well recovered of his wounds . . . very pressing for assistance, . . . has a numerous army and great numbers of cannon, but for want of discipline his force, I believe, could not withstand a large body of Europeans . . . he is desirous of giving Vizagapatam into my hands with any number of men and cannon I think proper, but as it is not under the Government of Bengal I can no other ways accept without your liberty'.

He added optimistically and inaccurately, 'There is no news of M. Bussy. The general account is that he had been defeated and plundered by Nizam Ali.' Nizam Ali, a younger brother of Salabat Jang, was a known enemy of the French and believed to have ambitions to replace his elder brother as viceroy.

Suddenly a great opportunity to expel the French from the long coastline of the Northern Circars had arisen. Dare Clive seize it? With the Carnatic in peril and turmoil in Murshidabad, it seemed a perilous undertaking. The Council and citizens of Calcutta with unusual unanimity rejected all thought of sending a single soldier out of Bengal. Clive pondered the situation. Madras clamoured for him to lend them every man he could spare; Pigot, with the backing of his old mentor Stringer Lawrence, insisted adamantly that, since the French had massed all their strength in the Carnatic, that province would be the place of decision and there the British in turn must mass all their strength—the classical military approach.

Clive was not convinced. Lally urgently needed money; if he was deprived of the revenue from the Northern Circars it would add considerably to his financial embarrassment; further, a British attack in that region would pin down the French troops he had left there and might compel him to detach troops from the Carnatic; and there was one more important consideration. Calcutta would lose command of all troops sent to Madras, but an army in the Northern Circars could be recalled if an unexpected danger threatened in Bengal. Madras was due to receive a complete British infantry battalion, and under such men as Lawrence and Pigot should be safe enough. A French attack on Bengal could be discounted unless Pocock suffered a disastrous defeat at sea, and Clive relied on his own personality to keep Murshidabad quiescent. In defiance of orthodox military doctrine he decided to send troops to Vizagapatam. It was the strategy of the indirect approach he had demonstrated so brilliantly at Arcot.

Such was Clive's dominance over the Council at Calcutta that, despite grave misgivings, the councillors reluctantly agreed to dispatch an expeditionary force to the Northern Circars with the cream of the Bengal Army. In a letter dated 15 September Clive explained his decision to Pigot, 'All here are much alarmed at so large a detachment leaving the place ... If I was to propose the troops proceeding to Madras, a negative would be given by every one but myself. I will not conceal from you that we are in no condition to withstand the French should there be any possibility of their paying us a visit during the absence of our troops. Our effectives are not above 280, and those the very scum of the men.'

The expeditionary force, consisting of 470 Europeans, 1,900 sepoys and six field guns, was placed under the command of Lieut-Colonel Forde. Clive had met and liked Forde while the latter was serving with the 39th at Madras. After Killpatrick's death, he prevailed on him to transfer to the Company's service and take up the appointment of major of the Calcutta garrison. To compensate himself for the loss of prospects consequent on his transfer, Forde asked for £5,000. The Council thought the sum exorbitant and thriftily offered £2,500. Clive, impatient of such haggling, made up the remaining £2,500 from his own purse, and the transfer went through.

Wind and tides caused many delays and it was not until 9 October 1758 that the little force put out to sea; but now the wind blew fair, and on 20 October Forde sailed into the harbour at Vizagapatam to find Ananda raj camped about twenty miles away. Seven weeks later on 9 December he met and defeated the French under the Marquis de Conflans at Condore about forty miles north of Rajamundry; but a rapid advance to exploit his victory and capture Masulipatam was frustrated by the maddening procrastination of the Indian chieftain; nevertheless the French in the Northern Circars had been struck a near fatal blow. In the Carnatic the crisis drew near as on 13 December Lally closed in on Madras.

Meanwhile at Murshidabad the intrigue against Rai Durlabh had reached the pitch of an open break. Towards the end of July Mir Jafar relieved his Treasurer of all his appointments. Scrafton commented to Clive, 'Unless Watts interferes strenuously and we openly protect him, be assured he is very short lived.' On 8 August while Mir Jafar was out hunting, Miran organised a riot of discontented and unpaid soldiers outside the palace of the Treasurer. A violent mob assembled and clamoured loudly for their pay. Scrafton personally intervened and prevented bloodshed; Mir Jafar, on his return, professed complete ignorance of the whole affair.

To divert the Nawab and extract him from the torrid atmosphere of his court, Clive, at Scrafton's suggestion, invited him to pay a visit to Calcutta. Mir Jafar accepted; on 11 or 12 August he went down the river with immense pomp and escorted by a large flotilla of boats, and was received with all possible honour. Clive fancied the visit a great success, but it was clear that there could be no reconciliation with Rai Durlabh. However, at Clive's request, as Warren Hastings who had taken over from Scrafton in Murshidabad informed him, 'The Nawab ordered the family in readiness to move immediately that their stay might not give you uneasiness or displeasure.' On 11 September Rai Durlabh with his family, escorted by a party of British soldiers under the command of ensign MacDowel, set off for Calcutta. But now events took a sinister turn.

On 13 September, when Mir Jafar was praying at a mosque, he found himself surrounded by a hostile crowd of troops apparently organised by his Commander-in-Chief, Khwaja Hadi. His retainers were jostled and he himself insulted. An informer told him that the incident was part of a carefully planned plot to provoke an affray in which, by an unfortunate mischance, he was to be killed. He managed to extricate himself successfully, relieved Khwaja Hadi of his post and replaced him by Mohammed Khan, a Pathan. During further investigations, a cavalry officer who had served in Rai Durlabh's army revealed that the Treasurer had bribed Khwaja Hadi with two lakhs of rupees to procure his assassination.

Clive treated the story with open scepticism. Then on 11 October Mir Jafar produced a letter he asserted had been written by Rai Durlabh to Khwaja Hadi; among others it implicated Clive, Watts and Scrafton in the plot for his overthrow. Clive remembered that, during the conspiracy against Siraj-ud-daula, Rai Durlabh had always rigidly refused to commit anything to paper, and thought the letter a forgery devised by Mir Jafar to prejudice the British against the Treasurer; he demanded that Khwaja Hadi should be interrogated. Khwaja Hadi, however, hurriedly trying to leave the country was killed at Rajmahal, apparently during a casual disturbance. Warren Hastings was certain that Mir Jafar had ordered his death; this opinion confirmed Clive in the belief that the letter was a forgery, and that Khwaja Hadi had been murdered to prevent him talking. Forde had departed with most of the troops, and now was no time for the British to become embroiled in Murshidabad. He contented himself with addressing a stern rebuke to the Nawab, telling him, according to Orme,

41 Murshidabad, the Great Mosque. Presumably the Nawab is about to come and pray, as a sepoy guard of honour has been mounted.

'that if he gave ear to such stories, there would be an end to all confidence between him and the English nation'. The rebuke sufficed and the incident appeared closed, but its after effects were to linger on. Mir Jafar had disclosed a want of firmness and sagacity and a willingness to listen to scheming intriguers that augured ill for the future, but in refusing to credit Mir Jafar's story it is possible that Clive erred. The Nawab had been in peril of his life, and in attributing that peril to the machinations of Rai Durlabh, although he may have been misled, he almost certainly only voiced what he himself believed to be true. The letter may have been a forgery planted by the Seths, but on the other hand it may have been genuine and Rai Durlabh included in it the names of Clive, Watts and Scrafton to make his confederate Khwaja Hadi think the plot had British backing. Mir Jafar may be forgiven for wondering about Clive's good faith. He had been nearly assassinated only two days after Rai Durlabh had left Murshidabad under British protection, and he might well think it a remarkable coincidence. Mir Jafar lived in a tortuous society in which the trusting were unlikely to prosper. Doubts about the part played by the British probably lingered, and led him to an intrigue with the Dutch that was to give Clive some anxious moments the following year.

While imposing his will, as he thought, at Murshidabad without firing a shot, and dispatching an expedition to the Northern Circars, Clive yet could spare the time to lay a firm foundation for the Bengal army that, in due course, was to become the main instrument in the conquest of India by the British. Until this time, the sepoy units had been mere aggregations of companies thrown together for a particular mission. Clive formed them into permanent battalions each of ten companies commanded by Indian officers and the whole under an Indian Commandant; but he added to the establishment a British captain to command on operations, with a lieutenant and an ensign to act as his field officers, a European sergeant major and a number of European sergeants. Each company was commanded by a subedar with under him three Indian officers called

Jemadars; it consisted of five havildars (the equivalent of the British sergeant), two tom-toms (drummers) and seventy sepoys.

As 1758 came to a close, although Madras was besieged and Calcutta stripped of troops, Clive viewed the future with equanimity. He wrote to his father: 'I am now projecting the ruin of the French in Golconda [the Northern Circars] for which purpose I have sent Colonel Forde with 500 Europeans and 2,000 blacks. My last letters advise . . . that the French were retreating . . . Be not uneasy at the loss of St David, which was scandalously given up. Notwithstanding this success the French are in a very bad way and will I hope be at the point of destruction by the latter end of next year'. With characteristic generosity, he added 'If you should have occasion for a sum of money to purchase commissions for either of my brothers or to answer any other purpose which may be to their advantage, you will apply to my attorneys who I desire may supply you accordingly.'

Edmund Maskelyne took the letter home; he was bound for England with a modest competence of £11,000 he had managed to amass during his service in India. He had resigned from the service at an unusual time, and the circumstances shed an interesting light on Clive's character. When Caillaud was promoted major in the Madras army, he passed over the head of his senior, Edmund Maskelyne. Edmund addressed a strong protest to the Council at Madras without avail, and then wrote several letters to Clive, claiming that he had been unjustly superseded because for some reason the 'old gentleman', Stringer Lawrence, had taken a dislike to him. He was Clive's earliest friend in India and his brother-in-law, but Clive also knew Caillaud and valued his professional talents highly. Since he thought Caillaud's promotion was for the good of the service, he never appears seriously to have tried to influence his old friend, Governor Pigot, to reverse the decision. The aggrieved Edmund resigned and went home, bearing Clive's letter to his father with him.

To Lawrence Sulivan, elected in April that year to be Chairman of the Court of Directors, he sent a detailed statement of his views on the future policy of the Company in Bengal by the hand of his secretary, John Walsh, also homeward bound. He summed up.

'May not so weak a Prince as Mir Jafar be easily destroyed, or influenced by others to attempt destroying us. What is it then can enable us to secure our present acquisitions or improve them, but such force as leaves nothing to the power of treachery and ingratitude . . . As the Company's privileges have been greatly extended so ought their views also; to conduct and carry on the affairs of Bengal to advantage not only requires servants of ability but many of them. Mr Watts has not I think had that justice done to his merits which his services at Murshidabad and since have deserved, therefore, I cannot blame him for resigning . . . Mr Holwell has talents, but I fear wants a heart, therefore, unfit to preside where integrity as well as capacity are equally essential . . . I think it a duty I owe my employers to call to your remembrance Messrs Vansittart and Dupré . . . the merit of the former shines with so peculiar and bright a lustre as must make his services coveted by every well-wisher of the Company.'

On 25 December 1758, knowing Stringer Lawrence had never managed to amass much wealth, he directed his attorneys to pay the 'old gentleman' an annuity of £500 per year for his natural life.

In the New Year of 1759 the torrent of intrigue at Murshidabad once again burst out in spate. The Seths had determined to unseat Mir Jafar; they feared that to ease his monetary problems he might raid their coffers. Far more intelligent than their ruler, they knew it was useless to appeal to Clive, but they assumed that with Madras besieged and most of the Bengal army in the Northern Circars, British military power in Bengal might be disregarded. Over the border the Nawab of Oudh, Shuja-ud-daula, was not averse to extending his dominions, and in his province the crown prince of the Moghul Empire, or Shahzada, Ali Gohar, having rebelled in the customary Moghul fashion against his father, was searching for money and men with which to form and equip an army. The Seths pointed out to him that Bengal could satisfy both his requirements. Shuja, for reasons of his own, agreed to assist the Prince and persuaded his cousin, Mohammed Kuli, the ruler of a small state which had Allahabad as its capital, to join the enterprise.

Towards the end of January 1759, Warren Hastings from Murshidabad informed Clive that the Seths were behaving rather oddly. On the pretence of going on a pilgrimage they had packed up all their possessions and seemed to be preparing to depart for good; at the same time the news had arrived that the Shahzada was approaching the borders of Bihar, and might be meditating an invasion. Mir Jafar alerted to this new peril, perhaps weary of the battlefield and uncertain of the British, started a negotiation to buy the Shahzada off. Clive had deprived himself of all his best troops for the benefit of Forde and had only a few Europeans and two newly raised sepoy battalions at his disposal. However, when he heard what Mir Jafar planned he wrote;

'I have just received a piece of information which I can scarcely give credit to, it is that Your Excellency is going to offer a sum of money to the King's son [Shahzada]. If you you do this you will have Shuja-ud-daula, the Mahrattas and many more come from all parts to the confines of your country who will bully you out of your money until you have none left in your treasury. . . . I beg Your Excellency will rely on the fidelity of the English and those troops which are attached to you.'

The letter was sufficient to revive the fighting spirit of the old warrior, but the intentions of Ram Narain, the not particularly faithful ruler of Bihar, excited doubt. Ram Narain faced a difficult decision. He knew that Mir Jafar disliked and distrusted him and would displace him if he could, and he in turn cherished no great respect or affection for his sovereign. Everything hinged on the British. Dare he throw in his lot with the Shahzada and risk the wrath of the terrible Clive. Clive wrote to him unequivocally pledging his support and saying that he was taking the field to march on Bihar. On 25 February 1759, Clive set out for Murshidabad. He had with him 450 Europeans and 2,500 sepoys. The Shahzada secretly sent him envoys, suggesting an alliance. Clive curtly warned them that if they approached him again 'he would take their heads for it'.

He reached Cossimbazar on 8 March and proceeded to upbraid Mir Jafar for his shortcomings that were losing the support of his people; having thus encouraged the Nawab, he then pushed on towards Patna accompanied by Miran and a large part of the Nawab's army. After the departure of Walsh, Clive had taken Captain John Carnac, late of the 39th, as his secretary. Carnac had become a close friend of Peggy Clive. Now that her husband was away, and only too aware of his reluctance to find time for private correspondence, she wrote to Carnac to obtain news of her husband. On 31 March she complained that she heard nothing from the 'Colonel' as she habitually referred to her husband, and remarked she found the society of Calcutta, 'so far as very insipid'. She had collected a small menagerie to amuse herself, 'I have lately added to my collection a young tyger, a bear, two porcupines, three of these new fashioned birds. The minor is often seen on Mylady's table having become a great favourite.' On 7 April she told Carnac significantly, 'Two mornings ago I cleared out Captain Carnac's room and had it cleaned,' and a trifle optimistically, 'I warrant you I'll take a dance or two with you on 23 June. At present I intend celebrating the anniversary of Plassey with a good deal of pomp and splendour'. And on 13 April 1759;

    Dum Dum   Good Friday
'I am glad the tygers have not yet devoured you, but I wish you would not all run into danger. . . . My salams and very good wishes to Lushington sahib.'

Inevitably Clive had to play a dangerous game, but it was one that he played to perfection. On 15 March Amyatt announced, somewhat prematurely, that Patna was lost and that he was leaving. Unmoved, Clive wrote to Ram Narain, 'What power has the Shahzada to resist the united forces of the Nawab and the English? Think what will then be your fate.'

Ram Narain thought long and earnestly. He took a leaf out of the book of the Raja of Tanjore and began a prolonged negotiation. At one time he insisted that any treaty he signed would also have to bear the signature of Mohammed Kuli. When he received this, he entered the Shahzada's camp, ostensibly to make his submission. The Imperial army did not impress him. A guard had been placed over his tent, but he pleaded that, as a Hindu, his religion did not permit him to drink with moslems, and under guise of getting some drinking water evaded his guard and escaped into Patna, where he at once ordered the gates to be barred. Shuja had gone and Mohammed Kuli took the lead. He did not credit that Ram Narain would have the temerity to defy him. He sent him various demands with which Ram Narain complied, but avoided doing anything that would endanger his city. Then, hearing that Clive was approaching, Ram Narain demanded an explanation from Mohammed Kuli of all the insolent messages he had been sent and remarked that he had only visited the Shahzada to perform the duty of a loyal subject to the son of the Emperor. Since the son of the Emperor was rebelling against his father, the argument was unconvincing. Mohammed Kuli, in a fury, determined to storm the city. On 4 April he launched a fierce onslaught which was only repelled with difficulty; on 5 April he renewed the attack. The stormers were gaining the mastery when suddenly they retreated, and next day the besiegers had gone.

At this time the British advance guard was only ten miles from Patna, but it was not their presence that caused the abrupt termination of the siege. Mohammed Kuli had neglected to take the elementary precaution of insisting that Shuja remained with the invading army. Shuja had returned to Oudh, and, taking advantage of Mohammed Kuli's absence with his army, had seized Allahabad and was in the process of annexing his state. The Shahzada vainly urged the outraged Mohammed Kuli first to capture Patna and then settle matters with Shuja; and Law, tardily arriving with his band of Frenchmen, he had a knack of arriving late, failed to make him change his mind, although he swore that Patna would fall in the hour. Mohammed Kuli rushed back to deal with his treacherous kinsman, fell in with an army from Oudh, was defeated, captured and killed.

The Shahzada, deprived of his allies, withdrew, but Clive pursued him to such effect that his army fell to pieces. As he wandered through Oudh with his dispirited band of fugitives, he dispatched piteous appeals to Clive to grant him asylum in Bengal. To allow such a potent focus of intrigue into the province was not to be thought of, and Clive politely declined. From the Emperor Clive received warm congratulations for his loyal and noble conduct in routing a rebel, together with a suggestion that he should secure the person of the rebel and open an English factory in the royal city of Delhi.

Clive was too wise needlessly to extend his commitments and refused the gracious offer; but much work remained to be done to re-establish Mir Jafar's authority over minor chieftains in Oudh, and Peggy was not to see her husband or John Carnac on the anniversary of Plassey.

In a letter on 5 April she assured Carnac how much his letters meant to her, 'I do assure you that the certainty I have of hearing by your means, keeps my mind in a state of tranquillity I never knew in that Creature's absence. Why are men of so much consequence to us. . . . Has the Colonel a decent coat? I rigged him out well, but I suppose ye are all by now in rags and tatters. . . . When will you come back and chatter again.' And on 24 April,

'I have many thanks to return to my friend the secretary for his obliging letters. I cannot help accusing you in part for the Colonel's idleness, he neglecting to write because he knows how faithful a correspondent you are. . . . When the Colonel arrives we shall live in which house he pleases as he is Commanding Officer at home. . . . You are a parcel of pretty creatures indeed to leave all your curtains dirty on the fall for three months together. If I had not gone to Dum Dum you might have found them on your return just as you left them. But I have taken care ye shall find your kennels in apple pie order. . . . I hope the plentiful showers will make the month of May tolerable.'

As time passed, and there was still no sign of the army returning, she wrote on 19 May. 'If the Colonel should stay the rains let him expect that I shall drown in my tears which is a worse death than if I was demolished in a southeaster. . . . For God's sake Carnac take care of yourselves, I would not have you sick for the worlds.'

On the Coromandel coast the French lurched from one disaster to another. On 17 February Lally abandoned the siege of Madras and marched back to Pondicherry, while in the Northern Circars Forde, against odds, stormed the city of Masulipatam and took most of the French in the province prisoner. Salabat Jang, advancing to relieve the French forces penned in the city, arrived too late and, seeing the utter ruin of his French allies, concluded a treaty with Forde by which he ceded Masulipatam to the British, ended his alliance with the French and guaranteed to allow no Frenchman in the Deccan north of the river Kistna. As Clive had forecast, Lally's great schemes had begun to collapse.

After the rout of the Shahzada, the Seths returned from their pilgrimage uneasily conscious that their conduct was open to question. With their habitual ingenuity they produced a scheme to placate Clive. They called to mind that at the beginning of the year he had approached them over a delicate matter which he hesitated to broach to the Nawab directly, that, as a nobleman of the Empire and the commander of 6,000 infantry and 5,000 Horse, he was due an annual income of three lakhs (£30,000) a year. It was customary to meet this income by assigning to the newly created nobleman a district, known as a jaghir which yielded the appropriate amount of revenue. When Clive made his request, the Seths, preoccupied with their current intrigue with the Shahzada, had disregarded it. Now it occurred to them that here was an excellent opportunity to recover their standing with Clive at no cost to themselves. They offered to negotiate him a jaghir in a remote part of Bihar. Clive brushed the proposal aside as little better than a polite form of refusal and let the matter rest. In June however, when he returned in triumph to Murshidabad, the Seths told him that Mir Jafar had acceded to their requests and, in view of his recent services, wished to grant him a jaghir in Bengal. The Seths had excelled themselves. On their recommendation Mir Jafar offered Clive lands to the southward of Calcutta already leased by him to the Company for an annual rental of £30,000 per annum. The Company would now pay the rent to Clive instead of into the viceregal treasury. Mir Jafar, in his puzzled way, had already noted that the Company never actually paid him any rent, always managing to offset it against sums of money it was alleged he owed the Company. No doubt the rascally clerks at Calcutta would continue to make their curious calculations, and he would never see a rupee in revenue from his lands; he was, therefore, happy to assent to this brilliant scheme of the Seths whereby he rewarded Clive at no real cost to himself.

Clive accepted the jaghir, and his acceptance was ratified by the Company. It made him a very rich man, but, as though pointing the moral to a fable, before he was finished it cost him dear. The propriety of his acceptance was subsequently questioned, but British commanders both before and afterwards, including Wellington and Nelson, were offered and accepted such gifts from foreign governments for the services they had rendered. Their services, rendered as part of their duty to the Crown, differed from those of Clive only in that his were rendered in the course of his duty to his sovereign, the Company. Even that stern moralist, Macaulay, did not cavil at his action. That such gifts might, in the long run, have undesirable consequences is obvious, but that was a matter for the legislators, not Clive.

Bengal appeared tranquil, and in July Clive at last came home to Peggy in Calcutta. As so often in that province, the calm existed on the surface only. Early in the year there had been rumours that the Dutch in Batavia were fitting out a large expedition destined for Bengal. In July Clive learned the expedition was on the point of sailing and wrote to Warren Hastings, bidding him request the Nawab to forbid it entry into his provinces. Mir Jafar assured Hastings he would oppose any such intrusion and sent instructions to the Dutch at Chinsura, expressly prohibiting the entry of any more Dutch troops into his realm.

Early in August 1759, a Dutch vessel containing Dutch and Malay troops arrived in the Hooghly. The Nawab demanded an explanation, and the Dutch replied that the presence of the ship was due to bad weather, and once it had taken aboard water and provisions it would sail. The ship duly left, but Clive remained suspicious. He stationed a detachment of troops with some of the Nawab's army at Tannah fort, erected batteries overlooking the ship channel and started searching all Dutch shipping. This annoyed the Dutch and provoked the series of minor incidents that might be expected. One such afflicted Lieutenant George Koehler who wrote to Clive on 8 October 1759, '. . . finding myself accused in a very extraordinary and unjust manner by Mynheer Zuyland and Trembly of Chinsura of treating the said gentlemen ill on 29 September last in searching some Dutch boats in consequence of orders received from Your Honor [sic] . . . by these affidavits you will see how unjustly I am accused'.

The Dutch, however, were preparing sterner measures than making 'unjust' accusations against the officers of the Company. Early in October, while Mir Jafar was visiting Calcutta, six Dutch vessels crammed with troops, anchored off the mouth of the Hooghly. It was a situation of peculiar delicacy. Holland and Britain were officially friendly states, and, if an incident in India precipitated Holland into joining France in the European war, Clive's head would answer for it. On the other hand most of the Bengal army was still in the Northern Circars, and if the Dutch allied themselves with a faction in Murshidabad the British position in Bengal would be gravely jeopardised. The Dutch presence was only explicable as part of a wider intrigue aimed at crippling British power in Bengal.

Mir Jafar assured Clive that he would compel the Dutch to withdraw their ships, and left on 19 October for the town of Hooghly with the proclaimed intention of making this clear to them. Warren Hastings who was with him observed, however, that when the Nawab interviewed the Dutch authorities from Chinsura, he treated them with suspicious cordiality. After the interview, Mir Jafar informed Clive

42 Boats on the Hooghly.

that the Dutch ships had been detained by the weather, and that as soon as it was favourable they would sail. As the weather was excellent, and as John Matthews in charge of Tannah fort had seen the Dutch ships lowering their masts, his statement seemed open to doubt.

Clive prepared for action. He did not intend that a Dutch attempt to reach Chinsura should go uncontested, or at least he was determined to give the Dutch that impression. He armed batteries commanding the narrow Tannah passage, and improvised a naval squadron out of three East Indiamen at anchor off Calcutta by mounting heavy cannon on them and thickening the sides of their gun decks with salt-petre sacks; he recalled the British detachment at Patna, and every able-bodied man in Calcutta was mobilised. Forde had returned from the Northern Circars as the Directors had rewarded his magnificent services by promoting Eyre Coote over his head; he was in ill-health and had resigned from the Company, yet he volunteered to command the troops.

For a period matters hung fire. The Dutch, too, had their political difficulties. Apart from the formidable problem of forcing their way past the British batteries, their own government might not welcome an incident which they appeared to have provoked, and the resolute action taken by Clive, linked with the absence of any signs of assistance from the Nawab, made them tread warily. They decided to clear the political ground by lodging with the Council in Calcutta a 'grand remonstrance', protesting against the British searching of their ships, which, they asserted, was an infringement of Dutch sovereignty, and they threatened reprisals.

The Council at Calcutta replied with a certain smugness that they had no intention of insulting the Dutch flag, but in taking steps to prevent Dutch ships coming up the Hooghly with soldiers on board they were only acting under the instructions of the Viceroy, himself vested with his authority by the Emperor, as they were required to do by the terms of their alliance. In addition, since Britain was at war with France it was incumbent on them to see that no French soldiers were smuggled into Bengal. They added unctuously that, if the Dutch so wished, they would present their case in the viceregal court and endeavour to save them from punishment for violating his orders. The blatant hypocrisy of the last part of their reply appears to have stung the Dutch into playing into the hands of the British.

In Murshidabad matters remained confused. Francis Sykes told Clive he had seen Miran and that he was ready to 'depart for Hooghly with all his troops . . . to act as you may think proper. He told me his father had informed him that the dispute had been compromised while he was at Hooghly ... and refused to let him have guns and ammunition'. But the Dutch had lost patience. On 13 November, Ensign Brown at Budge-Budge reported to Carnac that the Dutch had hoisted their masts and 'sails bent ready to sail', and on 15 November, Bernard Forrester, master of one of the East Indiamen, the Duke of Dorset, added, 'They [the Dutch] are determined to proceed up the river with their ships and stop at Sangaral to land their troops who it seems are destined to attack Tannah fort by surprise in the night, having large scaling ladders for this purpose'.

A crisis was fast approaching, and now the Dutch made an extremely stupid blunder. They attacked and captured some small British ships at the mouth of the Hooghly, landed at Fulta, destroying British property and hauling down the Union Jack, and barred the river to navigation by British ships. Clive had the justification he wanted for any action he took. On 16 November Alexander Scott, the master of another of the East Indiamen, reported to Clive, 'The Dutch this morning weighed at Fulta. The Dutch ships have taken the *Leopard* snow, *Monmouth* ketch ... with four sloops'. They also refused to allow the British squadron up the river to Calcutta. Alexander continued, referring to the Dutch Commodore, 'I should not regard him or his ships either, but since the captains think their orders are not sufficient to indemnify them if the ships receive damage or be taken or sunk ... it was resolved, if they would not let us pass, to keep close to them into Tannah reach and there do what we can to distress them'. The ships' captains were not worried by the guns of the Dutch, but by the financial implications of incurring damage in an unauthorised engagement.

On this Clive took the initiative. He ordered Forde to take his men to seize a Dutch building in Baranagar, advance on Chandernagore and take up a position near Chinsura, ready to intercept the Dutch if they tried to come up the river overland. He told his improvised naval squadron to shadow the Dutch ships, and he sent a strongly-worded letter to Mir Jafar. As the Dutch ships started up the Hooghly and an armed clash between the British and Dutch looked imminent, Mir Jafar, worried by the fear of a rupture with Clive, at last took action and gave orders for the Dutch factories in outstations to be closed down. On 22 November Warren Hastings wrote to Clive 'This evening Din Mahmud and Bahadur Ali Khan, Jemadars, surrounded the Dutch factory at Coleapore, everything goes on in this quarter as it ought. The Nawab seems as zealous in the cause as he was before remiss in it.'

43 The Dutch settlement at Chinsura.

Perhaps alarmed for the safety of Chinsura, on 22 November the Dutch troops disembarked near Sankeral point, just out of range of the batteries of Tannah; but their ships seemed reluctant to risk an action with the British batteries and dropped down the river again with the three British ships in attendance. By landing their troops, Clive believed, the Dutch ships were now weak enough for the British to attack them with a reasonable chance of success. He ordered Captain Wilson, the commodore of his squadron, to demand from the Dutch Commodore the return of the

British ships and seamen he had captured, under pain of instant battle. The Dutchman refused. Wilson at once attacked. After a stubborn action all but one of the Dutch ships were captured.

Forde at this time was at Chandernagore, having driven in a small Dutch force from Chinsura he had discovered lurking in its outskirts and taken their guns. He now stood with boats moored to the riverbank, ready to advance against Chinsura or sail down the river to succour Tannah fort. On 23 November he had news that the Dutch troops were marching up the river. Forde, confident that he could defeat them but uncertain of the political situation, wrote to Clive asking for an Order-in-Council authorising him to fight. It is related by Malcolm that Clive was sitting at a table playing cards when the note was brought over to him. Without leaving the table he picked up a pencil, scrawled across it, 'Dear Forde, fight them immediately, I will send the Order-in-Council tomorrow' and resumed his game.[1]

On the morning of 25 November 1759, Forde saw the little Dutch column, weary and footsore, straggling into view; it consisted of 700 Europeans and 800 Malays under a French soldier of fortune, but it lacked both cavalry and guns. Forde had with him only 240 European infantry, a troop of 50 European Horse composed of young Calcutta bloods taking time off from their counting houses, 800 sepoys, a detachment of 100 Horse from the Nawab's army and four guns. The experienced British commander lined his army up across the Chinsura road with one flank resting on a village and the other on an orchard, while along most of his front ran a deep wide nullah. The Dutch knew neither the ground nor the country, but they formed a line and pressed forward towards the British. They suffered severely from the British guns as they advanced, and then their ranks were disordered by the nullah. It was all over in half an hour. As the Dutch fell back in disorder, the cavalry charged home and turned their retreat into a rout. Strangers in a strange country, those that were not struck down surrendered.

[1] Forrester maintains Forde's letter referred to the Dutch on the outskirts of Chandernagore.

The Dutch now were helpless, and the Council at Chinsura pleaded for terms. They agreed that they were the aggressors and would pay the expenses of the British. This satisfied Clive and he gave them back their ships. Two or three days later Miran appeared with 7,000 Horse. Clive at once interposed his troops so that there could be no question of the Nawab's troops plundering the hapless Dutch settlement, and mediated on their behalf with the Prince whose quarrel he had in theory espoused. Terms were agreed with the Nawab whereby the Dutch, in exchange for permission to continue trading, undertook not to maintain more than 125 soldiers in Bengal, nor to enlist any locally. Any surplus to this number were to be sent away immediately. If the Dutch offended against the terms of the agreement they would be expelled from Bengal. The treaty ended all possibility of further Dutch adventures in India.

It had been a curious, almost inexplicable, episode. Bisdom, the Governor at Chinsura, was a friend of Clive's and opposed to the venture from the start, but seems to have been overruled by the rest of his council, perhaps from the idea that while the French broke the British power in the Carnatic, the Dutch should take the opportunity to expel the British from Bengal. From the Dutch correspondence it is evident that in November 1758 Mir Jafar entered into some form of agreement with them. At that time his trust in Clive's good faith had been shaken. Then in the spring of 1759 Clive saved him from the Shahzada and demonstrated, beyond any reasonable doubt, that he had been no party to the dubious intrigues of the year before. When the first Dutch ship arrived he had made clear to the Dutch that his views had changed, but they disregarded the warning and persisted in their original scheme. Once again the Nawab was on the horns of a dilemma. He now had every reason to be grateful to Clive, but to a certain extent he was pledged to the Dutch. He adopted a policy, to be made famous by a later British prime-minister, that of 'wait' and see', and his actions had the same ambiguity that characterised them before Plassey. Yet every overt action he took aided the British; had he openly sided with the

Dutch, Clive's difficulties would have been well-nigh insuperable.

Mir Jafar had a strong streak of passivity running through his character; when a situation was too difficult he simply drifted with the tide of events; it is possible that he is not the only ruler to have done so. It is difficult to censure his actions. Less than a year after Clive departed, the British did depose him, an action that bitterly divided British opinion in Bengal and one that Clive himself deeply resented. Mir Jafar was no pillar of rectitude, he would never have been Commander-in-Chief of an army in India had he possessed so unusual a virtue; he was certainly no gifted administrator; but within the context of the age he was an honourable man. Clive later said of him, 'The old Nawab, Mir Jafar, if ever a Mussulman had an affection for a Christian had an affection for me.' In his own way there can be little doubt that Clive returned that affection.

There is an interesting sidelight on the whole affair. Clive had much of his own fortune at stake; it was in Dutch hands, and his father was busily engaged in trying to extract it from them in Amsterdam. As a result of the payments made by Mir Jafar, the Company had a glut of money at Calcutta and refused to grant its servants bills of exchange on London. Clive had sent most of his money to Chinsura to be used for bills on Amsterdam.

But Clive had another antagonist now, one that perhaps was to give him one of the hardest fights of his life, the Court of Directors in London.

Chapter 15

INTERLUDE IN ENGLAND
1760–4

Although for Clive 1759 had been a year of splendid achievement in India, his relationship with the Court of Directors in London had steadily deteriorated. He paid little heed to their directions, and they in their appointments were more anxious to exploit their opportunities for patronage than to choose men of ability and judgement. He suffered a number of pinpricks, then came an appointment that roused his anger to a degree almost past bearing.

Coote, after his return to England, had been masquerading, not entirely at his own desire, as the hero of Plassey, on the grounds that it was on his, the professional soldier's advice, that Clive had advanced from Cutwa and won the battle. In consequence, when the Government agreed to raise a regular infantry battalion for service in Bengal, he was selected to command it. The Directors, gratified at receiving such assistance, and possibly under the impression that if an officer of the regular army commanded in Bengal his views would carry greater weight with the military authorities at home than those of an officer of the Company, conferred on him the appointment of Commander-in-Chief in Bengal. They wrote to acquaint an unreceptive Clive of their skilful piece of diplomacy.

Not only was the news personally unpalatable to Clive, he was infuriated that Forde, who had been Coote's senior in the 39th and had just concluded a brilliant campaign in the Northern Circars, should be superseded in this way by an officer who, except for his fruitless pursuit of Law, had never exercised an independent command in the field. Remembering the activities of Adlercron and the undefined relationship between Governors appointed by the Company and officers appointed by the Crown, he also doubted the wisdom of the decision. And not least the refusal to confirm Forde in his post as Commander-in-Chief in Bengal appeared a slight on his own judgement.

On learning he was passed over, Forde at once resigned, but Clive assured that ill-treated officer he would do everything in his power to have the appointment reversed. Coote with his regiment arrived at Madras in October 1759; but the still critical state of affairs in the Carnatic induced Governor Pigot, with the willing concurrence of Clive, to retain him and send Major Caillaud with 200 men to reinforce Bengal. Vansittart, at this time a member of the Council at Madras, drily wrote to Clive on 17 October, 'I am quite of the opinion that Caillaud with 200 of the Company's old troops would be more useful in Bengal than Coote with his whole regiment.' But by keeping Coote at Madras, it appeared to the Directors in London that, as had happened over their orders for reforming the Constitution of the Council in Bengal, their governors in India were flouting their authority once again. Sulivan, their chairman, deeply resented the activities of the 'rebellious gentlemen of Bengal', as he termed them.

During the autumn of 1759 Clive's health started to trouble him. He resolved to return to England as soon as the Dutch affair was settled, both to recruit his strength and to represent to the Directors the folly and injustice of their actions. He became so exasperated with the letters he received from England that he allowed his passions to overcome his judgement, and expressed his views with a freedom that was to harm himself and the Company's affairs in Bengal. The Directors themselves were not accustomed to mince their words; the following paragraph is an example of their epistolary style: 'We shall pass over the before mentioned triplicate of your letter by the Marlborough until your consultations are received. [Then proceeding to do nothing of the sort] Because from the lights before us there appear such flagrant instances of weak management, such gross neglects of our interests that were the facts properly established would oblige us to animadvert on your conduct in the severest terms.' Apparently noticing nothing incongruous, they signed themselves, 'your loving friends'.

But such diction is unwise to a superior, Clive, perhaps suffering at the time from fever, in a General letter to the Directors dated 29 December 1759 signed by all the members of the Select Committee, cast aside all restraint. Among other things it was stated: 'Mr Ellis will have a seat on our Board on his arrival. We beg to observe that by this nomination you have superseded eleven of your servants in this establishment whose fidelity and zeal to this establishment have never been questioned. . . . We might say the same thing with regard to your appointment of Captain James Barton to so high in your Council.'

The letter commented that the Company's servants in Calcutta were 'faithful to little purpose if the breath of scandal joined to private and personal attachment have the power to sway in one hour the merits of many years service'.

It concluded, 'Permit us to say that the diction of your letter is most unworthy of yourselves and us, whatever relation considered, either as masters to servants or gentlemen to gentlemen. Mere inadvertences and casual neglects arising from an unavoidable and most complicated confusion in your affairs have been treated in such language as nothing but the most glaring and premeditated faults could warrant.' The Directors were not only incompetent and corrupt, they did not know how to behave like gentlemen.

Before he sent the letter Clive had decided to resign and his preparations for returning home were already well advanced. He would have been wise to wait until he reached England before venting his wrath. The news that he was leaving caused dismay in Calcutta and Murshidabad, but he would listen to no pleading; apart from anything else, his failing health made a return imperative. In February 1760,

Margaret and he dropped down the Hooghly in the *Royal George* bound for England. It must have been a sorrowful moment for Peggy. A baby had been born to her a few months earlier and now lay mortally sick. But wind and tide waited for no man, and she had to embark and leave her baby behind to die. As the *Royal George* cleared the mouth of the Hooghly, a vessel with dispatches from Madras passed her going up the river. The dispatches contained the information that on 22 January 1760, Eyre Coote had utterly defeated the French at the battle of Wandewash. Lally was wounded and Bussy captured.

Clive stepped ashore in England towards the end of the summer of 1760, not only famous but exceedingly wealthy. He was received by the King and voted the thanks of the Directors, although some, including the chairman, Sulivan, silently nursed rather different emotions in which gratitude hardly figured at all.

In Bengal Vansittart, on his recommendation, came from Madras to be President. In July Miran died, struck by lightning and mourned by few. Vansittart first nominated Mir Kasim as the Nawab's heir, then losing patience with Mir Jafar's incompetence, deposed him and placed Mir Kassim on the *musnud*; it was an act that deeply divided the Company's servants in Bengal, many of whom, including Carnac, thought the action dishonourable and impolitic. As a result of the transaction, Mir Kassim ceded permanently to the Company the districts of Burdwan, Midnapore and Chittagong, ostensibly to pay for troops the Company would maintain for his assistance. The Council at Calcutta received a gift of 20 lakhs of rupees of which £60,000 went personally to Vansittart. The precedent set by Clive had been followed, but with little justification. Vansittart no doubt thought he acted in the best interests of the Company, but the deposition cast long and ugly shadows; it could appear that the Company was prepared to auction Bengal at regular intervals to the highest bidder, as Mir Kassim himself at one moment ironically suggested to Vansittart. Mir Jafar's overthrow started a chain of events that almost inevitably led to catastrophe.

When Peggy heard the news she wrote to Carnac, 'I am much surprised by the Revolution in Bengal. I may say sorry over our old Nawab, but I am no judge of such affairs'. She recalled, 'I cannot help putting in mind how carefully my Lord [once the "Colonel"] made me conceal myself when the black grandees came to visit, not suffering me to appear till I was asked for, thereby to increase their respect.'

Before coming to England Clive had written to William Pitt, for whom he cherished an immense admiration, suggesting that it was no longer appropriate for a merchant company to own such extensive territories and wield such power as the Company now possessed. He thought Britain could annex Bengal, Bihar and Orissa, without difficulty and should govern the three provinces as a colony under the Crown. He was confident that the majority of the people would welcome British rule, 'The natives themselves have no attachment whatever to particular princes, and as under the present government they have no security in their lives or properties, they would rejoice in so happy an exchange as that of a mild for a despotic Government.' The sentiments may be questioned, but both in the Carnatic and Bengal Clive's conquests could never have been won if the people of the provinces as a whole had not shown an almost total disinterest in the fate of their rulers.

Pitt, at this time immersed in the Seven Years' War and facing the prospect that a young and headstrong Prince might soon be King, was reluctant to add to his problems by introducing so contentious a measure. In 1757 he had been largely responsible for having the Company's charter renewed for twenty years in exchange for a handsome donation to the Exchequer. For the Crown to take over the Company a bare three years later might savour of sharp practice; besides he feared the proposal might provide the monarch with an income outside the control of Parliament, and he told Walsh who presented Clive's proposal, 'such a revenue would endanger our liberties'.

The proposal was dropped, and a century was to pass before Clive's far-sighted proposals were adopted. The news that he had made such a proposition was unlikely to endear him to the Directors; they might, not unjustifiably, think it an intolerable piece of presumption on the part of one of their servants to recommend to the Prime Minister that their company should be liquidated. Sulivan, their chairman, was a man of considerable experience and great force of character. He upheld whole-heartedly the idea that the Company existed solely to make a profit and should not become entangled in expensive military adventures. At first Clive and he behaved towards each other with a cordiality that neither felt. A clash between the two, taking into account Clive's imperious nature, sooner or later was bound to occur.

However, shortly after his arrival in England Clive's health collapsed. He suffered from gout and rheumatism and possibly from attacks of malaria. The strain of the past three years took its toll, and to add to his physical infirmities he fell into a fit of melancholia. Peggy wrote to Carnac, '. . . the disorder which prayed on his spirits, as well as his health, was of such a nature as to terrify me'.

Early in 1761, after sampling the waters of Bath, he seems to have recovered his health and zest for living. He was only thirty-six years old and determined to have a say in the government of his country. He took a house in Berkeley Square and stood for Parliament as the Member for Shrewsbury. He was duly elected on 27 April 1761. He arranged for one or two of his friends and relatives, notably Walsh, to stand as well, so that he could have a small personal following in the Commons. There were, however, difficulties. His cousin George Clive wrote to him from Penryn in April, 'We have found the mayor the only elector in Penryn and he was unfortunately against us.' It must have been a very exclusive constituency.

It is curious that nothing was done by the Government to recognise Clive's services immediately on his return to England. It was not until December 1761, that at his instance the Duke of Newcastle obtained for him an Irish peerage, and he was granted the title of Robert Lord Clive Baron of Plassey in the County of Clare. Clive had renamed an estate he acquired in Ireland, Plassey, so he could have the famous name in his title.

On 5 October 1761, his political ambitions suffered a reverse when the leader he revered, Pitt, failing to persuade his Cabinet to anticipate a declaration of war by Spain, resigned. In July 1762, the Duke of Newcastle followed his example, and Lord Bute assumed the leadership of the Government. Clive was not prepared to turn his back on his old political associates and resisted the blandishments of Bute who desired his support. He became independent and had the mortification of seeing Bute turn instead to Sulivan.

With Sulivan his relations were becoming strained. Sulivan adamantly refused to make Forde Commander-in-Chief in Bengal, and indeed after Coote's success at Wandewash he can scarcely be blamed for his refusal. Clive was pledged to support Forde and would not abandon his protégé. Then there was the matter of the intemperate letter to the Directors of 29 December 1759. When it was received the explosion of wrath could probably be heard the length of Leadenhall Street. To be accused of incompetence and nepotism was bad enough, but to be told that they were no gentlemen, that was altogether too much. All those who signed the letter were dismissed from the Company's service out of hand, thereby contributing not a little to the impending tragedy in Bengal. Sulivan, writing to Eyre Coote, had already complained, 'The ungrateful wretches late of Bengal have hurt my temper', and in the nature of things the most prominent of the ungrateful wretches came to hear of his sentiments.

Still Clive trod warily. The Court of Directors had one powerful weapon, they might deprive him of the rent of his jaghir. Out of London he bought property including a house, Walcot, near Bishops Castle which he had largely rebuilt. He moved in Court circles and was to have a royal god-parent for one of the daughters that Peggy provided him with at regular intervals. He, himself, maintained considerable state, and he was something of a dandy with a liking for bright colours. Peggy wrote in September 1761 to Carnac, 'We are very much taken up with the setting of the new Court. Our King and Queen are just married and half the people in England are run mad on the occasion.' And later, 'We are on a very good footing with our India acquaintance, the gentlemen are sociable and form themselves into a club and once a fortnight they meet at an assembly carried on by subscription for the entertainment of the ladies. . . . I have been to some of their balls when I meet a number of my old acquaintance.' Peggy also occupied her leisure hours when away from her babies by the study of music. Clive did not neglect family affairs. While in India he settled £2,000 on each of his five sisters and told them in round terms that it was high time they were married. Whether it was his advice or the money is not disclosed but two of them obeyed instructions within a matter of months. He also provided an annuity for his improvident father.

But affairs of state were soon to demand his attention. The war with France was drawing to a close, and he submitted a memorial to Bute suggesting what he thought should be the basis of the British proposals for a settlement in India. Coote had captured and destroyed Pondicherry and finally extinguished French power. Clive recommended that the French should be severely limited in the number of soldiers they were allowed to keep on the Coromandel coast, and be strictly forbidden to re-enter Bengal.

In the Treaty of Paris that ended the War, most of what he recommended was included. But the treaty contained one sentence to which he took exception. It ran: 'In order to preserve future peace on the coast of Coromandel and Orissa, the English and French shall acknowledge Mohammed Ali Khan as the lawful Nawab of the Carnatic and Salabat Jang for the lawful Soubah of the Deccan.'

Clive considered that French recognition of the two princes implied that France still had some standing in matters of succession. It seems a small point and the future was to prove that, although the French might intrigue with the Princes and send them adventurers of varying degrees of military skill, they would never succeed in re-establishing a military power in the sub-continent sufficient again to endanger the

British position. In such matters British seapower was more potent than legal niceties. However, in the event, and to Bute's marked displeasure, Clive joined the minority that voted against the treaty. At this time it might be misleading to describe Britain as a democracy, but power largely resided in Parliament. That establishment could be, and was, manipulated, but some form of consensus was necessary and such can rarely be achieved without compromise; but compromise was foreign to Clive's nature. His refusal to make the small concessions often necessary to attain great ends proved a fatal political handicap to him in his own country which, perhaps, he never understood so well as he understood India.

Bute fell shortly after the treaty was signed, and George Grenville succeeded him as leader of the Government. Both Pitt and Newcastle were in opposition; Clive had no wish to join them there, and Grenville was to become a close political friend. At the same time he had no wish to appear to abandon Pitt and Newcastle merely because they were out of favour. He solved a delicate problem by declaring himself again independent. The disunity, feuds, and manoeuvring for personal advantage that marked this period he viewed with disgust. For the time being, he decided to forsake his political ambitions and instead of the Commons to dominate the Court of Directors. It was a decision bound to lead to mortal strife with Sulivan. The constitution of the Company, like that of many other British institutions, was not a little odd. James Mill in his history of India Volume III remarked of the Company that supreme power was vested in the Court of Proprietors,

'In the first place they held the legislative power entire; all laws and regulations, all determination of dividends, all grants of money were made by the Court of Proprietors. To act under their ordinance and manage the business of routine was the department reserved for the Court of Directors. . . . In this constitution the Court of Proprietors be regarded as representing the general body of the people, the Court of Directors as representing an aristocratical senate and the chairman as representing the sovereign, we have an image of the British Constitution.'

Here Mill exaggerated somewhat. In many ways the Chairman possessed more power over the Company than the British Sovereign of that time over his realm, even when the Sovereign was George III. The Court of Proprietors, sometimes referred to as the General Court, elected the Court of Directors annually in the months of April. The Directors numbered twenty-four with thirteen present constituting a quorum. To qualify to be a member of the Court of Proprietors, a shareholder in the Company had to hold a minimum of £500's worth of stock; voting in the Court of Proprietors was by the counting of heads, irrespective of how much stock a shareholder might hold over, and above his qualifying £500. The twenty-four Directors had to hold stock to the value of £2,000; they possessed very considerable influence and powers of patronage, and the competition for office was keen.

Clive now adopted a simple expedient to gain control. Before the next election he bought up large quantities of stock, then split it down into £500 lots which he assigned to a host of nominees. There were no rules about how long the qualifying amount of stock should be held; it could be acquired a few days before the election and disposed of almost immediately afterwards. The device of splitting stock, as it was called, was subsequently stopped by enforcing a minimum period during which the stock had to be held before the holder was entitled to a vote. At the time Clive's tactics, although not altogether novel, were looked on as rather 'sharp'. It is difficult to see why; under modern company law the measure of control exerted by individual shareholders depends, in the last resort, on the amount of stock they hold and not the number of followers they can count among the other shareholders.

Sulivan became aware that his authority was challenged and a bitter struggle ensued. Most of the shareholders who had been in Bengal favoured Clive; there was always a tendency for shareholders who had been in India to vote according to the presidency in which they had served. However, Sulivan, who came from Bombay, was a formidable opponent. In a letter of 21 April 1761 to Carnac Clive described the election of that year. 'After a most violent contest whichever happened for the choice of the Directors we at last are worsted. We began too late and were wanting both in activity and experience. However, the knowledge we have acquired will enable us to engage on more equal terms next year for which we are sparring already.'

The last statement was only too true. After his victory, Sulivan with the ruthlessness of the great commander at once exploited his success. As chairman of the Company he ordered that payment of the rent on Clive's jaghir should at once be suspended, and he instructed the Company's lawyers to examine the possibility of claiming back all the payments that had already been made. Sulivan shows up badly; he was prepared to use all the resources of the Company to further a personal quarrel. In a letter of extraordinary venom he directed that every detail of Clive's title to the jaghir should be doubly checked.

Clive at once took steps to refer the matter to the Courts, and both sides prepared for a lawsuit of outstanding bitterness and duration. The legality of Sulivan's action was as dubious as his motives. He queried Clive's right to the jaghir on the grounds that only the Emperor was empowered to grant land and that, therefore, the grant made by Mir Jafar was invalid. However, that argument had no bearing on Mir Jafar's right to assign revenue from his own land how he wished; moreover the application of this argument, generally, would have invalidated the Company's rights to most of the territory it owned, both in Bengal and the Carnatic. Besides all this, the Court might well wonder why the legality of Mir Jafar's action should suddenly be questioned four years after the event. While both sides were mustering their arguments, news came from Bengal that overshadowed all else.

Vansittart, when he became Governor, found himself in an unprecedented situation and encompassed by difficulties that it was beyond his powers to overcome. The Company had been instrumental in placing Mir Jafar on the *musnud*, and now at its nod Mir Jafar had been deposed. As a result, the authority of the Nawab had been fatally undermined, and there were many adventurers, both British and Indian, eager to take advantage of a state of affairs where jurisdiction was so uncertain. The old question of *dustucks* and the right to the free movement of goods for the internal trade gave rise to the most flagrant abuses, which the officials of Mir Kassim were powerless to check. Vansittart saw the abuses, but was the prisoner of his own Council. The situation was aggravated in that his most experienced councillors, having signed Clive's injudicious letter, had been summarily dismissed; the remainder, with the notable exception of Warren Hastings, were interested only in accumulating a fortune in the shortest possible time. The vicious system, whereby the Company paid its servants an utterly inadequate salary which they were expected to supplement by their own endeavours, was an open invitation to corruption, one that most of its servants were happy to accept.

Mir Kassim was determined to free himself from the shackles of the Company. He began by removing from office those who owed their position to the British. In particular he took his revenge on Ram Narain, the Governor of Bihar, who in Clive's day had thwarted him when he tried to acquire that province for himself. He relieved Ram Narain from his office and imprisoned him. Vansittart made a few futile gestures of protest, but in the end did nothing effective. His acquiescence in this treatment of a friend of the British angered Clive, whose numerous friends in Bengal kept him well posted with events, and it was the beginning of a lasting breach between the two men. Having successfully displaced Ram Narain, Mir Kassim moved his capital from Murshidabad, dangerously close to Calcutta as he thought, to Monghyr 160 miles up the Ganges.

By February 1763, friction between the Nawab's officials and the British had reached a pitch when an explosion could not long be delayed. To limit the abuse of *dustucks* Vansittart tried to make the internal trade in betel-nut, tobacco and salt subject to the Nawab's customs and excise. The Council almost unanimously rejected his proposal. The Nawab, maddened by the contempt with which his officials were treated, declared free passage for all merchandise throughout his realm. The Council at Calcutta, horrified by a measure that would extend to all the privilege on which much of their wealth depended, had the effrontery to send two envoys, Hay and Amyatt, to protest.

The Nawab now demanded that Ellis, the British chief at Patna, and the British garrison in that city should be withdrawn. The majority of the Council, overriding their Governor, looked on this demand as a virtual declaration of war and authorised Ellis, if he thought fit, to seize the citadel at Patna. Ellis, appointed to his position at the behest of the Directors, was a stupid and violent man, unsuited to his post. While Mir Kassim was negotiating with the Council in Calcutta, he ordered his troops to storm the citadel. His men took it by surprise, but then he allowed them to disperse in search of plunder. The Nawab's army promptly struck back, retook the citadel, dispersed the sepoys, and after a hard struggle captured all the Europeans. It was the signal for a general conflagration throughout Bengal. Amyatt and his party were passing Murshidabad in boats returning from their talks with the Nawab. They were ambushed; Amyatt was killed and the remainder of his party taken prisoner. All over Bengal the property of the Company was looted and its officials imprisoned. Only in Dacca was the factory successfully defended.

In Calcutta, when the Council heard of Amyatt's death, it was resolved to reinstate Mir Jafar as Nawab. Major Adams took an army to Murshidabad, proclaimed the new Nawab, then drove forward to Monghyr where, it was rumoured, Mir Kassim was assembling his troops. As Adams pressed on against some violent opposition, Mir Kassim evacuated his capital and retired on Patna. He warned Adams he would kill all his European captives if Monghyr were attacked.

Ellis, himself, managed to send a letter to Adams, in which, with great courage, he said that the possible fate of the European prisoners should not be allowed in any way to affect the operations of the army. Adams seized Monghyr and thrust on towards Patna. Mir Kassim was as good as his word. He had all his European prisoners butchered, Ram Narain was thrown into the Ganges with a sack of sand tied round his neck, and two members of the Seth family he had taken as hostages were also murdered. Then he fled across the border to Oudh, where he was welcomed by the Nawab, Shuja-ud-daula. The Shahzada, who after the death of his father, had claimed to be Emperor taking the name of Shah Alam II, was once again sheltering in Oudh, and he now saw another chance of securing the support he needed to assert his claim.

In 1764, with an army 30,000-strong, the three Princes invaded Bihar. At Buxar, on the morning of 16 October 1764 they encountered a British army under Major Hector Munro consisting of 850 Europeans, 5,000 sepoys and 1,000 local cavalry. By the evening, after a bloody combat, the three Princes were fugitives and their armies no more.

In England the news of the looting of the British factories in Bengal and the massacre of so many British caused stupefaction. Peggy wrote to Carnac on 27 February 1764, 'The Lapwing brought us news of the new revolution in Bengal and the death of Mr Amyatt . . . we conclude you were not in the field at the time of their attack on Patna. . . . This day is held a general meeting of the East India proprietors. . . . I feel nothing but joy in the news of his [Mir Jafar's] being reinstated, where it not for the losses of the Company, for I have grieved much to hear of his deposition.'

The meeting of the proprietors on 27 February was adjourned to 12 March. To the proprietors there was one man and one man only to restore order to the chaos in Bengal. They voted to request Clive to go to Bengal as Governor and Commander-in-Chief. He, however, temporised, asking that the appointment might be endorsed by the Directors. The Directors duly endorsed it, but still Clive procrastinated; an election for the new Court of Directors was impending, and he wanted to be certain that he would be properly supported before he embarked on so delicate a mission. Since Clive had not accepted the offer, Sulivan sought to have it annulled, but the Court of Proprietors threw his motion out. On 28 March Clive in a letter to the proprietors began to show his hand; he bluntly refused to accept the offer, unless Sulivan was divested of the chairmanship and he could count on the support of the Court of Directors. On 12 April the new court was elected, twelve were adherents of Clive, twelve of Sulivan. Everything now depended on whom the proprietors elected Chairman. The following day the crucial election was held, Rous was to be chairman and Bolton deputy; both were friends of Clive. Peggy wrote to Carnac on 14 April, 'Mr Sulivan by a majority of one vote came into the direction, but being rejected of being chairman he went out of the court yesterday in a pet followed by some of his friends saying he wished the gentlemen a better direction. From this it is rumoured that Mr Sulivan intends resigning his place as he cannot be the leader. Mr Rous is chairman. ... He [Clive] goes in a month's time to India. He seems to think we shall embark at one of the ports most distant from London.'

Clive was ready to go but only on his own terms. The matter of his jaghir needed to be settled; the Proprietors confirmed that the Company would pay the rent for at least the next ten years, a compromise he himself had suggested earlier. He required authority to override the Council in Calcutta if he thought fit. It was agreed that he should be independent of the Council, but he was not given completely dictatorial powers, he had to act with the concurrence of a Select Committee; but this was to be composed of four friends, Carnac, Verelst, Sykes and Sumner. All members of the regular army were to be recalled from Bengal and the two senior Company officers there, Carnac and Caillaud, were to be granted the rank of Brigadier General. Sir Robert Barker was appointed to command the artillery. To try to stamp out the corruption that had played a significant part in the Bengal tragedy, it was ruled that all servants of the Company should covenant to hand over to the Company

any gift they received which exceeded 4,000 rupees in value. Clive himself swore that he would return not one penny the richer.

Before embarking he wrote two letters in which he set out his views on the policy to be followed; they are both of considerable interest, as they reveal among other things the reasoning behind the policy he pursued during his first term as Governor of Bengal. Since, after that period, he recommended to Pitt that the Country should take over the Company's territory in India, he cannot have regarded the results of the policy as entirely satisfactory. He wrote '... I think myself bound in honour to accept the charge of your affairs in Bengal provided you will co-operate and assist me in such manner that I may be able to answer the expectations and intentions of the General Court'.

He went on to analyse the mistakes that led to Mir Kassim's revolt: 'He was suffered to retire at a great distance from his capital, that our influence might be felt and dreaded as little as possible by him: he was suffered to dismiss all those old officers who had any connection with or dependance upon us; and what was worst of all our faithfull friend and ally, Ram Narain, the Nawab of Patna was given up. Either the princes of the country must be in a great measure dependent on us or we totally so on them.'

He suggested that the strong British party in Bengal who disapproved of Mir Jafar's deposition, once the Prince had been deposed, were culpable in continuing an opposition that led Mir Kassim to fear a reversal of policy within the Council, which might lead Mir Jafar to be reinstated. He continued:

'The encroachments made upon the Nawab's prescriptive right by the Governor and Council and the rest of the servants trading in the articles of salt, betel and tobacco, together with the power given by Mr Vansittart to subject our gomastahs or agents to the jurisdiction of the country government all concurred to hasten and bring on the late troubles; but still the groundwork of the whole was the Nawab's independency ... strict and impartial justice should ever be observed; but let that justice come from ourselves.

'The trade therefore of salt, betel and tobacco having been the cause of the present disputes, I hope these articles will be restored to the Nawab and your servants absolutely forbid to trade in them. ... If some method be not thought of and your council do not heartily co-operate with your Governor to prevent the sudden acquisition of fortunes which has taken place of late, the Company's affairs must greatly suffer ... for the good of the Company I would propose that you should always have in Bengal four or at least three thousand Europeans; to consist of three battalions of seven hundred each, four companies of artillery one hundred each, and five hundred light horse. ...

'I could wish that whatever emoluments are unavoidable may fall to those few who having been long are high in your service. Thus will the expense be hardly felt by the Company, in comparison to what it is at the present time, when, for want of due subordination, everyone thinks himself entitled to every advantage, and the juniors of your service be excited to exert themselves from a certain knowledge that application and abilities only can restore them to their native country with fortunes honourably acquired.'

In his second letter he stresses that the deposition of Mir Jafar and the war against Mir Kassim

'Have lost us all the confidence of the natives; to restore this ought to be our principal object; and the best means will, in my opinion, be by establishing a moderation in the advantages which may be reserved for the Company or allotted to individuals in their service. ... Nothing but extreme necessity ought to induce us to extend our ideas of territorial acquisitions beyond the amount of those ceded by Mir Kassim to Vansittart. ...

'It ought to be our plan to convince the Nawab that our troops are his best, his only, support against foreign enemies, and that our friendship will be his best support against the plots and revolutions of his own officers. ... The principal officers must be convinced that we will protect them from any capricious violencies of their sovereign; on the other hand the Nawab must be convinced that we will give them up to his just resentment the moment their ambitions alone lead them to strike at him.

'To carry this balance with even hand the strictest integrity will be necessary in everyone who shall have a vote in your councils abroad.'

The contradictions in this policy, in large measure caused by the break-up of the Moghul Empire, are only too apparent. To avoid being at the mercy of the Nawab of Bengal, the Company had to be sovereign and independent; yet at the same time it had to be nominally under the jurisdiction of a ruler who would himself be wholly dependent on it for the armed forces upon which, in the last resort, all authority depends. Clive foresaw that, in the political maelstrom that accompanied the fall of the Moghul Empire, if the Company appeared as a strong sovereign power it might excite the combined hostility of the Indian Princes, and either itself be engulfed or else forced to extend its commitments beyond its limited resources.

The system of dual control that he outlined might work for a period, if the demarcation of authority was clear enough and the Company restrained the more grasping of its servants. In the long run, however, it would require governors with the wisdom of Solomon and councillors with the forebearance of archangels if it was to succeed. One aspect Clive did however make clear. The aim of the Company could no longer be the traditional one of a joint-stock company, to provide the maximum profit for its shareholders; it had to earn its acceptance in India by the integrity of its dealing and its attention to the well-being of those over whom it ruled.

So Clive prepared to return to India to give a firm foundation to British power there, to restore Britain's reputation for fair dealing, and to purify the administration of the Company. He probably had little conception of the nest of vipers he was about to enter.

On 19 May 1764, Peggy Clive took her first opportunity of addressing Carnac as a general. 'I take this last opportunity before my leaving England of assuring my friend General Carnac of my concern for his last illness.... A band of music and a music master will employ me on this voyage.' But she was not to while away the hours of the long voyage out, amusing herself with her orchestra. On 27 February 1765, she wrote after a long interval, 'Last time I wrote I thought myself on the point of leaving England. That my health prevented it was a matter of great uneasiness to me.... I was obliged to stay with the little family here, but I could have torn myself sooner from them than him.... I am condemned to pass my life in a continual state of apprehension and suspense.... Colonel Forde remains fixed in Ireland and we see nothing of him here.'

Clive took with him Edmund Maskelyne as his ADC, Henry Strachey as his secretary, and Dr Ingham as his physician. Peggy Clive gave Strachey strict injunctions to let her know how her husband fared; no doubt she hoped for the faithful service she had received from John Carnac. On 4 June 1764, Clive sailed from Portsmouth for India on perhaps the most testing mission the Company had ever called on him to undertake.

Chapter 16

REFORM IN BENGAL
1765

Why did Clive, rich and famous, return to India? It was the country to which younger sons were sent to make their fortune, or at least relieve their families of their presence, or to which those returned who had squandered the fortune they had made. The long, dangerous and uncomfortable sea voyage, the heat and the fever that took so heavy a toll of life, what rich man would contemplate enduring them? As for Clive himself, his first thought after arriving in India almost invariably seemed to be, how soon could he go back to England? Why then did he go?

At one level the answer is clear enough. He was locked in deadly combat with Sulivan, and had lost the first battle; now he had a chance to reverse the verdict and, perhaps, score a lasting success. Then there was the matter of the jaghir; by going to India that was put beyond the reach of Sulivan's malice. He was, of course, a rich man without the money from the jaghir, but if the rent already paid to him was reclaimed, then he might face bankruptcy. Here, it might he thought, was motive enough. But high legal opinion, including that of the Solicitor General, favoured the view that his right to it would be upheld by the Courts, and a verdict in the Courts would settle the matter once and for all. On the other hand, the outcome of a lawsuit can seldom be predicted with certainty, and by accepting the Governorship of Bengal the matter would be decided without the expense of litigation. It is reasonable to suppose that these considerations were not without their influence, but undoubtedly there were others.

Clive had a strong attachment to the East India Company and a genuine desire to see it prosper; he was, moreover, a convinced patriot who had seen his great services to his country questioned and attributed solely to a desire for self-aggrandisement. To suggest that he returned to India only from a high and selfless sense of duty may be doing him more than justice, but equally to ignore these sentiments would be doing him less.

His voyage out was long and tedious. He was accompanied by Sumner and Sykes of the Select Committee, and colonels Richard Smith and Sir Robert Barker. Edmund Maskelyne writing to Peggy observed 'there never reigned a greater harmony among a sett of Gentlemen'. Unfortunately, Sumner took with him his wife, a female decidedly lacking in attraction. Owing to the incompetence of the young captain, the *Kent* had to put into Rio de Janeiro, and on 14 October Clive wrote a letter from that port venting his feelings to Peggy.

'We found Mrs Sumner a woman of a most diabolical disposition, ignorant, ill-tempered and selfish in the highest degree. . . . One blessed effect of this lady being aboard was that we have all caught cold, your humble servant being the greatest sufferer . . . for this lady being cool in nothing but body insisted that all the doors and windows should be kept constantly open. . . . She had been playing two humdrum tunes [on the harpsichord] for four hours every day since she has been aboard without the least variation or improvement. . . . I hope you are delivered of a boy for we have girls in abundance.' (That hope was to be disappointed.) Clive was unlikely to have suffered in silence, and the situation must have had its embarrassing moments for the unfortunate Sumner; it may have been the origin of the rift that was to open between Clive and himself.

Having touched at Madras the *Kent* at last made Calcutta on 3 May 1765. During the long voyage much had happened in India. The battle of Buxar had demonstrated the Company's military superiority in an unmistakable fashion, but

REFORM IN BENGAL 329

before the battle there had been several cases of serious indiscipline. At one time a large number of Europeans had deserted, at another a complete sepoy battalion had mutinied. Munro restored discipline by stern measures; he had the ring-leaders among the mutineers blown from the mouths of guns. It was related that the grenadiers among them claimed the privilege of being blown from the guns first, as they were entitled to the right of the line, an act of courage that affected even those hardened ex-marines among the European soldiers who, by a curious coincidence, had formed part of the firing party that shot Admiral Byng on his own quarter-deck.

The war in Oudh still dragged on. Shujah took refuge with the Rohillas, tribes of Pathans who had established themselves in Rohilcund, the wild and hilly country to the north-west of Oudh, where he raised a mixed army of Rohillas and Mahrattas to try to recover his province. Shah Alam, however, made his peace with the British and joined Carnac in his camp, claiming he had been forced to invade Bihar by Shujah, who now held the post of Wazir, or chief minister, in the non-existent Empire. Carnac went on foot to receive the titular Emperor and welcomed him with full regal honours. Shah Alam promptly sought to enlist the help of the British for a march on Delhi. To some at Calcutta his proposals opened dazzling vistas of power. At Panipat in 1761 the Mahrattas had suffered a shattering defeat at the hands of Ahmad Shah Abdalli and were still recovering from their wounds. The formidable Afghan conqueror, himself, had returned to his native land. The way seemed clear for the Company to render the same service to Shah Alam as it had done to Mir Jafar, and become the power behind the throne to which, in name at least, all India owed allegiance. The Council toyed with the idea and meanwhile placed Shah Alam in possession of the province of Oudh.

In May Shujah's improvised army, after half-hearted actions at Korah and Kalpi, collapsed. By now he had heard of Clive's arrival in Calcutta; realising he had little hope of regaining his province and confident that with Clive as

Governor he would receive just treatment, on 26 May he surrendered to Carnac. In Bengal, Vansittart had gone home and Governor Spencer from Bombay had replaced him. Mir Jafar had died. Despite the imminent arrival of Clive, Spencer created Mir Jafar's dissolute twenty-year-old son, Najum-ud-daula, the new Nawab, and although the Company's instructions regarding presents had arrived some three months before, he and the Council nonchalantly accepted gifts amounting to 14 lakhs on his accession. Sir John Malcolm in his life of Clive trenchantly observed of this transaction, 'Where small men attempt to imitate great, they reach only the defects and fail in every other part.'

For the rest, the members of the Council and the merchants in Calcutta were happily engrossed in the unscrupulous practices that had driven Mir Kassim finally to revolt. Clive himself gives a vivid picture of the young Englishman of the time newly arrived from home.

'As soon as he lands a *bunnia* worth £100,000 desires he may have the power of serving the young gentleman at four shillings and sixpence per month. The Company has provided chambers for him but they are not good enough; the *bunnia* finds better. The young man takes a walk about town; he observes that other writers arrived only a year before him live in splendid apartments or have houses of their own, ride upon prancing arab horses and in palankins. He tells the *bunnia* what he has observed. The *bunnia* assures him that he may soon arrive at the same good fortune; he furnishes him with money, he is then at his mercy.'

And Warren Hastings writing to his friend Vansittart on 25 April 1762, 'I beg to lay before you a grievance ... I mean the oppressions committed under the sanction of the British name, and through the want of spirit of the Nawab's subjects to oppose them. This evil I am well assured is not confined to our dependants alone, but is practised all over the country by people falsely assuming the habits of our sepoys or calling themselves our *gomastahs*. On such occasions the great power of the British intimidates the people from making any resistance.'

REFORM IN BENGAL

Britain had the power but no legal authority, the Nawab legal authority but no power. An intolerable situation likely to attract every unscrupulous adventurer of any race or creed, it was aggravated by the absence of senior officials. Most of these, with unremitting zeal, had made the largest possible fortunes in the shortest possible time by any means, legal or illegal, and had departed, leaving nothing but their deplorable example to guide their juniors. The seniors had at least some administrative experience, their juniors nothing but their greed. Of course there were honourable exceptions, but these were few.

Thus when Clive came to Calcutta he found a war in progress that had been won but which had yet to be concluded, a victorious army, but one that had shown signs of serious indiscipline, a corrupt society whose members, enthralled by the opportunities for rich and easy pickings, had abandoned all pretence to commercial or any other form of morality, and on the *musnud* a dissolute youth incapable of exercising what small amount of authority remained to him. Clive, writing home, claimed he had to cleanse an 'Augean stable'. For once he did not exaggerate.

His first task was to impress his authority on the Council. He related what occurred at his first council meeting to Carnac in a letter dated 5 May 1765.

'I then acquainted the Board that the Committee was determined to make full use of the power invested in them to the fullest extent; that the conditions of the country and the very being of the Company made such a step absolutely necessary. Mr Leycester then seemed inclined to enter into a debate about the meaning and extent of these powers, but I cut him short by informing the Board that I would not suffer anyone to enter into the least discussion of those powers; but that the Select Committee alone was absolutely determined to be sole and only judge; but that they were at liberty to enter upon the Consultations any minutes they thought proper, but nothing more. Mr Johnstone desired that some other paragraphs of the letter might be sent to the different subordinates [out stations] as tending I believe in his opinion to invalidate those orders. Upon which I asked him whether he would dare dispute our authority? Mr Johnstone replied that he had not the least intention of doing such a thing; upon which there was an appearance of very long and pale countenances and not one of the Council uttered another syllable.'

Clive has been criticised for taking up so extreme an attitude so soon after his arrival, before, it has been asserted, he had time adequately to study conditions in Bengal. It seems an odd criticism; apart from the constant stream of letters he had received from his friends in the province while he was in England, and the endless deliberations that almost certainly took place in the great cabin of the *Kent* on the way out, the real issue would seem to be, was he correct in the decisions he came to? not how long he took to make them; of the correctness of his judgement there can be no question. It is probable that the Council never expected him to enforce any of the Directors' instructions.

Having established the authority of the Select Committee, he went on to tackle the contentious question of presents. Here he appeared rather in the guise of the Devil rebuking sin, although it is doubtful if, until his previous actions were thrown in his face, such a comparison ever crossed his mind. Yet he had certainly made more money more quickly, during his time in India, than anyone present. To Clive, to compare the presents he earned, risking life and health in the service of the Company, with the large sums received by members of Council as a reward for how they cast their votes in the Council chamber was so absurd as not to be worth a moment's thought. When he accepted his presents he merely followed an accepted practice, while Governor Spencer and the Council accepted large sums of money from Najum for creating him the new Nawab, three months after the letter from the Directors expressly prohibiting such an action had arrived. Nevertheless, in the nature of things, the knowledge that Clive obtained his own fortune from the practice that he now sternly condemned was bound to cause accusations of hypocrisy and feelings of bitterness.

REFORM IN BENGAL

On 7 June the matter was debated in Council. Johnstone vigorously defended the presents received by Council members, as well he might in view of what he had accepted himself. On 14 June Clive wrote to Governor Palk at Madras, 'The gentlemen [Johnstone, Leycester and two others] were to receive 1,250,000 sicca rupees from the Nawab, 475,000 from Mohammed Reza Khan and 1,250,000 from Jagat Seth'. He went on that they actually received 625,000 from the Nawab, 225,000 from Mohammed Reza and 50,000 from Jagat Seth. It is not impossible that Clive was exaggerating, the figures are certainly high, and Clive when he wanted to make a point, did not always restrain his imagination; however, when the Nawab himself came to Calcutta towards the end of May, seeking to have Mohammed Reza replaced by Nundcomar, an unmitigated scoundrel more likely to pander to his pleasures, he complained that Mohammed Reza had distributed 20 lakhs to members of Council to secure his appointment.

When the question of covenents was discussed, Johnstone referred to the 'approved example of the President, Lord Clive, to himself'. To which Clive replied with some heat that there was a difference between an unsolicited gift, given to a victorious commander, and one to a councillor who had heroically cast his vote with the majority in the Council. Johnstone and Leycester were two men on whose conduct it is pleasanter not to dwell. Philip Woodruff, in his book *The Men Who Ruled India, The Founders*, selected the two, together with Robert Bolt, as prime examples of the depths plumbed by British merchants at this time. But Johnstone's sentiments were undoubtedly widely shared by those who had begun to wonder if the period of easy fortunes was over. However, there was no withstanding Clive, and on 11 May 1765 the members of Council, with who knows what reservations, signed the covenants.

Clive had made a beginning in Calcutta, but before he began seriously to purify the administration, it was clearly necessary to end the war, with Oudh and organise a stable government in Bengal. The opposition he had so far encountered he treated with a contempt that was, perhaps, a little unwise. At this time he felt exhilarated at the splendid prospect before him. With virtually untrammelled authority he confronted vast and complex problems; it was a situation he enjoyed. He shared with most great soldiers and statesmen the singular ability to see a complicated problem in its totality. He could reduce it to its essentials, propound his solution in clear and unambiguous terms, and then relentlessly press forward to a successful conclusion.

As he had shown in his letter to the Directors before he left England, he had noted the fatal mistakes made by Dupleix, and was resolved to keep the territorial ambitions of the Company within the bounds of its resources. The chimera of installing a puppet Emperor in Delhi he discarded out of hand. He intended to limit the Company's authority to the viceroyalty of Bengal, to turn Oudh into a friendly but independent buffer state, and to avoid antagonising the great Indian princes and other European powers, by retaining the Nawab as titular head of Bengal.

On 25 June he set out for Murshidabad, leaving Sumner, his Second-in-Council, to run affairs in Calcutta. It was the custom at this time for the heads of the major subordinates, as the out-stations were called, to be Members of Council. It was a useful perquisite for senior councillors, but it gave too much autonomy to the out-stations, and such councillors, when in Calcutta, were apt to place an undue emphasis on their own particular interests. Clive wanted the Council reduced from sixteen to twelve members, and left Sumner instructions to exclude from it the chiefs of the factories at Cossimbazar, Monghyr, Dacca and Patna.

Sumner, deprived of the physical support of his iron-willed chief, wrote pathetic letters to Clive saying he could not proceed with this re-organisation, as two general letters from London had been produced, in one of which it was stipulated that the chief of Patna must be a councillor and the other that the Council should consist of sixteen members. Sumner considered that only a unanimous decision by the whole Council could override such specific instructions, a unanimity that could never be obtained while such men as Johnstone were Council members.

To accept that the Council had any jurisdiction over the Select Committee was anathema to Clive, as he told Sumner in no uncertain terms. To others he said, 'Sumner's behaviour is so inexpressibly weak that I almost dread the thought of having him my successor'. The concluding paragraph of his letter to Sumner reveals the contempt in which he held his venal opponents and the confidence with which he contemplated the future; 'Be persuaded that the proceedings of the Committee will appear so very honourable so very disinterested and so evidently calculated for the interest of the Company that they will meet with universal approbation outwardly; for even the worst of men cannot, dare not, set their faces against measures which will defend themselves.' It was an optimistic forecast.

Despite the clammy heat of the monsoon Clive radiated confidence and energy. To Palk he wrote on 14 June, 'Now or never is the time for settling a firm and lasting peace. I am almost enthusiastic with the thought of acquiring great honour for myself in conjunction with the Committee and immense solid advantages for the Company.' At Murshidabad he made a momentous decision. Before landing at Calcutta he had largely abandoned his first idea of a dual regime in Bengal, now the incapacity of the present Nawab made it plainly impracticable. Instead he proposed that the Company should be responsible for collecting all the revenue in the province and for meeting all the expenses of its administration, allowing the Nawab a sum of 53 lakhs a year for his personal use. When the proposal was broached the young prince leapt at it, happily remarking, 'Thank God, I shall now have as many dancing girls as I please.'

By this arrangement the Company became the *Diwan* of Bengal.[1] To appreciate its significance it is necessary to

---

[1] Before acquiring the *diwani*, Clive sent home to his agents instructing them to raise or borrow as much money as they could and invest it in the Company stock, presumably as he thought the news would lift its value. He advised, confidentially, the Chairman of the Directors, Rous, to do the same. This has been advanced as another example of Clive's unscrupulous avarice. Admittedly it is more honourable for a member of a company not to make use of inside knowledge to make a personal profit, and two centuries later legislation on the point is contemplated. However, let the stockbroker who has never used an 'inside tip' cast the first stone.

hark back to the political hierarchy of the Moghul Empire in its heyday. Then in each province the Emperor appointed a nawab to govern the province, command the armed forces, and administer justice, but he also appointed a *diwan* who was responsible to the Imperial Court, not to the nawab, for all its financial affairs. The duty of the *diwan* was to collect the taxes, forward the correct amount to the Imperial treasury and then meet the administrative expenses of the Nawab. In practice, as has already been mentioned, with the decline of the Moghul power the nawabs tended to become independent rulers and therefore to appoint their own *diwans*; even so it was generally the custom to obtain the formal assent of the Emperor to a new appointment.

Clive planned a master stroke. Since the Company would now be responsible for all revenue, the tax collectors would take their authority from the Company, and anyone trying to dispute their authority would ultimately find himself in conflict with the Company. The situation that had occurred under Mir Kassim, when servants of the Company could intimidate or overawe officials appointed by the Nawab, would now be impossible. The Company would have both power and legal authority. But Clive planned something more. He intended to obtain a *firman* from the Emperor appointing the Company *diwan* of the Bengal viceroyalty in perpetuity. The Company would then occupy an unimpeachable legal position in the province that the Nawab would have no right to query. He would remain the titular ruler, but legally, as well as in fact, he would be little more than the pensionary of the Company.

However, first it was necessary to settle matters in Oudh. He called Sykes to Murshidabad to set up the new organisation and extract the necessary documents of authority, or *perwannahs*, from the young Nawab. Meanwhile, he continued up the river to Benares where Shujah-ud-daula awaited his arrival. He proposed to restore Oudh to that Prince. Shujah had experienced the strong arm of the British and after his previous actions could scarcely expect such generous treatment. If his realm was restored to him, Clive would secure his first requirement, a friendly buffer state on the

44 Shuja-ud-daula, Nawab of Oudh.

borders of Bihar. However, the precipitate action of the Council in granting Oudh to Shah Alam had created an obstacle to his plan, and some delicate negotiations might be necessary.

At Benares, Shuja received the British Governor with great ceremony. Clive explained his plans for Oudh, but pointed out that some provision would have to be made for Shah Alam. He told Shuja he would have to cede to the

45 Clive receiving the *diwani* of Bengal, Bihar and Orissa from the Emperor Shah Alam. Clive's clothing is singularly unsuitable for the time of year.

titular Emperor the state of Allahabad with an annual rental of 10 lakhs and the district of Korah with one of 18. He would also have to pay the Company an indemnity of 50 lakhs for the expenses of the war—the figure was inadequate, but Clive knew that at this time the finances of Oudh could support no heavier burden. Shuja accepted such lenient terms with alacrity; they were better than his fondest hopes. Now everything depended on the Emperor.

Shuja, Clive and Carnac went on up the river to Allahabad to meet Shah Alam. Although he was little more than an impecunious fugitive, he proved at first recalcitrant. A little reflection, however, convinced him that by acquiring Oudh he would only incur the unrelenting animosity of Shah Shuja, and that Clive's proposals were really in his own best interests; in due course he gave a reluctant assent. In addition to Allahabad and Korah, Clive offered him an annual income of 26 lakhs from Bengal, paid in monthly instalments, if he would recognise Najum as the Nawab of the Bengal viceroyalty, grant to the British the *diwani* of Bengal, Bihar and Orissa in perpetuity, acknowledge the right of the British to their possessions in the Carnatic and the Northern Circars and finally confirm Clive in his jaghir. The offer nearly doubled his income and the Emperor had little hesitation in agreeing to it. The *firmans* were duly executed and signed on 12 August 1765. The *firman* for the *diwani* of Bengal was presented to Clive with full Imperial ceremony a little marred in that Clive's canopy had to substitute for the Imperial Palace and a draped dining-room table with a cushion for the solid gold Imperial *musnud*, encrusted with precious stones, that adorned the Imperial Palace.

It might seem absurd for an Emperor lacking an army and an empire to issue a document beginning, 'At this happy time our royal *firman*, indispensably requiring obedience, is issued . . .'. But nonetheless the *firman* conferred a legal authority that could come from no other source. It gave the Company a recognised status in India, one that could not be denied either by any other prince nor, perhaps equally important, by any power in Europe. Perhaps the granting of the *firman* was the last great act of an Imperial government that but twenty-five years ago, although bruised and battered, was still accepted as the ultimate repository of sovereignty in India. It seemed a far cry from the days of the young writer in Madras, when the Nawab of the Carnatic was a great potentate to be honoured and propitiated, and the Emperor dwelt in Delhi in unimaginable splendour.

Clive agreed to station troops in Allahabad and be responsible for the safety of Oudh, while the Princes reconstituted the armies that had been shattered at Buxar; then towards the end of August he began to retrace his steps to Calcutta in triumph. In four months he had brought peace to Bengal on terms which, while securing the Company's interests, gave grievance to none and were likely to endure; he had obtained Imperial recognition and sanction to the British presence in India; he had laid a new framework for the administration of Bengal; he had introduced the system of covenants to the servants of the Company, and was in the process of stamping out corruption. It was altogether a remarkable achievement.

Clive at this time, despite the enervating monsoon heat, probably felt as happy as at any period in his life. On 24 August he wrote to Peggy, 'It must afford you great pleasure to hear that I enjoy my health better than in England, and that action as formerly agrees better with me than indolence and laziness.' In excellent health, conscious of his entire disinterestedness, and feeling more than a match for the problems of the hour, Clive rejoiced in his own powers like a lion gambolling in the spring. It was one of fate's many ironies that his last period in India, when he never made a penny, when all his endeavours were directed to promote the good of his country and the Company, was also to be the period that brought him suffering and obloquy that never altogether left him until the end of his days. But at the present there was nothing to warn him of the darkness that lay ahead.

In his absence, after a series of disputes in the Council, Johnstone and Leycester had departed, nursing a bitter hatred against the President who had foiled their endeavours to procure for themselves immense and ill-got riches, not that they departed poor men. When Clive arrived back in Calcutta he took the opportunity to replace the timorous Sumner by Verelst as his deputy.

At this time, although there were many in Calcutta who had little liking for the dictatorial methods of the man they styled 'King of Calcutta', the foremost men of the city were happy to attend his table. In the scurrilous and contemporary biography of Clive by a gentleman who called himself Carraccioli there is a vivid picture of Clive's daily life, quoted by Mervyn Davies in his book *Clive of Plassey*.

'The very furniture of Government House, the tapestries and carpets, the magnificent plate, the splendid equipages, were the envy of the settlement, and his frequent sumptuous costly entertainment their delight. His hospitality was ample, but in his private life his mode of living was not more lavish than was customary in a wealthy luxurious community. Dinner, according to the custom of the time, was served at 2 p.m., and a few friends of his Select Committee, or senior members of the Company dined with him. His table was served with delicacy and profusion, and all the most exquisite wines of Europe were at the discretion of his guests. If he were in a good humour, he would encourage a free circulation of the bottle, and by intervals stimulate mirth and jollity; but he soon relapsed into his natural pensive mood, and was after silent for a considerable time. His conversation was not lively, but rational and solid. As he seldom drank freely enough to be seen without disguise, he was impenetrable, except to a few confidants to whom he entrusted the execution of his schemes and designs. It was not often that his guests were allowed a greater lattitude of freedom, as he was always stately and commonly reserved. After dinner he took sometimes a little repose, as is customary in this torrid region.'

In the evening he might go for a stroll to enjoy the breeze that blew in from the sea, come home to supper and perhaps play some hands of cards. But it was not luxury that Clive enjoyed, it was power and the ability to manage men and events.

In Calcutta, as the monsoon rained itself out and the cooler weather of autumn drew on, his thoughts turned to how the Company might be reformed and the tendencies to corruption be eliminated. Most of the previous troubles had risen because the Company's servants were paid salaries that were nothing more than retainers to supplement an income they had to earn by other means. A member of Council, for instance, was paid £300 a year while his expenses, at the admittedly lavish scale affected by the British in Calcutta, would amount to something like £3,000. In these circumstances the affairs of the Company became only a vexatious interruption to the more profitable and indeed essential pursuit of private business. In the past the system had worked well enough, and the Company's servants had displayed sufficient diligence to send home its ships with adequate cargoes, so the Company made a profit and the Proprietors at home remained satisfied with the return on their money. But now that the Company had become a great sovereign power, an organisation in which the only full time employees were the Indian clerks and watchmen was utterly incapable of dealing with the manifold and intricate problems that constantly arose.

If the Company was to function efficiently, its servants would have to direct their attention primarily to its well being; but if they were to do so they would clearly need to be paid sufficient money to live at the standard to which they had become accustomed. But Clive knew only too well that the merchants of Leadenhall Street could not be made to understand that, in the long run, it was in the interests of the Company to pay its servants a generous salary. They had prohibited the acceptance of presents and issued stringent instructions restraining their servants from participating in the internal trade in India. The question of how, in these circumstances, their servants were to live at all had apparently escaped their attention. Clive produced a remarkably ingenious solution to the problem, which would not only enable adequate salaries to be paid, but would also establish a proper salary structure, in which long and faithful service, and positions of responsibility received their just desserts. Clive thought it particularly important to build up in each Presidency a cadre of responsible, experienced officials who had found it worth their while to spend a major part of their lives in India, instead of forever seeking how quickly they could turn an honest or dishonest penny or two, and then return to England at the earliest opportunity.

To this end he formed a Society to which he granted a monopoly of the trade in salt, betel-nut and tobacco. All the Company's servants above the grade of writer, and all officers of the rank of major and above were to be members and to have shares according to their rank. He directed Sumner to ascertain the average price of salt over the past twenty years and fix the price accordingly. Sumner and Verelst drew up a scheme which was approved and duly launched on 18 September. Clive's share as Governor he donated to Maskelyne, Ingham and Strachey, the members of his personal staff who were not officially servants of the Company and had no source of income. The Society did not defraud the consumer, the average price of salt had varied between 3s 6d and 7s per maund (80 lb) over the past twenty years and Clive set the price at 4s; even so the members of the Society made a handsome profit, and Maskelyne, Ingham and Strachey had no cause of complaint about their emoluments. The Society solved an intractable problem, but it did, of course, run directly counter to the instructions from the Company.

The collection of the revenues in the viceroyalty Clive left in the hands of the ex-officials of the Nawab. In this matter he had no choice. Apart from such matters as knowledge of the somewhat abstruse method of calculation used by the Moghuls to work out the land tax and the ability to speak the language, there were no Britons available in Calcutta to undertake the task of acting as collectors, to use the title such officials were eventually given; the Company's resources were fully stretched administering the territories it had already acquired. All Clive could do was to place Sykes at the head of the Department of Revenue, make him Resident at the Court of the Nawab at Murshidabad, and ensure that the senior Indian officials received adequate salaries. These could be concealed in the general expenses of collecting the revenue, whereas the salaries paid to any Britons in the employment of the Company would certainly be queried by the potentates of the General Court in London.

As 1765 came to a close, in Bengal order was slowly emerging out of chaos; the army officers had signed the covenants without much overt protest; Clive's bitterest enemies had left Calcutta; none in the Council dared oppose him. Although the first exhilaration had no doubt worn off, Clive almost certainly viewed the apparently tranquil future with a quiet confidence. It only remained to abolish Batta for the Army, consolidate the reforms he had carried out, and then return to England as the magician before whose magic wand the troubles of the Company vanished into a cloud lined with silver and gold.

He had already taken the first steps to abolish Batta and had decreed that from 1 January 1766 it would cease for all units in peace-stations. In the Council there were now four vacancies. He could see no one in Calcutta fit to occupy them. He had been corresponding with Palk about whether he could have some experienced men from Madras; he had asked for Kelsall, Floyer, Russell and Aldersley and expected them in a couple of months' time. It is unlikely that at this time Clive had the smallest premonition of the fearful ordeals the new year was to bring.

Chapter 17

THE BENGAL MUTINY
1766

Soon after arriving in Calcutta in May 1765, Clive appointed his chief artillery officer, Sir Robert Barker, to command an infantry brigade over the head of Sir Robert Fletcher, at that time serving with Carnac in Oudh. (Since both men had the Christian name of Robert it will be clearer to refer to them by their surnames only.) Fletcher objected strenuously to Barker's appointment maintaining that, since he was a gunner, he was unfit to command an infantry brigade. Fletcher should have known better than to expect Clive to rescind a decision, particularly for reasons that must have been fully known to him at the time that he made it. Clive wrote back on 28 June, flatly rejecting his contention. He concluded: 'With no disparagement of your merit which I shall always be ready to acknowledge, it is not in the eyes of the world equal to that of Sir Robert Barker'. Fletcher may have held a different view about what the eyes of the world beheld, and perhaps, in consequence, came to harbour a grievance that banefully influenced his actions during the fateful spring of 1766.

His protest, however, was only a symptom of a wider malaise; under Vansittart the Army had become accustomed to going its own way without paying overmuch attention to the civil authority. In May a case concerning Lieutenant Macpherson had come to Clive's notice. Before his arrival, the Governor and Council permitted a Captain Whitchcot to sell his commission to Macpherson and appointed the latter to take the precedence of the commission he had bought. This caused intense resentment among the other officers, and the Council so far met their complaints as to order Macpherson to rank as the junior captain; but the concession placated them not at all. The captains and lieutenants started to form an association to protect their rights, as they termed it, and refused point blank to accept Macpherson in the rank of captain.

Such an action had far-reaching implications as Clive instantly recognised. He wrote firmly to Carnac: 'I hear of a general association among the officers not to admit Captain Macpherson among them. ... I am determined that every officer upon the Bengal establishment shall have leave to resign before I give up the point in question. It is no longer a struggle between Captain Macpherson and the Corps of Officers, but between the civil and military which shall predominate.' It may be that the officers had some justice on their side, but junior officers who formed associations to exert pressure on the Government displayed a

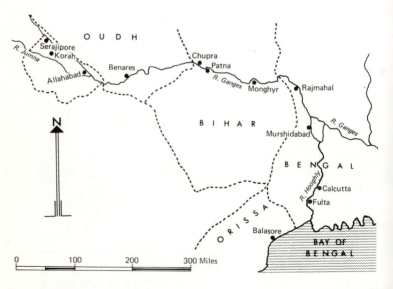

13 Oudh, Bihar and Bengal.

strange and novel understanding of their duties and responsibilities; plainly such threats could not be tolerated, and that they should ever have been made illustrated all too clearly the laxity that had prevailed during the recent past.

Clive attributed the trouble in part to the lack of field officers. There were none in the sepoy battalions, and it was not unusual for armies to be commanded by majors. As early as 11 May he wrote to Palk in Madras, 'I am determined on an absolute reformation. The army stands in equal need of reformation, but here we must act with caution until peace is established.'

On his way back to Calcutta after signing the peace treaty with Shuja, he considered that the time for the reformation had come. On 5 August 1765, he issued orders dividing the field armies into three brigades each consisting of one European infantry battalion, six sepoy battalions, a company of artillery and a troop of Indian light horse. In establishing these three little army corps of all arms, at a time when the divisional organisation was still unknown in Europe, Clive showed himself well in advance of current military thinking. In addition, he made a farsighted proposal to Colonel Richard Smith, commanding one of the three brigades: 'The officers commanding the sepoys [are] to run in that corps only, by which means all officers will understand the language without which it is impossible to bring the sepoys to that pitch of discipline which will make them truly formidable. . . . When the captains of sepoys are of rank sufficient to claim a majority, they will be undoubtedly intitled to it if deserving'. The adoption of this proposal fostered the fine understanding between British officers and their sepoys that, except for one black period, characterised the Indian Army whether under the Company or the Crown.

The three brigades were stationed in three important cities on the Ganges. The First garrisoned Monghyr in Bengal; technically it was under the command of General Carnac, but since as Commander-in-Chief he resided in Calcutta with Clive, Fletcher officiated in his absence. The

Second, under Colonel Richard Smith, at the request of Shah Alam was stationed at Allahabad with the function of protecting the border. The Third, under Colonel Barker, was cantoned at Bankipore, about two miles from Patna.

The new year came and with it the first signs of active unrest among the servants of the Company. On 13 January Clive sent a hurried note to Verelst,

'You will receive a letter from the Committee requiring your immediate attendance. The reason for this summons is no less than that a circular letter has been sent by Mr Majendie to all servants requiring their attendance at the Council House, where they accordingly met yesterday and signed a memorial to the Court of Directors against the measure of sending for the Madras gentlemen. . . . It will certainly be incumbent upon us to make proper examples of the ringleaders. Two of the Council have thought fit to take a principal part in this affair and have actually signed the memorial.'

It may seem an injudicious move to summon 'gentlemen from Madras'. Clive must have known that it would provoke bitter anger. Before he sailed for India, he had warned the Directors against appointing a Governor of Calcutta from outside the Presidency. When he explained his action to the Directors, he said there was no one in Calcutta fit to be appointed to the Council, but he must have been aware that the extraordinary powers possessed by the Select Committee which enabled them to override the Council had been granted only for the period of the emergency in Bengal; once it could be held that the emergency had been ended, those powers would lapse. When that happened, it would be essential for him to command a majority in the Council. He could count on the support of members drawn from Madras, who depended on his favour for their lucrative posts. In the event, during a crucial period he did obtain that support, but the price he paid for it was heavy. The appointment of these councillors blocked all promotions in the establishment at Calcutta and provoked intense hostility. The implication that no members of that city were competent to be councillors affronted even the few decent citizens.

Now Clive walked in an aura of hatred, and he and the Select Committee were subjected to a positive boycott. He wrote in a dispatch to the Directors 'All visits to the President are forbidden—all invitations from him and the members of the Select Committee are to be slighted—the Gentlemen called down by us from Madras are to be treated with neglect and contempt—Every man who deviates from this confederacy is to be stigmatized and avoided.' The gentlemen of Calcutta were decidedly modern in their outlook.

Although outwardly unmoved by this treatment Clive was grievously hurt. To Peggy he wrote '. . . I have undertaken a most disagreeable and odious task which my honor obliges me to go through with; I am become the slave of the Company and the detestation of individuals and my constitution cannot bear it long if I am not relieved by the Madras Gentlemen. . . . May our meeting be soon and untill that time may health and serenity of mind accompany you wherever you go.' It may be conjectured that Clive was desperately in need of what he wished for his wife, but so far he had suffered only a foretaste of what was to come.

Towards the end of March he left Calcutta for Murshidabad to review the collection of the revenue; it may be surmised he left with some relief. The gentlemen of Calcutta pursued their feud until the last moment, and on 29 March he sent a letter to Verelst thanking him for refusing to hire out a band to a number of young gentlemen who intended 'an insolent celebration of my departure from the Presidency'.

The affairs of the Company, however, were prospering. On 19 April he wrote Verelst a long and illuminating letter from Muti Jhil, just outside Murshidabad. His letter exposes clearly enough the problems caused by the sudden and vast expansion of the Company's power and his reluctance to involve it too deeply in the day-to-day administration of the province.

The revenue next year was expected to amount to 172 lakhs 'which is 12 lakhs more than last year;' he continued,

'If we can avoid giving umbrage to the European powers and to keep up the appearance of the present form of government, I think we ought not to exact a farthing of revenue from this province. [Presumably he means by imposing any taxes on the other European settlements.]

'For my own part I think (after we have made this year's experiment and find we have not overrated the countries by the regular payment of rent) that if Bengal was let out for 3, 5 or 7 years it would be for the advantage of the Company and individuals and add stability to our possessions by inspiring the inhabitants with just ideas of our justice and moderation. . . . The frequent complaints made by Mohammed Reza Khan of the power which the officers assume commanding sepoys and who are sent only for the purpose of collecting the revenues, hath made me resolve to new model the army.'

He proposed that the army should consist of a field force of fifteen sepoy battalions to be employed on active service only. There should, in addition, be eleven more battalions to be employed on garrison duties and to supervise the collection of revenue. Two would be stationed at Calcutta 'always commanded by the Town Major and the Barrackmaster', one at each of Midnapore, Burdwan and Chittagong, three at Murshidabad under Sykes and three more in Bihar under Middleton. The last six would have the express duty of collecting the revenue. 'These shall have but one commissioned officer each at their head who shall always reside at the city, and whenever detachments are made no European above the rank of sergeant shall command, that there may be no disputes about receiving and obeying the officers of the Government.' Without actually saying so, he really contemplated the formation of a gendarmerie firmly under the hand of the civil not the military authorities. It was an interesting conception and throws a lurid light on the recent behaviour of some of the officers.

Already a faint cloud had appeared on the political

horizon. A Mahratta army, rumoured to be 50,000 or 60,000 strong, was gathering about 150 miles to the west of Allahabad, and it was uncertain whether the Mahrattas contemplated marching on Delhi or invading Oudh. Colonel Smith took the whole of his 2nd Brigade, except for the European battalion, to Serajipore on the Ganges, about 100 miles to the west of Allahabad, to guard the border. The European battalion was left in Allahabad fort, because, as Strachey records, 'It was not thought proper to risque it in the field during the excessive heats of April and May.'

Clive was concerting arrangements with Shuja, Shah Alam and some Rohilla chiefs to counter a possible invasion, when on 20 or 21 April he received a curious letter from Barker with the 3rd Brigade at Bankipore. Barker forwarded the proceedings of a General Court-Martial following the setting fire to some quarters. Apparently the fire followed a dispute which, so Barker reported, 'arose from Ensign Davis's refusing to give up his commission to Captain Duff who would have forced it from him'. Looking into the cause of this strange transaction Barker, 'to his great surprise became acquainted with a combination which had been formed in the 3rd Brigade'. He had stumbled on an exceedingly dangerous conspiracy.

Since the new year, and possibly before, a number of officers had begun to form what they called a combination to resist the abolition of Batta; Barker suspected the conspiracy had originated in Fletcher's 1st Brigade at Monghyr. Batta was an allowance customarily paid to troops on active service. After Plassey, Mir Jafar had doubled the Batta of officers and paid it out of his own pocket. At the time, Clive had warned his officers that this was a purely temporary measure depending on the generosity of the Nawab. Strachey observes,

'The expense of this Batta was in the process of time thrown upon the Company who, unwilling to adopt such an expensive precedent notwithstanding the revenues of several districts of land had been signed over by the Nawab to the Company for defraying the charges of the army, repeatedly issued orders in the most positive terms that it should be abolished. But the situation of the political and military affairs in Bengal was so frequently critical and the superior servants in the civil branch so averse, perhaps through want of resolution, to abridge the officers of any emoluments that a remonstrance from the army never failed to convince the Governor and Council of the impropriety of such a deduction.'

Strachey gives a table showing the amount of Batta to which the various ranks in each arm were entitled; a short extract for the infantry, is given in the table quoted below:

Rank	Pay per month in sonaut rupees Rs	Field Batta per month in sonaut rupees Rs	Additional allc. in Arcot rupees (2% better) Rs	Total per month in pounds sterling at 2/3 per rupee (rounded off in pounds) £
Colonel	310	775	1,240	286
Lt. Colonel	248	620	—	108
Major	186	465	—	81
Captain	124	186	—	38
Capt./Lieut.	62	186	—	30
Lieut.	62	124	—	23
Ensign	50	93	—	17
Cadet	—	62	—	8

NB. The Batta of officers in cantonments is only half that enjoyed in the field. The Batta after crossing the Caramnassa [the river that marked the border between Bihar and Oudh] is double field Batta. In the Colonel's absence the next field officer commanding the regiment receives the additional Batta of the rank above him with 40 rupees per diem for his table.

It can be seen that the sums of money concerned were very considerable. Clive by his Society for the Salt Trade provided an adequate separate source of income for the majors and above, but the captains and subalterns would be hard hit by the loss of Batta and would have to reduce appreciably their standard of living.

However, with effect from 1 January 1766, double Batta ceased except for the 2nd Brigade at Allahabad, which was allowed double Batta in the field and single when in cantonments. Half single Batta was to continue for the troops in Monghyr and Bankipore but, as Strachey remarked, the rest of the army namely 'the detachments in the Presidency and the factories and other places were to be put precisely on a footing with the Company's forces on the coast of Coromandel, that is to say, they were to have no Batta at all'. Clive had been given no discretion by the General Court about carrying out this reduction, and he intended to fulfil his instructions to the letter.

The captains, lieutenants and ensigns, recognising at the outset that official protests to Clive would be useless, turned to what would now be called 'industrial action'; they decided they would withdraw their labour by resigning their commissions simultaneously. In each brigade associations were formed and 'Committees of Correspondence' appointed as the executive of the Brigade association or combination as they called it.

Every member swore a solemn oath of secrecy which was so well kept that the few senior officers, it appeared, knew nothing of what went on. A fighting fund of £18,000 was raised, to which it was suspected, although never proved, a large number of civilians in Calcutta were happy to contribute. Each officer executed a bond of £500 that he would not receive back his commission until double Batta was restored, and delivered his commission to his adjutant or quartermaster, as an earnest of his intentions and so that all could be handed in together at a predetermined time. Intense pressure was brought to bear on recalcitrant officers and, as already mentioned, it was a case of intimidation that brought the whole conspiracy to light.

Originally the commissions were to be handed in on 1 June, but now the plot had been discovered the date was brought forward to 1 May. After resigning, the officers were to continue serving as volunteers without pay until 15 May. An officer could, of course, resign when he wished, but mass resignation would amount to mutiny. It was hoped that by this manoeuvre they would be able to withdraw their services without being guilty of an offence. But none seriously expected that Clive would dare force them to a confrontation, and they made no proper plans for such a contingency. They did not yet know their Commander.

But they were playing a desperately risky game, with the prospect of death by hanging or a firing squad for the ringleaders if they failed. There was some evidence of a plot to murder Clive. In the Consultations of the Council in Calcutta it was recorded, 'In the height of the combination Captain Stainforth proposed to throw the die with any person to make a sacrifice of Lord Clive.' Clearly the proposal had been made in the course of a 'thick' night as a 'Mr Coggan' was asked if he would go to Captain Stainforth 'next morning to ask him if he recollected using such an expression. So far from denying it, he not only avowed the proposal but declared he continued in the same mind.' Clive himself was sceptical and thought the two officers were being framed by their comrades. He wrote to the Council, 'I have received your letter of the 14th [and] what you mention there relating to Captain Stainforth and Mr Hoggan not Coggan. . . . They came into the association last of all; when they wanted to withdraw they were threatened with death by some of the officers.'

Now the Mahrattas were on the move, the officers were confident that Clive would have to submit to their demand, and events began to move fast. The day after Clive received the Court-Martial proceedings, Verelst in Calcutta forwarded to him a 'Remonstrance' from the officers of the 3rd Brigade at Bankipore. The 'Remonstrance' spoke of the high cost of living and ended with a plea that the order abolishing Batta should be revoked. Verelst asked what action he should take. Clive directed that since it was not clear that the 'Remonstrance' had been seen by the 3rd Brigade headquarters, it should be returned with the request that it should be forwarded through the proper channels.

However, it soon became clear that most of the junior officers in all three brigades were implicated, and Clive faced the worst crisis of his career. He was uncertain how far the officers, having embraced such desperate measures, were prepared to go; nor could it be guessed how far their soldiers might support them. But he had no doubt of the tremendous issues at stake. Strachey noted,

'... to grant a request demanded as it were sword in hand might have been attended with the worst of evils; for where threats in this instance might have been found successful subordination and discipline would have been openly disavowed. The civil government might at length be totally overthrown by the military. The saving which arose from the saving of Batta was of trifling consideration compared with the dangers of yielding to the menaces of so unprecedented and mutinous an association. ... Submission would not bear a moment's deliberation.'

Subsequently there was reason to believe that the restoration of Batta would not have satisfied the officers, and that once it had been granted they intended to demand the abolition of covenants, the abdication of power by the Select Committee and an undertaking that no officer from outside should be allowed to outrank the officers on the Bengal establishment.

Clive, having determined to break the mutiny and in no circumstances to submit to blackmail, considered what measures were open to him to prevent an armed clash and perhaps the total breakdown of British power in Bengal. Whatever happened, he was determined not to negotiate. His first step was clearly to convince the officers through their commanders that they had no chance of success. This in itself should be sufficient; but if the matter were forced to an issue, he might have to replace most of his junior officers. But this might not be all; the officers having fatally compromised themselves might feel there was no turning back; then the attitude of their soldiers would be of paramount importance, and the attitude of the sepoy battalions decisive.

An Indian battalion with its own Indian commandant, its subedars and jemadars, could operate for a period without any British officers at all. Yet an action between loyal Indian troops and a mutinous European battalion scarcely bore contemplation; the odium that Clive endured now would be slight indeed beside what he would be called on to face if such a clash were to occur, and the political implications would be incalculable. As if this was not enough, over all loomed the menace of a large Mahratta army assembling just over the border of Kora. At this time Clive seemed to have little left to him save his courage; yet one priceless asset he did possess; with firm, clear leadership his countrymen have seldom failed to rise to an occasion, and in this appalling crisis he had the unstinting and unanimous support of the Council in Calcutta; it was to turn the scale.

On 29 April Clive formed a small *ad hoc* committee of himself, Sykes and Carnac to deal with the situation. They instructed the Council to recruit officers from among the free merchants of Calcutta and to request Madras to send immediately every captain and subaltern that could be spared and any cadets fit to be commissioned. At the same time he wrote to his three brigade commanders ordering them to find out who was holding the commissions, to put the holders under arrest and to try by Court-Martial any officer who showed the slightest signs of mutiny; he directed that the members of the court should be field officers, as any others would be certain not to convict. He also urged them to ensure the 'fidelity of the subedars of the black troops'.

The 2nd Brigade at Allahabad was a special case. With the Mahrattas near the border a compromise might be inescapable. But he told Colonel Richard Smith that he should only agree to a compromise as a last resort. He had one further card to play. When Mir Jafar died, he left Clive a legacy of 5 lakhs. Clive could scarcely refuse the bequest, but to conform with his covenant he had resolved to turn the money to a charitable purpose and to set up a trust fund for the benefit of soldiers' widows, their children and the disabled; he could show that he had not entirely neglected the welfare of his men.

As April gave way to May, he waited anxiously at Murshidabad for news. On 1 and 2 May nothing came from the brigades. Then one of the officers of his staff from the 1st Brigade showed him a letter he had received from his comrades at Monghyr dated 27 April, which informed him that he must resign on 1 May unless Batta was restored, and asserting, 'This is no hasty and ill-conducted scheme, but the settled resolution of the three brigades who are to a man resolved to send every officer to everlasting coventry who refuses to join in a scheme so just and honourable.'

A letter from Barker with the 3rd Brigade at Bankipore brought the news that he, Barker, was convinced all his officers would resign, but that there was 'no disposition to mutiny among the private men'. But 4 May came and went without a word from Monghyr. Clive again sent orders to Fletcher to search out the ringleaders and to ensure the fidelity of the subedars and the sepoys. He made preparations to go to Monghyr himself so as to be present on the crucial 15 May.

At last the news came from Fletcher that on 1 May forty-two officers of the 1st Brigade had handed in their commissions and that his officers were resolved to serve without pay until 15 May. About the same time an alarming letter arrived from Barker. His officers had handed in their commissions, but he added ominously that he had heard that the European other ranks in Fletcher's 1st Brigade proposed to support the mutinous officers.

Clive never wavered. He ordered boats to be collected at Monghyr, so that any officer who refused to withdraw his resignation could be sent down to Calcutta within twenty-four hours. Fletcher wrote on 2 May that he 'was convinced no disturbance would happen, even if the troops knew the conduct of their officers'. Clive curtly directed him 'to secure the captains who had been most active and send them down prisoners to Calcutta' and on 6 May left Murshidabad for Monghyr, taking with him Carnac and the officers of his bodyguard and escort of sepoys. Majors Champion and Polier, and Captains Smith, Pearson and Martin, his remaining loyal officers, he sent post-haste to Monghyr ahead of him.

In a letter dated 3 May, Fletcher told him that he had

done everything possible but could not alter his officers' determination to resign. They proposed to write to their friends in Madras to induce them not to serve in Bengal. Clive sent urgent instructions to the Council to stop all private mail between Calcutta and Madras. The members of the Council now took a hand, writing to Fletcher or to 'the officer commanding at Monghyr', and telling him they had learned that his officers had handed in their commissions. They expressed surprise at 'such an extraordinary and unwarrantable proceeding'. He was ordered to accept as many commissions as were offered, and to send down to Calcutta within the space of twenty-four hours anyone who had resigned the service, 'since no confidence could be placed in those who had deserted their duty in a manner so inconsistent with the character of officers and gentlemen'. All twelve members of Council signed the letter and its effect may well have proved decisive. Fletcher's brigade, as Barker had asserted, was undoubtedly the seat of the mutiny and Fletcher himself almost certainly implicated. The letter from the Council must have given him pause. Britain might be a long way away, but British justice was patient and its arm long. If he was associated with a mutiny against a Governor who was doing no more than execute the wishes of the Directors and enjoyed the support of every member of the Council in the Presidency, and if from that mutiny the Company's interests were damaged, he might expect short shrift when he returned home. If an armed clash did occur, he might find himself the enemy not only of the Company, but also of his country, and Fletcher was not an unscrupulous adventurer ready to spend the rest of his life in India living on his wits, even if his principles on one or two notable occasions appeared unduly flexible. Inconceivable though it might seem, Clive was not going to give way, and the scheme to humiliate and break him had become exceedingly dangerous. All this is only surmise; Fletcher always protested his innocence, but, as will be seen, his actions were decidedly curious.

As Clive and his party continued on their way to Monghyr, Strachey remarked 'the heat of the season of the year was so insupportable that many of the men had already died on the march ... but it was necessary to reach Monghyr if possible before the despatch of the officers'. While they travelled up the river, they met a courier going down carrying a bulky parcel addressed to the Council in Calcutta. Clive had it opened. It contained the commissions of fifty officers from Barker's 3rd Brigade. Clive impounded them and continued on his way. On 13 May his party was delayed for a day by a bridge that had been swept away by a spate.

Meanwhile Major Champion and his small group of officers had arrived at Monghyr on 12 May. They spoke to all the officers of the garrison, pointing out that Clive was inflexibly resolved not to give way on the matter of Batta, in which he was doing nothing more than carry out the instructions of the Company. They also spoke of Clive's solicitude for the welfare of his troops and the 5 lakhs of rupees he had donated to form a pension fund. They made little impression.

Matters reached a head on 14 May in a denouement difficult to explain except by a change of heart in the brigade commander. At 11 p.m. on the night of the 13th Captain Smith with two battalions of sepoys, fully armed and carrying ball ammunition, marched on to the brigade parade-ground and slept there with their arms beside them. Next morning Smith suggested to Fletcher that they should return to their normal parade ground, as from there they could command the main gates of the fort where the European battalion was quartered, and detachments could be sent speedily to any part of the garrison. In order to obviate suspicion, it could be put about that they were assembled ready to fall in and greet Lord Clive on his arrival, which was hourly expected.

Fletcher agreed; then that afternoon he sent Smith orders to march at once to the fort where the European battalion had mutinied. Smith was the only British officer with the two battalions. As he was marching to comply with his orders, he came across an officer who had resigned his commission. Smith asked him for assistance, but the officer hesitated. Smith told him what he could do with himself, and handed over command of the second battalion to its Indian commandant. When he arrived near the European barrack square, moving cautiously and by a roundabout route, he occupied the signal battery which overlooked the European's parade ground. Shortly afterwards the European battalion and the gunners assembled under their officers. Suddenly they found themselves confronted by long steady lines of sepoys with fixed bayonets. There was a startled moment of confusion. Smith took advantage of it to tell them that unless they returned peaceably to their quarters he would immediately open fire.

At this juncture Fletcher rode up, harangued the men and apparently distributed money to them, giving each man two rupees. The soldiers told Fletcher that they had been led to believe he would head them otherwise they would have never turned out. They assured him they cared nothing for their officers and would do whatever he told them. Fletcher then ordered all the officers to leave the fort and dismissed the parade. The officers who had resigned left and camped on the bank of the river a few miles away, and the men returned to their lines. Fletcher wrote to Clive that night, 'Some have been very troublesome and particularly those whom I have all along suspected and whose confidence I used every art to gain in January last, when I heard the whole were to form a plan for quitting the brigades without giving any warning. I went so far as to approve some of their schemes that they might do nothing without my knowledge.'

Next day Clive arrived, and on 16 May the brigade fell in for his inspection. He noticed the men were in good order but 'thinly officered'. He first addressed the Europeans. He explained why the Batta had been withdrawn, and said that the officers who had resigned were guilty of mutiny and would pay the penalty of their crimes. He told them of the provision he had made for invalids and dependants, and exhorted them to do their duty as soldiers. He then turned to the sepoy battalions and, addressing them through an interpreter, congratulated them on their conduct and promised them double pay for the months of May and June.

THE BENGAL MUTINY 361

His remarks were well received, and after the parade the men dispersed quietly to their quarters. Next day he sent a party of sepoys to mount a guard over the officers by the river; he ordered them to return within twenty-four hours to Calcutta and to move in small parties. Some of the subalterns declared they had not been members of the association and asked to be reinstated. On 18 May he left for Bankipore.

Barker with the 3rd Brigade had had his share of trouble. At eleven o'clock on the morning of 1 May his adjutant, Ensign Roberts, handed him a letter from his captains and subalterns resigning their commissions unless Batta was restored. Roberts added laconically that the parcel with the letter might be of interest. It contained the commissions of fifty of his officers. Barker believed that his adjutant was one of the ringleaders. He paraded all his officers and told them forthrightly that by their actions they were guilty of mutiny and desertion. They listened to him quietly, but declined to withdraw their resignations. Barker then turned to his adjutant and ordered him to return to Calcutta at once. Roberts replied that, since he had resigned the service, he was no longer subject to military discipline. He challenged Barker to send him back as a prisoner to Calcutta, 'that I may know where to apply for restitution'.

Barker, unimpressed by the implied threat, obliged him by placing him in custody and promptly dispatched him with another officer he knew as a troublemaker under guard to Calcutta. The remainder of his officers, without withdrawing their resignations, remained at duty as they had promised. When Barker returned them their commissions, they parcelled them up and addressed them to the Council in Calcutta. As already mentioned, Clive intercepted the courier.

An uneasy peace prevailed until 15 May. Barker was fortunate in his European infantry. Strachey remarked with, perhaps, unconscious irony, 'His European regiment consisted chiefly of new recruits who were yet unaccustomed to mutiny and showed not the least disposition to be troublesome'. On 15 May, when it was clear that the nerve

46 The fort at Allahabad.

of their Commander was not to be shaken, most of the officers expressed their readiness to continue to serve under Barker. When Clive arrived, Barker interceded on their behalf and Clive pardoned them.

In two of his brigades the danger of a large scale mutiny was over, but Clive felt uneasy about the conduct of the officers on their way back to Calcutta. He sent detachments of sepoys to piquet the roads and prevent disturbances. He also instructed the Council that if any officers created any trouble they were to be confined in the new fort and shipped home by the earliest available boat; the ringleaders were to be court-martialled.

There yet remained Richard Smith's 2nd Brigade at Allahabad. Here matters for a few days were serious. As at any moment the Brigade might be called on to operate against the Mahrattas, the officers did not resign on 1 May, but on 6 May they sent a letter to Smith at Serajipur informing him they intended to resign on 15 May, or on 6 June at the latest, in support of the other two brigades. Smith was wroth. He published an order: 'The Colonel cannot find words sufficiently strong to express his astonishment at the conduct of those officers who have applied to him for leave to leave the service at a time when an enemy's army so numerous is encamped at no great distance from us. . . . When honourable motives have no longer any influence, the service of such officers is no longer desirable. . . .' He ordered Captains Scott and Auchmuty, Captain-Lieutenants Clifton and Black, Lieutenant Ellerker and Ensign Maverty to proceed to Calcutta immediately.

The public rebuke deeply angered the officers. An intemperate correspondence ensued, resulting in the officers declaring their intent to resign by 20 May. Except for one officer, everyone in the rank of Captain and below was in the association. Major Smith, commanding the European battalion at Allahabad, suspected the officers of tampering with the loyalty of their men, and became anxious for the security of the fort. He ordered up the 8th Native Infantry Battalion from Serajipore 104 miles away. Strachey claimed that the battalion covered the distance in two days, a frankly incredible feat, but it was undoubtedly a fine battalion which Smith himself had at one time commanded; its swift arrival probably took the mutinous officers by surprise; once it had taken over the guards and duties, the fort was secure from any attempt by the mutineers to seize it by a sudden coup-de-main, and Smith had some troops on which he could rely. The officers now agreed to serve on until 1 June, but on 22 May Lieutenant Marvel and Ensign North requested an interview with their Commanding Officer. At the interview, in the name of the officers, they demanded that Smith should dismiss his adjutant, Lieutenant Peake, 'as he had gone back on his oath to the combination'.

The hot weather and the curious antics of his officers were unlikely to have encouraged a philosophical frame of mind in Smith, and this final piece of insolence was too much; his temper boiled over. He put Marvel and North under arrest and sent Lieutenants Brooke and Delderfield to get the 8th under arms. Then he went and put all the remaining officers of his regiment except four under arrest. He added that if they made any disturbance or did not apologise within an hour he would have them all shot.

His officers do not appear to have doubted the determination of their redoubtable Commander. The Combination collapsed, whereat he released all but six whom he sent under arrest to Patna. At Serajipore Colonel Richard Smith dismissed half his officers, but with the fiasco at Allahabad the mutiny came to an end. Letters of recantation deluged Clive's headquarters. He instructed Colonel Richard Smith to pardon whom he wished. He pardoned all the ensigns and most of the Lieutenants on the ground that they had been intimidated, but the Captains were subjected to a more searching scrutiny, and six were ordered to be court-martialled.

On 22 May Clive wrote to Verelst from Bankipore. 'All is well and we are in no immediate need of officers. . . . The mutineers all intend to gather at some place near Calcutta and make a triumphal entry . . . if any gentleman should be particular in the reception then immediate dismissal should be the consequence.' With the breaking of the mutiny the officers commanding regiments had an unrivalled opportunity for ridding themselves of incompetent officers; discipline was restored and the purged regiments were soon ready for action. Clive had endured perhaps the most taxing period of his life, and mastering the mutiny he considered his greatest single personal achievement.

But the Mahrattas were still in the field and measures had to be taken to deal with them. He went to Chupra about thirty miles west of Patna and conferred with Shuja about a possible alliance with some Rohilla and Jat chieftains. There on 9 June he wrote indignantly to Verelst, 'The King [Shah Alam] is a most infamous. . . . [Left blank in the letter except for an indecipherable initial letter.] He hath not only invited the Mahrattas but hath prevailed on them among other requests to demand the whole Soubah of Bihar. . . .' Shuja told him that at one moment he was on the point of quitting Colonel Richard Smith and joining the Mahrattas, Clive added 'you may as well keep that information to yourself'. The British peril during the mutiny had been great. Again from Chupra he addressed Verelst. 'As Shuja has complied with this treaty I shall order his country to be restored to him and Colonel Smith's brigade shall be removed to this place', and on the 26 June, 'By what I can learn the Mahrattas are much more apprehensive of us quarrelling with them than any of their quarrelling with us. The King has been the cause of all . . . assuring him [the Mahratta leader] that he had with great difficulty prevented us from crossing the Jumna . . . The King is a very good scoundrel and the sooner we are clear of him the better.'

Clive remained at Chupra with Shuja for a period trying to arrange a defensive alliance with the Rohillas and Jats, but negotiations dragged on; now that the immediate threat of a Mahratta invasion was over he was prepared to allow Shuja to negotiate terms on his own, merely requiring him to forward any draft treaty to Calcutta for approval before he signed it. The clearing up of the mutiny still exercised his mind. On 20 June he informed Verelst:

'Those whom we thought proper to restore should not be degraded. If they be obliged to sign a contract for serving a limited time it will be setting a sufficient mark to distinguish them from those who did not resign and who ought to be exempt from contracting.... All we can think of at present is to contract the gentlemen for a year or a year and a half, or such time as we may suppose will bring us the determination of the Court of Directors.'

It was finally decided that those who had recanted should contract their services for a period of three years.

Madras had sent a number of officers in response to the Council's request, and these Clive ordered to return; their presence was no longer necessary and a threatening situation was developing in the Deccan. Six officers were court-martialled and cashiered, as there was doubt if the company had the legal right to impose a sentence of death. There remained Sir Robert Fletcher. Clive ordered him to be court-martialled at Patna. Writing on 3 July Fletcher submitted a plea that he might be tried by Clive and the Council, but his plea was refused. On 19 June Clive had received an anonymous letter denouncing Fletcher; 'Be it known to Your Lordship that we have been led into the resignation of our commissions and therewith our whole support by a man who now stands behind the curtain deriding these miseries which his deluding arguments have brought upon us.' This was scarcely acceptable evidence; however, Fletcher was convicted on 15 September of engaging in Mutiny and failing to send Clive information about the officers' combination at the earliest opportunity. He was sentenced to be cashiered. The proceedings were signed by Colonel R. Smith, President.

The case had a curious sequel. After he arrived in England Fletcher campaigned ceaselessly against the verdict. The Directors eventually submitted the proceedings to Stringer Lawrence and Caillaud for review. They found the evidence insufficient to sustain the verdict and it was quashed. On 28 March 1771, Fletcher was appointed Colonel of Infantry on the establishment of Fort St George, Madras. William

Hickey, arriving in India for his first brief visit, observed that after he had gone ashore at Madras, 'We were conducted to a very handsome house in Fort St George. Here at one o'clock we sat down to an admirable dinner and were vastly comfortable, Captain Waddell promising to introduce me to Governor Bourchier the following morning for whom I had several letters, as I had likewise for General Richard Smith, the Command-in-Chief, Sir Robert Fletcher, Mr Dupré . . . and many other gentlemen high in the service.' The relationship between the Commander-in-Chief and the Colonel of Infantry he had once sentenced to be cashiered for mutiny must have been an interesting one.

Fletcher stayed on long enough in Madras to take part in the extraordinary transaction in 1776 when, at the behest of members of a Council whose activities did not bear scrutiny, the acting Commander-in-Chief arrested the Governor, Clive's old friend now a peer, Lord Pigot, and imprisoned him. Pigot died in captivity before a frigate could arrive from England, bearing the Directors' orders for his release and an invitation to the Commander-in-Chief to return home and explain his actions. Fletcher's complicity in the mutiny at Monghyr might not be provable beyond all reasonable doubt, but it seems not unlikely.

By the beginning of August, Clive was back in Calcutta. He was not altogether satisfied with the trading of the Salt Society, he found 'that the industrious native is still deprived of that share to which he has an undoubted and natural right, nor is it yet on that equitable footing which justice and humanity would, I am sure, incline this committee to establish', and he made some reforms to ensure that retailers should not demand too high a price.

His task, as he thought, completed he now planned to return home. He wrote to Peggy on 8 September.

'The situation of the Company's affairs will not permit me to leave India before the latter end of January when I have agreed to take my passage on the Britannia, Captain Rous. . . . I flatter myself with the pleasing hope of seeing Berkeley Square in July 1767. Mun [*Maskelyne*] Strachey and Doctor Ingham will accompany me, Mun with about £25,000, Mr Strachey 18,000, Doctor Ingham 16,000 and Mr Philpott 3,000 [*pounds*] all my other followers you know are dead.'

Such sums of money, earned after less than two years in the country, seem unduly large; at the same time, as Clive's last sentence shows, the hazards bore some relationship to the rewards.

By October all opposition among the civil servants had been crushed and the chief malcontents sent home, the discipline of the Army and the supremacy of the civil authority over it was restored, no enemy menaced the borders of Bengal, there was peace in the province and the Company's trade prospered. All seemed set fair. The relaxation of tension was too much for Clive and his health gave way.

He suffered some sort of mental breakdown, fever, fits, and acute depression. On 4 December Carnac wrote to Peggy, 'His nerves have been affected in the most violent manner; and it grieved me beyond measure to see a person endued with such extraordinary firmness so oppressed in his spirits.' Doctor Ingham assured Carnac that there was no danger and that Clive had experienced similar symptoms when he returned home in 1760. Clive was, however, incapable of work and compelled to spend between six weeks and two months in complete seclusion.

It is possible that, during the nerve-wracking tensions of the spring, he may have increased the amount of opium he was eating and that it affected him. In May 1765 he had written to a Mr Billey. 'I wrote to you a few days ago about procuring me 5 or 6 lbs of opium. . . . If any opportunity should offer wherein you think I may be able to serve you, I shall not fail to exert my influence on your behalf. . . . '

De Quincey, in his *Confessions of an English Opium Eater*, observed, when comparing the effects of the drug with alcohol:

'Whereas wine disorders the mental faculties, opium, on the contrary (if taken in the proper manner) introduces amongst them the most exquisite order, legislation and harmony. Wine robs a man of his self-possession, opium greatly invigorates it. Wine unsettles and clouds the judgement . . . opium on the contrary communicates serenity and equipoise to all the faculties active or passive.'

Opium, of course, exacts a terrible revenge for any benefits it may confer. De Quincey had periods when he was plagued with fearful dreams. How far the drug affected Clive it is difficult to say; certainly there is no good evidence that it ever affected his actions or that he was ever seen to be under its influence.

The Directors wished him to remain another year in India. They were full of praise for everything he had done except for the constitution of the Society for the salt trade, of this they disapproved strongly. 'With respect to the Company it is neither consistent with their honour and dignity to promote such an exclusive trade . . . we cannot therefore approve the plan you have sent us for trading in salt, betel-nut and tobacco, or admit this trade in any shape whatever.' They told Clive, 'We must enjoin on you to have particular regard to the good of the Natives, whose interests and welfare are now become our primary care; and we earnestly recommend to you that you take the most effectual means to prevent . . . the poor and indigent becoming liable to those grievances and exactions which we mean to prevent our people from being guilty of.'

These were admirable and enlightened sentiments, and ones not conspicuously shared by other eighteenth-century authorities. It was unfortunate that in pursuing them the Directors came to the conclusion that the Salt Society must be wound up. It is possible to understand their views; Clive, himself, had said with some force before he sailed for India that the trade should be restored to the Nawab. Now, however, that the Company had taken over the administration of the revenue, conditions had altered. The problem remained that there was still no provision for paying the servants of the Company adequate salaries. In conformity with the wishes of the Directors the Select Committee abolished the Society, although they sent home a letter explaining how it operated in the hope that the Directors would reverse their decision:

'... Under these regulations the trade can scarce be considered in the odious light of a monopoly, since we are rather agents for manufacturing salt than the proprietors of the trade. It is sold in Calcutta to the natives only, to the utter exclusion of all Europeans, at an easier rate than it ever could be procured when under the management of the government before we were admitted to participation. The natives transport it to all the different parts of the country under such limitations that it must reach the hands of the consumer at a stated and moderate price. Hereby the people feel the justice of your government; and your servants who have attained the highest stations, after a course of many years spent in an unfavourable climate, reap the reward of their services, and enjoy the means of securing that independence to which they have so equitable a claim.'

The Directors were, however, adamant, and in due course their servants, denied a legitimate means of reaping a reward for their labours, turned again to illegitimate, and peculation and extortion re-appeared.

Clive's health rendered it impossible for him to remain in India and he was impatient to be gone. On 29 January 1767 he embarked on the *Britannia* and sailed for England. It was unfortunate, both for him and his country, that he could not remain another year and consolidate the reforms he had made.

As with most of Clive's achievements, his policies during his brief eighteen months in India have been lauded to the skies or described as makeshift and misconceived. It can scarcely be denied that in this period he showed a phenomenal degree of energy. He placed the Company's affairs on an unshakable legal footing and completed a settlement that gave Bengal peace for nearly two centuries. From the Company's point of view he restored discipline in the army and among the Company's servants, and laid a sure foundation for the Bengal army that was to be the rock on which British Imperial power in India was to be based.

It is in the administration of the province that his work is most open to criticism. Here the unprecedented nature of the situation needs to be remembered. In 1756 Calcutta was sacked by the Nawab of Bengal. In 1757 Plassey was fought merely to place a Nawab friendly to the British on the *musnud*. As early as 1759 Clive perceived that the political power the Company was acquiring was inappropriate for a joint stock company, but his suggestion that the Crown should take over its responsibilities was rejected, and that by one of Britain's greatest statesmen and one that he revered above all others.

Parliament would not assume any responsibilities in India until events made it unavoidable. He returned to India in 1764 with the aim of producing a stable Indian Government in Bengal that would enable the Company to expand its trade without interference. He early recognised that the Company had to assume some political power in view of its military predominance and revised his plans, so that the Company took responsibility for the ultimate administration of the province; but he still tried, wrongly as it subsequently turned out, to limit the Company's political role to a minimum, and hoped, as he showed in his letter to Verelst of 19 April 1766, to keep the collection of revenue in Indian hands so far as it might be possible. Here it should not be forgotten that the Company had no legal authority over British subjects outside its own territories and the only sanction it possessed was the right to send those of its servants that misbehaved back to Britain. As for actually governing Bengal, Clive judged that at this time it was politically undesirable, and even had he judged it wise he lacked resources to form a proper British civil administration.

It can be argued that political and military power cannot be separated, and that the dichotomy, whereby the administration of justice remained under the Nawab while the ability to enforce the law remained with the British, was bound in the long run to produce an impossible situation.

Taking into account the pressing immediate difficulties that surrounded him, it is perhaps unfair to blame Clive for not legislating for a situation that, up to that time, had no historical parallel. Sir George Forrester's summary of his achievements after his second period of rule, although it has been challenged, surely still stands: '. . . during his brief second administration, the boy hero of Arcot, the winner of Plassey, proved himself possessed of many of the finest qualities of a statesman'.

Chapter 18

ENGLAND ONCE MORE
1767–71

Clive returned to England his health damaged and his spirit scarred. The long sea voyage brought some relief. From the Cape he wrote home to Peggy,

'I owe my recovery entirely to the bark which has had a most surprising effect upon my original nervous disorder, in so much that if it does not extirpate the complaint I am convinced it will make life much more tolerable than it has been, ever since I was first taken ill in Madras. I am still thin and weak but in every other respect recovered . . . Major Winwood who has been greatly affected with the same distemper which made so severe an attack on me hath promised to deliver this letter with his own hands'.

Winwood was travelling on a faster sailer than the *Britannia*, and Clive expected he would arrive in England some three weeks ahead of him. The efficacy of quinine, and the recurrent attacks that he suffered, suggest that among his ailments he numbered malaria. If he had been infected by the benign variety, he would be liable to have attacks of fever whenever he had been put under a prolonged strain, and it would accentuate the melancholia to which he was always prone.

When he landed at Portsmouth on 14 July he was still far from well. His fits of illness and depression, and perhaps the memory of the hateful six months of 1766, made him petulant and unreasonable and a little too ready to imagine slights even from his friends. He came back, however, to a warm welcome. Five days after he had landed George Grenville wrote cordially, telling him that he was sending Mr Whately, one of the Secretaries of the Treasury, to call upon him. Whately would inform him about the current state of affairs in the country and, in particular, about the dispute with the American Colonies which was giving rise to much concern. He added, 'I should be extremely glad to wait on you if I came to Town, but I suppose you will be going into the country. If you would make this place on your way thither you would do me a great honour and give me a very sensible pleasure.' Grenville, although out of office, still commanded a substantial following among the more moderate of the Whigs and was a leading member of the House of Commons. He was one of the few men whose opinions Clive respected, and he accepted his political advice and followed his lead on most issues of importance. Grenville seems to have cherished a warm affection for his formidable, but impetuous and occasionally unmanageable friend.

On 24 July Clive was received very graciously by the Queen and King and a few days later was given the congratulations of the Directors on the eminent services he had rendered the Company. But in early August his health collapsed and he left London for Walcot. He stayed at Wootton on the way and, no doubt, concerted plans to take his place in Parliament when the next General Election took place, an event that Grenville was convinced could not long be delayed.

Before he arrived in England, Walsh had brought a resolution before the General Court of the Company, conferring on him his jaghir for a further ten years. The affair was mismanaged and, to Clive's indignation, permission to introduce the resolution was only granted by a majority of twenty-five votes. However, in September the resolution was unanimously confirmed. The smallness of that first majority, however, had some sinister implications. There were men home from Calcutta who believed they had good reason to hate him; chief among them was John Johnstone whom he had expelled from the Council and driven out of Calcutta. Johnstone had wealthy and influential connections, and he had an obvious ally in Sulivan who was patiently scheming to regain his old pre-eminence.

Clive's foes could not be driven out of England as they were from Bengal, but from his sickbed at Walcot he failed to understand the situation and railed against his friends, bidding fair to alienate the less faithful. His old comrade of Plassey days, Luke Scrafton, was among the Directors, Rous was still Chairman, but they were no Select Committee with extraordinary powers to ride rough-shod over all opposition, they had to work within the limits of what was acceptable to the general body of the Proprietors, and a growing number, led by Johnstone and Sulivan, were beginning to question his achievements and suggest that he had been more than amply rewarded. The Directors had launched a legal action to recover from the members of Council who presided over Mir Jafar's second accession to power the presents they had received on that occasion. This aroused intense opposition and the Directors thought it prudent to withdraw. Clive from his sickbed saw none of their difficulties and felt he had been betrayed. Yet the Directors, in securing for him his jaghir, had shown considerable finesse, and their success revealed that Clive still had a powerful following among the Proprietors.

But the sick man at Walcot, conscious only of what he had achieved in India and the heavy mental and physical price he had paid, could not perceive it. He never really understood the processes of democracy, and its results he viewed with contempt. He tried vainly to make the Directors rescind their decision about the Salt Trade, and their refusal infuriated him. Writing to Verelst he said of the Directors, 'Their whole conduct towards me and my associates in the Committee has shown weakness, or something worse.... In short they appear very envious and jealous of my influence....' Scrafton took the brunt of the tirades from his great one-time master and bore all with exemplary patience.

However, Clive's failing health had to take precedence over all else. The waters of Bath brought no relief and he resolved on a visit to France. Before going he made preparations for the forthcoming General Election in which he proposed to stand for Shrewsbury. On 2 January 1768, he wrote to Doctor Adams who managed his affairs in the constituency, instructing him to be foremost in setting an example when it came to public charities, 'but encouraging drunkenness, luxury and debauchery is what I cannot reconcile to myself; and nothing but the necessity can force me into such a measure . . . I will follow your advice'.

On 19 January he wrote confidently to John Gale,

'We shall come very strong into Parliament:
    Lord Clive—Shrewsbury
    Richard Clive—Montgomery
    William Clive—Bishops Castle
    George Clive—Bishops Castle
    John Walsh—Worcester
    Henry Strachey—Pontefract
    Edmund Maskelyne—probably either Whitchurch or Cricklade'.

Towards the end of the month, with Peggy and a large entourage, he set out in some state for France, having prudently directed that £200 should be laid out in Shrewsbury for the relief of the poor. Henry Strachey remained in his house at Berkeley Square to keep watch on affairs in England. The travellers eventually came to rest in Montpellier, from which on 3 March Peggy wrote to Henry Strachey.

'I think there are none but old men in the place. . . . We had a very short walk after dinner and it being cold, we came in determined to write to friends and play at chess. My Lord gained his first victory. . . . My Lord went for a ride this morning and has made a good breakfast since the horses, Doctor Ingham says, were rather shy and troublesome from want of use. . . . We have found a very pleasant house to rent at Montpellier' [*L'Enclos de Despioch*].

Clive still felt depressed. On 22 April he wrote to Strachey,

'I suffer in the manner that I did on board the *Britannia* both from the bile and my former nervous complaint, but not more, which convinces me the roots of both disorders still remain and I much fear I must be unhappy as long as I live; though I am certain there is nothing mortal in either of them and in all probability I shall drag on a miserable life for fifteen or twenty years longer, as I have already done ever since the year 1752. That I am fitter and stronger than when I landed at Portsmouth is certain, that I can trot on horseback for fifteen or twenty miles together. With more exercise I have left off opium altogether. It is certainly true that my bones are much stronger.'

His strength and his interest in life were returning, and against the advice of their medical adviser, in September 1768 the Clives went back to England. He had been duly elected by the discriminating citizens of Shrewsbury and he now prepared to play his part both in the affairs of the Company and the Country. In February 1769, the state of the East India Company came up for debate in the House. In 1767, flushed with the increased revenue from Bengal, the Company had agreed to pay the Government £400,000 a year, and to export annually goods to approximately the same value, in exchange for its charter. The agreement had been for two years only, and now was due for review. Clive opposed reimposing such onerous conditions on the grounds that the Company could not afford them, but his arguments went unheeded, and the agreement was duly renewed without a division. During the debate 'Governor' Johnstone, the brother of John Johnstone, accused Clive of murdering Siraj-ud-daula. It was the first roll of thunder, presaging the approach of a deadly but still distant storm.

In April that year, Sulivan and his party regained control of the Court of Directors. It was, in part, as a result of political manoeuvres in Parliament occasioned by the great debates over the expulsion of Wilkes from the House of Commons. Grenville, to the fury of the Government,

47 Clive by Thomas Gainsborough. It is thought to have been painted in 1761 when Clive would have been thirty-five or thirty-six years old.

opposed the expulsion, and in consequence Wedderburn, a Scottish barrister of great ability and one of Grenville's most prominent supporters, lost his seat. Clive procured him another, an act of kindness that gained him a loyal friend and a valuable ally.

Clive, himself, was becoming disillusioned with public life; his advice in the Commons was disregarded; even when his friends controlled the East India Company his views had not been treated with the respect that he expected and now, with Sulivan at the head, matters were certain to grow worse. He contemplated retiring from public life altogether. He still kept up a voluminous correspondence with his friends in India, but he began to interest himself more in buying property and renovating the numerous houses he had come to acquire. He bought the estate of Claremont in Surrey and planned a splendid mansion for himself. Then in 1770, to his great distress, George Grenville died, a loss that, as the next two years were to show, he could ill afford.

During this time the financial situation of the Company had been deteriorating with increasing rapidity. Verelst, who had succeeded Clive in Bengal, attributed the trouble to a variety of causes. The unsettled state of Bengal for the past thirty years, dating from Alivardi Khan's long struggles with the Mahrattas through to the series of revolutions that had followed the deposition of Siraj-ud-daula, had impoverished the province, an impoverishment, he thought, increased by the large treasure that Mir Kassim was alleged to have carried off with him into exile. The annual tribute of 26 lakhs to the Emperor was a severe additional drain on its resources. Madras had managed to embroil itself in a costly and disastrous war with Hyder Ali of Mysore and had called on Bengal for financial assistance, while the resulting unrest in the Carnatic, no less than the military expenses, had seriously affected the revenue of the Company.

Even so there was nothing that sound administration should not have been able to overcome, but the administration was by no means sound. At home the Directors, now occupying positions of great influence and patronage, depended on the favour of the Proprietors for their annual re-election, and were no sooner elected, Clive claimed, than they started to plan for the next election. The temptation to pay out a high dividend, irrespective of the profit for the year, was one to which they succumbed with the utmost regularity. In India the old ills that Clive had sought to cure had reasserted themselves, and the Company's servants made large and rapid fortunes while neglecting the interests of their employer.

But there were also more fundamental causes; the whole economic pattern of trade in India had been dramatically changed. Whereas before India had been a net exporter and the European traders had been forced to pay in bullion for their outstanding purchases, pouring a steady flow of capital into the country, now the Company used the revenues of Bengal for its annual purchases, the investment as it was termed, and in real terms many of the goods exported to Europe went unrequited. Two more factors aggravated the situation. Tea, rapidly becoming an essential element in the diet of the true Briton, came exclusively from China, but the Chinese disdained the products of Europe and demanded silver in payment, much of which the Company now obtained from Bengal. The currency in India was based on silver; as the province was steadily stripped of that metal, it was clear that sooner or later there would be a monetary crisis. Clive recognised the evil while he was still Governor and had made an abortive attempt to introduce a new currency based on gold.

The second factor was the wealth accumulated by British merchants in India; they were faced with the problem, not unknown in the present day, of getting their money home. They could buy a large cargo and ship it back to England, accepting all the risks of the long sea voyage, or deposit their rupees with some European merchant in India against bills of exchange on his agents in Europe. When the Company, glutted with rupees, refused to execute any more bills, the returning merchants negotiated them with the trading companies of the French, the Dutch or the Danish; hence these companies, too, needed to export fewer goods from Europe to pay for their purchases. The whole pattern of trading had changed to the detriment of India; capital no longer came from Europe, the provinces were drained of silver for the trade with China, and as money became scarce industry declined. Then, to aggravate a bad situation, the monsoon failed in Bengal, and in 1769 that province was afflicted by a famine of appalling proportions.

While the Company's revenues fell away, its servants continued to return to their native land almost overburdened with wealth. The contrast was stark, and it seemed obvious that the prime cause of the Company's difficulties was the mismanagement, or worse, of the Company's servants in India. Something had to be done before the general public woke up to the situation, and Parliament began to interfere and perhaps take a large measure of control in the Company's affairs, a prospect that filled Sulivan with horror. He wished to send out Vansittart as Governor-General of Bengal. Clive blocked the appointment. As a compromise, it was agreed a delegation of three, Vansittart, Scrafton and Forde, should be sent out to inquire into the circumstances of the three Presidencies and correct abuses; they had the power to dismiss or suspend the servants of the Company as they thought fit. It was an interesting illustration of the influence Clive still possessed among the Proprietors that two out of the three should have been his known supporters. He wrote, rather grimly, to Scrafton, saying that he did not envy him his task and hoping that he would have better luck than he had enjoyed.

The three supervisors, as they were called, sailed on the frigate *Aurora* in November 1770. After rounding the Cape the *Aurora* was never heard of again.

In 1771, while the fate of the Supervisors was still unknown, Warren Hastings was appointed President and Governor of Calcutta, and on 1 August Clive wrote to congratulate him and give him some advice. Clive thought the system in which the Governor was only the first of a Council of twelve or sixteen was faulty: 'My plan of government, a Committee of five to be appointed out of the best and ablest men in Bengal'. He warned him, 'A general apprehension prevails of the mismanagement of the Company's affairs ... the late dreadful famine or a war with Shuja-ud-daula will plunge us into still deeper distress. A discontented nation and a disappointed minister will then call to account a weak and pusillanimous Court of Directors, who will turn the blow from themselves upon their agents abroad.'

He added; 'Be impartial to the public regardless of the interests of individuals where the honor of the nation and the real advantage of the Company are at stake, and resolute in carrying into execution your determination which I hope will at all times be rather founded on your opinion than others.' In these last sentences Clive revealed his own philosophy, but in his prophecy about the storm likely to break in England, he erred only in that it was already eddying round his head and was destined to blow itself out before ever it reached India.

During 1770 the stream of wealthy Britons pouring back from India had continued unabated. These gentlemen, the nabobs as they were termed, were far from popular in their own country. They behaved in strange outlandish ways they had learned in the East and had an indecent amount of money; they bought up the estates of their betters from the more impecunious members of the gentry, indulged in uncalled for and vulgar ostentation and gave themselves airs that aroused considerable resentment among the natives of Britain.

As stories circulated that the Company itself was in low financial water and was to send out men to check the exactions and corrupt practices of its servants, it became plain to the country at large that, as had long been suspected, these nabobs had made their money by a flagrant disregard of the interests of the Company they pretended to serve and by swindling and oppressing the unfortunate Indians with whom they had traded. Then the news of the Bengal famine began to seep home, and it was whispered that Britons, utterly steeped in villainy and forgetful of their race, had created their fortunes by cornering rice; it was they who were responsible for the fearful famine about which dreadful stories were brought home by every ship from India. (The last, of course, was a vicious slander, but one widely believed.)

A great wave of moral fervour built up against the alleged activities of Britons in India; it may have been largely compounded of self-righteous ignorance and shrewdly exploited by unscrupulous hypocrites for their own ends,

48 Lord North; he was afterwards created the Earl of Guildford.

but it was not entirely an emotion of which the nation need feel ashamed. That Clive himself, as the most conspicuous of the nabobs, should share in the general obloquy was perhaps inevitable, but his enemies, themselves heavily tainted by the crimes of which they were to accuse him, took advantage of the situation with undeniable skill.

Now the storm clouds were gathering about Clive, but

the beginning, in the spring of 1771, seemed innocuous enough. At this time the amiable and easy-going Lord North was Prime Minister of England. Among the crosses he had to bear two were of outstanding dimensions, the colonies in America and India, and at the moment India seemed the heavier burden. Although friendly with Sulivan, it was to Clive that he turned for advice on a subject about which he frankly confessed he knew nothing. Clive, at first, refused to be drawn, saying that Strachey under his directions was drawing up a scheme for India that would not be ready for eighteen months, and that he himself proposed to winter in Italy.

The popular clamour persisted and North dare not disregard it. Clive was undoubtedly the outstanding authority on India affairs and his help in any reform was clearly indispensable. In October 1771 North wrote to Clive from Downing Street 'The very intricate and dangerous situation of our possessions in India will probably make it necessary to bring them under the consideration of Parliament next session. . . . Your lordship from your extensive knowledge of it can be of great service to me . . .'. Clive agreed to help.

At this time Sulivan was Deputy Chairman of the Company and a member of Parliament. He heard of North's overtures with some dismay. Fearing what the Government, with Clive as its chief adviser, might not do he resolved to discredit his old adversary and at the same time to anticipate North by introducing a bill of his own. He organised a scurrilous campaign in the Press against Clive and employed Bolt and others of his ilk to publish pamphlets accusing him of every imaginable crime. As the year ended, the stage was set for Clive's last great battle; this time it was to be fought out not on the plains of India but on the floor of the House of Commons. Had Grenville lived the battle might never have been fought, and the history of England, America, and indeed therefore the whole world, might have been altered.

Chapter 19

THE LAST BATTLE
1772–4

In the new year of 1772, two rather curious incidents occurred. On 7 January Clive received a letter from the Secretary to the Court of Directors, enclosing a copy of some charges that had been laid against him concerning his last administration in India and asking for his comments. He was accused of creating monopolies in cotton and diamonds, of introducing a fraudulent gold currency and making a 'monopoly in salt, betel-nut and tobacco and other commodities which occasioned the late famine in Bengal'. The charges were unsigned, their content puerile, and they related to events more than four years old. It is difficult to imagine why they had been sent to him. Perhaps Sulivan intended the letter as a warning to Clive of what he might expect if he continued to meddle in Company affairs, or perhaps the Court of Directors may have felt that the charges, although anonymous, could not be entirely ignored. Clive returned them, remarking he was not prepared to comment on such a document and that from their records the Directors could see for themselves that they were baseless. Next month, on 7 February, Mr Purling, the then Chairman of the Directors, forwarded to him a 'sketch of an act for the better managing of East India affairs' and asked for his opinion. Clive replied that, in view of his relations with the Court of Directors, he could not comment officially on the proposals, but that he would be prepared to discuss them privately with the Chairman as a friend.

Purling answered regretting Clive should feel that there was any breach between himself and the Directors and accepting his offer of a private conversation; it seems that the discussion took place, but there is no record of its outcome.

Sulivan, the real power in the Court of Directors, may have been the instigator of both incidents, and certainly was of the second. It is interesting to speculate on his motives. Most of his money was in the East India Company stock and he had, therefore, a strong financial inducement to secure Clive's support; if they acted together Parliament would be certain to approve anything they proposed; the invitation may have been some form of olive branch, but on the other hand he may have only been hoping Clive might be tricked into revealing his arguments.

Whatever his reasons, he did not receive the response he wanted, and he now made preparations to pre-empt Lord North by introducing his own bill to regulate the affairs of the Company. He brought it forward on 30 March 1772, and during the debate that followed Clive came under attack. He defended himself with his customary vigour and characteristically turned defence into attack. He pointed out that he had been the victim of a scurrilous attack in the Press solely because, when he went out to India at the request of the General Court, he had done his duty. Then he dealt with the charges that the Directors had sent him in January, treating them with the ridicule that they deserved. He claimed, 'as to Cotton, I know no more about it than the Pope of Rome.' The charge about diamonds was equally absurd. The diamond mines in India were outside the jurisdiction of the Company and he had no control over the sale of precious stones. He had bought some diamonds, it was true, but he had done this so that he could bring back to England the money owed to him on his jaghir, without embarrassing the Company by drawing on it large bills of exchange. As regarded the charge about gold, well, he was no expert on currency; the export of silver from Bengal to China had reduced the amount of that metal available for minting into rupees, currency became scarce and trade was adversely affected. To remedy a difficult situation he had tried to introduce a monetary system based on gold; the Select Committee had taken the advice of an honest and expert man, but the project failed. He had not made a penny from it. As for the monopoly on salt, betel-nut and tobacco and other commodities, since the other commodities were not named, he could not answer for them, and had no idea what they were, but how a monopoly on salt, betel-nut and tobacco in 1765 and 1766 could prevent the rains falling and the rivers running and cause a rice famine in 1769, 'is past my comprehension'. He then turned his attention to the bill before the House. He recapitulated the past history of the Company, and now perhaps he aired the frustrations he felt he had been made to endure since his return to England. In graphic but immoderate terms, he flayed past Courts of Directors and the whole system for running the Company in England, he flayed past governments for their failure to regulate Indian affairs better, he flayed the Company's governors in India for almost everything they had done. At the close it appeared that everyone had been wrong about India but himself. As a speech it was generally judged a brilliant performance, but most thought its content ungenerous and injudicious. The bill was introduced without a division.

As it had not been introduced by the Government and had been so roughly handled by Clive, Sulivan may have despaired of having it passed. There is, unfortunately, no record to throw any light on his motives. Whatever the reason, he now seems to have resolved on the destruction of Clive. When the bill was given its second reading, a serving officer, Colonel John Burgoyne, made a very able speech in which he observed:[1] 'I beg leave to state the motives and principles on which I act. . . . I never conceived it possible that Parliament should be called upon by any men whatever to apply a remedy without information of the disease . . . to pass an act on divination'. He proposed a Select Committee to investigate the affairs of the Company. He

[1] Quoted from *The Rt. Hon. J. Burgoyne, Political and Military Episodes* by B. de Fontblanque.

49 Colonel John Burgoyne. He was later promoted to the rank of major-general.

continued: 'I mean an investigation of the facts to discover the common danger and common interest of the Company and the Nation. As to the servants, I scorn the thought of proceeding on a vindictive principle towards any of them ... when means can be found to make the offence impracticable in the future, example of the offender is unnecessary.' Admirable sentiments which were no sooner voiced than discarded.

It was said of Burgoyne with some aptness, '. . . his sentiments have probably procured him more respect than his battles'. In this instance, in view of the conflict of evidence offered the House and the total ignorance of matters Indian enjoyed by most of its members, his logic was unassailable. Edmund Burke spoke against his proposal, but it was passed without division. A Select Committee under his chairmanship, consisting of thirty-one members, was constituted 'to inquire into the nature, state and conditions of the East India Company and of British affairs in the East Indies', and Sulivan's bill was dropped. Clive and Strachey were both made members, as was Governor Johnstone, brother of that John Johnstone, perhaps, except for Sulivan, the most bitter of all Clive's enemies.

It was one of the more curious ironies of fate that Gentleman John Burgoyne, as he was known to his soldiers, should have been the man to preside over the proceedings of a committee that, despite its terms of reference, was to become nothing more than an inquisition into all Clive's actions; Burgoyne would have been better employed studying how Clive advanced up the Hooghly to Plassey; perhaps then he might have avoided disaster when, in America in 1777, he marched down the Hudson river to Saratoga.

The two campaigns, except in their outcome, bore a surprising similarity. Both involved an advance along a river; for success both commanders depended on the actions of another, Mir Jafar in India, General William Howe in America; neither Clive nor Burgoyne knew anything positive about the intentions or actions of the general whose co-operation was vital. Clive moved with great caution, securing each bound before he advanced to the next; Burgoyne happily ambled down his river oblivious of the possible consequences if Howe failed to play his part. Both had to make a vital decision, whether or not to cross the river along which they had been advancing. Clive paused at Cutwa and only went forward after prolonged heart-searching, Burgoyne, for the first time began to appreciate the perils of his position, but did nothing to guard against them. Both were surprised by a superior enemy, Clive in a position so well chosen that he could either fight or retreat, Burgoyne in a trap from which despite the utmost gallantry of his troops and, be it said, of himself, there could be no escape. For Burgoyne all this lay in the future, but now he, the man who was to do most to bring Britain defeat in America, was to cross-examine with singular malevolence the man who did most to bring Britain victory in India.

Burgoyne was a year older than Clive. His motives for what he did can only be guessed. He had no connection with India; probably at this time he was only interested in making a name for himself in the Commons; in this he succeeded only too well. Over the past few years there had been considerable jealousy between the troops of the Company and the regular army. Perhaps he also hoped to humble a general who had never been trained as a regular soldier.

At the first meeting the gallant Chairman was found to have no plan of action for his committee; with suspicious alacrity 'Governor' Johnstone stepped into the breach. He proposed that the inquiry should begin with the succession of Siraj-ud-daula and should particularly scrutinise how various individuals had acquired their wealth. This rather odd proposal was adopted, yet the starting point selected was arbitrary, and affairs in the Bombay and Madras Presidencies, for reasons unstated, were to be ignored. 'Governor' Johnstone's motives, however, emerged soon enough. Slowly, and with considerable address, he bent the inquiry into an indictment of everything Clive had done during his first tour in Bengal.

The Committee submitted its first report in May, but throughout the rest of the year its proceedings dragged on.

As it became clear that its only aim was to denigrate Clive, some of its members became disgusted with its methods and on occasion there was difficulty in assembling the quorum of seven members. Nevertheless, Burgoyne pressed relentlessly on, while all the time Clive became less and less a member of the committee and more and more the prisoner at the bar. He, the one-time absolute ruler of vast provinces, the arbiter of the fate of millions, had to submit to the cross-questioning of a virtually unknown chairman and of a man actuated only by malice; he had to listen while all that he had achieved was questioned and belittled.

He fought back with his customary courage, but he was speaking of events that happened fifteen years ago, and does not appear to have had full access to the records. He was asked for his reasons for attacking Chandernagore against the wishes of the Nawab, and forbore to mention how permission had been obtained. It was made to appear as though it was part of a deep laid plot to overthrow a friendly Nawab, perhaps in the hope of financial gain. The fictitious treaty with Omichand was thoroughly investigated and much was made of Admiral Watson's refusal to sign. Walsh was called on to give evidence. He is recorded as saying 'that a letter was carried by him and Mr Lushington to the committee and he returned with the treaties signed in the evening; that he cannot recollect whether he went to Admiral Watson; or now recollect the whole transaction . . . his idea has always been that Mr [sic] Watson refused to sign the spurious treaty, but permitted Mr Lushington to do it for him'.

Lushington could not be called, he had been murdered on the orders of Mir Kassim with the other British captives. A John Cooke gave evidence,

'that after the Battle of Plassey, he waited on Admiral Watson with a message from the Select Committee, that among other things this fictitious treaty was mentioned in conversation; that the Admiral said he had not signed it (shrugging his shoulders) but had left them to do as they pleased. This conversation, as the witness thought, was in

July, and the Admiral was then in good health and spirits. The witness further said he had no doubt that the Admiral knew his name was to it; and he understood from what dropped from him that he secretly permitted his name to be used. ... He further said that the Admiral's consent to having his name put to the fictitious treaty was never communicated to the Secret Committee.'

Captain Brereton, who had been a lieutenant on the *Kent* with Admiral Watson in 1757, said that

'he had often heard the Admiral speak of it; it was proposed to him to sign a fictitious treaty to deprive Omichand of thirty lakh, which he refused to do, as dishonourable to him as an officer and an affront to propose it to him. That it was then proposed somebody should sign it for him, which he also refused, and said he would have nothing to do with it, he was a stranger to deception, they might do as they pleased. ... Being asked if he ever heard Admiral Watson say who was the person that proposed to him to sign the fictitious treaty, said the Admiral did not mention the gentleman's name, but said, with a sneer, it was a member of the Secret Committee.
'As for the Admiral's signing the real treaty, he never heard him mention it particularly; he had heard him say he thought it an extraordinary measure to depose a man they had so lately made solemn treaty with.'

Excellent as Brereton's memory of his conversations with Watson appeared to be, the Admiral clearly did not think it necessary to confide in him that on one occasion he had written with his customary flamboyance to Siraj-ud-daula, threatening to set Bengal on fire if his requirements were not met. Clive, when re-examined on the subject, replied that 'he certainly would not have declared that Admiral Watson had consented to have his name put to the fictitious treaty if he had not understood so from Mr Lushington', adding contemptuously that he 'would have ordered his name to be put, whether he consented or not'.

And so it went on. The Committee tried to belittle the Battle of Plassey by comparing the number of casualties suffered there against an Indian enemy with those at Chandernagore against the French. It was pointed out that, if the Committee wanted a good butchers' bill, the number of casualties suffered in the attack on Siraj-ud-daula's army outside Calcutta might satisfy them. Sir Eyre Coote, as he had now become, was examined about the decision to advance from Cutwa. It was put to him that Clive decided to advance on Plassey after receiving a 'memorial' from him. Coote, who had little reason to feel much affection for Clive, to his credit emphatically denied that he had submitted any 'memorial', and declared that Clive changed his mind without consulting him. How any of these questions threw light on the problems facing the Company in 1772 Burgoyne never troubled to explain.

The presents given by Mir Jafar after Plassey were duly exhumed and it was then that under cross-examination Clive made a famous rejoinder: 'Consider the situation in which the victory of Plassey placed me. A great prince dependent on my pleasure; an opulent city lay at my mercy; its richest bankers bid against each other for my smiles; I walked through vaults which were thrown open to me alone, piled on either hand with gold and jewels. Mr Chairman, at this moment I stand astonished at my own moderation.'

During the summer, while the Committee pursued its vindictive way, the affairs of the Company progressed from bad to worse. Despite Clive's admonitions, the Directors had continued to raise the dividend. In 1772 they declared one of $12\frac{1}{2}$ per cent, the maximum permitted by Parliament, yet in July the Company was bankrupt with assets of under £1 million and liabilities of £$2\frac{1}{2}$ million. The Directors applied to the Bank of England for a loan, but the annual payment of £400,000 to the Government patently could not be met.

In the city the Company's stock slumped to an alarming degree, and the easy-going Lord North, already spending more time than he wished over the intractable problems of the American colonies, realised something would have to be done. The Select Committee had produced no concrete recommendations and with their present pre-occupations seemed unlikely to do so. In November he appointed a Secret Committee of thirteen to look into the Company. He explained the apparent by-passing of the Select Committee by suggesting it was undesirable for the Company to submit their confidential records for the scrutiny of an open committee.

During the summer, Lord Powis, Lord Lieutenant of Shropshire, died. Clive asked Wedderburn to sound Lord North about appointing him to the vacancy. Despite the proceedings of the Select Committee, Lord North welcomed the chance of doing Clive a favour. He wrote to Wedderburn on 18 September 1772:

'I think myself much obliged to you for your suggestion concerning Lord Clive; an opportunity of manifesting my respect to his merit and my earnest desire of being well with him is what I have long wished to find, though I have thought it right, at the same time, to be very careful of deceiving him by any engagement which I could not be morally sure of performing. ... I will promise my best offices for the obtaining of it.'

On 9 October Clive received the honour and in December became Lord Lieutenant of Montgomeryshire, as well. They were the last honours he was to receive from his country.

Meanwhile, the Company's financial crisis remained unsolved and in March 1773, the Directors were obliged to seek a loan of £1½ million from the Government, an enormous loan from an annual budget often less than £18 million. In early April Lord North successfully moved that the loan should be granted, but on conditions, and on 3 May asked for leave to bring in a bill to ensure the better management of the Company. Clive spoke in the debate that followed and at the end of a long speech, complained bitterly of the persecution to which he had been subjected.

'My situation for the past twelve months has not been an agreeable one. . . . It is very certain that much of the time and attention of the Committee, instead of inquiring into the state, nature and conditions of the East India Company, have been taken up in inquiring into the state, nature and conditions of their very humble servant the Baron of Plassey . . . whether these bitter persecutions proceed from the laudable desire of bringing a public offender . . . to justice, or whether they proceed from resentment and malevolence because I have done my duty to the public and dared to avow it. . . . I must humbly submit to the consideration of Parliament.'

After developing his theme he continued ironically; 'There are at present three poles on Temple Bar on which formerly were planted three Jacobite heads, but they have long since fallen down. . . . Suppose by way of pre-eminence my head was placed on the middle one. His majesty has bestowed such honour on me that I am entitled to supporters; suppose then one each side of me, were placed the heads of the late chairman and deputy chairman—such an example would have a wonderful effect.[1]

The bitter jest caused laughter, but some undoubtedly there were who would have rejoiced to see Clive's head on Temple Bar, and now, with Burgoyne as their figurehead, they prepared to strike. At a conference of ministers held to consider the report of the two Committees and consider how the Company might meet its debts, there was a singular dearth of ideas. The Attorney General, Lord Thurlow, claiming he had read the proceedings of both committees gave it as his opinion that Parliament should confiscate all presents made to individuals of the Company, on the grounds that the rewards came from services rendered to the State. The noble Lord, who does not appear to have been blessed

---

[1] These and the following extracts have been taken from the speaking drafts of Clive's speeches preserved in the India Office Library. The text differs in some particulars from those published; but at that time the recording of speeches was unauthorised and shorthand had yet to be invented. Clive may have altered his text when he spoke, but it is probable that on occasion published records owed something to the imagination of the scribe.

with an over fertile imagination, remarked that he could see no other solution. The gross injustice of such retrospective legislation was argued, and indeed it is difficult to understand how a proposal, unjust in itself and irrelevant to any but the most immediate problems of the Company, could be entertained for a moment. But the suggestion gave Burgoyne an idea.

On 10 May he laid the report of the Select Committee before the House. He declared the report contained a record of crimes 'shocking to human nature'. In particular he referred to the deposition of Siraj-ud-daula as a villainy of the blackest hue. He proposed, and the house accepted without division, that all acquisitions made under the influence of military force or by right of treaty belonged rightfully to the State. He added two other resolutions couched in similar general terms, and added significantly 'that persons who have acquired sums of money by presents or otherwise in India, if they had acquired such sums by virtue of their acting in a public capacity should be forced to make restitution'.

The hunt was up and the hunters closing for the kill. On 19 May Burgoyne, apparently oblivious of his original proposition that 'when means can be found to make the offence impracticable in the future example of the offender is unnecessary', introduced a resolution 'that at the deposition of Siraj-ud-daula, Clive obtained, through the use of his powers as a member of the Secret Committee in Calcutta, sums amounting to £234,000 and that in so doing the said Robert, Lord Clive, abused the powers with which he was intrusted, to the evil example of the servants of the public'.

Burgoyne made a long opening speech.[1] He started by unctuously proclaiming: 'The task of a public accuser was never a pleasing, but sometimes a necessary one. Envy and malignity were the vices of little minds', and he disclaimed them. He developed the theme of his motives and then went on: 'Instances of rapacity and injustice have occurred in our

[1] The content of this speech is taken from Sir John Malcolm's biography of Clive which, the author asserted, he obtained from the pencilled notes of a member who was present. Burgoyne's biographer, perhaps with some wisdom, failed to record it.

Eastern possessions . . . an inordinate desire for wealth has had full play'. He now put his first point, 'that it was impossible that any civil or military servant, in treating with a foreign Prince or state, could lawfully bargain for, or acquire property for himself. This principle had uniformly been departed from in all the transactions which had been laid before the House.'

He considered the history of the Company.

'In the year 1757, when the English ascendancy was established, the Company was raised, by the power of magic, from the situation of merchants to that of sovereign Princes . . . their servants looked with contempt on the slow returns of trade and merchandise, since they saw before them a shorter and surer way of opulence; . . . revolution followed revolution; and at each successive change the treasures of the Prince were ravished to glut the rapacity of the agents by whom it was effected. At last, when the whole treasure of the Prince was exhausted, they did not stop short, but took possession of the country itself.'

He now put forward his own version of the attack on Chandernagore; it appeared that

'by the treaty with Siraj-ud-daula the Company was confirmed in all the privileges they had formerly enjoyed . . . yet on the breaking out of the war with France it was thought proper to violate the treaty just concluded, by attacking Chandernagore. The Select Committee were not unanimous on this point. The violent councils of Clive prevailed. . . . When we broke with him and hurled him from his high eminence, Siraj-ud-daula had been guilty of no overt act of hostility.'

He then contended that the presents Clive received were 'contrary to justice and right'.

He treated of the various revolutions that had followed the overthrow of Siraj-ud-daula, and condemned the presents received by members of the Council on each occasion.

But, he maintained,

'Let it be remembered that the revolution of 1757 was the foundation and model of all the subsequent revolutions. Our vindictive justice must go back to the origin of the evil ... let it not be said that the magnitude of the offence and the wealth and dignity of the offender are to be deemed a sufficient justification. . . .

'I wish not to plunder or impoverish Lord Clive, or the subjects of this motion. I am willing they should remain in the possession of such rewards as a generous State would give. What I ask is for a bill for the satisfaction of sufferers out of the private estates of persons who received sums of money unwarrantably. Such satisfaction ought to be made to the Company to the discharge of their debts.'

He added generously, 'I have no desire, no wish, that after satisfaction has been made, any odium should remain against the accused. I have offered them an opportunity of bringing their characters from under the cloud which has surrounded them and of justifying themselves to the world.' In nobility Burgoyne's sentiments were not to be found wanting.

That in some of his contentions there was justice cannot be denied, but the underlying vindictiveness of the speech showed through as the speaker proceeded. Restitution should be to the 'sufferers', who for some obscure reason suddenly became transformed into the Company; but the Company itself did extremely well out of each revolution. If the *diwani* of Bengal had been improperly acquired, then it ought to be restored to the Nawab of Bengal. If the Company's servants accepted gifts illegally, then the gifts should be returned to those who made them, or, in view of the lateness of the prosecution, to their heirs. And if it was illegal for individuals to accept gifts, was it any more legal for the Company to do so? Burgoyne's passion for justice did not extend to the Indians for whose tribulations he professed such indignation. His solution to the Company's difficulties was no more than to prosecute some of its servants and one in particular. One does not have to look far to find the real motive for the resolution.

Sir William Meredith seconded the resolution, adding that the lapse of time could not improve a claim to wealth that had been acquired illegally. For good measure, and inaccurately, he said; 'Others have fought against European enemies, he [Clive] against wretched Indians—a circumstance not to be forgotten in estimating the comparative merit of officers.' What this had to do with the resolution Meredith omitted to point out, and he himself appeared to have forgotten Clive's campaigns in the Carnatic.

Wedderburn, at this time Solicitor General, made a spirited defence of Clive. Lord North, professing his readiness to examine the evidence, proclaimed that 'any abuse of public authority was a pernicious example' and threw in a few more unexceptionable platitudes, but did nothing to help Clive in his extremity. With public feeling running as it was, there was no question of his peril. He faced disgrace and financial ruin. He now made a speech through which his true greatness shines clear. He attacked no one, aspersed no motives. He began:

'After so many years faithful and successful service rendered to the state, after sixteen years enjoyment of my fame and fortune uninterrupted and unimpeached, after so many marks of public approbation received, I confess I thought it impossible that a motion could be introduced into this House tending in its consequence to deprive me both of honour and fortune. So circumstanced, I am persuaded the House will not accuse me of vanity and presumption if I say I have rendered the state some service.'

Of presents he said: 'Presents in India are coeval with the Company. As soon as we began to raise fortifications the Company's chiefs began to receive presents. . . . There has not been a commander of his Majesty's Squadron, nor a commander of His Majesty's Land Forces, nor a governor, nor any chief who has not received presents.'

He went on to recount his campaigns in the Carnatic,

then turned to justify his conduct to Omichand. Of Admiral Watson's refusal to sign the fictitious treaty, he observed: 'Under such circumstances, when the lives of so many individuals were at stake, as well as the very existence of the Company, I should not have hesitated a moment in ordering Mr [sic] Watson's name to be put to the treaty, even without his consent.' He added that he still believed that Watson did give his consent.

He spoke of his year-long ordeal at the hands of the Select Committee. 'For my part I look upon myself as in a state of bankruptcy. I have now nothing to call my own, but an estate of £500 a year in Shropshire which has belonged to the family for some ages. I can retain this, and upon that income perhaps enjoy more health, more happiness, more tranquillity and more peace of mind, than in the midst of my wealth, accompanied with so much envy and detraction.'

Referring to the resolution, 'Then am I condemned by an

50 The House of Lords as it was when Clive was a member. The scene depicted is the death of Chatham by J. S. Copley.

ex post facto resolution for receiving presents sixteen years ago which, without I had been an angel from Heaven, I could not possibly have known to be an offence or illegal.' He concluded: 'I am not now afraid to encounter adversity. I am ready to stare bad fortune full in the face, and I have but one favour to ask of the House, which is that when they come to decide on my honour they will not forget their own.' As he sat down, for a few moments there was silence; then it was carried that the House should adjourn. On 21 May, Clive's evidence to the Select Committee was read out and Clive made a short statement ending, 'Take my fortune but save my honour.' He then left the House.

An amendment was immediately proposed to divide the resolution into two, separating the first statement from the condemnation. This was accepted. Now Mr Rose Fuller moved that the reference to the Select Committee in what had become the first resolution, should be deleted. This reduced it to no more than a statement of the amount of money paid by Siraj-ud-daula to Clive, and vitally altered its content. His amendment, therefore, started a warm debate which covered all aspects of Burgoyne's original resolution. The verdict when it came was unmistakable. For Fuller's amendment 155, against 95. Party loyalties seem to have been disregarded; Lord North, to Clive's abiding disgust, voted against the amendment. After this vote the second resolution was rejected without a division, and at four o'clock in the morning Wedderburn moved an addition to Burgoyne's truncated resolution; 'That Lord Clive did, at the same time, render great and meritorious services to this country.' His addition was passed unopposed.

On this occasion, at least, Parliament spoke for Britain and justice. The size of Clive's presents may have been undesirable, the precedent unfortunate, but there was no basis in law for asserting that the presents were illegal at the time they were made, and Burgoyne's claim that the money rightfully belonged to the Company was absurd. Clive undoubtedly turned a number of his actions to his own considerable financial advantage; but there is no evidence that he ever did this to the detriment of the Company, or ever allowed the prospect of personal gain rather than the public interest to decide his course of action. Less than fifty years later, Wellington, who had the good fortune to serve the Crown and not a joint-stock company, received vast rewards from foreign potentates, the morality of which has never been questioned.

Parliament had vindicated Clive, but the wounds he had received in his year-long ordeal proved mortal. When he left the Commons after his final defence, he also left public life for good. On 30 May he wrote to the Mayor of Shrewsbury thanking him for the congratulations of the Corporation on the defeat of the House of Commons resolution. In October, writing to recommend Commodore Hughes to his old comrade of his days in the Carnatic, the Nawab Mohammed Ali, he expressed a certain defiance: 'Your excellency . . . a high situation will always create envy, and bad men are always endeavouring to deprive others of what they themselves cannot hope to obtain. . . . Parliament has done me ample justice.'

After the tumult had died, Lord North introduced his bill for the better regulation of the Company; it was largely based on a memorial submitted by Clive and made provision for the Governor of Bengal to become Governor-General with authority over the other two Presidencies. Warren Hastings was appointed the first Governor-General, and on 11 October Clive wrote to congratulate him, adding 'my influence may be not inconsiderable as I am at present very strong among the new qualified Proprietors'. But that spark of the old spirit speedily flickered and died. During the rest of the year his formerly voluminous correspondence dwindled to a trickle. He could still rouse himself on behalf of an old comrade. Carnac was back in England, nearly destitute; his attorney in India had just died revealing that he had misappropriated nearly all his money; it was imperative he should go back to India, and on 13 November Clive wrote to, the now Lord, Pigot at Madras telling him of Carnac's misfortune; he also mentioned, 'I shall probably set out on my tour of Italy before your Lordship's answer can reach London.'

At the end of November he departed for the Continent. He seemed to wish to be away on his own. Peggy and the faithful Strachey stayed behind. Strachey sent him news, hoping to re-awaken his interest in public affairs. On 3 December 1773, he urged Clive to return to the House of Commons, 'Lord North, I am told, is highly sensible of your conduct towards him and expresses himself on all occasions with the greatest cordiality. ... He certainly made a determined point of serving Carnac.' And again on 16 December, 'The newspapers every now and then throw out a little abuse about you, but I have the honour to have a larger share. They have discovered that I have a most malignant and vindictive heart.' Peggy Clive had been to Court and been received by the Queen; she scribbled on the back of one of the sheets of Strachey's letter that gracious inquiries had been made about her husband. But Clive drifted round Italy, seldom bothering to reply and sometimes failing to tell Strachey his new address.

On 18 February 1774, Strachey wrote, 'In the Court of Directors the Administration cannot carry any question without the assistance of your friends. This they are perfectly convinced of'. Peggy added cheerfully: 'Mrs Wedderburn expects us to call, but the others only early; as they win or lose a great deal of money I shall only call in at the latter end of the feast. ... My best wishes attend your three companions ... be sure to bring me some good music. Your affectionate little wife.'

But Clive was unmoved. In one of his infrequent replies he made his feelings clear; 'After what I have been "*Caesar aut nullus*" is my motto' and 'my constitution is such that no consideration shall prevail upon me to enter again into public engagement'. And then to emphasise the irrevocable nature of his decision, he scrawled in 'whatever' between 'consideration' and 'shall'.

In June he was back in England, but his trip abroad this time had done him little good. Black gloom persisted and he suffered intense pain from gall stones. He tried the waters of Tunbridge Wells, but 'the waters seem to be mere chips of porridge, they do neither good nor harm'. In September he cast around to find a new employer for Henry Strachey, and then, on 22 November 1774, he died by his own hand in circumstances never fully revealed. With great secrecy his remains were conveyed to Styche and interred in the church at Moreton Saye. An inscription says no more than that his bones lie within the church. Unlike Westerham, where Wolfe is commemorated and Montcalm not forgotten, Market Drayton has not thought fit to raise a memorial to him.

Peggy pursued the quiet country life she far preferred to the turmoil of London and died at the age of eighty-three. His eldest son, Edward, succeeded to the title, and for a period was Governor of Madras, where the young Arthur Wellesley thought well of his ability. He married Henrietta Herbert sister of George, Earl of Powis. When the Earl died the Earldom lapsed and was subsequently conferred on Edward as a reward for his services. In accordance with a provision in his Uncle George's will, Edward's son adopted the arms and surname of Herbert and dropped that of Clive.

Clive had one other son who survived him, Robert, who was born in 1769 and who lived until 1832. Only two of his daughters, Rebecca and Charlotte, reached maturity.

Epilogue

CLIVE, THE MAN

Clive was born out of his time. As a boy he was solitary and thrown on his own resources. His formative years were spent in an India where despotism flourished unquestioned and where to be a Briton was to be a man of authority and responsibility. He learned early an Imperial outlook and imperious ways, better fitted perhaps to the great days of the Roman Empire than the Britain in which he was born.

Uninterested in the small beer of life his gaze remained fixed on the mountains. Gleig, in his *Life of Clive*, quotes a conversation Boswell recorded between Doctor Robertson and Johnson:

'Doctor Robertson expatiated on the character of a certain nobleman that he was one of the strongest minded men that ever lived; he would sit in company quite sluggish while there was nothing to call for his intellectual vigour, but the moment that any important subject was started—for instance how this country is to be defended from a French invasion—he would rouse himself and show his extraordinary talents with powerful ability and animation. *Johnson*. "Yet this man cut his throat. The true strong and sound mind can embrace equally great things and small".'

Gleig felt certain that the 'nobleman' was Clive and unquestionably the description fits him well.

Although he despised small talk, nature had endowed him with a certain eloquence and he had the tendency to exaggerate which often accompanies that quality. He was quick tempered and outspoken, and sometimes overhasty in his judgement of individuals, but if he excited a hostility a cooler tempered man might have avoided, he was always generous and loyal to his friends. He loved display and his lavish style of living to some seemed unduly ostentatious. But then he had to create an impression, he had to lead and be great. Like Hotspur, he was ready 'to pluck honour from the pale-faced moon'. In eighteenth-century England greatness and wealth walked hand-in-hand, and so he sought money, not through avariciousness, but as a symbol and ingredient of power. His quest led him down some dubious by-ways. But for all that, his integrity and courage were absolute. It may be that, while in courage he towered over his contemporaries, in his standards of conduct he reflected too faithfully the less scrupulous attitudes of his day; but he never did an act which he himself thought dishonourable or demeaning, or which he hesitated to acknowledge.

His health constantly affected his activities, but in a curious fashion. He was capable of immense spurts of energy, then suffered an intense reaction. He complained to Strachey that he never felt really well after his illness in 1752, but this was a patent exaggeration, written in a fit of depression. He maintained that the climate of India never agreed with him, but in August 1765, when the hot humid weather of the monsoon was at its worst and the energies of the most active apt to wilt, he wrote home to his wife that he was in excellent health. He seemed to possess a temperament like a tightly compressed, highly tensile steel spring, that reacted to a challenge with tremendous force, but that once the challenge was over lay uncoiled, limp and slack; and perhaps behind his formidable appearance and manner there lurked an inner vulnerability which he was at pains to conceal.

In his reasoning he was intuitive and in argument combative, seeking only to impose his own viewpoint—often with good reason—but his intolerance of opposition and the inflexibility of his opinions, often expressed with unnecessary candour, made him many enemies. He could rule but not persuade.

In his public life, he was, above all else, a man of action. He was a soldier after the pattern of Julius Caesar, unshackled by convention, instant of decision, a master of improvisation, a leader almost capable of winning victory through the sheer force of his own personality. Although there was little of speculation or philosophy in his nature, he possessed a mind of tremendous power within the range of his interests. He could master great issues, peer through the veils of the future and see what lay beyond, and in his campaigns he was a soldier-statesman who saw a battle not as an end in itself, but only as one aspect of a policy for attaining a political objective. He liked, however, great issues and grew impatient of the petty details of day-to-day administration.

As a statesman, despite the almost overwhelming extent of the opportunities that appeared to open before him, he never lost his sense of proportion. In Bengal he assessed with care how much the Company could undertake without overstraining its resources and then refused to overstep his self-imposed limits. He might appear unyielding and even extreme in his decisions, yet in the end he almost always favoured moderation. Perhaps it was symptomatic of his approach, combining as it did vision with a keen sense of reality, that while Dupleix and Bussy insisted on going abroad mounted on elephants, he never rode anything but a horse. His insight into Indian affairs was remarkable. Had he known and understood his own countrymen as well as he did the Indian Princes with whom he mingled, he would not now occupy an unmarked grave in an obscure country church, that may itself be under sentence.

He died aged forty-nine, a year younger than Stringer Lawrence when that warrior stepped ashore at Madras, on the threshold of a new career that was to bring him a secure, if not particularly prominent, niche in the history of his country. A year after Clive's death the war with the American Colonies broke out. It was the political type of struggle to which his genius was particularly well attuned. It may be it was a war Britain could not hope to win, but if any man could have won it, that man was Clive; and after victory he would have insisted on a settlement that was just, moderate and far-sighted.

It has been argued that his health would not have permitted him to shoulder once again such vast new responsibilities. This is debatable. His health seemed peculiarly to depend on the state of his mind. During 1773 Lord North was happy to seek his advice, and his own last great speech showed that, at least until the last year of his life, his intellect was unimpaired.

It has been suggested, it is true, that he returned from his last tour of Bengal broken in mind and body, but there is no evidence to show that he was any more ill in 1767 than in 1760. During 1767 and 1768 he engaged in a massive correspondence; his letters may betray the petulance of a man not in the best of health and one unaccustomed to seeing his wishes thwarted, but give no evidence that his mental powers were declining. It may have been more palatable to suggest that he returned to England a sick man with a fevered brain and committed suicide in a moment of mental instability, rather than to accept that his own countrymen hounded him to a premature grave, for to the orthodox Englishman of that era suicide smacked of weakness and sin.

But after the past year when he had been subjected to the abuse of the public and had to listen to all his achievements questioned and disparaged he may have felt with Marcus Aurelius, 'And as for death, if there be any gods, it is no grievous thing to leave the society of men'.[1] For he was a man cast in the mould of a Roman Emperor, and like a Roman he died unconquered by any but himself.

---

[1] The *Meditations of Marcus Aurelius* translated by Meric Casaubon.

Appendix 1

A note on spelling and pronunciation

The spelling and pronunciation of Indian words and names present certain difficulties. The official language of the Moghul Court was Persian, from which developed Urdu, the language of the Camp, which might be termed a form of Persian, to adapt a once well-known phrase, 'modified for India'; it was written in the Arabic script. When the British came to India, they listened with varying degrees of intentness to the unfamiliar sounds of the local language and tried to develop a system for spelling the words in the Roman alphabet, by using phonetically equivalent English syllables.

Over the years a reasonably consistent method of spelling evolved. For instance the Arabic alphabet has two 'a's, a long 'a' pronounced as the 'a' in 'car', and a short 'a' pronounced as the 'u' in 'but'. In Clive's day the long 'a' was rendered, for some reason, 'au' or 'aw' as in the old spelling Punjaub, and the short 'a' by 'u' as in bungalow. In addition there is in Urdu a plethora of 'h's which crop up in all sorts of unexpected places. Those with more sensitive hearing, suspecting they might be missing some subtle distinction, were apt to put in 'h's almost at random, but generally the Briton of the time sturdily ignored them.

This was the state of affairs when, in the second half of the nineteenth century, some well-intentioned, but perhaps misguided, scholars decided to provide Urdu with a proper system of spelling by producing equivalents from the Roman alphabet, letter by letter, for the Arabic. All was now confusion, and the well-known principle of British spelling that from the written word it should be impossible to deduce the pronunciation was firmly reinstated. 'H's sprang up in all directions, and diphthongs such as kh and gh were produced to render sounds that the Englishman had long recognised as impossible to pronounce as the 'ch' in loch.

The confusion has persisted; generations of Britons brought up to the spelling 'Cawnpore' were not prepared to change lightly to 'Kanpur', although recently cricketing journalists have been doing their utmost to re-educate them. Yet in many ways the old spelling was much easier for the ordinary British reader. 'Meerut', for instance, is possible to pronounce, while its transliterated equivalent 'Mirath' is likely to baffle most. The old 'Goorka', having been transliterated into 'Gurkha', has been mispronounced ever since, and a like fate will almost certainly befall the new state of Bangladesh.

In the absence of a practicable general rule, the following principles have been observed. So far as place names are concerned, the spelling in the Bartholomew Atlas of 1944 has been preserved, it seems a good combination of the old and the new. For the names of people, unless they have come down to history with a particular and consistent spelling, such as Omichand who would be unrecognisable as Aminchand, the correct transliteration, so far as it has proved possible to discover, has been observed. Indian families had no surnames and 'ud-daula's and Ali Khans were apt to be tacked on according to taste; these, which to a European eye might show a false family connection, have therefore been used sparingly.

As for the spelling of the Anglo-Indian terms with which the Britons of the day delighted to sprinkle their letters, in the main the old spelling has been preferred, except where the new spelling has already gained general acceptance, e.g. 'Nawab' has invariably been used and not the customary eighteenth-century 'Nabob'. When quoting from letters, in the interests of clarity, spelling has been corrected in accordance with these general principles.

Appendix 2

Glossary of Anglo–Indian terms

Arzi, araz   A petition or request.
Aurang   A goods depot or group of warehouses.

Badshah, padshah   Emperor.
Bakshi   Paymaster General hence also Commander-in-Chief.

Chauth   Right to a quarter of the revenue of a state. Conceded by Emperor to the Mahrattas for the states of Southern India.
Choakey   Police station, customs or toll house, military patrol post.
Chop   Imperial or royal seal.
Choquedar   A sentry; later, a night watchman.
Choultry   (Southern India) large shed with only three walls; rest-house.
Coffree   An African, generally an African soldier.
Cos, Coss   Measure of distance, variable, generally about two miles.
Cossid   A Courier or running messenger.
Crore   100 lakhs = 10 million. One crore of rupees = £1 million approx.
Cutwal, Cutwall   A magistrate or chief of police.

Dandi   A boatman—used chiefly on Ganges.
Dewan, Diwan   Head financial minister responsible for transmitting taxes to the Imperial treasury.
Dhobi   Washerman.
Dhooli   Covered litter.

Durbar	A court, also the executive govt of a state.
Dustuck	A pass or permit.
Factor	Originally the chief of a factory or trading centre, latterly the third grade of Company civil servant.
Fanam	Silver, or debased gold coin varying from 36 to 42 to the Pagoda, worth from 2d to $2\frac{1}{2}$d, depending on where minted.
Faujdar, phousdar	A military commander of a fort or a district.
Gentoo	A Hindu.
Gomasta	An agent.
Griffin	A newcomer to India.
Jemadar, Jemidar	Commander of a body of troops; in the Company's Indian Army, the commander of an infantry platoon.
Killadar	Commander of a fort.
Koatey, koti	A lock-up.
Lakh	100,000, especially of rupees = £10,000 approx.
Maund	A measure of weight = 80 lb.
Mohur	A gold coin varying in worth from 10–14 rupees; eventually stabilised at 16 rupees in nineteenth century.
Moor, moorman	An Indian Muslim.
Musnud	Large cushion used by Indian Princes as a throne.
Mussoola	A surf boat used at Madras.
Naib	A deputy to the ruler, the governor of a minor province.
Naik	Leader, headman; in the Company's Indian army, a corporal.
Nawab	The muslim ruler of a province or viceroyalty; subsequently debased to the ruler of a large tract of land.
Omra	A noble or high official at the Imperial Court.

Pagoda	A Hindu temple. Also a coin in use at Madras worth 36–42 fanamas or $3\frac{1}{2}$ rupees = 7s 6d.
Pattamar	A runner or courier, a lateen rigged packet boat.
Palankin, palanquin	A covered litter, see illustration.
Peon	A foot-soldier, often only armed with sword and buckler, hence an orderly or messenger.
Pergannah	A sub division of a district.
Perwannah	A grant or letter under the royal seal.
Peshcash	Tribute or rent; present to a great man.
Petta	A suburb outside the walls of a town or fort.
Polighar, polyghar	A minor feudal chief in Southern India.
Raja	A hindu King, later debased to include a great noble.
Ramzan, Ramadan	Ninth month in the muslim calendar, to be passed in fasting.
Riot, Ryot	A peasant or small farmer.
Rupee	A silver coin, the main currency throughout India. Coined in different places with differing degrees of fineness. Arcot rupees were originally the first minted coin of the Company. Sicca rupees were originally new and therefore full value rupees; became the standard Company rupee. Value fluctuated—2s 2d.
Sahib	An honorific title given where the old esquire would be used in British letters.
Sanad, sunnud	A patent or deed.
Seerpaw	A dress given by a Prince as a mark of favour.
Shroff	A money changer or banker.
Sipahi, sepoy	A soldier. In the Company's army generally an infantryman.
Subah, soubah	A large province or viceroyalty.
Subahdar	The ruler of a large province; a viceroy.
Subedar	A company commander in the Company's army.
Tank	An artificial pond.
Tappy	The post, meaning a collection of letters; a post office.

Topass	A half-caste Indian claiming Portuguese descent.
Vakil	A lawyer, advocate or representative.
Wazir	Chief minister in an Indian Muslim state, equivalent to the European 'chancellor'.
Writer	Junior grade of covenanted Company civil servant.
Zemindar	A man responsible for collecting the Imperial revenue, including some for himself, from a given area of land; the post was hereditary and hence a zemindar was in many ways the equivalent of the eighteenth-century British squire.

Appendix 3

Proposed treaty between the Company and Mir Jafar

Proposals:
1. An Alliance Offensive and Defensive against all Enemies Country or European.
2. The French fugitives to be taken and delivered up to us. All their Factorys to be delivered up to us in order to be destroy'd. The French never to be permitted to resettle in this Subahship. In Consideration of which the English Company will annually pay the Amount of Duties usually paid into the King's Treasury on the French Trade or a sum not exceeding 50,000 Rs annually.
3. Restitution of the Companys whole Loss by the taking of Calcutta & their Out Settlements, also Restitution for the Losses of all Europeans by Ditto as may be fairly stated by Adm Watson, Governor, Colonel Clive, Wm Watts Esqr., Major Killpatrick, & Becher. Blacks & Armenians are not included.
4. That the whole of our Phirmaund be compli'd with and all other Grants ever made to us particularly in the Treaty with Sei Rajah Dowlet.
5. That the Bounds of Calcutta to extend the whole Circle of the Ditch dug upon the Invasion of the Morattas also 600 Yards without it for an Esplanade. The Inhabitants dwelling within our Bounds to be entirely subject to the English Laws & Governmt.
6. That we have Liberty to fortify & Garrison our Factorys of Cossimbuzar & Dacca as we think proper and a sufficient Esplanade be granted us round each. That Convoys too & from our Settlement to another be permitted to pass without Interruption or Molestation.

7 That the Moors shall erect no Fortifications within twenty miles of the River side from Hughley to Ingelee.
8 That a Tract of land be made over to the English Compy. whose Revenues shall be sufficient to maintain a proper Force of Europeans and Sepoys to keep out the French and assist the Government against all Enemies.
9 That whenever the English Troops are called to the Assistance of the Government that the Extraordinary Expences of the Campaign be made good by the Government.
10 That an English Gentleman in Quality of Envoy be permitted to reside at Court, have audience whenever required & be treated with due respect.

Bibliography

MANUSCRIPTS
Clive Papers, India Office Library
Powis Papers, National Library of Wales
Sutton Court Collection, India Office Library
Verelst Manuscripts, India Office Library

BOOKS
Atkinson, C. T. *The Dorsetshire Regiment* (1947)
Beveridge, Henry *A Comprehensive History of India*, Vol. 1 (1871)
Biddulph, Col. J. *Stringer Lawrence, Father of the Indian Army* (1901)
Cambridge, R. O. *Account of the War in India between the English and French, 1750–61* (1761)
Cambridge History of India, Vol. 5 (1935)
Catto, W. E. *The Calcutta Light Horse* (1957)
Complete History of the War in Hindustan, 1749–61, Anon. (1761)
Dalton, C. *Memoir of Captain Dalton H.E.I.C.S.* (1886)
Davies, A. M. *Clive of Plassey* (1939)
De Quincey *Confessions of an English Opium Eater* (1889)
Dodwell, H. *Dupleix and Clive, The Beginning of Empire* (1967)
    Madras Despatches, 1744–55 (1930)
Edwardes, M. *The Battle of Plassey* (1963)
    A History of India (1961)
Forde, Col. L. *Lord Clive's Right-hand Man: A Memoir of Colonel Francis Forde* (1910)
Forrest, Sir G. *The Life of Lord Clive*, 2 vols (1918)
Fortescue, Sir J. *History of the British Army*, Vol. 2 (1899)
Gleig, Rev. G. R. *The Life of Robert, First Lord Clive* (1861)
Grant, Robertson C. *England under the Hanoverians*

Hickey, *Memoirs of William Hickey*, 3rd edition (1919)
Hill, S. C. *Bengal, 1756–7*, 3 vols (1905)
Love, H. Davison *Vestiges of Old Madras*, Vol. 2 (1913)
McCance, Capt. *History of the Royal Munster Fusiliers*, Vol. 1 (1927)
Macaulay, Lord *Historical Essays* (1908)
Malcolm, Sir J. *Life of Lord Clive*, 3 vols (1836)
Malleson, Col. G. B. *Rulers of India – Dupleix* (1890)
Mill, J. *History of India*, Vol. 3 (1817)
Minney, R. J. *Clive* (1931)
Orme, Robert A. *A History of British Transactions in Indostan*, Vols 1 and 2 (1803)
Owen, Sidney J. *The Fall of the Mogul Empire* (1912)
Ram, Gopal *How the British Occupied Bengal* (1964)
Scrafton, Luke *Reflections on the Govt., etc. of Indostan With a Short History of Bengal* (1763)
Spear, Percival *India, A Modern History* (1963)
Strachey, Henry *A Narrative of the Mutiny of the Officers of the Army in Bengal in the Year 1766* (1773)
Trevelyan, G. M. *Illustrated English Social History* (1951)
Watson, Steven *The Reign of George III, 1760–1815* (1960)
Williams, E. N. *Life in Georgian England* (1962)
Williams, Capt. John *The Bengal Native Infantry* (1817)
Wilson, Sir Charles *Clive* (1902)
Wilson, Beckles *Ledger and Sword* (1903)
Wilson, C. R. *Records of Old Fort William* (1906)
Woodruff, Philip *The Men Who Ruled India – The Founders* (1953)
Wylly, H. C. *Life of Sir Eyre Coote* (1922)
        Neill's Blue Caps: The Royal Dublin Fusiliers
Yule, H. and Burnell, A. C. *Hobson Jobson: A Glossary of Anglo-Indian Colloquial Words and Phrases* (1968)

Postscript

Three aspects of Clive's life have excited controversy, his relationship with his family, his ability as a general, and the circumstances of his death. It may be worth considering them in more detail.

There is an astonishing paucity of information about his early life; this in itself may be significant. He was first adopted, in all but name, then thrust back to his family to be sent out to India at the age of seventeen. This suggests a disturbed childhood; then there is the remark of his father, 'Why the booby has some sense after all.' It could be the deprecatory remark of an affectionate parent, but such an assumption seems out of character, for Clive subsequently deplored the way his father boasted about his achievements. It is more likely that his father meant precisely what he said, that until hearing of his successes in India he thought him a senseless booby.

Most revealing of all is the failure of his family to write to him after he had gone to India. Clive's voyage there took fourteen months, but many ships did it in six. He might have expected two or three letters to greet him on arrival at Madras, but it seems clear he found nothing. What loving mother, having packed her young son off to the ends of the earth for an uncertain period, would not write to him at the earliest opportunity, or, if she found letter writing difficult, make certain that his father wrote? Unless a trunkful of letters still exists undiscovered in Powis Castle, it seems logical to assume that his family viewed the departure of young Robert with an indifference that scarcely argues much affection.

His military ability was denigrated in his lifetime—not amazingly. He, the talented amateur, was used by the elder Pitt as a weapon with which to taunt his unsuccessful generals; he called him a 'heaven-born General', a phrase which must have infuriated them and most regular officers, and the desire to disprove the claim would be only natural.

It was, for instance, asserted that he never fought against the French. But at the siege of Arcot there were 150 French soldiers; at Arni, Orme asserted, there were 300 French against 200 British, at Kauveripauk 400 French against 380 British. If it was meant that he never fought against a French commander, the claim is still not valid. D'Auteuil surrendered to him at Volcondah and the forts at Covelong and Chingleput were both commanded by Frenchmen.

It is suggested that luck played a large part in his successes, that he captured Arcot by a stroke of luck, as the defenders had fled, that after the siege of fifty days he was relieved mainly owing to the intervention of the Mahrattas, another stroke of luck. (But a few years later 500 Europeans managed to hold Calcutta for only three days against an Indian army unequipped with a siege-train.) His tactical skill at Arni could not be denied, but at Kauveripauk he was ambushed and only luck, aided perhaps by some instant treachery, saved him. He, of course, captured Covelong and Chingleput by luck, helped no doubt by treachery; no other explanation is possible, for Lally did not attempt to attack Chingleput when he had with him the regular soldiers of France and it lay square across his line of communications as he advanced to besiege Madras. No wonder Napoleon's first question about a general was 'Is he lucky?'.

He has been censured for not fighting Siraj-ud-daula's immense host in the open near Calcutta when he had no cavalry nor any transport with which to move his guns; his subsequent expedient of using seamen was unpopular, worked badly, and might have been disastrous in a pitched battle. He has also been condemned on the grounds that, when he did attack that host, his plan went awry and the casualties were heavy; nevertheless his attack caused Siraj-ud-daula to retire and excited the admiration of the French and the Dutch.

The capture of Chandernagore is advanced as an example of Clive's failure when opposed by 'proper soldiers' like the French. The contention ignores his circumstances. He was deficient in siege guns and time was vital. He had neither the time for a formal siege nor sufficient men to attempt anything else. At Badajoz, Wellington with more than 20,000 men took three weeks to capture a fortress manned by 5,000 French. The fortifications at Chandernagore bore little resemblance to the formidable ones at Badajoz, but sieges in the eighteenth century could not be hurried.

The Battle of Plassey was disparaged almost from the time it was fought, and the tactical skill displayed by Clive in his advance up the river and the choice of his battle position ignored. It has been termed a non-event, a mere political transaction. It is true that the larger part of Siraj-ud-daula's army did not take part, that the casualties, about 80 out of an army of 3,000, proportionally less than half the 5,000 suffered by Wellington out of an army of 75,000 at Vitoria were very light. Yet battles are to be judged by their results, not by the number of casualties. At Plassey a battle was fought and an utterly decisive victory gained. Siraj-ud-daula's army was irretrievably shattered and he himself turned into a fugitive. If the battle had been a mere sham, it might have been expected that Mir Jaffar would ride arrogantly into the British camp to receive the congratulations of Clive on the victory he, Mir Jaffar had provided for him. But by all accounts Mir Jaffar was decidedly nervous when he rode into the British camp, and never thereafter dared openly to oppose the victor.

It is said Clive feared to go to Madras to face French regular troops under Lally and a careless remark he wrote to Forde is quoted to substantiate the claim. For Clive to abandon Bengal to the Calcutta Council, that had lost their city once, to place himself under Pigot, Stringer Lawrence, and probably some regular lieutenant-colonel newly out from England would have been an act of arrant folly.

In a remarkably percipient analysis of what would happen after Lally landed in the Carnatic, he foresaw that the French had little chance of success unless they beat the British fleet, and this he was confident they could not do. His sure political and military judgement enabled him to strip Bengal of his best troops when all Calcutta clamoured against his decision, and despite the pleas of both Pigot and Lawrence for help in Madras, to send them to the Northern Circars. It cannot be denied that he never fought a battle on a large enough scale to prove conclusively his claim to rank among the greatest of the military commanders, but there is nothing to suggest he would have found such a test beyond his powers.

About the closing years of his life a similar degree of controversy has continued. Some have seen him return from his second governorship of Bengal a broken man, a mere shell of his former self. But his correspondence after his return lacks little of its former force or clarity. It is unpleasant to think that his grateful countrymen hounded him to his death; far pleasanter to suppose, as R. J. Minney strongly argued in an article in volume 13 of the Army Historical Journal, that physical pain from illness so sapped his self-control that in a moment of weakness he almost accidentally took an overdose of opium. But an overdose of opium could be so easily explained away. Laudanum was the recognised, indeed the only, specific for acute physical pain; and then why the need for the intense secrecy with which his family surrounded his death, why was he lodged in an unmarked grave only to be found by accident a century and a half later? That he died in an unmistakable fashion by his own hand seems the only logical explanation.

That his suicide was largely caused by the way, however unadmitted, he was put on trial before Parliament and had to listen while all his achievements were vilified, the mute testimony of his correspondence bears powerful, if indirect, witness. From 1757 onwards his correspondence, year by year, filled numerous letter-books and box after box of records, even when he was ill. Then after May 1773 the flood dries up as suddenly as if dammed. A few random letters, a declaration that he to whom public life was all would take no further part in it, a letter or two on behalf of a friend, and then silence. Melancholy though such a conclusion must be, it seems inescapable that the ordeal through which he had passed robbed him of all desire to continue living. In the words of his own quotation, *'aut Caesar, aut nullus'*, and it was clear that although Parliament refused to condemn him, even accorded him a modicum of praise, for the future it must be *nullus*.

Index

Abdul Wahab, brother of Mohammed Ali: at Volconda 95
Adams, Major: advances against Mir Kassim 320
Adams, Doctor: Clive's agent in Shrewsbury 376
Adlercron, Colonel 39th Foot 171
Ahmad Shah Abdalli, Ruler of Afghanistan: threatens Bengal 203; defeats Mahrattas at Panipat 329
Aix la Chapelle, treaty 74
Alivardi Khan, Viceroy of Bengal: defeats Sarfaraz Khan 162; Viceroy and dies 163
Allum Khan 125
Amyatt, Peter, Agent at Patna 295; negotiates with Mir Kassim, killed 320
Ananda raj, Raja of Vizianagram: takes Vizagapatam 286
Angria, Tulaji, Pirate Admiral: breaks with Mahrattas 155; flees to Mahrattas 158
Anwar-ud-Din: appointed Nawab of Carnatic 47–8, 49; sends army to take Madras 61; defeated and killed 84
Arcot 40; advance on 100–1; siege of 107–9; storm 110–11
Arni, Battle of 113–15
Aurangabad, capital of Nizam-ul-mulk 38, 40

Balaji Rao, Peshwa of Mahrattas: offers British help 226

Barker, Sir Robert: appointed to command Bengal Artillery 322; appointed to command a Brigade 345, 349, 351, 357; mutiny of officers 361–3
Barnett, Commodore Curtis: arrives Madras 49; dies 50
Barthélemy: in Madras 61; repels Mahfuz Khan 62
Batta, field allowance 344, 351; scale 352; reduction 353; officer conspiracy over 353–4
Bayley, Daniel 20, 35
Bengal Sepoy Army: organisation 291, 347, 350
Benyon, Richard, Governor of Madras 25
Bisdom, Adrian, Governor of Chinsura 306
Blacktown 29, 32
Bolt, Robert, a corrupt merchant 333, 384
Bombay 39; arrival of Clive 153, 155
Boscawen, Admiral Edward 70; attacks Pondicherry 71–4; leaves India 84
Boswell, James; record of Dr Johnson's conversation with Dr Robertson 405
Bourchier, Ann, wife of Secretary to Madras Council: writes to Margaret Clive 153
Brereton, Captain, R.N.: evidence about fictitious treaty 392
Bristow, British agent at Ingeram 286

INDEX 425

Budge-Budge 178; action 181–4
Burgoyne, Col John: recommends a select committee 387–9, 390; lays proceedings of committee before Parliament 396–8
Burslem, Rev., schoolmaster 21
Bussy, Charles Castelnau de: captures Gingee 90; to Aurangabad 91; hostility in Deccan 154; ceded Northern Circars 193; sacks Vizagapatam 273; recalled from Deccan 283
Bute, Lord: becomes Prime Minister, prefers Sulivan to Clive 314

Caillaud, Major John, later Brigadier General 282; goes to Bengal 309; Brigadier General 322
Calcutta 161; siege 169–70; action outside 199–202; Black Hole 170
Campbell, Captain Dugald: killed at Budge-Budge 187
Carnac, John 146; accompanies Clive to Bihar 295, 321–2; Brigadier General 322, 331, 346, 356; Clive's breakdown 368; ruined by attorney 402
Carnatic, geography 38, 40
Champion, Major on Clive's Staff, sent to Monghyr, 357; speaks to officers of Fletcher's brigade 359
Chandernagore—French settlement 192; attack on 208–12; terms of surrender 212
Chingleput 135; captured by Clive 136–7
Chitpur Tank 194, 198
Chunda Sahib 42, 43; ransomed and invades Carnatic 83; at Tanjore 85; defeated by Nazir Jang 87; victory at Volconda 97; blockades Trichinopoly 98; detaches troops to Arcot 104; captured and killed 132–3
Clive, Edward, son to Robert Clive: Governor of Madras, becomes Lord Powis 404
Clive, Margaret 135; marries Robert 144–6; arrives Calcutta 272, 295, 297–8; returns to England 311, 312–14, 321, 326, 328, 349; letter from France 370, 403–4
Clive, Rebecca 19
Clive, Richard, Robert's father 17; character 19; return of Robert to England 146–8
Clive, Robert, Lord: early life 17–22; sets out to India 22; arrival at Madras 25, 31; attempt at suicide 33; home sickness 33–4; escape from Madras to Fort St David 57–8; duel 59–60; actions at Fort St David 66–7; at siege of Pondicherry 71–4; incident with Rev. Fordyce 74–6; at siege of Devicotta 80–1; illness and trip to Calcutta 92; at Volconda 94; proposes attack on Arcot 98–9; captures Arcot 100–2; actions at Timeri Fort 103; besieged by Raja Sahib 106–8; repels storm of Arcot 109–11; defeats Raja Sahib at Arni 113–16; captures Pagoda at Conjeeveram 116–17; defeats Raja Sahib at Kauveripauk 118–20; destroys Dupleix's monument 121; accompanies Lawrence to Trichinopoly 122–4; action outside Trichinopoly 125–6; detached north of Cauveri 127; action at Samiaveram 127–31; captures Pitchunda Pagoda 132; returns to Madras 135; captures Covelong and Chingleput 135–7; achievements in Carnatic 138–42; forming of character 142–3; illness and opium 143–4; marries Margaret Maskelyne 144; sails for England 146; elected to Parliament 149; election declared invalid 151; returns to India as Deputy Governor Madras 151–2; Gheria and dispute over prizemoney 155–9; relationship with Watson 156–7; appointed C. in C. Land Forces for expedition to Calcutta

Clive, Robert, Lord—*contd.*
171–2; situation at Fulta 177–9; action at Budge-Budge 181–7; recapture of Fort William, incident with Coote and Watson 187–90; Clive's view of situation in Bengal 193–4; efforts to negotiate with Siraj-ud-daula 195–8; dispute with Council over independent authority 196; attack on Nawab's camp outside Calcutta 196–202; treaty with Siraj-ud-daula 203–5; negotiation with French at Chandernagore 205; rejected by Watson 206; attack on Chandernagore 207–12; terms granted by Watson 212; proposal for Governor-General in India 214–15; demands Siraj-ud-daula expels French 217–19; conspiracy against Siraj-ud-daula, 221–6; fictitious treaty with Omichand 226–30; negotiation with Mir Jafar 226–32; break between Siraj-ud-daula and Mir Jafar 232; advances up Hooghly 233; lack of information from Mir Jafar 238; halt at Cutwa 238–40; Council of War at Cutwa 240–1; decides to advance to Plassey 242–4; position at Plassey 251; dispositions 253; action 254–60; flight of Siraj-ud-daula 261; considerations on battle 262; resites Fort William 273; imposes order on Bengal and Bijar 275–7; presented with Jaghir 278; becomes Governor of Calcutta 279–80; prescient letter to Pigot 280–1; quarrel between Rai Durlabh and Mir Jafar, conspiracy against Mir Jafar 285–91; sends Forde to Northern Circars 286–8; reorganises sepoys 291–2; letter to Sulivan on Company policy 292–3; annuity to Lawrence 293; attack by Shahzada on Patna 294–7; allocation of Jaghir to Clive 298–9; Dutch expedition to Bengal defeated 300–7; strained relations with Directors 308–10; return to England 311; proposal for Crown to take over Company 312–13; illness in England, elected to Parliament, peerage 313; quarrel with Sulivan 314; objection to treaty of Paris 315–16; endeavours to obtain control of Company, fails 317–18; Sulivan suspends Jaghir 318; consequent on chaos in Bengal sent back as Governor 321–2; views on troubles in Bengal 323–5; sails 316; situation in Bengal and abuses 328–31; impresses authority on Council 331–5; settles with Shuja and Shahzada, acquires diwani of Bengal 335–40; mode of life in Calcutta 341; reformation 342–4; formation of Society for trade in Salt, Betel-nut and Tobacco 343; introduction of four civil servants from Madras 344; indiscipline of army and re-organisation 345–8, 350; protests by civil servants in Calcutta 348–9; officers' conspiracy against abolition of Batta 351–5; determines to break mutiny 355–64; mutiny collapses 364–6; court-martial of Fletcher 366–7; breakdown in health 368–9; Directors order dissolution of Society of Salt, Betel-nut and Tobacco 369–70; achievements 370–2; return to England 371; difficulties with directors 374–5; ill health 376; visit to France and re-enters Parliament 376–7; makes a friend of Wedderburn 378; difficulties of Company 379–80; appointment of supervisors, lost at sea 381; dislike of Nabobs 382–3; North decides to reform Company with his advice 384; Sulivan resolves to anticipate North and

Clive, Robert, Lord—*contd.*
introduces bill 385–6; speaks
against it 386–7; Burgoyne
proposes select committee to
include Clive 387–9;
proceedings of committee 390–
3; Company bankrupt 393–4;
North appoints secret select
committee 394; becomes Lord
Lieutenant of Shropshire and
Montgomeryshire 394;
complains of select committee
proceedings 394–5; Burgoyne
lays committee proceedings
before Parliament and moves
resolution against Clive 396;
replies 399–401; resolutions
nullified 401; effect on Clive
402; departs to continent 403;
commits suicide 404; his
character 405–8
Coiladdy Fort, engages Lawrence
124–5
Cole, description of first Siege of
Madras 56
Conjeeveram 103; siege of Pagoda
116
Cooke, John, evidence about
fictitious treaty 391–2
Coote, Eyre, Captain, later
General Sir: at Budge-Budge
182–6; quarrel over Fort
William 187–90, 191; action at
Hooghly 191; outside Calcutta
200–2; at Chandernagore 211–
12; promoted major 237;
captures Cutwa 237–8;
disagrees with Clive 241; at
Plassey 253, 258–60; pursues
Law 269–71; returns to
England 275; appointed C. in
C. Bengal 308, 311, 315; gives
evidence to select committee 393
Cope, Captain John: attack on
Devicotta 79; joins Mohammed
Ali 86; repulsed at Madura 94;
killed near Trichinopoly 117
Cossimbazar 161
Covelong Fort 135; captured by
Clive 136
Cutwa Fort: captured by Coote
237–8; Clive at 239–44

Dacca 161; surrenders 162; 320
d'Aché, Admiral: arrives
Pondicherry 278; action with
Pocock 279, 281–2
Dalton, John, Captain 74; at
Devicotta 80–1; at Volconda
96–8, 125; attacks d'Auteuil
131; joins Clive 132
d'Auteuil, Louis, with Nazir
Jang 87; advances to Utatoor
127–8; retreats 131; captured
by Clive 132
de Bury: attacks Cuddalore 66
de Gingins, Captain Rodolphe:
goes to relieve Trichinopoly
94–5; defeated at Volconda
96–8; retires to Trichinopoly
98, 117, 125
Devicotta, attack on 79–81, 98
Diwani of Bengal 339
Drake, Roger, Governor of
Calcutta 166–7, 175, 190;
demands Clive accepts
authority of Council 196;
recalled 279
Dupleix, Joseph-François 48–9,
51; ransoms Chunda Sahib
83–6; defeats Nazir Jang 89–90,
112; strikes in Central Carnatic
117, 123; sends d'Auteuil to
succeed Law 127, 132; intrigues
with Mysore regent 133;
superseded 134

Easton, doctor, headmaster
Clive's school 21
Eckman, Captain Peter:
commands Madras garrison
53–4
Ellis, William 310; captured at
Patna 320; killed 321

Farrukhsiyar, Moghul Emperor:
treaty with British 161
Fletcher, Sir Robert 345, 347,
357–60; responsibility for
officers' mutiny, court-
martialled 366, 367
Floyer, Charles, Governor of Fort
St David 58; superseded 92
Forde, Lt-Col Francis 287;
campaign in Northern Circars

INDEX

Forde, Lt-Col Francis—*contd.*
288; captures Masulipatam 298; returns Calcutta 302-3; defeats Dutch 305, 326; perishes in Aurora 381
Fordyce, Chaplain Fort St David: affray with Clive 75
Fort d'Orleans 208-9
Fort St David 49; arrival of Clive 58; French attacks 66-7, 69-70, 292
Fort St George, description 52-4; first siege 51-7; second siege 292
Fort William, captured by Siraj-ud-daula 169-70; recaptured 187; resited 273
Forth, doctor: writes of Nawab's dispositions 178
Fowke, Joseph 75
Fox, Robert 151
Fullerton, Captain 30
Fulta: arrival of British 171; Clive at 175-6; Dutch attack 303

Gaskell, Nathaniel 19
Gheria, pirate stronghold, expedition against 156-8
Glass, Ensign, 107, 116
Gleig, Rev. C. R.: reference to Clive's character 405
Goa 39
Godeheu, French Governor-General: succeeds Dupleix 134; treaty with British 134
Golconda 39, 132
Grant, Major Archibald 253
Grenville, George 316, 374; espouses cause of Wilkes 377; dies 379
Griffin, Commodore Thomas, R.N. 66-7, 69

Hastings, Warren 289; actions against Dutch expedition 300-7, 330; appointed Governor of Calcutta 381; appointed Governor-General in India 402
Hayter, Lieutenant, R.N.: withdraws from Council of War before Plassey 240

Holwell, J. Z., member of Calcutta Council 176, 196
Hon. East India Company 17; organisation in India 30; Constitution 316-17; situation of a young writer 330; salaries to servants 342; role in Bengal 371; situation in 1772 393; asks for loan 394
Hooghly—Port: attacked by Killpatrick 190-1
Hughes, Commodore, R.N. 402
Hyderabad 38-40

Indian Armies: character 64-5, 233-5
Ingham, Doctor: accompanies Clive to India as his physician 326, 343, 368, 376

Johnstone, 'Governor' 377; member of select committee 389, 390
Johnstone, John, member of Calcutta Council 331-3, 340, 375

Kauveripauk—Battle of 118-21, 122
Keene, Lieutenant Madras Europeans, at Kauveripauk 119-20
Kelsall, Sergeant, Irish deserter 128-9; shoots at Clive 131
Khudadad Yar Lutuf Khan 223-4, 232
Khwaja Wajid, prominent Armenian merchant 167, 195
Killpatrick, James 108-9; joins Clive at Arcot 112; goes to Calcutta 160, 183; attacks Hooghly 190-1; returns Calcutta 194; arrives Chandernagore 233; at Plassey 253; advances 258-60; dies 273
King, The Reverend 20
Knipe, Major 67
Koehler, Lieutenant George: searching of Dutch ships in Hooghly 300
Krishan Dass, son of Raj Ballabh: takes refuge in Calcutta 165

INDEX

La Bourdonnais, François Mahé 50; attacks Madras 51, 55–7; quarrel with Dupleix 57
Lalgoody 127
Lally de Tollendal, French Governor-General: arrives Pondicherry 278; moves against Tanjore 281–2; recalls Bussy from Deccan 283, 285, 287, 298
Latham, Thomas, Captain of HMS *Tyger* 189–90, 280
Law, Jacques: commanding at Trichinopoly 117, 123; engages Lawrence 125; retreats to Sriringham Island 126, 128; surrenders 132–3
Law, Jean: chief of French factory at Cossimbazar 212, 228, 246; views on Nawab's actions 249; returns to Patna 269; crosses into Oudh, 271
Lawrence, Major Stringer, later Major General 67–9, 71; at Devicotta 79; joins Nazir Jang 86–8; returns to England 89; returns to India 122; at Trichinopoly 123–33; wins battle of Bahur 136; quarrel with Saunders 143, 283; annuity from Clive 293
Leycester, Ralph, member of Calcutta Council 331, 333, 340
Lostock School 21

Macpherson, Lieutenant: dispute over promotion 345–6
Madras 24–5; description of 26–32, 38; first siege 51–7; Lally abandons second siege 298
Mahfuz Khan, deputy Nawab 47; attacks Madras 61–2; defeats de Bury 66; captured at Ambur 84
Mahratta Confederacy 40–2, 149
Majendie, Calcutta merchant: intrigues against Clive 348
Manikchand, Governor of Calcutta 171, 176–8; defeated Budge-Budge 183–4
Manningham, Charles, Councillor Calcutta Council 176, 279
Market Drayton 21, 404
Maskelyne, Edmund 36, 57, 67, 145; returns to England 292; returns to India with Clive 326, 328, 343, 367; fortune 368, 376
Maskelyne, Nevil: brother to Edmund 144
Masulipatam 40; captured by Forde 298
Meredith, Sir William: seconds Burgoyne's motion against Clive 399
Miran, son of Mir Jafar 269, 277, 288; to Patna with Clive 295, 306; struck by lightning 311
Mir Jafar Ali Khan 165; joins conspiracy against Siraj-uddaula 225, 232, 238, 247–9; at Plassey 254, 261–3; debt to Company 266, 276; relationship with Clive 278; nearly assassinated, 288–91, 294, 299; Dutch invasion 300–7; deposed 311; reinstated 321; dies 330; legacy to Clive 357
Mir Kassim 311; imprisons and drowns Ram Narain 319
Mir Madan 257
Mirza Omar Beg, confidant of Mir Jafar 227
Minchin, Captain, garrison commander at Fort William 170
Mohammed Ali Khan, Governor of Trichinopoly 47; joins Nazir Jang 87; defeated 89, 92, 94; dispute with Mysore regent 133; recognised as Nawab by French 134; letter from Clive 402
Mohammed Kuli 294; fails to storm Patna 296–7
Mohan Lal 222
Moll, Cornelius 30
Monakji, commander of Tanjore army 132
Morari Rao, Mahratta chieftain: seizes Trichinopoly 43; withdraws 47, 87; dispute with Mohammed Ali 132; joins French 139, 143
Morgan, John 30
Morse, Nicholas, Governor of Madras 31, 48; surrenders Madras 56–7

430 INDEX

Munro, Major Hector: defeats Shuja and Shah Zada at Buxar 321; mutinies before battle 328
Murshid Ali Khan, Viceroy of Bengal 162
Murshidabad, Capital of Bengal: great mosque 166; Clive enters 266
Murtaza Ali Khan 42–3, 46–7; at siege of Arcot 107
Muzaffar Jang 83, 87; Viceroy 90; killed 91

Najum-ud-daula: succeeds Mir Jafar 330, 332, 335
Nazir Jang 83; invades Carnatic 86–8; killed 89
Newcastle, Duke of: obstructs Clive's entry to Parliament 149; obtains peerage for him 313
Nizam Ali, younger brother of Salabat Jang 286
Nizam-ul-mulk 39; intervenes in Carnatic 46–7; dies 83
Norbett, Father: description of Madras 27
North, Lord 383; asks Clive's advice 384, 393; appoints secret select committee 394, 399; votes against Clive 401, 402–3
Northern Circars 39; Ananda raj takes Vizagapatam 286; Clive intervenes 287

Omichand, Hindu merchant 165, 205; Watt's opinion of him 220; demands money for services 226; false treaty with 226–9, 267, 391
Orme, Robert 135

Palk, Robert, Governor of Madras 335
Paradis, Louis, Swiss engineer officer 62; defeats Mahfuz Khan 63–4; attacks Fort St David 66–7; killed 72
Peyton, Captain Edward, R.N.: action with La Bourdonnais 50; superseded 66
Pigot, George 135; Governor of Madras 159, 215; requests Clive's return 286–7, 309, 402
Pitchunda Pagoda 124, 127; captured 132
Pitt, William, refuses to annex Company's Indian possessions 312; resigns as Prime Minister 314
Plassey, Battle of: description of ground 251; British dispositions at 253–4; battle 254–61; Clive's skill at 262
Pocock, Admiral George 197; at Chandernagore 210–11; sails to Madras 278; action with French 279, 281–2
Pondicherry 38, 40; first siege 71–3; captured by Coote 315
Poona 38, 41
Prince, Richard, Deputy Governor of Madras 106
Princess Louise, East Indiaman 23
Purling, Chairman of Directors: asks Clive's advice 385–6
Pye, Captain: at Budge-Budge 182–3

Raghoji Bhonsla 42, 162
Rai Durlabh, Dewan of Bengal 168; joins conspiracy against Nawab 225, 253, 267; quarrel with Mir Jafar 275, 288
Raja Sahib: goes to retake Arcot 106–11; defeated at Arni 113–15, 117; defeated at Kauveripauk 118–21
Raj Ballabh, chief minister at Dacca 165
Ram Narain, Governor of Bihar 271; revolts 275; reconciled 277, 288–9; struggle with Shah Zada and Mohammed Kuli 294–5; imprisoned 319; killed 321
Renault, Governor of Chandernagore 206–7; defends Chandernagore 209–12; reconstitutes French council at Chinsura 215–16
Revel, Lieutenant: at Conjeeveram 116
Rose Fuller, M.P. 401
Rous, Boughton, Chairman of Directors 322

INDEX 431

Safdar Ali, Nawab of Carnatic 42; moves family to Madras 43–4; assassinated 46

Sahoji: claims Tanjore 79; pensioned off 81

St Frais, Law's deputy: joins Siraj-ud-daula 246; at Plassey 255–6, 258, 260

St Thomé, Battle of 63–4

St Thomé Street, Madras 34

Salabat Jang, Viceroy of Deccan 91; rivalry with Mahrattas 149, 154; asks for British assistance 159, 193; treaty with British 298

Salt, Betel-nut and Tobacco monopoly 343, 367; disapproval of directors 369; abolished 370, 375, 387

Samiaveram 127; action at 128–31

Sandwich, Lord 148; letter to Clive 151

Saunders, Thomas, Governor of Madras 91; plans attack on Arcot 98–9, 122; negotiates peace with French 134; returns to England 159

Scott, Alexander, master of East Indiaman: reports Dutch attack 303

Scrafton, Luke: visits Siraj-ud-daula outside Calcutta 197–9; at Cossimbazar 220–1; tries to visit Mir Jafar, 230; payment after Plassey 266; warns of conspiracies 285, 375; perishes in Aurora 381

Seths, Jagat, banking firm: conspire against Siraj-ud-daula 219; rule on Mir Jafar's debts 266, 278, 285, 291, 293; negotiate Jaghir for Clive 298–9, 321

Shah Zada, Ali Gohar: becomes Shah Alam II 293, 297; defeated at Buxar 321, 329; grants diwani of Bengal 339, 351, 365

Shaukat Jang, Governor of Purneah 165; rebels against Siraj-ud-daula, killed 174–5

Shuja-ud-daula, Nawab of Oudh 275, 294; seizes Allahabad 296–7; defeated at Buxar 328–9, 330, 337–9, 351, 365

Siraj-ud-daula: succeeds Alivardi Khan 165; moves against British 166; right to Bengal 168; quarrel with Calcutta 167–8; captures Calcutta 169–71; character 173; defeats Shaukat Jang 174–5, 194–7; action outside Calcutta 199–202; concludes treaty 204; forbids attack on Chandernagore 205; permits it 207, 212–13; invites in Bussy 217; expels Law 218; dismisses Mir Jafar 232, 245; reconciles himself with Mir Jafar 246–7; advance to Plassey 249–53, 260; flees to Murshidabad 261; captured and murdered 269

Sivaji 40

Smith, Captain: goes to Monghyr 357; helps crush officers' mutiny 359–60

Smith, Colonel Richard: accompanies Clive to Bengal 328, 347–8, 351, 356; mutiny of officers 363–4

Smith, Major, commanding European battalion at Allahabad 363–4

Speke, Captain, R.N. 189; wounded at Chandernagore 211

Spencer, Acting Governor of Calcutta 330

Sriringham Island 93, 126, 131; Lawrence crosses on to 132–3

Stainforth, Captain 354

Sterling, tutor, Hemel Hempstead 21

Stewart, Captain of *Winchester* 25–6

Strachey, Henry 343, 355, 358, 361, 368, 376–7, 403–4

Strahan, seaman: captures Budge-Budge, reprimanded 186–7

Styche 17

Sulivan, Lawrence 292–3, 313; quarrel with Clive 314, 317; suspends payment on Jaghir

Sulivan, Lawrence—*contd.*
318; loses Chairmanship of Directors 322, 327; regains control 377; sends supervisors to India 381, 384; introduces bill to regulate Company 386; resolves to destroy Clive 387
Sumner, William: member of select committee with Clive 322; Clive dislikes wife 328; weakness 334–5, 343
Surat 39
Sykes, Francis 302–3, 336; resident at Murshidabad 343, 356
Symonds, Ensign: at Kauveripauk 120

Tanjore 38, 40
Tannah Fort 178, 187
Thurlow, Lord, Attorney General 395–6
Trichinopoly 38, 40, 43; description of 93–4, 117; intrigues for 133–4

Utatoor 128; action at 131

Vansittart, Henry 309; Governor of Bengal 311, 318; break with Mir Kassim 319; his mistakes 323–4; perishes in Aurora 381
Verelst, Harry: goes to India with Clive 322, 341, 348–9, 354, 364–5; officers' mutiny 366, 375; Governor of Calcutta 379
Vernet, Chief of Dutch Factory at Cossimbazar 169
Vizagapatam 39, 197; Bussy sacks 273; captured by Ananda raj 286
Volconda 95; action at 96–7, 131–2

Walsh, John: visits Siraj-ud-daula 197–9; stands for Parliament 313; has Clive's Jaghir confirmed by General Court 374, 376; questioned about fictitious treaty 391

Warrick, Captain, R.N., commands Naval detachment in action outside Calcutta 199–202
Watson, Vice-Admiral, Charles 155; relationship with Clive 156–7; attack on Gheria 157–8, 159, 160; sails for Calcutta 171–2; arrives Fulta, 176–7; advance up Hooghly 179–87; quarrel over Fort William 187–90; blocks agreement with French 196, 199, 202; treaty with Nawab 204; blocks treaty with French 206; attacks Chandernagore 207–12; demands passage for British troops to Patna 223; refuses to sign false treaty 228–9; supplies Clive with seamen 231; attitude to advance on Murshidabad 265; dies 272; attitude to false treaty 391–2
Watts, William, Chief of Cossimbazar Factory 167–8; surrenders factory 169, 174; returns to Cossimbazar 205; obtains permission for attack on Chandernagore 207, 220; conspiracy against Siraj-ud-daula 221–37; payment after Plassey 266
Wedderburn, Alexander, Barrister: Clive procures Parliamentary seat for 378; recommends Clive for Lord Lieutenancy to North 394; defends Clive 399, 401
Weller, Captain 39th Foot 182–4
Wellesley, Arthur, Duke of Wellington: at Sultan petta Tope 140, 150; presents received 402
White Town, Madras 28, 32
Wilson, Captain: attacks Dutch ships 304–5
Winchester, East Indiaman 22–3

York, Ensign with 39th: action outside Calcutta 201